Environmental Change and Human Survival

Some Dimensions of Human Ecology

Stephen Molnar

Iva M. Molnar

Washington University

Prentice Hall
Upper Saddle River, NJ 07458

Library of Congress Cataloging-in-Publication Data

Molnar, Stephen.
Environmental change and human survival : some dimensions of human ecology / Stephen Molnar, Iva M. Molnar.
p. cm.
Includes bibliographical references and index.
ISBN 0-13-176041-6 (pbk.)
1. Human ecology. I. Molnar, Iva M. II. Title.
GF41.M65 2000
304.2—dc21 99-29823
CIP

Editorial Director: Charlyce Jones Owen
Editor in Chief: Nancy Roberts
Managing Editor: Sharon Chambliss
Editorial/production supervision
and interior design: Mary Araneo
Marketing Manager: Christopher DeJohn
Cover Art Director: Jayne Conte
Cover Designer: Kiwi Design
Cover Art: José Ortega/SIS, Inc.

This book was set in 10/12 Palatino by A & A Publishing Services, Inc., and was printed and bound by Courier Companies, Inc. The cover was printed by Phoenix Color Corp.

Printed in the United States of America

10 9 8 7 6 5 4 3 2 1

ISBN 0-13-176041-6

PRENTICE-HALL INTERNATIONAL (UK) LIMITED, *London*
PRENTICE-HALL OF AUSTRALIA PTY. LIMITED, *Sydney*
PRENTICE-HALL CANADA INC., *Toronto*
PRENTICE-HALL HISPANOAMERICANA, S.A., *Mexico*
PRENTICE-HALL OF INDIA PRIVATE LIMITED, *New Delhi*
PRENTICE-HALL OF JAPAN, INC., *Tokyo*
PEARSON EDUCATION ASIA PTE. LTD., *Singapore*
EDITORA PRENTICE-HALL DO BRASIL, LTDA., *Rio de Janeiro*

To Jessica Nicole
and all of the children of the 21st century

Contents

Tables

Figures

Preface

Today, we live in a world largely of our own making, surrounded by technological developments of the last century. This does not mean that we are entirely free of environmental influences, only that humans are increasingly able to manipulate these influences. As a result, we are active participants, a controlling force in the complex web of linkages between the living and inanimate worlds. It has not always been this way, though. The development of our knowledge and skills has occurred over millennia with a rapid acceleration during the past 200 years. In effect, we have created a new ecological niche for our species, the urban–industrial niche.

To understand this niche, or place in the natural world, we offer a perspective of human ecology by examination of the linkages between human actions and environmental inputs. In turn, these inputs affect human health, survival, and population growth or decline. Chapter 1 describes world environments, climates, and some of the restrictions they impose on human survival. Chapter 2 considers general ecological concepts and discusses their applications to the human species. Though this is a book that deals with recent and contemporary populations, a historical context must be offered. Chapter 3 offers such a context as it traces demographic and cultural developments. These developments are traced through a series of demographic landmarks as our species increased in numbers over the last few millennia.

Radical and rapid changes in human society, population numbers, and especially technology accelerated during a period referred to as the Industrial Revolution. This revolution laid the foundation for the modern world we enjoy today. Chapter 4 sketches the history of major events and offers details of the sustained population growth, intensification of environmental change, and technological achievement. Over this 200-year period, the feedbacks between human action and environmental use became clearly established. Human diet departed significantly from that of previous generations, and health began to approach its modern dimensions. As the development of natural resources proceeded, population gains were sustained and Europe, especially the Western region, became a crowded continent. Measures of these changes are outlined by the description of the interactions among diet, disease, demography, and development; the four Ds introduced in Chapter 1 as defining a web of human ecological linkages.

Chapter 5 describes the basics of population dynamics. Fertility rates, life expectancy, and population structure with its generational changes are considered with examples from contemporary societies of the developed and developing world. Diet needs, food energy requirements for work and reproduction, and for child growth are outlined in Chapter 6. The diversity of diet and growth among several traditional small-scale societies is considered in contrast to industrialized societies. Special attention is given to the impact of diet changes on the health of these traditional peoples. The impact is seen in epidemiological transitions as development proceeded with expanded contacts among populations throughout the world causing significant lifestyle changes. Chapter 7 outlines these changes and their affects on peoples of the developing world. The health influences of both the "old diseases" and the new viral diseases are considered.

Chapter 8 emphasizes development, in its several forms, as the driving force of population growth and demographic transition. Control of food production, expansion of disease prevention, and rapidly expanding travel and communication networks all have affected an unprecedented population growth. The doubling and doubling again of numbers of humans during the twentieth century have, in turn, driven environmental and social changes and have required new adaptations. Our survival of these changes depends upon a clearer understanding of populations, society, and their adaptations. The book concludes with a restatement of the linkages between human actions and the measurements of environmental stresses.

Acknowledgment of specific influences after years of study, teaching, and writing is nearly impossible. The many discussions with my colleagues at Washington University, St. Louis have certainly added to my appreciation of the scope of human ecology. They and the students that I have had the pleasure of teaching deserve acknowledgment for their numerous and varied inputs. Appreciation is also extended to the University of Arizona for a visiting scholar appointment. My coauthor and I wish to thank the Prentice Hall staff for its able guidance of the manuscript through the various stages to final production, especially Mary Araneo and Sharon Chambliss. Our compliments to the graphics department for the excellence of the graphs and line drawings; we especially thank Tracy Molnar for help with the original graphs. Finally, the comments and criticisms of the various reviewers were most helpful, especially those of David J. Boyd of the

University of California, Davis and Jane H. Underwood of the University of Arizona. The reviewers' sharp eyes and insightful comments guided us toward our goal of producing a book with an ecology-development theme. Any responsibility for falling short of such an ambitious goal is, needless to say, strictly our own.

Chapter 1

Human Environments

A World of Linkages

The twentieth century has been one hundred years of vast changes in all phases of human existence. It has been a time of rapid technological innovation spanning the entire scope of human endeavor: from food production to the control of many diseases, from surface and air transportation to space exploration, from a mastery of many sources of energy to the harnessing of nuclear power. The reach of human ingenuity has even extended to the control and alteration of many life forms through "genetic engineering." Note also must be taken of the explosive development in the capacity to communicate transglobally through satellites and computers, fax machines, cellular phones, and computer networks. This list may be expanded on and on with new innovations added with ever increasing frequency.

Yet, even during a century of such impressive achievements, there has been a growing awareness that something is amiss. There has been an uneasy feeling throughout the last decades, especially, that we may be approaching some yet to be defined environmental limit to the world as we have come to know it. True, we can fly ever faster, communicate further, prevent or heal illness and, with the aid of plant genetics, we also can produce surpluses of food far beyond the imagination of any previous generation. But we have come to recognize that there are costs connected with all of these activities. These costs may be measured in terms of environmental and social changes or in depletion of resources and increasing pollution, but the extent of the costs may not be realized until future generations confront them.

The state of the world has been reported annually in a series of volumes by that name since 1984. These volumes contain data on the essentials for human survival and offer an evaluation of environmental conditions. The list of data ranges from food production to energy systems, from forest products to biodiversity; water supplies and problems of pollution are also covered (see Brown, et al., 1999 for the most recent coverage). The theme of these volumes has been discussed over the years in publications too numerous to mention. General news periodicals have also reviewed the issues as well. *Time* magazine made Earth, "Planet of the Year" (January 2, 1989) and discussed an "endangered earth" plagued with droughts, deforestation, pollution, global warming, and a whole host of the problems confronting our world today. Many of these problems may be attributed to uncontrollable industrial growth as we continue to use natural resources as we always have—carelessly. Another factor was the young, rapidly growing populations in many of the underdeveloped countries.

Some measure of progress has been made since 1989, but many of the same problems still persist. Exactly ten years later, *Newsweek* published a detailed world map showing the locations and types of events that threaten society and environment. Pollutants still fill the waters and atmosphere, but many of the sources have been moved to new localities. Global warming and a decline in the ozone layer of the outer atmosphere have now reached measurable levels that leave little room for dispute. But added to the list is a growing number of what are called "local wars" or areas of civil strife. What has been perhaps the worst development is the increase of AIDS cases and the spread of HIV infection into a full-blown epidemic in several parts of the world. The appearance of these reports, ten years apart, awakens even the most optimistic of us to a realization that perhaps not all is well with humans and their world.

Besides the multiplication of environmental problems, one of the most obvious changes has been the rapid growth of our species, an event unparalleled at any time in our history. Within the last 150 years, we have doubled in number and then doubled again. Most of this population growth has taken place in the past one hundred years; there were 1.6 billion people in the world of 1900, a number that more than doubled by 1965. At the time of this writing, the world's population is approaching the 6 billion mark. From one perspective, this rapid growth may be seen as a landmark of human mastery of the environment, fewer infants die and life expectancy has increased by 50 percent. This may be taken as evidence of successful adaptation[1] of *Homo sapiens*, though such success has not been enjoyed by all people in all nations. The increased number of people has placed an extraordinary burden on resources, space, and on society's infrastructures. Social

[1]*To adapt* refers in a general sense to adjustments of an organism to its environment. The very existence of individuals or a group is evidence of successful adaptation to the conditions encountered, but there are broad differences in the means of adaptation. Degrees of success can be expressed only in relative terms; the comparisons of some measures among groups or populations .

institutions, whether at family, community, or national levels, have been strained to keep pace with the population increases. These institutions must integrate the technological innovations of industry, transportation, and communication in such a way that health and well being may be maintained and expanded for the benefit of present and future generations.

In the last few decades of the twentieth century, questions have been raised with increasing frequency about the impact of this explosive population growth and technological expansion on the environment. The children of the twenty-first century will have to cope with the crowded, polluted environments in a world whose resources are rapidly being depleted. Such an awareness of intergenerational transfer of problems is not new, of course. Over a century ago, George Marsh, in his *Man and Nature* (1864), described the effects of industrialization on the environment and warned of declining resources, increased pollution, and overpopulation. Colonial expansion, several wars, and an explosion of industrial development delayed acceptance of Marsh's wise observations until about fifty years ago, with a renewal of environmental awareness.

This renewal may be traced to a number of publications, like "Man's Role in Changing the Face of the Earth" a symposium collection of papers that dealt with the various effects of human action on the environment (Thomas, 1956). These papers successfully took up the issues first described by Marsh nearly a century before, but it was Rachel Carson's, *Silent Spring* in 1962 that captured the public's attention. This landmark book raised an early warning about pesticides and clearly explained the holistic view of nature with all of its complex linkages among life forms. The destruction of one small part of nature or even a single species could have broad ramifications and cause unanticipated effects. Her acute observations of changes in the natural world and the threats to future generations alerted us to the dangers of chemical pollutants. The increased and often careless use of pesticides by agriculture and industry, together with population growth, threatened the balance of our environment as many species were forced to extinction. Other writers also added to this holistic view of the human condition within a changing environment. Writing from the perspective of a medical microbiologist, Rene Dubos (1965) described changes in human health as a facet of environmental transition. He expanded his theme with an economist, Barbara Ward, in their book *Only One Earth* (1972).

These themes are being carried forward into the contemporary scene by many other writers who have continued to warn of environmental degradation as a consequence of overpopulation. Some of the problems of development and rapid population growth have been acknowledged, while other concerns have been rejected by various critics who see ecologists as alarmist opponents to progress. These critics claim, for example, that the decisions made at the earth summit in Rio De Janeiro in 1992 and at the Cairo population conference two years later were based on outdated information (Bailey,

1995). The risks of global warming were also criticized as being ill founded (Balling, 1995).

There has been some agreement among even the most vigorous of opponents that pollution and resource depletion do pose difficulties for economic growth, but some critics have a firm confidence in scientific solutions. Substitutes will be found for scarce materials, and pollution will be reduced with the improvements of manufacturing processes. Such faith in technological solutions has been a dominant view since the time of the Industrial Revolution. Other critics, less confident in technology alone, see the problem as more social and political than economic or technical, and argue that solutions should be sought in better regulation of industry.

Fortunately, the environmentalist movement of the 1960s, though often criticized, has paved the way for acknowledgment that there are serious problems confronting us and that these problems will intensify with each decade. Events over the last twenty years have proven many of the concerns to be justified and not merely the responses of emotional alarmists. Years after they had been deposited, pollutants often reappear unexpectedly. The spreading of industrial solvents within the water table of the city of Tucson is one example. A volatile solvent was disposed of by pumping it into the ground through injection wells. When first disposed of, the solvent (TCE) was expected to evaporate without harming the environment since it is highly volatile, but twenty years later it was detected as a flume spreading into the water table miles from its injection point. This forced the closing of several wells from which Tucson draws its water.

Another example is offered by the industrial buildup along the U.S. border with Mexico. Many of these industries are major sources of pollution for the Rio Grande River from El Paso-Juarez to Brownsville-Matamores, turning the river into one vast waste disposal ditch endangering those who live along its banks. One of the most dense concentrations of these border industries is found in Tijuana, Mexico, a city with a population of about 2 million people. Sewage and unregulated industrial wastes from the border factories, or *maquiladoras,* run into the Tijuana river that flows north across the border and regularly pollutes ocean and beaches of San Diego (Simon, 1997). Not even the hundreds of millions of dollars spent on sewage treatment and ocean outfalls are expected to completely alleviate the problem as the border area grows.

The weather has also awakened us and provided graphic evidence of the consequences of human disruption of environments. A strong, late season hurricane in October, 1998 blasted over Central America destroying roads, bridges, and banana and coffee plantations. The effects of its high wind and days of nonstop rain were made even worse by the previous decades of rain forest destruction to clear land to support large, growing populations. Mountain- and hillsides had little plant cover so the fierce rains washed out thousands of tons of mud to cover roads and entire villages.

Honduras and Nicaragua were hit the hardest, with an estimated 10,000 dead and five billion dollars in damage.

Periodic climatic shifts also add to the burdens faced by a crowded globe. The exceptionally long hot summers of drought from 1988 to 1994 ruined valuable food crops in many parts of the world, while during nearly the same period, monsoonal rains have caused widespread flooding throughout India and Southeast Asia. The return of a new "El Nino" event in 1996–1997 was blamed as a cause of heavier rainfall in parts of the Americas and for droughts in Southeast Asia. In the United States during the 1997–1998 season, much of the South alternately suffered a blistering summer drought, followed by some of the worst floods in history. One news item in December 1997, commented on the terrible weather of the year and predicted that if it continued, the years 1997–1998 would go down in history as "climatic choas." The weather did continue its erratic gyrations, and the year was a period of climatic chaos.

The erratic weather pattern affected many points of the globe. After months of drought conditions, thousands of acres burned in Florida; the fires spread rapidly, closing major interstate highways and causing whole communities to be abandoned. Even worse droughts have occurred in Sudan, East Africa, resulting in widespread famine. These and other events are but a few examples that, together with many human-caused catastrophes of pollution, destruction of watershed and top soil and urban overcrowding have helped to shake us from our complacency. We are made to recognize that our species is, after all, a part of the complex web of life in the biosphere.

Humans have seriously depleted the earth of many resources; from forests, water, and top soil. We have spent wildly but not wisely in a rush to industrialize. This list includes our squandering of fossil fuels as well, despite the current glut of oil supplies. The continuation of these supplies are sensitive to the precarious political situations of the countries with the petroleum deposits or pipelines.

In the process of industrial development, carbon dioxide levels and several other gases continue to rise, creating what is called a "greenhouse" effect. This trapping of more solar heat than is lost through radiation back into space has contributed to a global warming. Though scientists may disagree on the rate or its long-term effects, there is no question of the increase of greenhouse gases. Concerned scientists have warned of the dangers ahead if the present rate of pollution is continued and the earth's average temperatures rise. They have been countered by critics who claimed that such warnings are exaggerated. Resources are not being depleted at the rate claimed, and the burning of fossil fuels has not altered the outer atmosphere to any critical point. Whichever position one chooses, the earth's environments are to be nurtured and protected and are not to be carelessly used without regard to the future of the growing populations.

The recognition of these problems and concerns is but a first step and must be extended to acknowledge the numerous and complex linkages between human action and environmental consequences. Every extraction of a natural resource, at whatever the level, has an expanding effect radiating throughout the world. There are far reaching side effects resulting from most human activities. The burning of low grade, high sulfur coal in China, exhausts from millions of automobiles, and fuel oil burned to generate electricity sends up clouds of carbon dioxide, sulfur dioxides, and other substances into the atmosphere, which knows no international boundaries.

The accident and near meltdown at Chernobyl, Ukraine's nuclear power plant, has firmly documented how interdependent nations and regions are when it comes to the spread of pollutants. Children throughout Northern Europe were in the path of atmospheric fallout from the radiation leakage emitted hundreds of miles away. They were treated to reduce the uptake of radioactive iodine by their thyroid glands and thereby prevent cancer later in life. The success of this treatment will only be revealed in the years to come.

Nuclear accidents and the difficulty of disposing of wastes from nuclear power plants have led to widespread contamination. The discovery of radioactive contamination from dump sites at weapons manufacturing plants in Washington, Colorado, and Ohio are additions to a growing list. Even in Japan where there is a major commitment to nuclear power but with a high regard for safety, there has been radiation leakage from nuclear plants that date back several years. News of these leaks are often suppressed but were brought to public attention in April of 1997 when the twelfth occurred within three years at one plant alone. This caused an outburst of criticism of the industry from the nation's prime minister. The worldwide news coverage that followed served to alert us that such problems were not confined to any single country. The international web of nuclear materials is now global with a continuous exchange, storage, or dumping of wastes. These added to an extensive array of toxic chemicals and other industrial waste products, have created a number of "hot spots" that effect the health of all living organisms (Wargo, 1996).

It is relatively easy to list the numerous risks we confront in our modern world. Such a listing feeds the cynical pessimism rapidly spreading throughout all levels of society and contributes to a feeling of helplessness. But what to do? Can world conferences like the Earth Summits twenty years apart (Stockholm, 1972 and Rio, 1992) or the World Population Conferences (Bucharest, 1974, Mexico City, 1984, and Cairo, 1994) offer solutions or mobilize national efforts? Is there a collective will to take action or are we even ready to recognize that our planet is of finite space and limited resources? If not a collective will or agreement on a course of action, at least there is an agreement that problems exist that need to addressed. Do we continue to follow a more optimistic course that looks to technology and economic expansion as an answer, or do we acknowledge some limits to industrial development?

The mix of global politics and economics at these conferences has provided evidence of the difficulties confronting international cooperation on family planning issues or the regulation of environmental pollution. A clear example of linkages between political decisions and global results was offered by the recent conference in Kyoto, Japan, 1997 to discuss climate and the problems of global warming. There was, to put it briefly, a complete lack of agreement on the action needed to reduce air and water pollution. The less-developed nations wish to have fewer pollution restrictions so their industries can catch up with the developed world. They argued that the more-developed nations, especially the United States, create greater amounts of hazardous wastes and are responsible for far more air pollution than all of the less-developed world. Therefore, such nations should bear a larger share of the control effort (Dunn, 1998). As would be expected, industrialists of the more-developed nations rejected these arguments.

We all share the same planet and its atmosphere; every farm, mine, oil well, or timber operation depends on the earth's resources and is linked together across political boundaries. Brown, pesticide-laden dust from intensely farmed arid lands has been blown all the way to the Arctic and has been found deposited on the region's ice and snow surfaces. The smoke from forest fires in Central America polluted the air over much of the southern United States. Chemical discharges in major rivers that flow across national boundaries (Europe's Rhine and Danube rivers are frequent examples) and coastal and harbor oil spills are too numerous to list. The global warming from greenhouse gases and depletion of the ozone layer caused by chlorinated hydrocarbons are other examples. Within all of these industrial–environmental links are the people, the willing or unwilling participants in these processes.

It is not sufficient to state that "everything" is linked to "everything" else on the planet, however. Nor can one pass with "You cannot do only one thing in the environment" or "Every action has multiple consequences." These or similar statements scarcely define or describe the nature or the extent of the linkages that involve humans in their manipulation of their environments. Such observations do not lead to an understanding that is sufficient for problem solving. Likewise, the comment that every activity may have unwanted consequences does not clearly focus our attention on the web of world linkages or on the political decisions that affect broader environmental consequences across time and international borders.

We must learn just what components of society and environment are linked and how the interactions work at each level of complexity throughout social and environmental interchanges. What will happen, for example, to human or to other species when alternative water supplies or food sources are secured? Just how sensitive are we to changes in diet or to waterborne pollutants that have been encountered over the past few generations? In another example, what behavioral responses might be stimulated by population crowding as a result of the development of dense urban areas? Generally, how do groups or individuals react to change in human and natural systems at various levels, and what might be the measures of these reactions?

Some guidance may be gained by a review of past events. How did past societies cope with crises of change? As Butzer (1990) argued, such an understanding is critical for the formation of effective management of resources. The impact of rapid change on indigenous peoples offers another body of information. Their ecological framework had been so different than either the developed or developing world that indigenous people provide several contrasts of human–environmental interactions. As their homelands have been overrun, resources destroyed, and their lifestyles changed, a measurement of the several responses provide some clues to human adaptation.

CENTRAL ELEMENTS OF HUMAN ECOLOGY

We shall start with an overview of four elements central to human ecology: *diet, disease, demography,* and *development.* Though each has some unique features and affects a population in specific ways, these elements are linked and interdependent for human survival. Should food supply decline, then dietary deficiencies will influence health, and in turn affect mortality, which will have an intergenerational impact on the demographic structure of the society. Most frequently, the individual and collective behavior within society determines the degree of linkage through the selection of the forms of environmental use.

Diet, is listed first because of the obvious dependency on basic nutrients for energy, growth, and tissue maintenance. The nutritional requirements of *Homo sapiens,* though, may be satisfied by a broad range of animal and plant products, which the human digestive tract can use as food. The acquisition of these foods, their quality, and their quantity are factors that influence health, well being, life span, and the size and age composition of a population. Variations in diet are linked closely to the other three elements.

Disease is considered as the next element because of its close relationship to nutritional status and to a people's use of space. Detrimental aspects of the environment are often expressed in a human population by a decline or depression of health due to malnutrition, infectious organisms, or exposure to some toxic pollutant. Such exposure, of course, often can be readily related to human activities and use of space, which influences contact with toxins and pathogenic organisms. Recognition and/or treatment of a disease also influence its impact on health.

Demography, the third element, is a study of the nature of population structure and the change in its composition from generation to generation. It can be a key measure of adaptation and, hence, is a major focus of our concern. The size and age distribution of a population, its fertility rate, and its morbidity/mortality rates all give evidence of a society's success in coping with the environment. For example, the number of newborns who survive the first year of life and, after this crucial first year, the number of children reaching their fifth birthday are sensitive measures for comparative population studies. Demography also provides data like age distribution, which enables projections and predictions to be made of the future demands on resources. The obtainment of the resources required to satisfy the needs of a population of a given size requires a certain degree of technological skill and an expertise in the use of space that, in turn, influences food needs and health.

Development, the fourth element of human ecology, examines the use of the environment to suit society's purposes. Growth of or change in population composition as a response to human or naturally influenced events requires a more efficient use of resources, or, put another way, an improvement in methods of gaining the means of survival. Therefore, the term *development* identifies linkages to the other three categories primarily because it encompasses the use of space, natural resources, and all of the various features of the environment in general. Defined in this way, development means much more than its current usage in reference to development of natural resources or industrial development as in "developing countries" or "developing" economies.

LINKAGES

Interaction among these four elements may be explored to determine how human adaptation can be defined or measured. We shall consider in the following examples and in subsequent chapters levels of organization of human–environmental interaction. The first level concerns the survival of small-scale societies and the strategies employed to acquire the necessities of life. As an example, hunting or pastoral nomads are described in contrast to sedentary agricultural societies (Lee, 1969; Chagnon, 1983). Larger agrarian communities differ significantly from each of these smaller societies by the addition of complex political structures to regulate and control access to resources. Control of water rights in arid lands, distribution of plant seeds and fertilizer or development of roads and canals have all been added to elevate the complexity of human survival networks. The development of resources and conflicts among the international communities add still another layer of complexity and inject political considerations as a major influence.

The larger the population, the more apparent are controls that extend beyond the simple extended family level. Groups of human populations within an environment and their relationships to other organisms form a community established through coexistence and maintained in what has been described as a system of feedback networks called an *ecosystem*. Beyond these local communities, whole regions, even continents, are brought into more and more frequent interchange. These interchanges cross national boundaries within which local political issues often influence use of broader regional or even worldwide environments. This system of causes and effects at the human level has become especially apparent within this century but, unfortunately, the implications have only been appreciated within the last few decades.

Air pollution problems, such as acid rain—the hyperacidity of rain because of its sulfur dioxide content—is global, and many nations produce this pollutant. There has long been an awareness of the problem, and technical solutions have existed for more than forty years, but it has not been easy to bring the political and economic considerations together with the technical solutions. Likewise, the use of lead additives in gasoline, a decision made in 1922 to improve fuel combustion properties, caused a continuing increase in atmospheric lead far above that level reached a century ago through the burning of another fossil fuel, coal. Ice cores taken from the Greenland ice cap showed that lead concentration increased by a factor of twenty between 1750 and 1967. An estimated 400,000 tons of lead compounds were released into the atmosphere in 1970 (Montague and Montague, 1976). On a positive note, there has been an improvement since the introduction of unleaded gasoline in 1970; the quantity of lead compounds injected into the atmosphere has declined by a factor of seven over the past twenty years (Goudie, 1994). These compounds are washed out by rainfall and are picked up by plants and animals to become widely dispersed in the food chain. City air contains high concentrations, as well as the air over the communities near lead mines and smelters. From the beginnings of the industrial age, sulfates, nitrates, and carbon dioxide concentrations in the atmosphere have also increased, in addition to lead. These and other pollution problems offer many examples of political–environmental interdependencies.

Population growth, food distribution, famine, and disease control are other areas to explore in seeking an understanding of the more complex linkages within ecosystems of the modern world. Demography is central to this understanding but less so than in other species because, paradoxically, we are so adaptable. Our ingenuity in behavioral adaptation and our physiological acclimatization enable us to achieve numerous responses to climatic stresses. We can survive under most of the environmental conditions found on the planet. In modern times, the measure of adaptation has become more than a matter of survival, however. The length and quality of life are significant considerations for individuals and their society. Human populations, therefore, must be viewed within a worldwide context and the measure of biological success, or "fitness," requires more than a simple count of numbers of people.

When populations expand due to any number of causes, there will be a ripple effect extending over generations. The increase of Western Europeans in the eighteenth and nineteenth centuries contributed to colonial expansion and the occupation of many world regions. This increase offers a historical record of a population impact with global dimensions. A recent example was the slight increase in birth rates in China in 1987 due to a change in birth control policy. The rise of just three births per thousand that year meant that there were 22.3 million births compared to 18.9 million over the preceding twelve-month period. Because of China's size of over 1 billion people, this seemingly simple change in population policy added 3.4 million new people to the 85 million annual increase in world population. This may be taken as a linkage of events in the broadest sense of the word. Political decisions responding to social needs and preconceptions about quality of life within one country can have far-reaching international repercussions.

Other illustrations of demographic processes have been the disproportionate growth of minority groups that can have important political consequences, as in the example of the former USSR. The end of the cold war, leading to the dissolution of the Soviet Union, has been attributed to many causes but tensions among ethnic minorities and demographic differentials are seldom mentioned. Tajikistan and the other southern Republics, encompassing most of Central Asia—from the rich oil fields around the Caspian sea to China—contain roughly 60 million people. This is three times the number living in the area fifty years ago and is due to a retention of high birth rates while mortality declined. These populations, mostly followers of the Islamic religion, had a higher fertility rate and, hence, a population growth rate three times that of the European Russian majority of the Soviet Union. Such a high growth rate of ethnic minorities likely have had far-reaching repercussions for Russian society. Interestingly, since their breakaway from the Soviet Union, most of these now independent nations have halved their fertility rates between 1992 and 1998 (see Chapter 5).

These former states of the old USSR are now established as independent republics. Some have maintained close contacts with Russia, while some look to Iran in the south or to Turkey to the west for economic and possibly political alliances. Within several of these new republics, certain ethnic minorities have revived their traditions and are battling for political recognition. The economic impact caused by the discovery of rich oil deposits and the wealth to be gained by building pipelines to the West have further added to a need for political alliances or for ethnic dominance.

Even smaller, more localized regional demographic differences can initiate a broad range of world events. The higher fertility rates of minority groups may contribute to political upheaval a generation or more in the future. Some scholars have pointed to Lebanon as an example. When that nation gained independence following World War II, government representation was apportioned among Christian and Muslim factions according to their relative population. Over the last forty years, the fertility rate has been nearly twice as high among the Muslims, and they now make up a majority of the population, but the parliamentary representation established in 1946 has been retained. This could be seen as one of the contributing causes of the civil war that was bitterly fought from 1973 until the 1990 cease-fire, a conflict that has affected the entire Middle East and beyond. The Muslims in Israel have nearly twice the fertility rate as the Jewish population, a factor that adds to an already difficult relationship.

The eruption of war among Croat, Muslim, and Serb ethnic groups of the several Balkan republics of the former Yugoslavia that broke up in 1989 serves as another example of how ethnicity can be manipulated for political purposes. The wars fought at a vicious, often genocidal level relate to a complex of issues leading to the quest for political control of territory. Frequently, ancient ethnic conflicts have been described as the root cause (Kaplan, 1993; Sells, 1996). Though there is some historical basis for such a thesis, it is more likely that political advantage has been taken of the demographic differentials among ethnic groups. The high birth rate of Albanians has been cited as a threat to stir up Serbian nationalism, for example.

At the time of this writing, there is an uneasy peace in the Bosnian republic and its capital city lies in ruins divided among the former waring factions. The Balkan ethnic conflict continues, however, in nearby Kosovo where the Albania majority is fighting against their Serb rulers. In an effort to halt Serbian army attacks on Albanian civilians, NATO planes are bombing Serbia. Ethnicity, demography, and politics is a dangerous mix and can easily turn genocidal. The current fighting in the Balkans and the recent mass killings in Rwanda serve as grim reminders (see discussion of genocide in Lemarchand, 1994).

During these and other conflicts, some still continuing, farming has been impossible; planting is not done nor are crops harvested. One of the major markers of the twentieth-century development is that so much surplus food has been produced even during times when certain lands have failed to produce. What is more striking is that this surplus could be moved about the world to relieve famine. Tons of food have been delivered to Bosnia, to several African countries, and to many of the other trouble spots around the world where either natural or man-made catastrophe has prevented a local population from feeding itself. Support of the world's rapid population growth over future decades will require ever more efficiency of agricultural production.

A simple way of viewing population dependence on food productivity is through a consideration of energy transfer from agricultural effort to satisfaction of nutritional needs; the more people there are, the greater food energy required. Providing this energy has been one of the great achievements of our recent history, and there are numerous linkages between food acquisition, population growth, and the maintenance of larger numbers of people. These achievements have multiplied and accumulated since the start of the food producing revolution 10,000 years ago, when humans began to domesticate plants and animals.

From this early milestone, technological skills and new plant and animal species have added to productivity, increasing the numbers of people supported. Most increases were gradual and occurred over long periods of time, but there was a dramatic leap into a new era following the discovery and colonization of the Western hemisphere. The plants brought from the New World and adapted by European farmers increased agricultural production enormously and may be called the first "Green Revolution." Similar population increases had occurred in Asia since the times of the earliest agricultural revolution. These increases accelerated, especially in China and India, when certain food crops from the New World were introduced. Food production and improvements in technology are examples of development in its broadest sense, as outlined in Chapter 3.

For most of the last 150 years, however, development has increasingly occurred not because of local events but through massive changes brought about by outside forces and imposed at all levels of society. This form of development has usually taken the course of extraction of raw materials in exchange for manufactured goods or the planting of desirable "cash crops" like tobacco, sugar cane, or cotton. The European countries—in their African, Asian, and Latin American colonies, especially Britain in India—provided examples of a succession of the enormous changes that can be imposed over a very short space of time, even within one or two generations. The linkages that interconnect these changes have been far reaching, touching all levels of society throughout the globe and may be seen as the foundation for political events continuing even today in nations of these former colonies.

Economic development has contributed to vast geographic shifts in populations. The need for a cheap labor force to work the sugar, cotton, or tobacco plantations led to the transport of Africans to South America, the Caribbean, and to the southeastern United States. This forced migration introduced populations that soon replaced the Native American peoples of these regions, especially in the Caribbean. The vitality of Africans, even under the harsh conditions of slavery, far exceeded that of the indigenous peoples. On the other side of the world, in the Pacific, early contact, along with the later exploitation of the coconut palm for its oil forever changed many of the island environments and the lives of the diverse peoples spread over the vast reaches of the Pacific.

Historically, some of the well-known exchanges can be seen in the stories of European explorations of the eighteenth century. The Pacific discovery by Captain Cook of an easily grown tropical plant of high food value (the breadfruit) led to a series of voyages to transport seedlings to the Caribbean. The first attempt made by Captain Bligh's ship, *Bounty,* was aborted by the famous mutiny when mutineers seized the ship and sailed away to eventually land at the uncharted island of Pitcairn, after setting the captain and part of the crew adrift. Years later, Captain Bligh successfully completed his mission and the sugar cane planters on the British-controlled islands in the Caribbean received the breadfruit trees to grow as a cheap food energy source for their slave workers. This connection extended the economic viability of the sugar plantation system for a longer period than would have been possible given the broad fluctuation of sugar prices and the rising costs of slave labor replacements.

Since these early eighteenth- and nineteenth-century examples of development and change, there has been an exponential increase of external economic forces exerted on formerly isolated populations. Their lands have been mined for its minerals or exploited for oil, and plantation cash crops have displaced the traditional plantings. Polynesians who had depended on fish, taro, and coconuts now rely instead on spam, canned fish, and refined white flour. The Arctic Inuit (Eskimo) went to work for wages and purchased packaged foods in a company store, displacing their traditional diet. Subsistence farmers in Africa plant the maize and cassava for their dietary staples and have generally abandoned many of the native plants used by previous generations. Former nomadic hunters and foragers of Africa and Australia gathered around missions, towns, and cattle stations and became dependent on handouts of foods of lower nutritional value than that of their traditional diets.

The results have been all too clear. The change in diets to foods of lower nutritional value reduced their health and general well being. Indigenous people began to suffer heart disease, hypertension, and diabetes. Alcoholism was epidemic in many groups. Vitamin deficiencies appeared where none had ever been reported. Generally, the "Western diseases" common to the more-developed world may be attributed directly to economic development and dietary changes (Latham, 1978; Trowell and Burkitt, 1981).

In addition to economic development affecting a change in diet, which in turn influenced health, there are instances where development radically alters health through a change of work habits, time allocation, and use of land. The changes from subsistence activities to wage labor has had profound effects. Men often must leave for months at a time for seasonal migrant labor; and women are left to tend crops, if any, and care for the household. When women are employed by factories or on plantations, the effects on the family may be even worse. Participation of women in the labor force adversely effects child health. A woman's employment outside the home reduces the duration of breast feeding and alters child care in general. The family's diet also suffers in many ways, especially that of the children. One recent study demonstrated how a change in female work–time allocation during agricultural development contributed to an increase in xeropthalmia, a vitamin A deficiency disease of the eye (Huffman, 1987).

The development-health linkage appears to work like this: Families with working mothers, who recently became employed in garment industries or manufacturing assembly plants, had greater family incomes and a higher food budget but a radically altered diet. Protein and total food energy increased but the intake of vitamin A declined because of a decrease in the consumption of fresh vegetables. This change in dietary pattern can be related to the number of hours spent outside the household (Nurse, Weiner, and Jenkins, 1985). The negative affect on family nutrition likely occurs because less time is spent on food selection or in the tending of vegetables in their household gardens. There was the tendency for these working mothers to purchase those prepackaged and more readily available items, usually the refined, processed foods of high caloric content but lower in vitamin content.

Similar effects on family health and nutritional status may be seen among traditional agriculturists upon adoption of modern farm technology. With the introduction of plows and tractors as alternatives to hand labor, more land can be brought into production. These new methods are labor saving and more time efficient for the men whose agricultural role had been the heavy work of clearing and preparing the land for planting. Though the male work loads were reduced, female labor increased because they were responsible for the weeding and harvesting of the crops. With an expanded acreage under cultivation, less time is available for the care of their family; infants and the younger children receive less attention and suffered accordingly.

Technological improvements in food preparation also influence female labor–time allocation. The introduction of mechanical grinding of grains is labor saving but lowers the quality of the diet through the removal of the bran from the wheat or rice. A reduction in food quality is costly in terms of health, as demonstrated nearly a century ago. For example, the removal of the husk and the polishing of rice resulted in beriberi, the thiamin(B_1) deficiency disease that was once widespread throughout Southeast Asia following the introduction of mechanical processing of rice by steel roller mills. Other deficiency diseases are also known to occur following introduction of a new food supply or change in processing. Pellagra, another vitamin B deficiency disease, once prevalent among farm laborers of Southern Europe and sharecroppers in the southeastern United States, is the result of overreliance on maize(corn) as a major dietary component (Roe, 1973).

International economics play an increasingly important role as one of the linkages in the global ecological system. The oil price increases during the early 1970s sent the world economic system into a wild upward spiral of inflation. In addition to its economic effects, the price increases had a major impact upon the health and well being of millions throughout the underdeveloped countries. The increase in fuel energy prices drove up the costs of all petroleum-derived products. The impact of the price rise of fertilizers and insecticides contributed significantly to higher food prices. The less-developed countries, most of whom had to import these petroleum products, were especially hard hit during this period. Crop yields declined and there were few alternatives except an appeal for food aid. In addition, these countries were forced to make hard economic decisions that influenced population health over the next decade. One such decision involved a scaling back of insect control programs that contributed to a rise of the mosquito-borne diseases.

These examples, taken from contemporary cases, illustrate several levels of interrelationships that often include ever larger numbers of people and span greater distances. Increasingly since the age of European exploration, what occurs in one formerly remote, isolated area can, and often does, influence other regions, sometimes on a global scale as in the examples of the dumping of toxins in many underdeveloped countries. Millions of metric tons of toxic wastes are shipped from the Western industrialized nations each year to be dumped in several countries of the less-developed countries and Eastern Europe (Stebbins, 1992). Waste disposal has become a major enterprise, and the United States finds it less expensive to ship wastes thousands of miles than to find a dump site nearer home. Recent news describes plans to construct giant incinerators in Somalia for the treatment of Europe's industrial wastes. Somalia, with its war-torn and shattered economy, views this development as a benefit. The Marshall islands in the Central Pacific, where nuclear tests were carried out in the 1950s had considered offering some of its uninhabited atolls islands as storage sites for wastes from Taiwan's nuclear power reactors. In response to strong opposition, the Marshall's government blocked any further discussion and announced a ban on the introduction of foreign nuclear wastes into its territory.

Neighboring islands had also protested this offer, as had other nations. They rejected the disposal of toxic wastes of any kind in their territory. The reasoning is that if developed countries refused to bury the wastes in their own ground then it was too dangerous to accept. The needs to dispose of vast amounts of wastes remains, but the industrialized world's attitude is "Not in my backyard." Germany sent containers of contaminated pesticides to Albania for disposal in 1986. Albania refused to accept the cargo, but Germany would not take the pesticide load back. Where it is remains a mystery. New York City, unable to continue to dump sewage plant sludge in the ocean, has made a deal with Arizona and Texas farmers who are paid to spread the sludge on their cotton fields as a soil conditioner. This is continuing despite the protests of environmentalists who point to the high bacteria count and industrial residues in the sludge that they consider a health risk to local residents. Then there are the stories of ships and barges that have left major ports loaded with incinerator ash, compacted toxic material or sludge bound for countries where the materials would be dumped. The country would have a change of heart and reject the toxic cargo, so the ship would ply the sea lanes looking for another site. One shipload was rejected by countries from Sri Lanka to the Philippines until the ship finally turned up empty and with a new name in Singapore two years later. These and other stories illustrate the creation of something called garbage imperialism, since the developed nations have run out of dump sites they are seeking "colonies" where the debris of industry can be deposited (Stebbins, 1992).

CLIMATES AND SEASONALITY

Another perspective of the interactions between populations and their environments may be gained by considering the influence of seasonality, the periodic shift in climate that causes changes in disease organisms and vectors and affects crop production. The linkages to seasons may be seen as a reflection of the adaptability of our species to the demands of the environment and may be measured in several ways. The recent studies of poverty, disease, and seasonality in tropical regions offer numerous examples that may be summarized in this way. In subsistence farming areas, where food reserves are often low, the time prior to harvest is a time when food is in shortest supply and market prices are highest. Unfortunately, this is when the greatest physical work is needed but there is little chance of fully supplying a population's food energy needs. The average body weight among all age groups goes down and the children grow poorly during this season. It is also during this period when disease rates are at their highest. Household chores and cooking are neglected because of the heavy agricultural workload borne by the women (Bayliss-Smith, 1981). The alteration between wet and dry periods of the tropics place the heaviest burden on females in their reproductive years. The net result can be a broad fluctuation in the population's health from one season of the year to the next. Of course, this seasonal dependence has changed materially with a move away from subsistence farming, increased trade, and with urbanization.

Weather patterns and geography can also influence populations in an even broader sense and serve to link the fate of nations. Because climates, air currents, and gravity carry pollutants in air or water across national boundaries, decisions regarding the use of resources made by one political unit will frequently influence neighboring or distant cities or nations. The increased flow and the loads of silt carried by major rivers out of the Himalayas, like the Ganges, offer one of many examples of the international ramifications of local political decisions. The Ganges River feeds water and nutrients into a vast fertile area upon which tens of millions of India's burgeoning population depend. With the successful exploitation of hybrid seeds, agrochemicals and irrigation, northern India has taken full advantage of the productivity made possible by the "Green Revolution" that has led to a surplus of grains, especially wheat. But continued high productivity depends increasingly upon efficient control of river flow that has become evermore difficult each decade with increased run off from denuded mountain slopes.

The Ganges begins its life in the streams flowing out of the Himalayas, gradually increasing in volume as several rivers arising in Nepal join the Ganges along its course. These rivers, forming the major part of the drainage of the southern Himalayan slopes have, for millennia, added nutrient ladened silt to produce fertile plains along its 1550 mile course to the sea. This building of the river valley and the delta at the river mouth had been a gradual process and was a great benefit to the dense populations of India and Bangladesh.

The seasonal flooding from the summer monsoon rains was an anticipated and a welcomed event over hundreds of years. In the last fifty years, however, floods have become more extensive and destructive; 59 million hectares were covered in 1987 compared to only 25 million hectares in 1960. The worsening of flood conditions in the nation of Bangledash at the river's mouth have been even more dramatic. Peak flood levels in the delta, formed by the Ganges and Brahmaputta(Jamuna), have risen by two meters over the last sixty-five years. But even this peak was exceeded in September 1988 and 1991 and again in 1997 when both rivers overflowed their banks and covered nearly three-quarters of the country at its peak flood stage.

Though this densely populated nation of 124 million, living on the Ganges–Brahmaputta delta, had been subject to the devastating effects of cyclone winds, floods, and epidemics for generations, the floods of 1991 exceeded any others in recorded history and reportedly killed over a hundred thousand people. The causes of these increased flood conditions and the source of the 1.5 billion tons of sediment deposited on the delta are numerous but not difficult to identify; in addition to population increases that force more people to occupy low lying coastal areas, one has only to look to the northern Indian states and to the countries occupying the watersheds of the southern slopes of the Himalayas, especially Nepal.

The tiny nation of Nepal, about the size of the state of Arkansas, has experienced a rapid population growth since 1950. It has nearly doubled in population and reached 15 million by 1980; the continued high growth rate of 2.2 percent per year raised the population to 23.7 million by 1998. To feed these additional millions, greater food production and an expansion of agriculture was greatly encouraged by international agencies who provided the necessary seed, fertilizers, and technical assistance. Such expansion required more land, and deforestation proceeded rapidly and eventually included even the steeper mountain slopes. Between 1964 and 1984, Nepal lost over half of its forests. By the mid 1970s the consequences became all too clear and plans were made to reverse this trend; an aggressive reforestation program is now underway.

The people throughout Nepal have enthusiastically supported the conservation programs and marked advances have been made. However, the scarcity of agricultural land and the heavy demand for fuel wood (wood provides 90 percent of the cooking fuel) are still problems to be confronted. Forests grow slowly while the needs for forestry products and agricultural land rapidly expand; farming priorities of land use are difficult to restrict. In the meantime, soil erosion continues to add to the silt load of the rivers that eventually reach the Ganges–Brahmaputta delta. Thus, the needs and political decisions of a nation of about 19 million people influence the fate of nearly 400 million others living down stream. The population policies, environmental resources, and conservation decisions have and will continue to have a major impact on the most densely populated areas of India and Bangladesh. Again, the importance of the observation that you cannot change your environment without affecting others far away is of significance.

Political borders whether in developing or developed countries are not necessarily boundaries or barriers that restrict the effects of human action on natural environments. Witness the pollution of the Rhine and Danube rivers, which drain highly industrialized countries of Europe and carry a heavy load of pollutants. Likewise, the Mississippi drains a vast area of the United States and deposits top soil sediments and pollutants in the Gulf of Mexico. Or note the condition of the Colorado river, whose waters are increasingly diverted to irrigate desert farmland or supply burgeoning urban centers of California and Arizona while there is little water, but with a high saline content, reaching Mexico at the head of the Gulf of California. Air currents loaded with industrial pollutants, auto exhaust fumes and, from time to time, radiation particles are, likewise, a continuing concern for international communities.

SPATIAL USE AND URBANIZATION

Another kind of adaptation provides additional examples of connections between human populations and their environments. Since humans began a transition to sedentary life some 10,000 years ago with the earliest establishment of village life, influences of population density became an important factor in survival. The more people, the greater the host reservoir for a variety of organisms, many of which are disease causing. With denser populations, the transfer of such agents of disease from person to person is more frequent. Many of the "plagues" of the past were dependent upon particular conditions that were related to or caused by human activity. The skeletal remains of populations from these earliest periods of sedentary life, beginning in the Neolithic, show more frequent signs of disease and a short life expectancy by Bronze age and later. Additionally, sedentary life required a considerable change in the use of space and resources. Waste disposal became a problem, and polluted air and water were threats of major proportions. With the rise of the city, human populations became increasingly at risk with higher morbidity and mortality rates. Historical records provide us with even clearer evidence that, for most, life was short, morbidity was high, and disease epidemics were frequent events.

From the first cities built on the deltas of the great rivers of the Middle East and probably in China as well, our species' destiny seems to have been urban. There has been an increasing trend towards more and larger cities in modern times. Before the 1800s, cities of the world seldom reached 100,000 in population, Rome, London, and Mexico City excepted. Stimulated by the rise of technology during the Industrial Revolution in Western Europe, cities began to grow and London passed the 1 million mark by 1800. There were eleven cities of 1 million or more in the world, by 1900, and six of these were in Europe. Since then, the rate of urban growth has accelerated and has been greatest in the lesser-developed countries(LDC).

In 1950, 700 million lived in cities of 100,000 or more. As of mid-year 1998, 44 percent of the total world population of 5.9 billion lived in urban centers; the LDC (excluding China) counted 39 percent of its numbers in large urban conglomerates with an annual growth of 2 to 5 percent. Even India, a country that is still largely rural, 26 percent of 988.7 million people live in urban centers. Growth is especially rapid in urban giants of Asia like Beijing (11 million), Bombay (over 15 million), Shanghai (14 million), and Delhi(10 million). High population growth rates, reduction in numbers of agricultural jobs, and loss of land has driven millions to seek jobs in the city. The daily migration into Calcutta (population 12 million) alone is an estimated thousand per day, and cities throughout Latin America also experience high rates of growth. In Mexico, the flow of people into Mexico City (17 million) and urban centers along the northern border continues at daily rates estimated in the thousands. Such rural–urban migrations will continue as people seek employment and escape from rural poverty. This uncontrolled urbanization phenomenon places an enormous burden on outdated social and environmental infrastructures

Calcutta, India, is trying to meet the needs of 12 million people with a system designed for an urban population of about 2 million. The transportation facilities are near collapse and lack of housing forces millions to live several hours from their place of employment. The sewers and water systems are likewise wholly inadequate for such numbers. Cairo (10 million), Egypt, as well as other African cities, provide additional examples of the daunting task to provide life support systems for large, rapidly growing urban conglomerates. The lack of clean water and proper waste disposal contributes to periodic outbreaks of the "old" diseases that historically have plagued mankind. The latest example is the rise and spread of cholera from Lima, the crowded capital of Peru, surrounded by a sprawl of shanty towns. The few cases brought into Europe and North America by travelers and some imported foods suggest how vulnerable we all are, especially with increased travel and during the periods following natural disasters that disrupt water supplies and sewage systems. The "old diseases," tuberculosis, cholera, typhoid, typhus, and the like, have not gone away. They just remain in the background until environmental changes provide the right conditions to increase the spread of the pathogens (see Chapter 7).

The highly developed, industrialized world is not free of the problems of city growth by any means. Daily reports describe traffic gridlock and pollution-laden air. The difficulties of waste disposal from millions of urban residents are well known. Garbage-laden barges are towed about in search of disposal sites, and train loads of sewage sludge are transported 2,000 miles, as described. Between waste disposal problems, air pollution, crowding, traffic gridlocks, and housing shortages, the human endurance is heavily taxed with little relief in sight. If urbanization is, in fact, our destiny, an overview of the urban environment should provide many examples of linkages among disease, demography, development, and even diet.

As viewed from a historical perspective, the increase in population redistribution, change of settlement patterns, and the rise of technology are often seen as evidence of progress. Since human progress is equated with economic growth, a series of positive correlations have been identified by many authors. The increase in numbers of people, economic advancement, an increase in wealth, and a rise in average income are interrelated and contribute pressures for further technological advancement. Development and expansion of technology, it is argued, are responses to these pressures. Economists often point out that population growth stimulates technological innovations to meet the new needs. There is a technofix to meet mankind's problems. One level of events (population growth) stimulates a response (development of technology), followed by other pressures (environmental depletion), stimulates a search for alternate resources, and so on. There are numerous unintended consequences or side effects. These feedbacks among environment, population, and human actions lead to ever-escalating costs to the environment and society, caused by an expansion in population and the attendant exploitation of the environment.

We do not always know what the side effects will be nor which linkages operate, or how they may work at different levels of complexity. Theoretically, we should be able to establish some model or models to evaluate or predict the responses or changes in human institutions to those pressures brought about by the major variables. More people will require more space, more energy, etc. However, the confounding factor is the unpredictability of human populations in their search for satisfaction of biological needs and their perceptions of what these needs are. Humans, as individuals and especially in groups, often fail to respond as expected. The choices or options open to us are broad and the alternatives are many. Thus, it becomes necessary, even essential, to view human adaptations in special ways.

A most significant part of our preparation for the twenty-first century should be the establishment of a means of evaluating human adaptation. In order to compare populations under differing circumstances, we must have objective measurements to evaluate ability to respond and to adjust to the newer stresses of environmental change. These measures become especially important as populations go through a transition of lifestyle and environments, often at rapid rates. The subsistence farmers caught up by the development of large-scale commercial farming, as in the example of the rice farmers in Southeast Asia when the hybrid rice of the "Green Revolution" was introduced, or remote tribal communities of the Amazon rain forest impacted by mining, oil exploration, or lumbering operations, are examples of societies who must meet the demands and burdens enforced upon them by a changing world. Such groups respond in various ways; some adapt successfully and are able to maintain their society, but most, sadly, do not. Some become extinct as a culture, and some are able to sustain a few remnants of the past. Many of the old ways disappear, just as in developed societies, traditions and practices change over the generations.

This is a book about change and adaptation—the human capacity to adjust or to cope with the stresses generated within a changing environment. The following chapters are an examination of the evidence for linkages among human actions, the natural world, and altered environments. The emphasis throughout will be on the degree and kinds of interactions or the covariation of the physical and behavioral environments at several technological levels of human existence, since we hold that these environmental features cannot and should not be examined separately.

Chapter 2

Humans and Ecological Concepts

World environments place limits on human survival. Available water, hours and intensity of sunlight, animal and plant life, mean annual temperatures, and seasonal changes are the major components that set the boundaries of human habitation. This is true for other species as well, since much of the globe is inhospitable to many life forms. Over one-third of the land areas are either covered with polar ice caps, arid desert, or is at elevations over 3,000 meters. In fact, of all land areas, nearly one-half are uninhabited by humans or can be occupied only under special conditions.

The life-support potential of the habitable regions of the earth may be evaluated by defining a series of divisions that establish areas or zones relative to their distances from the equator. Within each of these zones further divisions are made, biogeographical regions called *biomes,* that have differing combinations of climate, precipitation rates, altitude, terrain, and natural geological features. Certain biomes favor particular life forms more so than others, as in the growth of a combination of plant varieties that, in turn, support a variety of animal life. This is illustrated by the hardy herbaceous scrubs growing at higher elevations or the drought resistant plants of arid lands or the lichens and mosses of the Arctic tundra.

The *tropics,* for example, include a range of biomes from grasslands to deserts, from rain forests to montane regions—all defined by rainfall, altitude, and physical location on continents or islands (Figure 2–1a and b). This zone between the Tropic of Cancer at 22° North latitude (northern hemisphere) and the Tropic of Capricorn at 22° South latitude (southern hemisphere), is a global region of intense solar radiation with little seasonal change. The region can be subdivided by amounts of rainfall into dry or wet

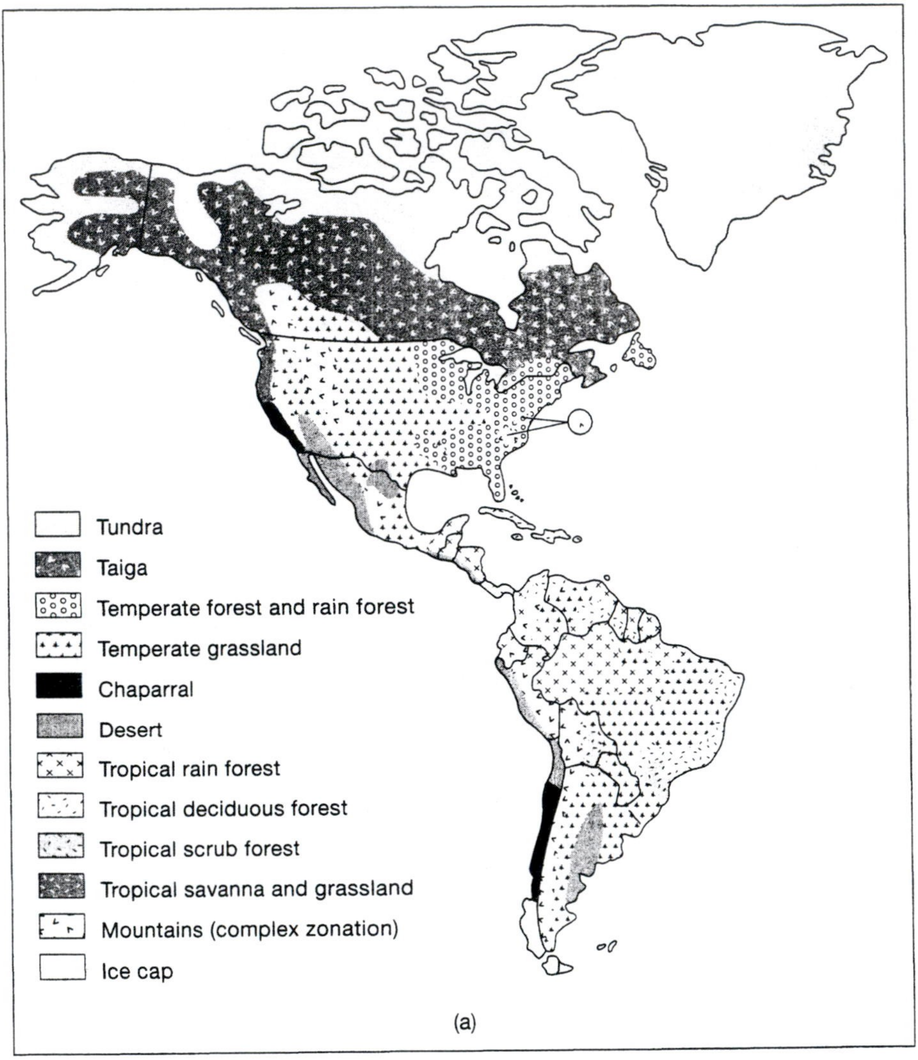

Figure 2–1a The Distribution of the Major Biomes of the World (Western Hemisphere)

From *Ecoscience: Population, Resources, Environment.* P. Ehrlich, A. Ehrlich, and J. Holdren, 1977. Reprinted by permission of the authors.

tropics. Dry tropics include semiarid grasslands with scattered scrub woodlands and deserts where rainfall averages less than 200 centimeters per year, as contrasted the wet tropics with high annual rainfall of 250 or more and thickly forested areas of a great variety of plant species (part b of Figure 2–1a). Each of the other regional divisions support a particular combination of life forms that is well adjusted to the local conditions. Compare the major

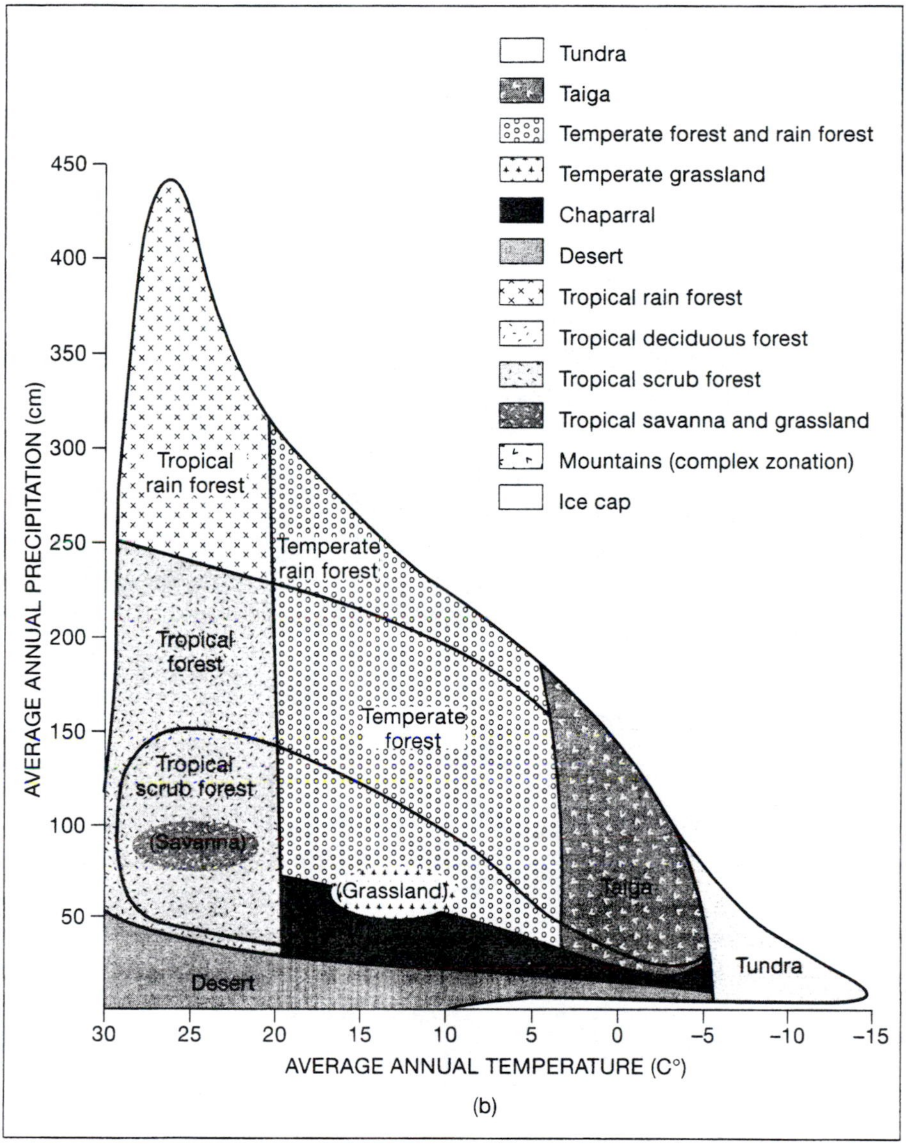

Figure 2–1a (con't.) The Relationship of Biomes to Precipitation and Temperature

The broken line encloses the range of values within which either grasses or woody plants may dominate, depending on local conditions. The figure is simplified, and the positions of the divisions are approximate.

From *Ecoscience: Population, Resources, Environment.* P. Ehrlich, A. Ehrlich, and J. Holdren, 1977. Reprinted by permission of the authors.

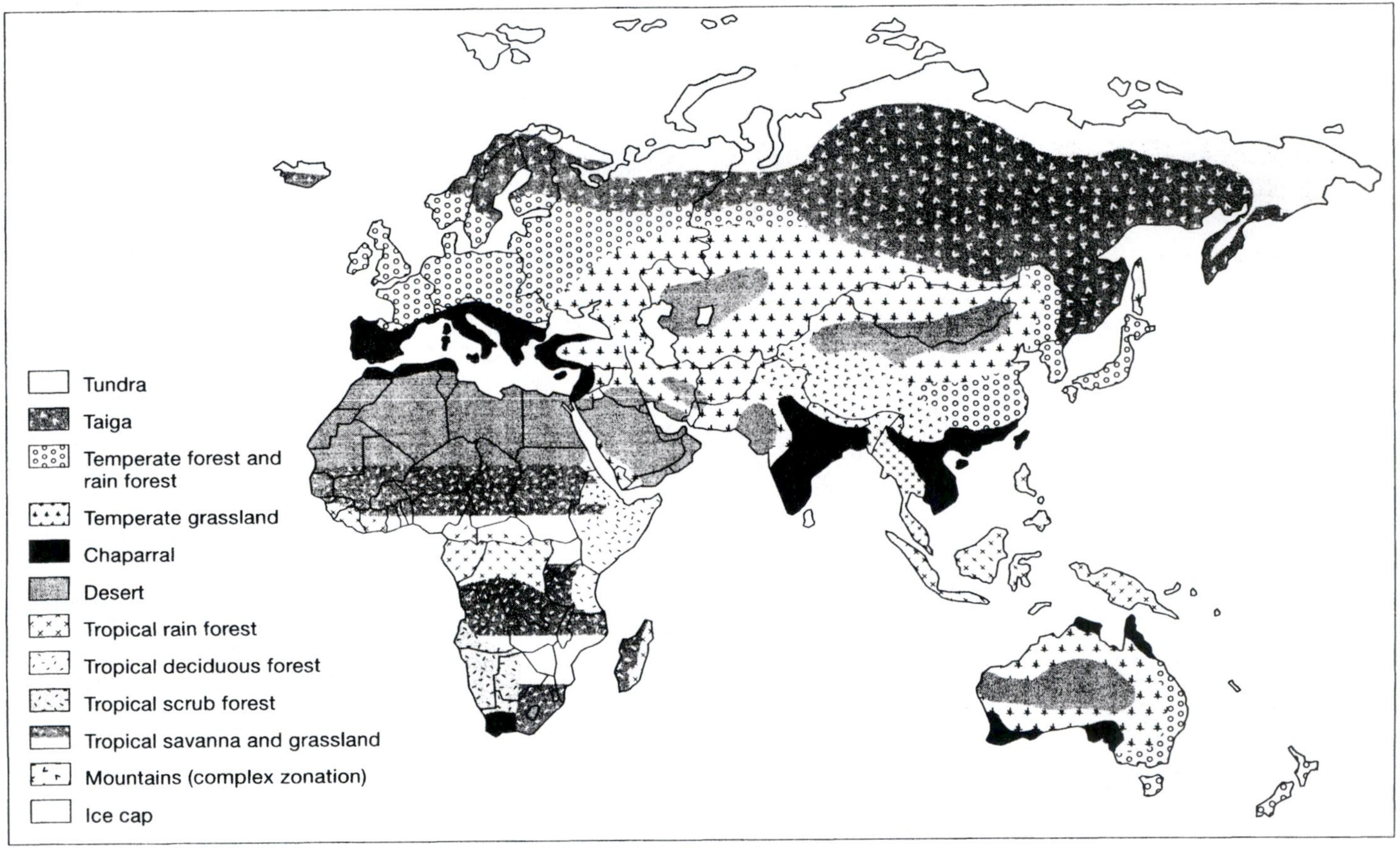

Figure 2–1b The Distribution of the Major Biomes of the World (Eastern Hemisphere)

From *Ecoscience: Population, Resources,Environment*. P. Ehrlich, A. Ehrlich, and J. Holdren, 1977. Reprinted by permission of the authors.

tropical biomes of the continents in Figures 2–1a and 2–1b and and note that it is within these tropical divisions that we find the greatest diversity in contrast to the temperate zones.

Seasonal changes in temperature increase with the distance north or south from the equator. The subtropical zone is still mild in temperature, and rainfall varies from slight to moderate. It contains biomes of mountains, deserts, forests, and grasslands. More extreme cyclical changes occur further from the equator in the temperate zone, with well-defined seasons and extremes in temperature and daylight hours between summer and winter; this is in contrast to the year-round intense solar radiation of the tropics. Further, still from the equator starting at 65° North or 65° South latitudes, are the polar regions of the Arctic and Antarctic with the harshest weather on the planet. In these zones of intense cold, there are reduced numbers and varieties of life forms; numbers of plant species diminish, as do the mammal species that feed upon them. The seas of these polar regions, however, abound with crustaceans, fish, and marine mammals.

These geographic and climatic features have dictated, to a large extent, the course of human history. The positions of the continents, water resources, and climates have influenced the distribution of human populations. Some parts of the world were more easily exploited, while others present severe challenges to human survival. Our earliest ancestors were limited to a few habitats, but over hundreds of thousands of years they learned to adapt more effectively through a complex system of behavior and technology. As our species advanced over time, use of environmental resources became increasingly efficient until most of the planet could support ever larger human populations—even before recent historic times. The archaeological record describes a journey from humble beginnings at a level of small-scale societies with limited environmental impact to a dominant role in the biosphere. It has been a long trip of many hundreds of thousands of years. No matter what achievements have been made, there still remain certain limitations on human habitations.

Viewed within a biosphere perspective, we are skillful, adaptable, and inventive, traits that continue to open up opportunities now as in the past. Our ancestors were able to survive changing conditions; if the cold temperatures exceeded their physiologic abilities, then they built shelters or wore special clothing for protection. If a preferred or necessary food was in short supply, then our ancestors acquired an alternate one, perhaps rendered digestible by special treatment and by cooking. If predators or competing human groups threatened, then weapons were made. Through these methods, more biomes were opened to early human occupation. As such skills were acquired, humans moved out of tropical regions as documented by archaeological skeletal remains. There is a wealth of anthropological literature that argues for a recent origin of *Homo sapiens* who spread out of Africa approximately 100,000 years ago (Stringer and McKie, 1996). This position is countered by even stronger arguments for an earlier origin and occupation of the temperate zones of the Old World (Brace, 1995). Whichever side one takes—a recent or an earlier origin—the fact is that most regions had been occupied by 100,000 years ago.

However, each environment that our species moved to required special skills to gain the resources needed to sustain life. These ancestors of humanity possessed these skills and were continually learning and improving over the millennia. Higher levels of specialized technology were reached a few thousand years ago, which offered even more options and broadened the environmental reach of our species. In other words, behavioral adaptation has enabled us to compensate for our physiological and anatomical limitations. This ability to compensate through behavior, learned and transmitted across generations, placed *Homo sapiens* in a unique position. We are part of the web of life of the planet and bound by its physical and biological laws, but our behavioral flexibility has reduced environmental constraints and allows for many exceptions. Understanding of this web of life and the human behavioral diversity requires a study of ecology.

ECOLOGY: CONCEPTS AND DEFINITIONS

The term *ecology* is frequently used to indicate breadth, or inclusiveness, of a study, as in the example of "ecological scarcity," ecological ethics," "ecological model," or "ecological transition." The authors of such phrases intend to convey a concern with the number and complexity of elements affecting an outcome. In the health sciences field, an increased recognition of socioeconomic influences has given rise to a frequent use of *disease ecology*. The diversity of population responses to environmental and social variables has led to a descriptive term, *demographic* or *population ecology*. Comparative studies of Western and non-Western societies in reference to social organization and how natural resources are used may be described as *cultural ecology*. Somewhat similar in its approach is *behavioral ecology*, but its study is broadened to include cross-species comparisons within an evolutionary context.

Some uses of the ecological concept stress the behavioral dimensions, and others emphasize variables within the natural environment that limit or enhance a species's chance of survival given particular behavioral attributes. But all applications of the concept seek to extend an investigation's scope to encompass a network of interactive feedbacks that occur among organisms and components of their environment. These broader and popular uses of the concept have led to many abuses, such as a frequent substitution of the term *ecology* when the meaning is clearly *environment* or when only one or a few feedback loops are defined. This wider use, however, has had the beneficial effect of drawing attention to the complexity within the natural world.

A way of understanding the scope of ecology is to consider it as comparative natural history, close to the original meaning of the Greek word *oekos*, meaning "household." The concern with the structure and function of the natural environment directs attention not only to the communities of living organisms, but to numerous interlocking systems within the environmental space occupied. In the biosphere, the flow of energy, the natural cycles of vital substances like water, oxygen, nitrogen, carbon, and mineral resources, all contribute to living organisms' life cycles. Another way of describing the perspective taken by ecologists is to note their view of a natural world as a collection of interacting systems of whole communities considered to be components within an abiotic (nonliving) and biotic (living) environmental complex. As Odum stated, "The role of the ecologist of the future is to promote the holistic approach" (Odum, 1989). The attempts to fulfill this role require a greater emphasis on human–environmental relations. Where previously much of the concern had been with "natural environments," that is, communities of plants and animals growing without human interference, today, more attention is paid to the many consequences of human action.

The impact of the human species is seen globally, in every corner of the world, regardless of how remote a region may be. It is this impact that prevents the study of a "natural ecology," environments uninfluenced by humans. Since the earliest appearance of *Homo sapiens*, there has been environmental destruction and changes exerted by human activity. The notion of "aboriginal man" as a conservationist, respectful of "Mother Earth," has been overdone in recent years and is reminiscent of a nineteenth-century romantic belief in the "noble savage" in tune with nature. Those of us who hold such an idealistic notion ignore or deliberately misconstrue much of the prehistoric evidence that documents the degradation or alteration of environments caused by premodern populations.

Ever since the discovery and use of fire some million years ago, humans have been disrupting natural environments in several ways. Influences were slight at first and mainly limited to disturbances of natural vegetation and animal herds, but human effects multiplied as populations increased and technology advanced. The firing of grasslands to encourage plant growth or as a hunting method did much to alter plant communities and affect wildlife. The collection and distribution of seeds and plant parts further extended the human influence on environmental change. Even more radical changes began to occur with plant domestication and sedentary village life. Beginning from this time, about 12,000 years ago, human action disrupted many "natural" plant communities (Goudie, 1994). So consideration of a world of biomes without *Homo sapiens* as a participant is not practical. The impact of human behavior increased exponentially with each technological advance. Environmental disruption parallels the march of human technological progress and population growth.

Given these problems of environmental disturbance, consideration of our species in the context of any biome raises questions about human ecology. Can valid distinctions be made between the ecological systems of humans and systems of other life forms, or do the same general rules apply to all organisms? Except for a few early observers, like George Marsh who wrote about human impact on the natural world in the nineteenth century, ecological studies have concentrated on lower life forms. More recently, general ecological principles are being applied to studies of human environments. In his description of demographic and economic transformations in a Spanish community from prehistoric times to the twentieth century, Karl Butzer explained the application of ecological principles: "Ecology allows a structured organization of unlike variables, emphasizes function, and hence interchanges between component parts" (Butzer, 1990:685).

Doubts have been expressed, however, about the applicability of these principles to our species because of the wide range of options open to us and because of the role played by social processes. Is there, in fact, such a thing as "human ecology" or is the system we so label actually only a system of decision-making processes used to define human needs (either perceived or real)? John Bennett raised this question in his exploration of technological change and society. He noted that human ecology is a variable of and, at the same time, a history of *Homo sapiens* absorbing nature into what he described as a socionatural system. Bennett described this incorporation of components of the natural environment into the human social system as, "...the increasingly complex cases of resources exploitation and economic handling that have endless ramifications in human institutions and the natural world" (Bennett 1976:22). Is political decision making, in fact, the key linkage to human–environment studies?

Human ecology needs to be clarified in respect to the implications that human activities, or human cultures,[1] have on the environment. The capture of energy, the elaboration of technology and population dynamics all bear a relationship to the environment, as is the case with other animal species. Groups or communities of organisms and their environments survive through a series of feedback controls to form a system, as we shall discuss. Human action, because of its flexibility and dominance, impacts the environment in unique ways, however. In its complexity, the means of satisfaction of our basic needs goes far beyond that of any other species. It involves an elaboration of perception of these needs and use of a social organization to fulfill them. Though *Homo sapiens* is part of the overall environmental complex, our conscious control of interaction can and often has changed the nature of a biome.

---

[1]Culture is broad in its concept and application; those activities, technologies, traditions, beliefs, and language humans transmit across generations by learning processes will be used as a definition throughout. Where any special meaning or attribute of behavior, adaptation, or culture is introduced it will be defined.

ECOSYSTEMS

The behavior of populations, together with biotic and abiotic environmental components, form a network of interaction above the level of individual organisms. This network of population, group, or community of living organisms is examined by application of a simplified model of the real world. Such models are considered *systems* of regularly interacting elements. These models encompass the whole of the needs of communities of organisms that retain a relationship through time and space. This grouping of interactive plant and animal communities within a common habitat form an organized unit, or *ecosystem*.

One of the more essential and obvious parts of the systematic interactions within the community is the flow of *energy*. Considered as a unit, the ecosystem may be viewed as an open system with a continuous input of energy. Solar radiation provides this input through the process of *photosynthesis*, the conversion of water and carbon dioxide into complex molecules of sugars and starches by green plants and by certain types of algae. The chlorophyll in plants catalyzes these chemical reactions while the sun provides the energy that is then stored as a component of the chemical bonds within the molecular structures. This is nature's way of capturing, utilizing (in the case of plants), and storing light energy; all of the planet's energy, including the fossil fuels, has been gained in this way.

The total stored energy within the earth's ecosystems includes fossil fuels, plants and algae, bacteria, and the more complex organisms who feed upon these sources. Species use different portions of the stored food energy, depending on the degree of their biological complexity; nonvertebrates generally have fewer choices than do vertebrates. Among the vertebrates, many mammals have the broadest access to several levels of the available stored energy. Humans have the ability to use any and all parts of the earth's energy supply, either from living or fossilized forms.

The potential energy available may be divided into several *trophic levels,* nutritional or food levels depicted in Figure 2–2. At the first level are producers of the energy chain, the *autotrophs*, or self-feeders. These are the plants and algae that satisfy their energy needs through the photosynthesis process. Though the autotrophs are able to use or store only about 1 percent of the light energy received, the total plant life still represents an enormous quantity. The second level is composed of herbivores, animals that consume the plants. At the third level are the carnivores who feed on the herbivorous animals of the second level, while there are carnivores who feed on other carnivores at a fourth level. Some species are diverse enough in diet and adaptation to utilize more than one of these levels, as in the case of omnivores who will satisfy their needs with combinations of plants and animals. Finally, capturing energy from all levels are the *decomposers,* who feed upon the wastes of decomposing organic matter. The dead and decay-

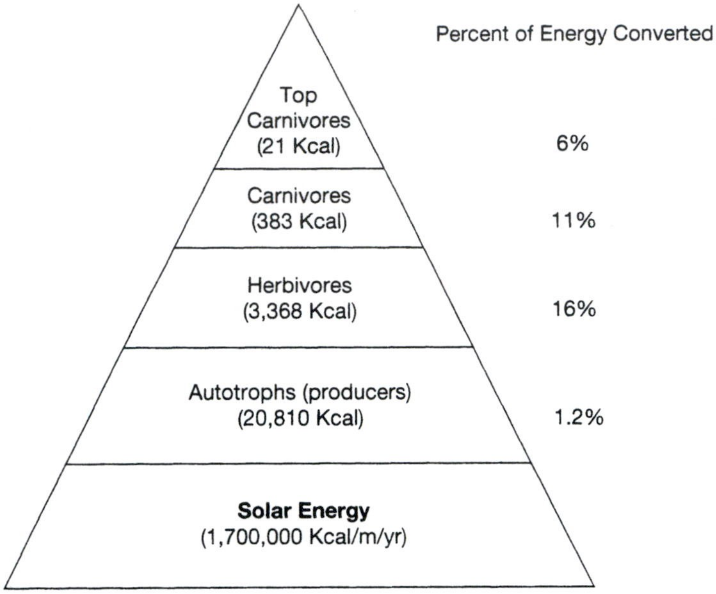

Figure 2–2 Examples of Efficiency of Energy Conversion between Trophic Levels
Adapted from Emmel, 1973 and Odum, 1989.

ing plants or animals provide food for a variety of bacteria, worms, bugs, or mites; in aquatic environments varieties of molluscs serve the function of the decomposers.

Energy, however, is lost in a transfer from one level to another, according to the *second law of thermodynamics*[2], which may be stated simply: "In any conversion of energy from one form to another, some energy is 'degraded.'" Essentially, this means that in the process of conversion, say from solar radiation to storage in plant tissue or from plant to animal tissue, a large portion of energy becomes unavailable to organisms at the next trophic level. In the example of the autotrophs, plants convert solar energy to stored energy in the form of chemical bonds of the carbohydrate molecules. But only approx-

[2]The experiments, observations, and theoretical interpretations of natural systems rely on two laws to explain energy flow—the laws of thermodynamics. The *first law* states that energy can neither be created nor destroyed but only converted or transformed into another form. Food energy into animal, whose conversion of the carbon bond energy is dissipated as heat or motion, is one example. The burning of fossil fuels are others. Because the process of transformation always involves a dispersal of some energy into unavailable forms, the *second law* states that in any transfer, some energy is dispersed or lost to the system. In practical terms this means that organisms use only a small portion of the energy stored at each of the trophic levels. This process of loss during conversion within a system has given rise to many lengthy discussions about how organisms maintain organized systems in the face of this increasing disorder, a transformation of energy to unavailable forms (see Lotka, 1956; Pianka, 1974).

imately 1 percent of the solar energy penetrating the atmosphere is stored. The balance that cannot be absorbed is dissipated as heat or is used in plant respiration processes. There is also a loss in the transfer to higher levels in the food chain. Thus, the grazing herbivore consumes quantities of plant material but is only able to use or "store" in its tissue about 10 percent of the energy represented by the chemical compounds in the plants. Again at the next trophic level, carnivores use only a portion of the total energy contained at the herbivore levels. This energy "flow" is often diagramed to enable measurement and estimates to be made of the biomass supported in any environment (Figure 2–3). Such a diagram is useful but only deals with average exchanges or flows of energy measured as kilocalories per square meter per year.

The efficiency of transfer, or rather the utilization of the available food resources from one level to the next, will vary from species to species, depending upon their digestive processes; it even varies among individuals because of age and gender differences. But rough estimates may be made of the quantity of living matter that can be maintained at each trophic level given certain conditions. The pastoralist is able to gage the *"carrying capacity"* of range land. He knows, from experience, that a certain number of animals can be supported in a given area for a period of time during a certain season. Beyond that limit, any surplus of animals will not have sufficient feed and will suffer weight loss, lowered fertility, shortened life span, and a

Figure 2–3 Solar Energy Flow (kcal. per square meter per year)
From Odum, E. P. 1989. Reprinted by permission of Sinauer Associates, Inc.

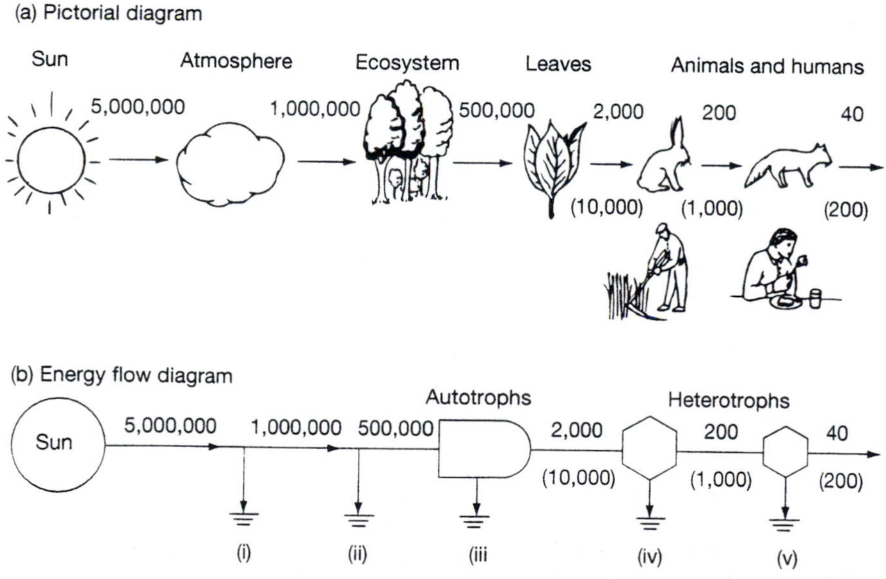

higher mortality rate. Seasonal declines or unusual climatic conditions can force a reduction of herd sizes through natural processes or by the decision to slaughter extra animals or remove them to other pastures. Some range lands in the great plains of the western United States require up to ten acres to support one steer, while the thicker grasses in the eastern plains of Kansas, a single acre may be sufficient. A stark contrast is seen in the case of Central Australia where as many as 100 acres may be needed (Goudie, 1994).

The ecologist, concerned with food energy resources within a total ecosystem, deals in trophic levels and the energy transfer between them. The carrying capacity is evaluated in terms of *biomass*, a measure used to estimate organic matter and the nutritional requirements of the animals within a given environment. The total weight of organisms possible at any level is related to the biomass of organisms at the level that supplies them. The inefficiency of transfer—the loss of energy between levels—must be considered, of course. A certain area in a particular climatic zone will capture and store solar energy in alfalfa, for example. Herbivores feeding on this type of grass are relatively easy to estimate compared to, say, carnivores or omnivores. A cow or steer will eat as much grass as five sheep, and ten rabbits eat as much as one sheep (Wagner, 1978).

Homo sapiens occupies a dominant position in the ecosystem that allows a wide choice from among resources. We are omnivorous in our diets and we can feed at any level of the food chain. Though our inability to digest complex compounds like cellulose limits our food choice to certain plants or plant parts (for example, grass seeds can be eaten but not the grass stems), there is still a variety of plant species that we may choose from. Herbivorous or carnivorous animals are also food sources, as well as insects, birds, etc. Such a diversity of food energy resources makes it difficult to describe our position within an ecosystem. We can and do freely move from one trophic level to another, which is a particular advantage to hunters and foragers of wild plants.

The variation of food chain levels may be compared to one another in order to estimate differences in energy requirements and biomass equivalents of humans subsisting by foraging; examples have been taken from studies of food gathering by Aboriginal Australians and the San of southern Africa. Each food choice yields a certain amount of energy for a given cost. That is, the work needed to obtain and prepare a food for human digestion must be compared to the metabolic energy gained. This is likely to influence food selections and season of gathering. Certain food items are more rewarding for the effort expended to collect them; such rewards vary with locale and season.

Knowledgeable foragers, it is argued, take a rational approach and practice what is called an optimal foraging strategy (Winterhalder, 1981). Decisions to hunt a given animal or to collect certain plants are not made randomly but are based on past experience with food yields in given environments and seasons. Likewise, the cultivator prepares a garden plot and selects certain plants that have been most productive in the past. Also, the pastoralist of East Africa maintains herds of mixed species, some keep goats and sheep used for meat while the cattle provide milk and blood. Of course, taste and food preferences play a major role in these decisions

As more complex cultivation technologies were developed with the use of irrigation systems and draft animals, higher yields of certain cereals enabled the support of denser human populations. At this point several thousand years ago, there was a greater dependence on a narrower part of the food chain (cereals, domesticated varieties of wild grasses) with less input from animal sources. This remains true today for hundreds of millions of people even with the growth of modern agriculture that has been providing an ever wider range of food choices. Taste and economics have become the more dominating factors in food selection in the developed world rather than a necessity to satisfy hunger.

The role of economics is clearly seen in the last 50 years as animal protein and fats make up a larger proportion of our diet. People in the more-developed countries annually consume between 700 and 800 kilograms of grain per capita, by far the world's highest. Most of this is consumed indirectly, since the bulk of grain production of the developed countries is fed to poultry and livestock to produce high-quality protein products. By contrast, people of the lesser developed countries of the world consume between 150–200 kilograms per capita per year. Almost all is consumed directly by humans in their daily meals and little used as animal feed grains (Brown, 1997).

In other words, feeding at different levels of the food chain may support greater or lesser numbers of people given the same energy inputs. Preferential use of food grains make all the difference. For example, an estimated 10 kilograms of grain are required to produce 1 kilogram of beef. This quantity of animal flesh also represents a large investment in land, labor, and fossil fuel energy. If all humans consumed grain directly rather than indirectly as we do when eating beef or poultry, a greater number of people could be supported by a given area of agricultural land. The decision to select one option over the other is directed by culture and political considerations as much as by environmental resources. Farmers in India's Ganges River Valley and the Punjab produce grain surpluses that are marketed and consumed directly by the buyers. Little is used indirectly through the herbivore step in the food chain because of costs and sometimes because of religious sanctions.

Beyond consideration of food chains and energy flows, the holistic approach represented by *ecosystem analysis* can be but a simplified version of the real world. Considering all of the biotic and abiotic components of the communities and their interactions within a given space is the object, of course. At this stage, even in the age of computer science, each and every variable may not be used nor even identified. For example, when grassland models are used to describe biomass (so many tons of beef supported on a given area of land), little consideration is given to micronutrients. These nutrients influence health, longevity, and especially the reproductive cycle of the animals. In certain areas of the world where cattle or sheep have done poorly, deficiencies of some micronutrients, essential for animal metabolism, were eventually identified as the primary cause. A range of nutritionally important trace elements, such as copper, cobalt, iodine, magnesium, nickel, and zinc, to name a few, have been found to be lacking in some soils. The plants grown on these deficient soils plus the animals that feed on them will suffer from various degrees of nutritional deficiencies. Humans can also be sensitive to micronutrient deficiencies: Low levels of zinc retard growth and sexual maturity; a lack of iodine results in depression of the thyroid gland; and magnesium deficiency effects mineralization of bone.

Such a lack in the environment–nutrition interactions of animal models did not retard progress in animal husbandry. It was sufficient to know which pastures supported how many and what kind of livestock, a kind of an energy-flow model—so many animals could be produced in a certain area. Though only an approximation of reality since micronutrient knowledge was lacking, the measures of energy inputs (pasture) and outputs (number of animals) provide a stimulus–response model—in engineering terms, a "black box," a model where inputs and outputs may be measured while the exact inner workings are unknown. Such a black box approach applied to ecosystems has had some successes and can point to the existence of key components in certain communities that contribute to their ecosystem functioning. In other words, we do not have to know all of the interacting variables in order to consider groups or communities of populations in a given environment.

Ecosystem analysis treats species as components of a mutually interdependent community that has a tendency towards a state of equilibrium. A series of *feedbacks* or linkages act to restrict the number of organisms to a level below the nutrient limits of their environment. That is, population sizes may vary somewhat but they tend to remain at or near an average size over time. This population *set point*, depending on the species, may be regulated by a combination of fertility rates, food supply fluctuation, and mortality rates. An example is climatic variation that influences plant growth and microbe increases that, in turn, will effect higher organisms throughout the food chain. Unfavorable climate may result in a depression of food supply, resulting in starvation and excessive mortality. A period of favorable climate and an expanding food supply would have the opposite effect, fueling population growth. The excessive population would then be at greater risk upon the approach of a new cycle of food shortages.

Periodically, there may be a weakening or a breakdown of the feedback regulating mechanisms, and populations would tend to increase far beyond the average set point within the community. This frequently occurs among several species of fast-breeding rodents. Females of several species of mice are fertile at about 13 days old and, if bred, can give birth to a litter of 6 pups just 20 days later. Immediately after giving birth, the female is fertile and could conceive; over a period of 20 month she is capable of producing 24 litters. A period of high rainfall and favorable temperatures encourages exuberant plant growth. The rodents feeding on this extensive food supply expand dramatically with literally a growth explosion far exceeding an average carrying capacity of their environment.

Such rapid rodent population expansions occur periodically in many parts of the world, and, occasionally, there are major health consequences for human populations. In the "Four Corners" area of the southwestern United States, following a season of high rainfall in 1992 there was an exceedingly large production of piñon pine nuts, the natural food supply of rodents of the area. This excess of piñon nuts contributed to a large increase in rodents that led to increased human contacts with a virus carried in droppings and urine. Drying out quickly in the arid climate, the particles were blown about in dust, distributing the virus over large areas and even into houses (Grady, 1993 and Chapter 7).

Feedback to regulate population growth and to maintain a certain number of individuals may also be described by such regulatory mechanisms of input–output, stimulus–response models, but the variables are more numerous and complex than those encountered in any typical engineering problems. Most mammal populations, for example, have a reproductive capacity to double their number each generation. Animals with longer gestation periods of several months can rapidly increase also. Even elephants, the slowest breeding of mammals (gestation of 22 months), could increase their numbers substantially, given optimum environmental conditions (as is the case since elephants have been declared a protected species in certain game preserves of East Africa). Theoretically, a single pair of elephants might contribute to 15 million descendants in 500 years if all animals bred at their maximum potential. But our planet is not overrun with elephants now nor was it in the past. Some other factor or factors besides food supplies have kept the species nearer replacement levels.

The experiences of both slow- and fast-breeding mammals demonstrate that species seldom reproduce at their theoretical maximum. Mice living around grain storage elevators, for example, do not reproduce to the theoretical maximum that the unlimited food supply could support. There are, however, periods of rapid increases, or "blooms," followed by "crashes," when a population's growth overshoots the resource limits of their environments. The next generation, decimated by starvation and disease, crash as their numbers exceed the ceiling or limit of their environment. The oscillating curves in Figure 2–4d and e illustrate this phenomenon of

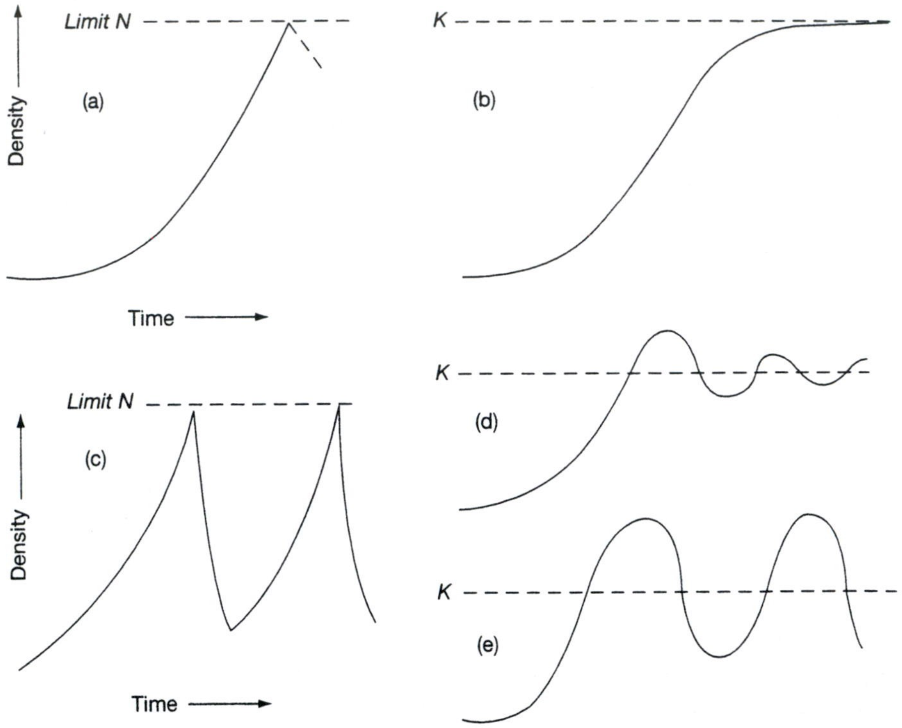

Figure 2–4 Population Growth Curves

Population growth forms: the *J*-shaped (exponential) form (a), the *S*-shaped (sigmoid) form (b), and some variants (c). The severe oscillations that would result from "boom and bust" cycles of exponential growth (d,e). The dampened and undampened oscillations that occur when sigmoid growth overshoots the carrying capacity, *K*.

From Odum, E. P. 1989. reprinted by permission of Sinauer Associates, Inc.

punching through the ceiling, *K*, and falling back below the maximum carrying capacity. Some species, however, seem to keep reproducing at high levels, decimating their food supply in the process and then moving on to new areas. Migratory herds in Africa may be used as examples. The Serengeti Plains of East Africa was once filled with large populations of herbivores of the antelope family that wandered freely, following the cycle of rainfall and growth of grasslands. Unusually dry periods, occurring every few years, would reduce the pasture growth, and the herds would reach the carrying capacity limit. Figure 2–4 a or c could describe this fluctuation. The increase of human agriculture and pastoralism encroaching on the herbivores range has interrupted this natural cycle and reduced the limit.

Predator–prey interactions describe another link in the population growth cycle. The rabbits introduced into Australia for sport some 200 years ago have grown from an an original stock of twenty-four pair to uncounted millions. In a favorable environment without any natural predators, they keep multiplying and in the process the rabbits have covered most of the continent, destroying vegetation. Their spread has ruined pastureland and their extensive burrows have contributed to erosion and have even undermined building foundations.

The rabbits have survived all attempts at control, even recovering from the intentional introduction of the myxomatosis disease caused by a deadly virus. At first, this virus caused a rapid decline, leaving only a few survivors. Those that survived had some degree of inherited resistance to the virus, and these survivors rapidly reproduced a new relatively immune breed of descendants. Recently, a new virus that causes a rabbit hemorrhagic fever has been discovered (rabbit calicivirus, or RCV). It has proven effective and is being released in test areas despite some opposition from naturalists. But the virus has been picked up and transported thousands of miles by flies, mosquitos, and fleas (Preslar, 1997). How effective it will prove to be in the long run is hard to predict, but as of now the RCV has reduced rabbit populations by as much as 90 percent. With their high reproductive rate (a female can breed at four months and then produce six litters per year) chance favors a repeat of the earlier attempts of control by the myxomatosis virus.

This Australian experience shows how lack of predation was an important factor in rapid growth, expansion, and environmental destruction by an exotic species. Where it exists, predation balances population sizes and species diversity in an ecosystem. The mountain lion and wolves preying upon deer populations, or foxes on rabbits and rodents are examples that regulate food chains. Certain species, however, have no predators, elephants or gorillas, for example, are only threatened by man. The feedback loops that have controlled their population sizes over generations must be of another source. Infectious and parasitic diseases have contributed to holding such populations far below their natural reproductive potential. Food supply is also a likely limiting factor that, together with increased crowding caused by humans expanding areas of cultivation, have limited the numbers of the larger primates as well as many of the large herbivores.

In the case of humans, explanations of achievement of reproductive potential and actual population sizes are much more complex, as expected. There have been intense studies of reproductive behavior to formulate a number of theoretical models to explain regulatory mechanisms that may limit the numbers of humans born each generation. Food supply, female workload, birth spacing, crowding and residence patterns, and disease are among those factors that have been offered as mechanisms to explain human fertility rates. However, all these components and linkages are overwhelmed by human decisions to consciously control reproduction by cultural means. The decisions on who are suitable mates and at what age they may marry have worked and still work to limit reproduction. Add to this the lengthy historical and folklore records of the birth control methods, abortion, and infanticide, and we can understand that population control has been and still is accomplished with some success.

Nomadic hunter–foragers may have strictly regulated reproductive rates by a number of methods, which included infanticide. Simple horticultural peoples also recognized the necessity of limiting population size, and they followed cultural practices, such as regulating age at marriage, that kept reproductive rates far below maximum. In fact, there is no evidence of any population, at least within the last 200 years, reproducing at maximum rates.

A few religious isolates in developed countries, living with the benefits of modern medicine and nutrition, are known for averaging as many as eight or ten children, as illustrated by the Amish and Hutterites of North America (Hostetler, 1985; McFalls, 1979). Fertility rates for most ethnic and national groups are usually far below this number, around four or five for populations of developing countries. Nations of Europe and North America, today, have fertility rates from 1.5 to 1.8, which contrasts to the highs of 6 or 8 of previous centuries and in some countries of the lesser-developed world today (see Chapter 5).

CONCEPTS OF ADAPTATION

In the broadest sense, adaptation is an adjustment or modification that an individual or population makes to meet the demands of their environment in order to survive. These adjustments may include either biological or behavioral components and often an interaction between the two. The behavioral component allows a range of activities enhancing survival; the range is broader in some species than in others. The biological component consists of either short-term adjustments (acclimatization) or genetic adaptation, gene frequency changes in a population over long-term exposure to forces of natural selection. Some genetic adaptations convey resistance to disease, endurance of environmental stressors like high altitude or temperature, or the ability to digest certain food sources. Such adaptations are well documented in many organisms, but it has been more difficult to identify in humans because of our biological diversity and an ability to alter environments.

Acclimatization is the ability of an individual organism to physiologically adjust, for example, to fluctuations of temperature or variations in food supply or to disease-causing organisms. The habitats of many species are restricted because of specific dietary needs or because of limited abilities to endure heat or cold. The range of habitats of reptiles, birds, or fish offer many examples; tropical birds, like the parrot family, colorful reef fish around tropical islands, or alligators and crocodiles of warm water swamps are but a few.

Some animals, especially mammals, have a genetically determined ability that enable a maintenance of individual physiological homeostasis. This ability enables them to acclimatize to a range of temperatures and other climatic conditions. The result has been a continuous interchange, the creation of dynamic process that contributes to survival from generation to generation within changing environments. Organisms, including humans, must be able to acclimatize or adapt to these changes. As Ernst Mayr describes, "Organisms are doomed to extinction unless they change continuously in order to keep step with the constantly changing physical and biotic environment" (Mayr, 1982:484).

Humans have avoided extinction and have multiplied and evolved because of our exceptional ability to acclimatize. But when environmental stresses exceed this ability, we may adapt through behavior. There are, however, several problems that confound the understanding of the adaptation concept as it applies to humans. First, we possess an extraordinary ability to manipulate natural environments and to create new ones, allowing a great many choices to satisfy our real or perceived needs. Second, we have rapidly increased our population size, but also have acquired the ability to regulate further growth. Third, our species encompasses a broad biological diversity both within and between populations dispersed about the globe.

Such variation in response leads to the critical question of how do we evaluate adaptation of a person or a population? Can we not take the mere fact of survival as evidence of success? The population's survival from generation to generation does not tell us whether one or the other form of behavior, technology, or acclimatization has been the most efficient contributor however. If a people had used a different kind of shelter or exploited other food plants or practiced cultivation instead of food collecting, then would they have been "better" adapted?

To understand the relative degrees of adaptation, we need a means of comparison. If we consider exploitation of certain food sources, we can compare behavioral adaptation. Maize (corn) is poor in certain nutrients (niacin, a vitamin and tryptophan, an amino acid) but, by soaking it in lime water prior to grinding, the nutrient value is enhanced. Native Americans learned this advantageous processing technique but Europeans did not and suffered the nutritional consequences. In other words, Native Americans were well adapted to a maize-based diet. Other food adaptation methods are illustrated by the repeated soaking and washing of harmful food toxins from certain root plants, like cassava (manioc) or from seeds of cycad palms (fedireco nuts). Special grain storage methods had to be devised to prevent the growth of poisonous molds that could cause severe neurological symptoms. These storage methods were adaptations to cold damp climates, practiced in Europe since the Middle Ages (Jackson, 1988; Lieber, 1970).

Measures of Adaptation There must be certain criteria for measurement of the degree of success or failure in response to environmental variations and stresses. Evaluations must be on the basis of a conformity between populations or individuals and environment determined by comparison of some biological or behavioral attribute. If we consider one group of *Homo sapiens* better adapted to solar radiation than another group because of their skin pigmentation, for example, then the differences must be expressed in measured units to define degree of melanization. The relative interference of this pigment with penetration of ultraviolet energy through the skin can then be evaluated. When fair-skinned people move to regions of high solar radiation of the tropics or dark-skinned people shift residence to the northern temperate zones, physiological evaluations may then be made in terms of risks of too much or too little ultraviolet radiation. Given the precolonial distribution of such populations, skin pigment appears to be a genetic adaptation. But since modern times, clothing, suntan oils, and vitamin supplements have alleviated some of the advantages or disadvantages of melanin density. Hence, human behavior has interfered with the natural selection for a genetic adaptation.

Child growth is also a useful measure to compare adaptation to varying environmental stresses. If a child's weight gain or stature increases or slows down under differing nutritional intakes, for example, the metabolic processes are adjusting to levels of energy and protein intake. Such individual responses are measurable in terms of several morphological dimensions of bone, tooth, and body development. These dimensions vary between generations; children in many countries grow faster and reach larger adult sizes than did their parents or grandparents. This suggests an improvement in childhood environments, with an abundant food supply and a decrease in disease as a result of a more efficient adaptation in recent generations.

The efficiency in the satisfaction of a population's energy needs is another comparative measure that is frequently used. Humans, for example, have certain basic requirements to maintain basic metabolic functions, about 2,000 kilocalories food energy per day for an adult male and 20 percent less for a female. To satisfy an increase of metabolic needs during physical activity, more calories are required depending on effort, and a balance of *energy out* (or work) compared to *energy in* for the total of the population can be calculated (Ulijaszek, 1995). This provides a measure of a human population's adaptive efficiency within an ecosystem, that is, the human energy expended to gain the material to meet their needs, food, clothing, shelter, transportation, and protection. The flow of energy between populations and their environments at each of several technological levels can thus be compared.

Agriculturists, using modern machinery, expend a minimum of human or animal power in food production but a high level of fossil fuel energy. By contrast, indigenous populations of small-scale cultivators of the tropics are able to subsist by technologically simple means that depend upon small energy inputs for large surpluses of food produced. By this measure they are more successful and "better adapted" than modern mechanized agricultural societies. They are less well adapted if costs are evaluated in terms other than an energy equation. Mechanization and large inputs of fertilizers and fossil fuel enable the production of large quantities of food and fiber on relatively smaller acreage. There were minimal fallow periods than were necessary for the small-scale cultivators who had to practice a shifting cultivation, leaving land idle for up to twenty years in tropical areas. Thus, the change of technology and behavior (the use of land) increased crop yield and has raised the potential of food production several hundredfold.

Measuring inputs and outputs in terms of calories alone seldom reveals the integrated nature of a population's adaptation, however. It neglects the "short fall," that is a failure to gain the maximum potential of the resources in the environment. It also does not account for a measure of well being or quality of life, nor is account taken of that significant area humans are particularly concerned with, the states of health or disease. These states are, according to Dubois (1965), "expressions of the success or failure experienced by the organism in its efforts to respond adaptively to environmental challenges." The satisfaction of needs, biologically determined or behaviorally defined, are intertwined in a very intricate manner, and measurement of adaptation will be difficult. A start may be made by considering population size stability or increase over time: That is, demography, the population dynamics due to changes in mortality rates, birth rates, and life expectancy. Additionally, degrees of adaptation may be derived by comparisons of values gained from measures of individuals over their life cycle: from birth weight throughout growth to work performance capacity of adults and fertility rates under differing dietary regimes.

ADAPTATION AND ECOLOGICAL NICHE

Adaptation or adaptive responses are terms frequently used to note reactions of populations to changing demands of the environment or as conformity between organism and environment (Pianka, 1974:187). But are these responses actually adaptive in the sense that they tend to maintain a stable state and enhance population survival chances? Or are they merely reactions to stimuli that may or may not be positive and advantageous to the group? Environments are not static and can change at a very high rate, requiring rapid responses by the inhabitants. Some species cannot readily adapt and hence become extinct. Humans can be quick to respond and, as a species, have proven to be highly adaptable, which will in turn contribute to further environmental change. This change alters the *ecological niche,* or environmental position, occupied by the population. An understanding of ecological niche requires a consideration of both past and present conditions. The human geographer, Carl Sauer, emphasized, "Current situations must be comprehended as a moving point in order to gain a knowledge of human processes" (quoted in Leighly, 1963:361).

The dynamic nature of ecological niches dictates a broad comprehension of their meaning. One view may be that the term refers to the sum total of all adaptations within an ecological unit, the ways that an organism exploits or uses its environment. Because of the broad use of the concept of ecological niche, there has been careful attention to its definition. Several authors describe niche in ways that emphasize subsistence base, or nutritional role. Others have noted the organism's place in the biotic world, or its status in relationship to food resource and potential predators. A broader, more comprehensive view was given by Odum (1989) when he described an organism's niche as its "profession" and its habitat as its "address." What he meant is that the organism's role in the community is related to structural adaptations, physiological responses, and behavior (learned or inherited). Considered from whatever perspective, one can see that our species has had a diverse number of "professions" to choose from. Forager, fisher, cultivator, hunter, or intense agriculturist and industrialist are "professions" that are or have been ways of gaining a subsistence from the world's biomes.

Regardless of the niche selected, the very process of humans adapting will alter a niche to varying degrees. As described by Baker (1984), adaptation to new environments provoked new stress formation that, in turn, demanded new adaptations. Figure 2–5 illustrates this cycle of events and the problems confronted by a population. The processes by which we cope with a stress and meet our biological needs alters the environment. The change, in turn, introduces new stresses and will continue as a neat circle of feedback loops. If isolated from external influences, the stimulus–response linkages could strike a balance and enable a population to reach an equilibrium. This would be theoretically possible except for the dynamics of internal and external stimuli.

A significant stimulus is provided by the natural fluctuation of the environment. Alternating climatic cycles, or seasonal shifts and changes in quantity of food resources, are a few areas to consider that would occur over shorter time periods. Expansion of neighboring populations and the resulting increased contact and competition for resources is another important stimulus to consider in measuring stability or change. This expansion can cause major environmental alterations as well as inject new population groups into a habitat. Competition and conflict result, and a larger, stronger, or better-adapted group would, over time, dominate. Witness the fate suffered by indigenous peoples upon contact with European colonists equipped with iron tools and weapons; or note the competition among pastoralists and cultivators.

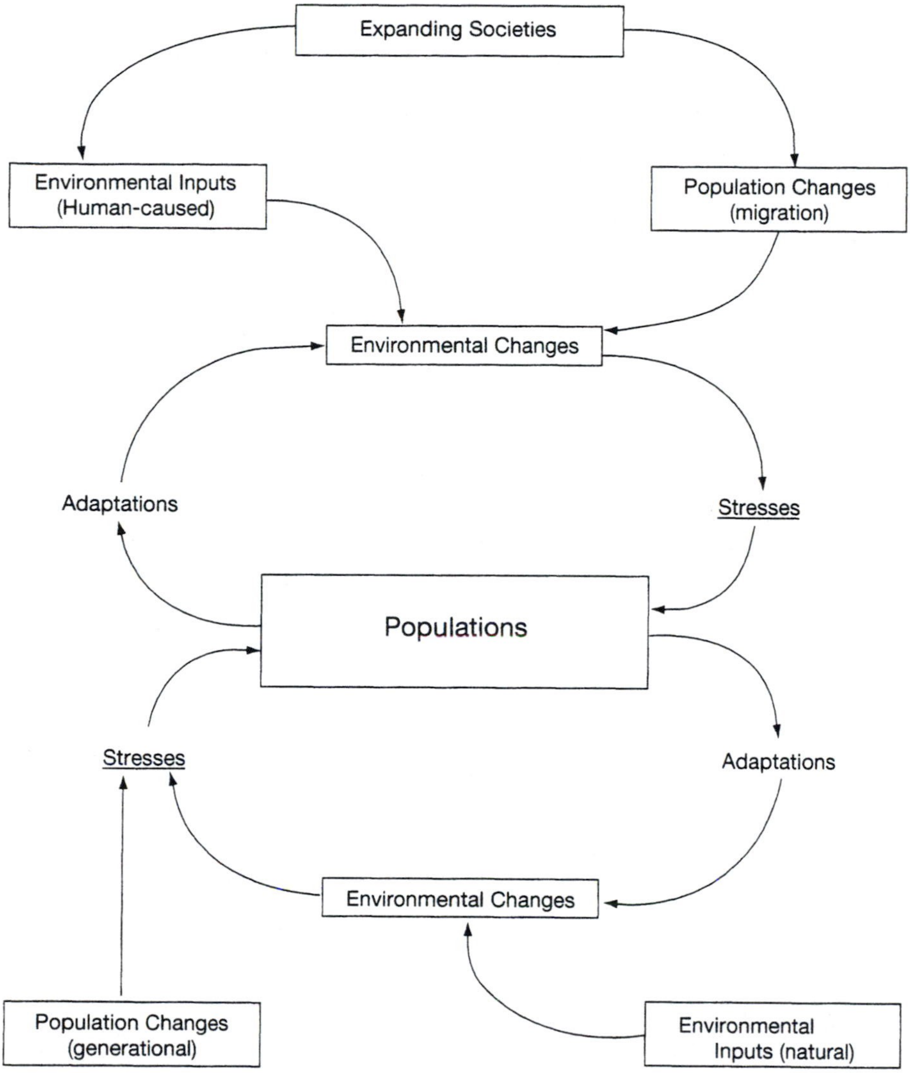

Figure 2–5 Adaptation and Linkages

Of equal importance are the natural generational changes experienced by the population due to increases or decreases of fertility rates, variations in mortality, and changes in age group sizes because of these events. As an example, the recent reduction of infant and child mortality experienced by many lesser developed countries has led to a disproportionate percentage (40 percent) of the population under 15 years of age compared to only 20 percent in the slow-growing populations of the developed countries.

Another example of both internal and external demographic influences is the experience of Australian Aboriginals. After maintaining slowly growing populations of low fertility for perhaps thousands of years, the shift to sedentary life in central Australia over the last century has broken this pattern. The length of the female reproductive period has been extended by several years and average fertility rate has doubled from three to six children per woman completing her reproductive years (Cowlishaw, 1981; White, 1977).

The details in the diagram in Figure 2–5 do not exclude the possibility of other forces for change. The different influences could be partitioned out, identified and added to the diagram; insect vectors of disease, improved farming, or technological inventions are examples. The diagram is meant to convey that niche changes may be, and frequently are, caused by some of the very adaptations made by the population. The more a society changes within an ecological system and the greater the population increases, the more adaptive responses will be required just to keep even (Baker, 1984). The story of the use of these responses can best be told by a description of *Homo sapiens'* place or niche, within the web of interaction of living and nonliving components of the environment.

THE HUMAN ECOLOGICAL NICHE

As pointed out, *Homo sapiens* can pick and choose from the resources at several levels of the food chain, and we have been successful at exploiting all of them. The Inuit (Eskimo) gain most of their food by hunting marine and terrestrial mammals, a diet that places them on the food chain as a carnivore. At the other extreme are nearly complete vegetarians, foragers, who depend upon a gathering of wild plants for a majority of their food, or peasant farmers subsisting upon grains and legumes to supply all of their dietary needs. In between range all of the rest of us who consume a diverse combination of plant and animal foods. If our goal was to merely define human ecology on the narrow basis of diet, we would still end up with an identification of several niches. But if niche means a "profession" practiced by an organism in its environment determined by the sum total of all adaptations, then niche number would be even larger, so large in fact, and so diverse that the meaning of human niche may be lost.

Our ability to adapt depends upon our skills in environmental manipulation. The human niche is best described by these learned socially transmitted skills (culture), and cultural classifications could be and have been used to distinguish among groups of human populations who depend upon either specialized or simpler technologies. This division would first establish a hunting and foraging niche, but even this encompasses subspecialities dependent upon certain plentiful, but narrowly defined resources, like marine organisms, migrating herds of large herbivores, or the harvesting of wild tubers and grass seeds. Though the hunting–foraging niche was one occupied for most of human existence, it was a niche of great diversity and not subject to simple classification.

Over the course of time, our ancestors devised many new methods of exploiting the environment, as evidenced by the prehistoric record. These methods underwent profound, sometimes rapid changes, with sweeping effects throughout following generations. Improved technological methods contributed to an increase of scattered populations as hunting–foraging bands extended throughout a variety of tropical, temperate, and arctic environments. Though the demands encountered in each environment varied, a similar "profession" was followed throughout the ranges of human habitation until near the end of the Pleistocene (Ice Ages). People began to concentrate on a narrower range of food resources, those in plentiful supply, easily collected within a smaller area. In other words, their subsistence base became more specialized.

As populations grew and the readily available, nutritionally richer foods were exploited more and more heavily, the bands had to search further afield or more intensely exploit the local resources. One may describe or reconstruct a period about 10,000 to 15,000 years ago in this way. Concentration of larger numbers of people in communities dependent on increased food specialization would be at risk from even slight environmental variations. Changes in climate, plant blights, or animal diseases could quickly change the flora and fauna of an area. The quantity available around the settlements probably would be inadequate to meet the needs of the now enlarged human population. Alternate food sources would have to be sought or their foraging would have to encompass a larger area. Given these population pressures and increased use of more marginal resources, the people began to experiment with cultivation of plants through attempts to enhance the growth of favored species. Several possibilities are considered in discussions of origins of cultivation (Flannery, 1973; Cowan and Watson, 1992).

Humans then entered a period we call the Neolithic (New Stone Age), equipped with long experience in food acquisition by foraging. Their extensive knowledge of their biomes enabled people to shift to a reliance on the domestication of plants and animals. This agricultural revolution occurred around 12,000 years ago when populations in several world regions shifted to a more sedentary lifestyle dependent on foods they could grow or the wild plants they could collect in the immediate vicinity. The acquisition of these new skills added a variety of new econiches related to environments and the differing types of species domesticated. This period of transition from a nomadic existence was a true revolution in human ecology.

Former nomadic foragers in China, Africa, the Valley of Mexico, and the Middle East gradually settled into a horticultural niche. Though the Middle East (especially the foothill areas around the Tigris and Euphrates rivers) is seen as the earliest agricultural sites, other world centers were not far behind in plant domestication. These new skills enabled the accumulation of surpluses and, with the development of storage methods, crop surpluses could balance out food shortages over short periods of climatic changes. Humans were not only adapting more effectively to their local environments but were radically changing them as well. With an expanded and more reliable subsistence base, populations grew at greater rates than at any previous time.

With each step of growth and technological progress, humans advanced further afield from their earlier beginnings within the restricted zone of the tropics. They gradually shed more and more of the environmental limitations that had restricted their earlier ancestors. But this progress in adaptive developments did vary since some biomes, because of climate and soil, could not sustain the sedentary life of the cultivator. There were other resources, however, that could and did support large numbers of humans, but these resources could only be successfully exploited by nomadic hunters or by pastoralists. Such groups could readily move with the seasonal changes. Other examples are to be found within the humid tropics where the high rainfall and thin soils could provide opportunities only for cultivators who practiced a form of crop rotation that required long fallow periods. They would cut and burn small plots of forest, plant their gardens in the ashes, and then move on after one or two growing seasons. The flora of the abandoned plot would gradually recover over several decades when the burning-planting-harvesting cycle could begin all over again.

The Arctic and subarctic, on the other hand, where the periglacial conditions of the Ice Ages persisted, required special cultural adaptations as documented by the survival of Inuit (of the New World), or Reindeer hunters and pastoralists of Siberia. In contrast, the high-altitude, montane environments of the Andes and Himalayas presented unique resources and climatic challenges that have been met by the millions of people who have occupied these rather harsh areas for nearly a thousand years (Browman, 1974). In sum, the varied conditions under which modern and premodern humans have existed required a development of a diversity of cultural adaptations, which encompassed social as well as technological aspects. Throughout the eighteenth and nineteenth centuries we could still find many examples of a continuation of this diversity. The spectrum of human activities has now expanded even further to include not only a continuation of nomadic and horticultural groups, but societies enjoying the benefits of space age technologies. Such persistence of cultures, reflective of our earlier prehistoric adaptations, has puzzled and perplexed social scientists for generations.

Often, there has been a temptation to equate people of these simpler technologies with a primitive mental state. Because of our expectation of human progress over time, or a "transformation to higher levels," we have tended to view societies in terms of advanced or retarded stages of development. In other words, it had been argued that "primitive" cultures persisted in certain parts of the world because of a biological inferiority of the people, hence, they possessed a kind of "unevolved mentality." The lack of agriculture, the persistence of stone tools, the failure to use certain marine resources, or a continuation of nomadism were thought to be evidence of "evolutionary failure" (see discussion in Berndt and Berndt, 1988). To organize human cultures on some technological scale imagined to represent progress is, in itself, a regression to an eighteenth-century world perspective. Such a racist view is seldom advanced today, but we still struggle for a comprehension of cultural diversity.

The persistence of simpler technological societies remains a puzzle largely because of a lack of understanding of evolution theory; there is an erroneous concept that evolution proceeded through "progressive stages" towards a final goal, man. A vagueness in the application of the concept of adaptation has often added to the confusion. Whatever the explanation, such small-scale societies that have persisted at simpler technological levels may lend insight into the variety of human techniques of environmental exploitation. This evidence may reflect certain conditions existing in earlier periods of human prehistory, such as the use of stone tools, hunting traps, fire, etc. However, such societies cannot be considered as "living fossils" as once thought of, nor are they remnants of earlier stages of evolution. The persistence of hunting and gathering was, for the groups that continued this mode of adaptation, a rational response to their needs given the environmental resources, or in many cases, such a lifestyle was forced on them through the competition with more powerful neighbors.

CONCLUSIONS

The ecological concepts that have been developed to explain the interaction of living systems with their environments apply to humans in the sense of a restraint or limitations. We have evolved biologically and behaviorally over the millennia to the point that we have weakened the bounds of these restrictions. Humans have shifted to the center of a "web of life," part of nature but yet more in control than at any time in our history. A special kind of ecosystem has developed, which we control and manipulate. Capturing energy, overcoming seasonal cycles, and reproducing and maintaining populations at levels never previously reached have been some landmarks of our specie's development. This development has been achieved through human's adaptive ability and at costs to the natural world. In a true sense, as Ortega y Gassett observed, "Man does not have a nature but a history." It is history of experience that drives the next generation; the direction is guided by the environment.

Chapter 3

Demographic Landmarks of a Successful Species

Today, with our space-age technology and billions of people covering much of the globe, it is easy to forget a few basic facts of our history. The first fact we should recall is that, until just a few thousand years ago, our ancestors were neither numerous nor in control of much of their environment. These ancestors lived in small nomadic bands and depended upon the collection of plant materials, insects, and hunting for their food supply. Second, though environmental knowledge and the development of varieties of food resources improved following the agricultural revolution, population sizes were still very closely restrained by local resources for several millennia. Third, as with communities of other species, there were numerous environmental conditions that limited human progress. Even after the development of agricultural skills and the adoption of a sedentary lifestyle, temporary or even minor changes in climate could result in major losses of life when droughts, frosts, or plant pests destroyed food crops. Nevertheless, slow advances were made, and populations increased. Finally, such a record of advancement might suggest a continuous growth as long as exploitation of natural resources expanded to keep pace with our needs. Population gains could be cut back drastically, however, as limits were reached or when radical environmental changes occurred. We may clarify this question of limits by a review of demographic milestones and the probable linkages to technological and environmental elements over the past few millennia.

LANDMARKS OF POPULATION AND DEVELOPMENT IN THE ANCIENT WORLD

Starting with the Neolithic Age, when we began a subsistence revolution relying on domesticated plants and animals, local populations scattered about the globe began to increase, at first slowly and then with a gradual acceleration. Though it took some 100,000 or more years to reach a level between 5 and 10 million people, only 4,000 years were required for our species to grow to 86 million (Table 3–1). This represents an annual increase of a little less than four-tenths of a percent, or an average addition of four new people per thousand population each year. Though slight, this growth acceleration at 4000 B.C. represents an important episode of achievement in human–environmental linkages.

Agriculture subsistence had become well established in most world regions and supported further population increases. There were between 270 million and 350 million people by the beginning of the Christian era, a thirtyfold increase in 8,000 years. Each generation gained gradually in numbers. The number entering their reproductive period increased, and they in turn bore offspring who survived in greater numbers and bore more offspring in their turn. Though this geometric growth[1] led to increasing increments of size in some regions, the overall world average population gain was still slow. For the first thousand years A.D., populations in some areas were barely maintained as classic civilizations rose or fell. According to the archaeological remains and the scant historic records, these population fluctuations were closely linked to agricultural developments.

Several major centers experienced rapid population increases and have been identified as primary examples of agricultural origins and, later, the development of the earliest civilizations. These regions include the Middle

[1]Geometric increase may be compared to a savings account earning compound interest.

TABLE 3–1 World Regions, Ancient and Preindustrial Estimates (in millions)

Regions	8000 B.C.	4000 B.C.	A.D. 1	1000	1500	1650	1750
World	5–10	86	270–350	275–345	440–540	545	735–805
Asia	–	–	145–235	125–218	210–350	330	404–490
Africa	–	–	25–45	25–50	36–72		60–95
Europe	–	–	35–50	36–55	60–70	100	120–135
North America	–	–	1–2	2–3	2–3	(1)	2–3
Central & South America	–	–	6–15	20–50	30–60	(12)	13–18
Oceania	–	–	1–2	1–2	1–2	(2)	

Note: These figures represent the best available population estimates. The accuracy increases after 1650 AD.

Source: Adapted from McEvedy and Jones, 1978; Deevey, 1960; Durand, 1977.

East and Egypt, where wheat and barley were the dietary mainstays, and Asia, including parts of China and India with a dependence on millet and rice (Chao, 1986). While these transformations from hunting–nomadic lifestyles to sedentary agricultural existence and then on to classic civilizations were being experienced, similar events occurred somewhat later on the other side of the world.

In the New World there is evidence for development of major agricultural centers in parts of Mexico, Central America, and Peru. In the valley of Mexico, maize was the major part of the subsistence base by 5000 B.C., supplemented later by beans and squash (Heiser, 1981). Potatoes and grains appeared as major dietary components in the Andean highlands from about the same time; these hardy food plants were later added to the diets in many other regions of North and Central America[2]. From these early beginnings in each region, plant domestication spread, and other, secondary, agricultural centers proliferated over vast areas and became an established agricultural dependent lifestyle based on a select number of food crops (outlined in Table 3–2). Technological skills continued to improve, intensifying environmental usage as populations grew with the expanding food (Matthews et al, 1990).

Now with a population increase of severalfold, there were even greater disturbances of natural environments. Food foraging and hunting in many areas could not return much for the effort they required. The foragers

[2]The growth of maize and potatoes depended on altitude; maize grew well up to about 3,500 meters but only the potato plant could be productive above 4,000 meters.

TABLE 3–2 Agricultural Development

Crop	Date	Area	Source
Wheat & Barley	7000 B.C.	Near East from Anatolia to present-day Iran	Matthews
Root Crops (Yams)	7000 B.C.	New Guinea	Golson
Millet	6000 B.C.	Northern China & Wheat spreading to rest of Greece	Matthews
Rice	5500 B.C.	China earliest 9000 to 7500—widespread dispersal probably 5000 B.C.	Fagan
Squash	5200 B.C.	Tamaulipas & Tehuacan	Cowan & Watson
Maize	4500 B.C.	Southcentral Mexico	Matthews
Wheat	4500 B.C.	Poland & Germany	Matthews
Cotton, lima beans, Squash	4000 B.C.	Peru	Thorne& Raymond
Wheat & Barley	4500 B.C.	Baltic & Southern Scandinvia	Matthews
Potato	4550 to 3100 B.C.	Andes—Peru	Wenke
Maize	2500 & 1800 B.C.	Mexico	Fagan

Sources: Adapted from Matthews, et al, 1990; Golson, 1982; Fagan, 1992; Cowan and Watson, 1992; Thorne & Raymond, 1989; Wenke, 1990.

had to wander further afield in their food search, and an increasing scarcity of natural products forced many onto an ever thinner margin of survival. True, some populations, protected by their isolation, could continue a traditional lifestyle, and a few larger groups were well supported by renewable resources like salmon, or large herds of annually migrating herbivores. Such groups eventually gave way to external pressures and shortages and began to adopt new subsistence strategies. Growth and change began to influence human culture to degrees not previously experienced. The estimates of population sizes in the pre-Industrial world show that we had come a long way since our ancestors first experimented with plant cultivation and sedentary life.

The combined effects of increased population densities interacting with the needs for advances in food production resulted in several major technological developments. River flood plains were exploited for their fertility and annual renewal of soil fertility. Then ditches were dug to divert water flow and, eventually, there was a dependence upon irrigation systems. The control of these hydrological works and the concentration of people resulted in the establishment of urban centers. The best documented of the earliest regions where this combination of events occurred are Mesopotamia and Egypt. About 6,000 years ago, large urban centers were established and became our earliest civilizations. These larger more complex societies with their monumental architecture, writing, and metallurgy of Western Asia and Egypt are considered to be the beginnings of human history. Developments of urban societies in regions of China, the Indian subcontinent, and Southeast Asia followed within 3,000 years, or perhaps sooner. Likewise, as an outgrowth of earlier agricultural efforts and population expansion, urban centers began to appear in the other regions as well, notably in Peru, Mexico, and Guatemala (see Fagan, 1992).

Each of these Old and New World civilizations left behind major architectural remains as a significant record of their achievements. Some still stand today, as in the case of Egyptians or Mayan pyramids: Some structures lie buried under silt or are covered over with modern city buildings and roads. The worldwide scope and antiquity of these marvels of human technology may be appreciated by the short list in Table 3–3, which offers some estimates of age and population sizes.

By the time of the earliest cities in Mesopotamia (5000 B.C.), only about three thousand years had lapsed since the initial agricultural revolution. From this period, the pace of social and technological change quickened each millennium until one major achievement followed another at ever-shorter time intervals. Each episode was marked by an increasing effectiveness of environmental control, principally the regulation of water supply, and improved agronomy with reliance on a calendar system to mark the seasons for planting or harvesting. Human technological and social progress appeared to have been accelerating throughout this period. Irrigation technology, aqueducts, the plow, harnessing of draft animals, wheeled carts,

TABLE 3–3 Ancient Civilizations and Urban Population Centers

Date	City	Region	Population	Source
8350 to 7350 B.C.	Jericho	Palestine	2,000 or more	Wenke
6250 B.C.	Catal Huyuk	Anatolia	4,000–6,000	Wenke
3100 B.C.	Memphis	Egypt		Wenke
3000 B.C.	Uruk	Sumeria	50,000	Wenke
2600 B.C.	Mohenjo-daro	Indus	40,000	Wenke
2200 B.C.	Greater Ur	Sumeria	250,000	Darlington
1750 B.C.	Shang Dynasty	China		
735 B.C.	Rome	Italy	500,000–	Pleket
A.D. 1		China*	1 million	Wenke*
500 A.D.	Teotihuacan	Valley of Mexico	100,000–200,000	Wenke
600 A.D.	Cahokia	Illinois	20,000	Thorne
1250 A.D.	Cahokia	Illinois	30,000–40,000	Wenke
1100 A.D.	Cuzco	Peru	200,000	Ency
1275 A.D.	Pigjiang lu (Suzhou)	China	329,603	Marme

*One of the world's first national censuses was conducted in China in A.D. 1–2 and tallied 57,700,000 people, at least 10% of whom lived in recantangular wooden towns with populations of up to 250,000 (Wenke, 1990).

Source: Data adapted from: Darlington, 1969; Marme, 1993; Pleket, 1993; Thorne & Raymond, 1989; Wenke, 1990.

wheel-made pottery, monumental architecture, writing, and even indoor plumbing head a long list of achievements.

One of the major landmarks of technological progress, and one that lends names for various episodes of ancient civilizations, was the improvement in the use of metals (Table 3–4). Metallurgy was first applied to the manufacture of ornaments and items of jewelry. Later, metal's value as sub-

TABLE 3–4 Landmarks of Development

Age	Time	Area	Source
Paleolithic	1 million B.C.		
Mesolithic	15,000 B.C.		
Neolithic	8-10,000 B.C.		
Copper	4600 to 4200 B.C.	Balkans	Fagan
Copper	3500 B.C.	Aegean & Greece	Fagan
Copper	3000 B.C.	Northern Europe	Fagan
Bronze	2500 B.C.	China	Wenke
Bronze	2000–3000 B.C.	W. Asia, Crete, Iran Mesopotamia, Aegean	Wenke
Bronze	2000–2500 B.C.	Hungary	Kovacs
Iron	1260 B.C.	Hittites	Fagan
Iron	400 B.C.	W. Africa—Mali	McIntosh
Iron	1000 B.C.	Kabuye in E. Africa	Van Noten and Raymaekers
Iron	500 B.C.	China	Wenke
Industrial Revolution	1760 to 1850 A.D.		see Chapter 4

Source: Data from Wenke, 1990; Fagan, 1992; Kovacs, 1977; McIntosh and McIntosh, 1981; Van Noten, F. & J Raymaekers, 1988.

stitutes for stone tools was recognized and the manufacture of implements began. Instead of pounding raw metals, like copper, out of rock outcrops containing nearly pure metals, innovative individuals found that they could more efficiently extract this metal by heating the ore to high temperatures, and the *Copper Age* (4600 B.C.) was born in the lands bordering the Eastern Mediterranean. This episode was followed by the Bronze Age (2000–2500 B.C.) when it was discovered that the addition of a small amount of tin to the melted copper would produce a stronger, harder metal. The application of these metallurgical skills was eventually applied to iron, a more difficult metal to work with, requiring higher temperatures and special treatment. But iron tools were harder and weapons stronger and shortly human technology had entered the Iron age (1500–1000 B.C.). Iron was probably first used by people (Hittites) living around the southeastern part of the Black Sea to make trinkets and items for harnesses for their horses. The iron working technique spread through the Middle East, to Greece, and up the Danube river valley, then through Europe to become an important material for weapons and tools, from about 500 B.C. Africa should be mentioned because, as with so many cultural innovations, the sub-Saharan region is seldom seen as an area of invention and origin. The conventional wisdom often relates that iron was brought across the Sahara by trade routes from the Phoenecians in North Africa. True, the earliest dates for iron implements in West Africa are from about 400 B.C., but 600 years earlier, people in East Africa were smelting iron. What is most important is that they were doing so with advanced methods using what may have been an early form of blast furnace (Van Noten and Raymaekers, 1988).

While the Classic civilizations around the Mediterranean were evolving, peoples in other areas, including the Western hemisphere (the New World), were developing complex societies dependent on an advanced management of resources. The agriculturists of the American Southwest farmed an arid land 2,000 years ago by skillful use of surface waters. The remains of vast irrigation systems and deep mounds of debris mark their ancient town sites, as can be seen in the area of Maricopa county around the modern day city of Phoenix, Arizona (Haury, 1976). On the other side of the world, perhaps as early as 9,000 years ago, people living in the highlands of New Guinea were practicing an efficient form of agricultural development. They dug long, deep ditches in valleys of high rainfall to drain swamps. This provided large areas of reclaimed fertile land on which they grew vast quantities of root crops (Golson, 1982).

Peoples living along the northwest coast of Europe, who exploited the maritime resources, are other examples. Living in an environment and climate extremely different from New Guinea or the North American Southwest, the prehistoric (6000 B.C.) populations in what is now Denmark, made skillful use of their local natural resources. So efficiently did they gain their subsistence from the sea with their fish traps, harpoons, and other implements, that agriculture was not adopted as a major means of subsistence until some several thousand years after farming was first introduced into river basins of southeastern Europe. While these prehistoric Danes and Frisians practiced a sedentary form of collecting, reindeer hunters-herders far to the north continued a nomadic existence, surviving by preying on these large herds just as their ancestors had during the last glacier advance (Clark, 1977).

In addition to these examples of exploitation by plant domestication are the numerous peoples who retained many of the subsistence strategies of their nomadic ancestors. Such societies varied—from the horse nomads of the Central Asian grasslands (ancestors of the Tartars and Mongols) to the pedestrian hunters of the great plains of North America. These Native Americans preyed upon the buffalo even before the introduction of the horse (about 1750 A.D.) enabled them to increase their hunting efforts.[3] In stark contrast are the numerous Arctic peoples living even today in an environment as harsh as any suffered by their ancestors during the height of the Pleistocene glacial advances. The Siberian tribes subsisting by hunting and trapping, the reindeer hunters and the Eskimo exploiting marine mammals and fish also illustrate the range of opportunities available in even the harshest of environments.

The tropics have offered an even greater environmental variety to be exploited by a diversity of cultures. In the Americas, this variety extended from complex civilizations like the Incas of the Andes or Mayan of Southern Mexico and Guatemala to numerous sedentary or seminomadic horticulturists of the tropical forests of Central and South America. These horticulturists, a few persisting into the last few decades, planted their gardens and then wandered off for a time to hunt and gather, returning when time to harvest. The African and Southeast Asian tropics likewise contained both foraging–hunting peoples and farmers, ranging from simple horticultural communities to large complex urban societies. The archaeological and ethnographic records are filled with such examples of the increasing diversity of cultures over time. As such cultural diversity was developing, our species was growing in number.

Total world population gain was still slow and unevenly distributed. Many populations of ancient historic times appear to have grown very rapidly over a short time span, only to suffer sharp declines within a few generations. Expanding numbers of people, for example, would place a heavy burden on a food supply that could be reduced drastically by a temporary shift in climate or by the arrival of an insect pest, sharply affecting crop yields. The fall of several early civilizations were marked by famine and loss of life following an erractic turn in the weather. Depletion of soil fertility due to intensive agriculture or saliniation (the accumulation of salts) after

[3] The Spanish provided horses to their Aztec allies as early as 1541, but it took several hundred years before the horse became an established part of the culture among the peoples of the Northern Great Plains (see Ewers, 1967:495; Roe, 1955:54).

many years of continuous irrigation is another primary cause of the decline of the societies in Mesopotamia (Darlington, 1969).

Half a world away in Arizona and New Mexico, the problem became one of lesser rainfall. Many of the densely populated Pueblos in the Southwest, which had flourished between 700 and 1200 A.D., had to be abandoned because of extreme drought that began about 1250 A.D.. The many terraces and irrigation ditches that had enabled the Anasazi people to farm and build dense village settlements in this semiarid region proved to be inadequate to cope with a near century of drought. Likewise, the societies dependent upon irrigation systems in fertile river valleys a few hundred miles away suffered severely and never recovered. When the Spaniards arrived in the sixteenth century, many of the Southwestern pueblos were occupied but the large-scale farming projects with their dense settlements no longer existed (Fagan, 1992). Considering these examples, plus the archaeological record of classic civilizations of the Middle East and around the Mediterranean, one cannot escape the conclusion that populations undergo an oscillation between expansion and contraction influenced by external forces. These classic civilizations lend some evidence of these cycles of rise and fall but do not always provide the reason. Changes in climate, declines in crop production, crowding or warfare, followed by famine and disease, all contribute to losses of people and their cultures.

Most of the population numbers mentioned are but rough estimates based on archaeologically derived data like structural ruins, traces of the remains of irrigation canals, and trash middens around ancient occupation sites. These data are, not surprisingly, subject to a wide range of errors and a considerable difference in interpretation. Some writers argue that population estimates are often too low, especially those made for peoples of the New World and throughout the Pacific. By about 1000 A.D., the range of error is reduced for parts of the world, and descriptions of population sizes can be offered with more confidence as written records become available. Historical narratives from Greece and Rome are helpful but the earliest documents dealing with population size are from China, with recorded tax rolls and census data in the first Imperial Census, 1 A.D. Then the next known census comes in the "Doomsday Book," a record gathered in 1033 A.D. by the victorious Normans to inventory the conquered lands of England and Wales. These data offer greater accuracy and significant regional differences of populations are well established from this time.

REGIONAL DISTRIBUTION OF POPULATION INCREASES

The periodic expansions or declines of populations were distributed unevenly through time and across space. China, because of its large size, its complex civilizations, and some of the earliest population statistics, provides an interesting case in contrast to southern Europe. From the first census, China increased from 90 million to 150 million people over the next 150 years. Growth continued for several hundred years despite periodic episodes of severe famine and warfare that caused high mortality. Statistics gained from dynastic records dating from the Han dynasty of 2 A.D. until the Ching dynasty of the early twentieth century plot a series of advances interspaced by significant declines in population (see Chao, 1986:231). For example, the eleventh century was a time of major advance, when China's population doubled and continued to grow into the following century (when it stabilized at about 125 million (Durand, 1977).

The Mongol invasion in the thirteenth century contributed to a major population loss through warfare and the destruction of the country's infrastructure and irrigation works. The inevitable famine, disease, and death followed. For about the next fifty years there was a slow recovery, until the middle of the century when the country was struck by a series of epidemics resulting in high mortality. The greatest loss occurred during the 1393 plague epidemic, when death rates were so high that population declined to a low of 90 million. Again, there was a slow recovery for the next four generations, and there was an estimated 150 million people. By the middle of sixteenth century, the population began to grow at a faster rate and recovered even more rapidly, overcoming the short periodic declines.

By contrast, over the first thousand years of the Christian era the populations living around the Mediterranean showed little gain and began to go into a decline after 400 A.D. In fact, the whole of Europe was an example of little average population change from an estimated 40 million. This stagnation was, in part, a result of the political turmoil initiated by a collapse of the Roman Empire. With the loss of Roman administrative control and military protection, Europe was beset with economic problems and overrun by periodic invasions of nomads from the Central Asian steppes (Darlington, 1969). Much of Europe was forced into regional isolation and entered what historians refer to as the "Dark Ages." By the twelfth and thirteenth centuries, there was a slow European recovery, resulting in an estimated 79 million people by 1300 A.D. (Table 3–5), gains that were lost later in the century when the plague and other epidemics swept over the continent. Overall, the period from the sixth to the fourteenth century was a time of slight increases interspaced by periods of heavy mortality, during which time up to 40 percent were lost among those populations occupying the area formerly included in the old Roman Empire (Wrigley, 1969).

The Middle East, the region that led the world into the "great agricultural transition" and created the earliest civilizations, was reduced from 45 million to 30 million by 1000 A.D. and, thereafter, the population remained relatively steady for the next 750 years (McEvedy and Jones, 1978). This decline was regional in scope and seemingly reflected the turmoil generated by the collapse of empires and declines of central political

TABLE 3–5 European Populations (1200–1900) (in millions)

	1200	1300	1400	1500	1600	1700	1800	1900
Europe	58	79	60	81	100	120	180	390
England & Wales	2.5	3.75	2.5	3.75	4.25	5.75	9.25	33
Ireland	0.6	0.8	0.6	0.8	1.25	2.5	5.25	4.5
Netherlands	0.6	0.8	0.6	0.9	1.5	2	2	5.25
Scandinavia	1.5	1.75	1.25	2	2.25	3	5.25	12.5
France	10.5	16	11	15	10.5	22	29	41
Germany	6	9	6.5	9	12	13	18	43
Russia	9	9	9	12	15	20	36	100
Spain	5.5	7.5	5.5	6.5	8.5	8	11.5	18.5
Italy	7.25	10	7	10	12	13	19	34
N. W. Europe	25	38	25	35	48	57	80	150

Source:Durand, 1977; Schofield, 1985; Wrigley, 1969.

control of resources. Even the rise of Arab influence and the spread of the Islam religion in the eighth century did not appear to stimulate population growth. Islam's influence did stimulate trade and cultural exchange around the Mediterranean, however, from the Arabian peninsula to Spain and North Africa.[4]

Significant contrasts were also seen in Asia. China's population increased by 250 percent during the first 1,700 years, while other Asian regions were growing more slowly or remained nearly static. The Indian subcontinent, which includes the area of today's Pakistan and Bangladesh, showed no increase between 1 A.D. and 1000 A.D., but then grew by 50 percent over the next 500 years. This growth acceleration continued and added another 33 percent to the regional populations by 1750 A.D.

The numbers of people in the Americas are more difficult to estimate and are generally biased by the European colonists' wish to view the New World as an empty land. The Incan, Mayan, and Aztec empires impressed the explorers with the magnitude of their architectural achievements, but the search for gold distracted from any interest in matters of environment or population. Not until nearly a century after contact, with the beginning of European colonization, was there much concern with practical matters of environmental resources and agricultural prospects. By then it was much too late to gain more accurate estimates of the native peoples. The early estimates of about 10 million have proven to be much too conservative. More careful review of archaeological evidence and the records of earlier European explorers now place the total nearer to 40 million for North America and about the same for Central and South America. Mexico alone is estimated to have had nearly 20 million at the time of Spanish contact (Reff, 1992).

[4] "The century following the beginning of Islamic religion saw a large number of conversions and a rapid spread of the faith. This increase stemmed from socioeconomic causes rather than from religious motivation. (Sills, 1968)

The large empires described in the earliest journals of the Spanish explorers like Cortez (Mexico), Pizzaro (Peru), and De Soto (Lower Mississippi valley) were soon destroyed and untold numbers of Native Americans died in wave after wave of epidemics. The inhabitants of the New World were extremely sensitive to European-type diseases and they suffered high mortality from the first exposure to these diseases. The inhabitants of the Caribbean Islands were the first to suffer but a better record is available for what transpired in Mexico. Smallpox, for example, was reportedly introduced into Vera Cruz by an infected slave when Cortez and his group landed in 1514 A.D. The infection killed about one-half of the population in Tenochtitlan (Mexico City) and enabled a handful of Spanish soldiers to conquer the Aztec empire within a few years.

The Native Americans throughout the Western Hemisphere proved to be so susceptible to smallpox that the virus spread rapidly between villages, causing the deaths of entire populations hundreds of miles from the point of introduction before any Europeans ever reached the area. Measles, several other types of what we call "childhood" diseases, and respiratory infections likewise were nearly as destructive to these "virgin populations," people with no prior contact with the viral and bacterial microbes so common among Europeans (Crosby, 1976). By the time of the arrival of English settlers, nearly a century after the first Spanish contact, whole areas of the New World had been decimated. The large urban settlements along the Mississippi and Ohio river valleys had been vacated by epidemics. The populations along the eastern seaboard of North America had thinned out, and Mexico, of which we have some of the best documentation, declined from about 20 million to less than 2 million (see Verano and Ubelaker, 1992, for a review).

Africa, except for the Mediterranean coast and Egypt, has proven to be a dilemma for the historical demographer. Despite the frequent Spanish and Portuguese contacts with the large flourishing empires of the western coastal areas, little was known of the peoples of the interior or in the eastern areas. Much of the continent remained a mystery to Europeans before more recent exploration and colonization. The populations of whole regions of the continent have been adequately estimated only since the end of the nineteenth century. However, early Arab traders' descriptions of their contacts with the West African Empires of Ghana and Mali suggest that the region supported populations in the millions. One wrote of the 200,000-man army that the king of Ghana could put into the field, and noted the large gold supply of the empire (Fagan, 1992:477). Such a military force could only be sustained by a large population under control of a complex social infrastructure. The scope and size of these early West African empires are only now becoming appreciated since archaeological excavations in the last few decades (McIntosh and McIntosh, 1981).

Toward the end of the "Middle Ages," at about 1400 A.D., pronounced world regional differences began to appear. Many groups grew at rates of up to one-half of one percent annually. China, for example, underwent several periods of rapid growth, until it contained about 430 million, or 40 percent of the world's people by 1850. The Indian subcontinent, likewise, increased until there were approximately 20 percent of the total world's people contained within its borders by the nineteenth century. After 1850, growth slowed for a time in Asia, however. But even these impressive gains were exceeded by the populations of the Western World. Europe and those world regions settled by Europeans, mainly North America, posted only slow gains following the Middle Ages until 1650 A.D., and then began to grow rapidly, a doubling in size every generation into the twentieth century. By 1900, Europeans and their descendants in North America made up about 30 percent of the world total while Asia went into a population decline from 64 to 58 percent (Figure 3–1a and b). These numbers and their distributions reflect a decline or rise throughout the world until modern times and demonstrate that population size is not stable nor is growth continuous, even in recent times. The causes of such instability are numerous and may have important implications for future populations.

Figure 3–1a World Regions, 1000–1750

Data selected and adapted from Deevey, 1960; Durand, 1977; McEvedy and Jones, 1977.

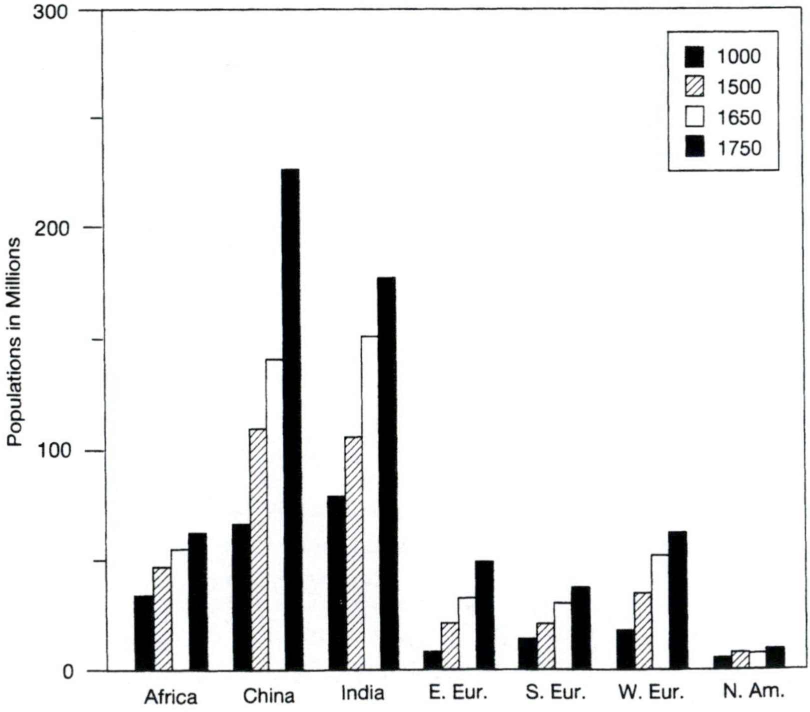

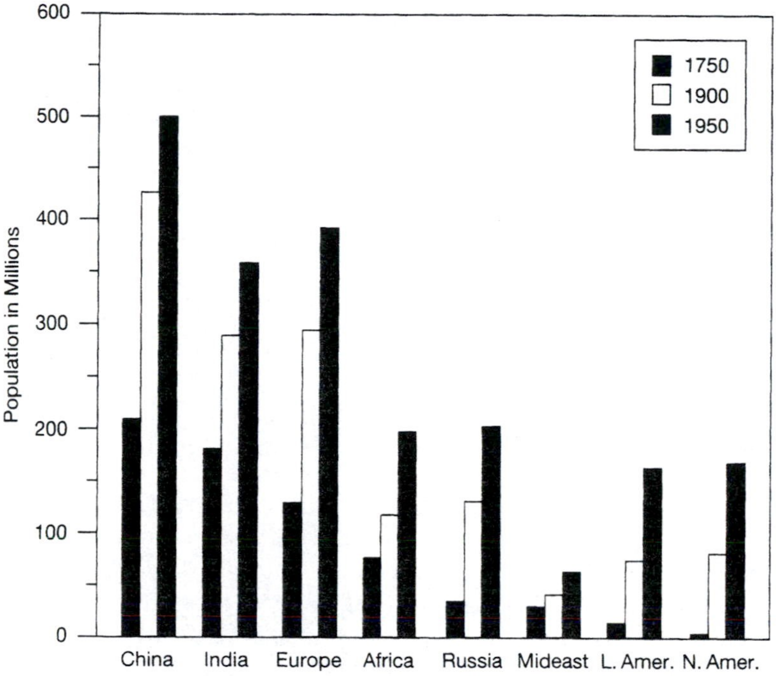

Figure 3–1b World Regions, 1750–1950

Data selected and adapted from Deevey, 1960; Durand, 1977; McEvedy and Jones, 1977.

SOME FACTORS CONTRIBUTING TO POPULATION GROWTH

Generally, the rise and fall in the numbers of people inhabiting different world regions may be explained by reference to three key factors. These are closely interrelated and not necessarily in any particular order. Health status is the first factor to consider, especially its effect on the differential between birth rates and mortality rates. Birth rates were frequently higher in the past than today, about 45 per 1,000 population. Countering this CBR (crude birth rate) was the excessive mortality suffered by many generations, between 30 and 35 per 1,000 population and, during certain periods, mortality would surge to even higher levels.[5]

Waves of epidemics periodically struck with devastating effects. In Europe, whose records are best known, there are frequent mention of "fevers" (caused by any one of several infections), the "pox" (probably smallpox) and "bloody fluxes" (dysenteric diseases). Throughout the Mid-

[5]By comparison, populations in the developing countries of Asia today record a CBR of thirty and a CDR of ten; this is in contrast to the CBR of 14 and CDR of 9 of the developed countries.

dle Ages, whole communities would be decimated with a high loss of life and severe disruption of economies. As European cities expanded, the crowded conditions would increase transmission of "herd" diseases. These were infectious disease types dependent upon large host populations; most notable for their high mortality and rapid spread from person to person were smallpox, typhus, measles, and whooping cough. Airborne respiratory diseases, probably also including influenza, were acute among dense populations of these ancient cities. Polluted water was also a major source of illness and was particularly threatening to children. The continued outbreak of "fevers" during times of economic crisis was a special fact of life. Add to this health burden that most famous of all episodes in the history of disease, the "Black Death," or plague, and the wonder is that European populations were able to persevere at all.

Introduced into Europe in 1346 A.D. from the Middle East, this deadly bacterial disease spread quickly among cities in southern Europe and then moved northward, accounting for about 25 percent mortality. The disease is caused by a bacteria that is preserved to this day among wild rodent populations throughout the world, causing periodic outbreaks among human populations. Fleas carried by the rodents act as vectors transmitting the bacteria between individuals, either rodents or humans. Periodically, when certain conditions bring humans into close contact with infected rodent populations, there is a transmission of the bacteria from the rodent, by way of the flea vectors, to humans who then suffer from various forms of the plague disease.[6] Because of its hosts and vectors, distribution of plague bacteria is especially sensitive to the numbers and habits of rodents and to human lifestyle. The crowded, mostly wooden dwellings of the fourteenth century cities provided close and frequent contacts between humans and rodents and the fleas that they carried.

The plague spread quickly as ships trading between Mediterranean ports carried infected rats among cargoes in their holds. Once ashore, the rats mingled with the local rodent populations, infecting them as well as humans. Overland transport of cargoes and humans continued the spread inland far from the sea ports. Once introduced, no urban center, town, or village was spared the high loss of life. The few survivors of an outbreak of plague epidemics fled, further spreading the disease. Entire villages were abandoned in the fourteenth century, some never to be reoccupied. In effect, the epidemic changed the settlement landscape of whole areas of Western

[6]The growth of the bacteria may be confined to the bloodstream and, after a short period, accumulated in the lymphatic system, causing swelling of the lymph nodes; hence the term "bubonic plague." Most deadly to crowded populations is the pneumonic form. Infection can increase rapidly to the point of reaching the lungs. The bacteria can be expelled by coughing, and infection can be thus transmitted from person to person, rapidly spreading throughout dense urban populations without assistance from the rodent-flea vector route.

Europe in particular. By 1352, the plague had run its course and 25 to 50 million people had perished, according to estimates by church officials. Some areas were even harder hit, with a loss of up to half of their population.[7] This episode has become one of the best documented of the many other "plagues" our ancestors suffered before modern times (McNeill, 1977).

Though the "Great Plague" ended in 1352, outbreaks continued to occur as often as three or four times within a generation in parts of Europe. A second and then a third pandemic spread through Europe in 1361 and 1369 and there were periodic outbreaks for the next century. People were convinced that plagues were a permanent part of nature, to be endured with the other hardships of their lives. Then the plague mortality in Europe began to decline somewhat during the early part of the seventeenth century. The mortality went down to 10 percent and, compared to the previous high of 50 percent, it would be considered an improvement.[8] Also, the intervals between outbreaks lengthened to a twelve-year cycle, and further lengthened until plague was no longer recalled as a threat. London suffered its last epidemic in 1650.

Unfortunately, after several plague-free generations, the disease reappeared in southern France in 1720. The epidemic struck with as much deadly force as during the first pandemic. Half of the population of Marseilles died, while Toulon lost 60 percent and Arles 44 percent (Gottfried, 1983). This was the last plague epidemic in Europe, but this dreaded disease of the Middle Ages has not disappeared from the planet, and occasionally there are local outbreaks. Parts of Asia, especially, continue to be a plague reservoir, with periodic epidemics spreading quickly along trade routes through crowded populations; the last epidemic spread throughout Mongolia and northern China around 1900 (Dubos, 1965). Since then there have been reoccurrences, but these have been kept isolated to a few hundred local cases by fast action of health officials using modern antibiotics.

The various epidemics and plagues in preindustrial Europe were dramatic events that attracted the attention of the writers of the period, and vivid descriptions have been handed down over the centuries. What is scarcely noted, except by the most careful demographers, is that there were consistently high rates of mortality between the peaks of the major epidemics. Young children, even during the best of times, suffered high death rates. As many as half of all children born alive would die before their fifth birthday, a rate that was retained well into the twentieth century by popula-

---

[7] Many histories of the plague have been written and, though there is some variance in dates and mortality rates, all depict a time of extreme crisis in which plague epidemics followed crop failures and famines worsened by wooden dwellings hospitable to large rodent populations. See Gottfried, 1983 and McEvedy, 1988 for recent reviews of the plague times.

[8] To put these mortality rates in perspective and the impact on society at the time and for generations to come, consider the one-half million deaths in the United States out of a population of 100 million from the Influenza epidemic of 1918.

tions of some world regions. Add to this another 15 percent of the children lost before they reached adulthood and the surprise is that populations could increase at all. However, human reproductive potential is great, as we shall describe. After episodes of excessive mortality, birth rates would rapidly increase and populations would recover. Within even a single generation, European populations of the sixteenth and seventeenth centuries rebounded with excess of births over deaths that were even higher than had existed before an epidemic.

Such recoveries occurred many times in human history as populations oscillated back and forth from high to low peaks of growth. Reliable recorded evidence is lacking, however, for most of our history. We know that populations went through wide swings in ancient and even recent times, but this knowledge is based on interpretations of partial census or tax records, historical, and archaeological evidence. The earliest reliable European census data comes from Central Sweden and lists the course of birth and mortality rates since 1691 (Ohlsson and Bengtsson, 1984; Post, 1985). This region recorded a surplus of births over deaths for a five-year period (1691–1695), followed by a decline during the next five-year period. This demographic pattern, for this region, of about 38,000 was followed for a generation. There were slight population gains cut back by losses. Then the gains began to increase, and the population grew slowly (Figure 3–2a). From 1749 onward, census data becomes more reliable, and there is a clearer relevance to economic events. Figure 3–2b shows birth and death rates between 1749–1914 and indicates the impact of crop failures and disease on population growth by the mortality peaks. At times, populations were growing at a rate of 1 percent per year but then there were surges in death rates where more people were lost than were added. This was not an unusual demographic response, as shown by church records and historical accounts from several other European countries. There are less reliable figures from England for the eighteenth century that are based on an analysis of baptismal and burial records from 200 English parishes; the period from 1690–1749 records 207,227 baptisms and 180,188 deaths.[9] This small population gain provides little surplus to compensate for losses during times of high mortality; and net population gain was correspondingly slower.

Another factor is the satisfaction of dietary needs, the most basic influence on growth and maintenance of any biological population. The linkages among population, food, and health are not difficult to trace. The more poorly nourished members of a society suffer a higher mortality rate. The fluctuation of population with food shortages, as shown in Figure 3–2b, suggests this and is demonstrated by more accurate recent data.

There are certain minimal food energy requirements for normal

[9]From a study of a national sample of Anglican parishes throughout England and Wales, cited by Razzell, 1974.

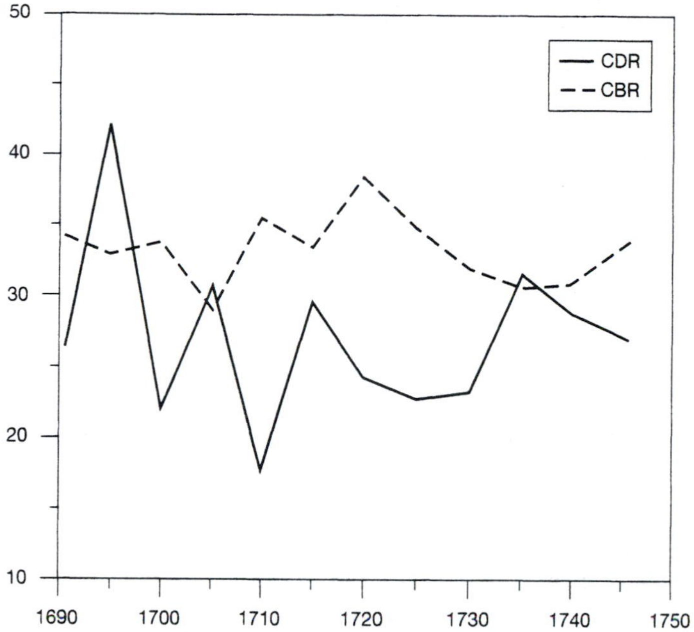

Figure 3–2a Crude Birth and Death Rates from Narke, Sweden

Data selected and adapted from Utterstrom, 1965.

Figure 3–2b Crude Birth and Death Rates, Sweden, 1751–1984

From Merrick, 1986. Reprinted by permission of Population Reference Bureau, Inc.

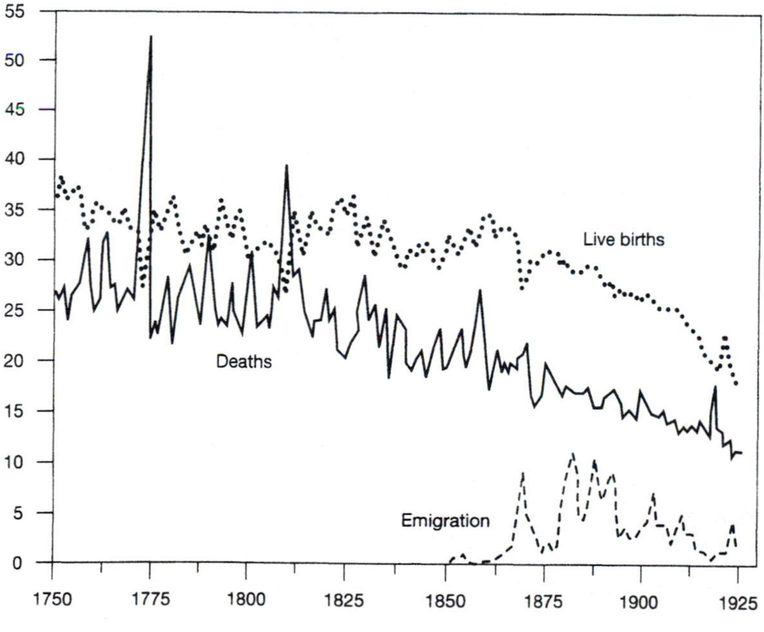

growth, reproduction, and work energy expenditures as we shall discuss in later chapters. If all requirements for each individual given their age, gender, and workloads are added, then the sum represents the total energy needed to maintain that particular population. These requirements may be translated into a system, the energy gained per unit of effort, and then related to "carrying capacity" of a given environment. That is, the available resources suitable for use as human food and the technology needed to exploit them can provide for a certain population size. This ability to obtain the needed food energy, of course, has varied over time and from place to place, sustaining smaller or larger numbers of people at different levels of health.

Climatic Fluctuations and Population Linkages

Since the days of classic civilizations, even minor environmental changes could and did cause a population crash. Over periods as long as a decade, yields from the traditional crops might be sufficient to meet local needs and could even provide some surpluses. These surpluses would enable the people to survive a bad year, perhaps even two but not more. Crop failures followed by famine, epidemics, and large population losses have been related to periodic climatic changes. The linkages of natural phenomena with demographic variables has led to an extensive study of European weather history as it has affected agricultural settlements from Neolithic to recent times.[10] The results have plotted numerous shifts in climate and agricultural opportunities, especially in Northwestern Europe.

The milder weather of the post glacial period (the Atlantic Phase) encouraged settlement and plant domestication but began to change about 5,000 years ago with more frequent colder and wetter winters (the subboreal phase). Life for the Bronze Age farmer became more difficult about 1800 B.C. with lower mean annual temperatures and erratic rainfall patterns. About 1 A.D., the climate began to shift to more favorable conditions marked by a warming trend between 400–1200 A.D.. This moderation of climate encouraged expansion of agriculture, particularly in Northern Europe, and even vineyards spread through England and Germany. During the peak of this warming trend (800–1000 A.D.) Norse settlements were established in Greenland, Iceland, and Vineland (probably Newfoundland).

These colonies thrived for several centuries as did the growing farming communities throughout Northern Europe but then, about 1200 A.D., things began to go wrong. There was another climatic shift that has been called the "Little Ice Age"(Ladurie, 1971). The winters gradually became longer and colder and were interspaced by cool, wet summers; the heavy winter snow-

---

[10] For example, see Silverberg, 1969 for a broad overview; Ladurie, 1971 and Parry, 1978 for careful analysis of climatic changes and the effects on crop yields.

falls were followed by torrential spring floods. Grain crops did not ripen and hay used to feed the stock rotted in the fields. Among the communities hardest hit were the Norse colonies. These remote settlements of sub-Arctic latitude were isolated from their Scandinavian homeland as the arctic pack ice extended further and further south, blocking shipping lanes. After the colonies lost contact with their mother country they managed to survive for nearly a century. The colonies were now dependent on their own resources and with the increasingly colder weather and shorter growing seasons there were frequent crop production shortfalls. The people endured extreme hardships as year after year they could not fully supply their food needs. After holding on for nearly a century, extinction was the ultimate fate of these remote, isolated colonies (McGovern, 1981:404).

People across Europe suffered comparable hardships. The cool, rainy summers reduced crop yields to less than half the usual production. England suffered its worst famines in 1315, 1316 and again in 1321, and each famine was a direct or indirect cause of large losses in life. Similar experiences were shared by most of Europe. Records show that France posted severe crop shortfalls in 1308 to 1319; Germany also suffered from 1312–1320. To make life even more precarious in this century, Europe was visited by the most devastating epidemic in human history, the Black Plague, described previously. The effect of these episodes of erratic climate, crop losses, plagues, and high mortality is shown by a reduction of population. Between 1300 A.D. and 1400 A.D., population declined by 1.5 million people in England alone. The total loss in Europe was probably about 19 million (see Table 3–5). When the climate began to moderate, harsh living conditions and food shortages began to ease.

Farming outputs increased with improved weather but there were still more cyclical changes to occur. Climatic shifts continued to be quite radical. There were times of extreme cold separated by decades of warmer temperatures, alternated with summer droughts, or sometimes cool, wet summers. It was a time of erratic weather that included several phases of the "Little Ice Age." Over this period, populations grew, but only slowly as the gains made over four to six generations were cut back again by some catastrophe of weather, famine, or disease (John, 1977). It was not until 1650 A.D. that populations rebuilt to their pre-fourteenth-century levels (Post, 1985).

The history of Europe is filled with such accounts of crop failures following unusually bad weather cycles (Ladurie, 1971). Frequent famines were a fact of life in human history and especially in Northern Europe of preindustrial times (Table 3–6). The oldest and most complete famine record comes from Finland. This country was especially hard hit by the "Great Famine" of 1696–1697 when, following several years of poor harvests, severe weather conditions caused almost total crop failure in large areas. Malnutrition and disease killed between a quarter and possibly a third of the total population, even higher in some areas when relief ships were late in arriv-

TABLE 3–6 Major Famines of History

Area	Time	Estimated Deaths*
Rome	450 B.C–436 B.C	many thousands
Rome	79 A.D. and 80 A.D.	10,000
England	310 A.D.	40,000
India (Kashmir)	917–918 A.D.	many thousands
Egypt	1064–1072	—
England	1069	—
London	1257–1258	20,000
India	1344–1345	many thousands
Italy	1347	—
Russia	1600	500,000
Eastern Europe	1601 (three-year famine)	500,000
India	1660–1661	—
Finland	1697	—
Russia	1765	—
France	1769	5 % of population
Bengal, India	1769–1770	over 100,000
Hungary	1772	—
Bohemia & Poland	1778	168,000
India (Bombay, Hyderabad)	1790–1792	—
Ireland	1821–1823, 1826–1827	—
	1845–1852	about 1 million
Bengal, India	1833	—
Northwestern India	1837–1838	800,000
Bengal, India	1865–1867	—
China	1875–1878	1.5 million
India	1876–1878	5 million
Northern China	1876–1879	9 to 13 million
Russia	1891–1892	—
Punjab, India	1899–1900	one million
Ethiopia	1882–1892	—
Russia	1920's	5.5 million
Northern China	1920–1921	500,000
China (Hunan)	1929	2 million
Russia	1932–1933	3 to 10 million
Bengal, India	1943–1944	1.5 million
China	1959–1961	over 15 million
Biafra, Nigeria	1969–1970	hundreds of thousands
Ethiopia	1972–1974	—
Bangladesh	1971–1974	—
Ethiopia	1984–1985	—

*These estimates cover a wide range but become more accurate in the last 150 years. The loss of life during the Irish famines is the subject of much dispute to this day, but estimates of 1 million lost during the last great famine (1845–1852) is probably the most accurate.

Source: From W. A. Dando, 1980; C. Riskin, 1990; N. S. Scrimshaw, 1987; C. Haub, 1994; and L. F. Brown and G. W. Finsterbrisch, 1972.

ing (Parry, 1978). Desperate, starving people consumed grain seed stocks and the next season's plantings were delayed until the seed stock could be replaced by importation from other areas. Hence, harvests continued to be smaller, and the original famine crisis had a ripple effect that continued for several years.

Periodic food shortages in Scandinavia continued to impact population, as is recorded for Sweden several times during the seventeenth and early eighteen centuries when changes in growing season length and early frosts destroyed much of the grain crops (Soderberg, 1981:255 and Utterstrom, 1965:545). During times of poor harvest the excess of births over deaths was only 2 per 1000 population, as compared to a gain of 8.4 more births than deaths during periods of excellent harvests. Death rates approached or even exceeded birth rates several times. As tax and census records become more reliable beginning in the eighteenth century, we can see how closely a population may have been linked to agricultural productivity. Even into the late nineteenth century there were effects on the social system: higher wheat prices appeared to influence lower marriage rates and, in turn, lower birth rates (see Post, 1985).

Agricultural Development and Population

Population growth oscillations before 1500 A.D. were inter spaced by natural and man-made disasters that caused short periods of population decline. Recovery was rapid in most regions and losses were quickly replaced over the next few generations once the "good times" returned. After European trade and colonization expanded to encompass the whole world, the population dynamics took on entirely new dimensions. Growth and change occurred over much shorter periods of time, and problems related to a persistent surplus of people began to appear.

Whenever the resources and wealth of a colonial empire are mentioned, we generally think of gold, silver, and precious stones, and of the spices so avidly sought throughout the Middle East, China, and India. The search for these precious commodities were the major driving force behind world exploration, which is well marked in our history by Columbus's search for a shorter route to the Indies. The greatest impact on European and Asian societies, however, was made by several plants native to the New World, especially potato, manioc, and maize, the principle dietary staples of millions of the inhabitants of the Western Hemisphere. From the time of their introduction by Spain and Portugal in the mid-sixteenth century, these plants were gradually incorporated into expanding agricultural economies. The impact of these food resources was quite far reaching, influencing Africa, India, and China, as well as Europe (McNeill, 1992).

Coincident with the increases of Chinese populations of the seventeenth and eighteenth century was the introduction of new food plants that became important components of China's agricultural base. These plants, maize, sweet potato, and peanuts, were of American origin, and added an important supplement to millet, soy beans, and rice, the dietary mainstays (Chao, 1986). The peanut, believed to be the first to gain wide acceptance, was probably introduced by Portuguese traders around 1516 A.D. (Ho, 1955).

Imported into Canton, the peanut soon became an important crop and was planted along the lower Yangtze river valley, some 600 to 700 miles to the north. Its importance grew over the next three centuries, even in the rice growing areas where the peanut was used in crop rotation serving the function of soil enrichment as did soy beans. The sweet potato was the next plant to be introduced (1560 A.D.) and quickly became a significant part of the subsistence in some areas over the next few decades. The sweet potato plant had the advantage of growing well on poor soils and on plots too steep or rocky to grow any other food crop. It soon was considered the "poor man's" staple and spread throughout the north, taking precedence on the hills and slopes of the upper reaches of several major river valleys. This food crop radically increased food production and sustained larger populations on more marginal lands. As the more fertile agricultural lands were taken up, villages were established further and further up the hillsides, especially along the Yangtze valley.

The spread of maize, that most important dietary staple of Native Americans, likewise, followed a similar pattern. After introduction through seaports or by overland routes from India, maize was quickly adopted in several regions in the seventeenth century. By the 1700s it, too, was an important crop that broadened the food base of the ever-growing Chinese population. It was a timely addition because they had reached the limits that rice cultivation alone could support (Ho, 1955).

A frequently asked question is, "Did these new plants contribute to or even stimulate population growth?" Alternatively, "Did an increasing population place such pressures on the existing agricultural system that new cultigens were quickly adopted?" Because other significant variables are involved in population growth, there are no simple answers or a single formula to plot correlations. Population expansions, as well as declines, are related to more than simply food productivity; political and environmental factors are also important elements. Close correlations are seen, however, between new plant introductions, increased agricultural productivity, and a rise in human populations. An interesting dimension of the question is provided by the history of the demographic impact that European exploration had on worldwide contact and development of technology.

European populations kept pace with the world average for the first sixteen centuries and, as Table 3–1 on page 52 showed, most of the growth occurred after 1000 A.D. By the middle of the seventeenth century, Europe began to pull ahead of the other world regions and shortly led Asia and the other regions in population growth rate; 20 million people were added between 1500–1600 A.D. and then another 20 million in the next century. This brought the continent to what often has been called, the "eve of the Industrial Revolution." At this point in history, roughly around 1700 A.D., several Western European countries had founded or were about to found colonies around the world, from the Americas to Africa, and in several parts of South

Asia. These colonies provided a steady flow of raw materials that became one of the foundations of wealth over the following centuries. Equally important is the space that the colonies provided, space for excess populations. But the influence of the New World cultigens was most important, an influence that may be evaluated by comparisons with traditional European food production systems.

"FAMINE PROOF" NEW WORLD CROPS

Because of these experiences with climatic variables affecting crop yields and survival, the inclusion of maize and potato into European agriculture had a major demographic impact. No indigenous food plants produced as high a yield as did these two plants. Maize gave a 200 to 1 yield, compared to the 10 to 1 return from the best harvests of wheat, rye, or barley. The food volume from a potato harvest was likewise higher with the added advantage of the plant's ability to grow on poor soils, unsuitable for grain cultivation. A family could be sustained on less than a quarter of the land area required for most grain crops (Connell, 1975:122). These yields enabled an enormous gain in food energy production. People tended to avoid the new foods and were reluctant to change their traditional subsistence, however. But change they did, sometimes in response to political pressures and sometimes out of need during periods of famine when their traditional crops failed.

The first impact on traditional agriculture was probably caused by the importation of maize (corn), which spread throughout Spanish-controlled areas of southern Europe and even into some adjacent regions. By 1530, the plant was being grown in Tuscany and Venetia in Northern Italy. From there maize spread into the Danube basin and within 200 years of its first introduction into Spain, parts of the Balkans and Hungary made intensive use of this crop. By the end of the eighteenth century, maize became the largest grain crop in these areas (Crosby, 1972). Maize was also adopted throughout southern France and spread north to a line from Bordeaux to Alsace (Langer, 1975).

Maize's economic value to wealthy landowners was soon discovered. The high food yield for work effort made it a cheap crop to use as food for agricultural laborers who were often provided only with modest shelter, their food, and little else. Any work the peasants engaged in beyond the basic effort needed to meet their immediate dietary needs was directed towards cultivation of more desirable and profitable crops, like wheat and barley. This kind of payment for labor cost the landlord little. In fact, maize became such an important part of the peasant diet that, for most of the year they subsisted on little else. This monotonous maize diet, though profitable for the landlord, proved to be costly to the peasant laborers. The social and health consequences of overdependence on a maize diet provide an example of interrelationships among diet, disease, demography, and development. The low cost of a basic maize diet for workers helped to support development of the more profitable agricultural products of grains, fibers, and meat. In other words, cash crops were produced cheaply because there was an alternative to more expensive traditional foods. The health consequences to the farm workers were, however, profound because of a dietary deficiency disease.

Maize is nutritionally deficient in some essential amino acids and niacin, one of the B vitamins. Diets mostly limited to maize were not only monotonous but deprived the consumer of a critical vitamin, niacin, affecting growth and normal functioning of several of the body's systems. The results were seen as skin lesions and a sensitivity to sunlight, chronic diarrhea, and impaired mental functioning. This disease came to be called pellagra and was widespread among farm laborers in Southern Europe and remained a major problem well into this century (Roe, 1973). Though the disease was described by a Spanish physician in the eighteenth century, its connection to diet was not made, and maize continued to be used by hundreds of thousands of farm laborers over the centuries. The medical profession ascribed the health problems of the peasants to an inferior heredity, or "bad blood."[11] All the while, maize, despite its cause of health problems, was viewed as a gift from the New World, a valuable resource to be nurtured.

The social and demographic impact of a second New World plant, the potato, was even more profound, acting as a stimulus for rapid population growth and political change. The incorporation of the potato into the northern European diet is, perhaps, better documented than maize. The Netherlands began to use the plant soon after its importation. The potato grew well in sandy soils and flourished in the northern European climate. By the late sixteenth century, it had spread widely and became a "cheap" food among the peasantry. As was the case with maize, the potato became a major part of the diet of the poor, selected not by choice but through necessity. It quickly gained value as an emergency food in times when the major grain crops of wheat or barley failed. As an example, the Hungarian famine of 1772 caused the Hapsburg government to order that more land be planted in potatoes. Likewise, famines in Russia, following a succession of crop failures that depleted grain reserves, forced the adoption of the potato (Crosby 1972:184). From these starting points, the plant gained prominence in Central and Eastern European agriculture as it had a century earlier throughout Northwestern Europe.

Whenever the subject of the potato and its population impact is considered, the discussion frequently turns to Ireland. The plant was imported

[11]Pellagra continued to be a major problem among Italian farm workers well into the twentieth century, just as it was widespread among sharecroppers in the southeastern United States until 1940. It took heroic efforts by teams of health researchers, led by Goldberger, to establish the dietary deficiency causes of pellagra beyond all question.

and adopted into parts of the British Isles shortly after its arrival on the continent, somewhere around 1650 A.D. Its spread was slow at first, but by the end of the century, Scotland and Ireland came to depend heavily on the plant. Within another 100 years, historians write that poor tenant farmers were eating little else. It is somewhat ironic to note that with the introduction of this plant into the British Isles, it became most widely adopted among those regions with poor soil and sparse population in contrast to the experiences on the continent. Most of Europe used the potato as a supplement or as an emergency ration throughout the grain-producing regions to protect against potential food shortages—a crop of last resort. However, the increasing reliance on the potato is arguably a major contributing factor to population growth, and Ireland offers the best documented case.

Ireland was an agrarian society of a few small farms and, following the conquest by the English, development was suppressed. It was maintained as a nation of many tenant farmers who paid high rents. Throughout the fifteenth, sixteenth, and seventeenth centuries, there had been little change in agriculture, the economy, or in the population. Even after the beginning of the eighteenth century, the majority of families survived at or near only subsistence levels. Technological developments and social changes that took place in England and throughout Western Europe, in general, did not appear to find their way into Ireland. The people of Ireland were held back by an oppressive land tenure system, a low state of economic development, and a relatively sparse population under the rigid control of a few, mostly absentee, landlords. Such conditions offered little expectation of improvement in the economy, in living conditions, or of increases in population. Given these lowly expectations, demographic events occurring over the next century surprised contemporary scholars and still are a point for argument among historians today.

However, it may be interpreted that what occurred was purely and simply a population explosion. The Irish began to increase rapidly from 2 million in 1732 to over 8.2 million by 1846, plus another 1.75 million who had emigrated (Connell, 1975:279). What is particularly striking about this sudden demographic acceleration is that it was achieved by an oppressed rural population without the aid of industrial development. Also, there was no marked improvement in living standards, contrary to the experiences of populations in Western Europe.

Historians have examined this period exhaustively and the sum of their studies describes a situation unparalleled in human history. It might be comparable to a "laboratory model" devised by some inhuman scientist who wished to study humans in order to observe population dynamics, particularly fertility and population growth, under minimal environmental conditions and marginal subsistence. But there was no evil genius, no plan, no design, and no predictors of the events that unfolded over the next few generations. What happened in Ireland was more than a century of unanticipated and extraordinary population increase influenced by the ready availability of a new, plentiful, and cheap food resource. This food resource allowed for societal changes that enabled a suppressed population, under severe economic hardship, to support an unusual change in family formation tradition.

The principle change following the introduction of the potato was a radical increase in fertility rates. Throughout much of a 100-year period (1740 to 1840), marriages occurred at earlier and earlier ages. Women were marrying at an average of age sixteen rather than twenty or twenty-four, which had been the tradition. In some districts, fourteen- and fifteen-year-old brides were the rule. A first child was typically born within the first year of marriage, and seldom did a family stop with one child (Connell, 1975). The fertility rate went up to an average of 6.5 children per woman, from the near replacement rate levels of previous generations; and the nation's population grew correspondingly. For several generations, all was well as the population more than doubled in size. This increase is even more impressive if we count the estimated 1.75 million who migrated before 1846. Each generation these additional people were added to an already politically oppressed, economically deprived population who remained poor tenant farmers. Besides an increase in population density, the major difference compared to previous centuries was that the bulk of their dietary requirements were satisfied by a single plant.

The potato flourished in most of the soils of Ireland and was as highly productive as elsewhere in Europe. Small plots of land, as little as one or two acres, could produce ten tons of these starchy roots, enough food to sustain a family of six for a year. In addition, the foliage and peelings could provide forage to support a cow and a few pigs. Beyond these small family plots, that were usually rented, the family worked to produce for the landlords wheat, rye, and barley for export. Because of the availability of a cheap, plentiful food supply and the need for labor, the young were encouraged to marry and establish a household years earlier in life than was the case elsewhere in Western Europe. A small plot of land could always be found to rent for the newlyweds.

This new agricultural system and the newer social system appeared to work well. The landowners of large estates had a plentiful supply of cheap labor, and the tenants had an ample and nutritious, though monotonous, food supply. Except, that is, when potato crops failed, as happened several times from 1741 and into the nineteenth century. The most famous were the crop failures, and the following famine, of 1845–1848, during which upwards of a million or more people died of starvation; another million emigrated. Other famines followed, in 1863 and 1879, that added to the death toll of what had become a crowded island, and increased the flight of many of the survivors. By 1881, Ireland had lost one half of its peak nineteenth-century population (Kennedy, 1973).

The problem centered on the overreliance on a single food crop, the potato, and its susceptibility to a particular fungus, Phytophtora, causing what has become known as "Late Blight." Following a series of unseasonably cool and wet summers, the fungus attacked the potato crops throughout Western Europe. This spread of the fungus had happened several times before, but the summer of 1845 was the worst. The cool, damp weather hastened the multiplication and spread of this plant-rotting fungus. The entire potato crop was lost, leaving the people without an alternative source of food. People in numerous communities were forced to dig up immature plant roots and to eat their seed stock, but even these seed potatoes blackened as the decay of the fungus destroyed them. Trying to cut away the decayed parts of the plants left little for human consumption and even animals would not feed on the affected plants. Out of desperation, the starving turned to foraging for wild plants and even ate the bark off the trees. The "emergency" food, the protector against famines, had failed. But it was more than just monoculture dependence (reliance on a single plant) that was at fault; the land tenure system was the major contributing cause of the loss of life.

A sad commentary on the history of the times is that, even during the worst of the famine, agriculture continued to be a profitable enterprise for the landlords. The productivity of food grains increased with many thousands of tons shipped out of the country, mainly to England. Livestock exports also increased since more acreage was dedicated to pasture land as the small tenant farmer, unable to pay his rent, was evicted. Between 1846 and 1850, 50,000 tons of grain and 90,000 tons of meat from Ireland's farms supplied the English markets. This note on the agricultural economy of Ireland is mentioned to illustrate that a failure of one plant does not necessarily mean failure of all. There can still be an ample supply of alternative foods.

Eyewitnesses of the actual conditions in Ireland record the many grim scenes of whole families dying along country lanes or outside of alms houses that were unable to take them in. The witnesses also describe tenants, without cash to purchase the available foods, starving rather than use those grain stocks they needed to pay their rent. This 1845 famine and the others of the later decades occurred in the midst of plenty. Political and economic forces are often of greater significance to human ecology than are the environmental factors. An even more poignant example of political economic forces is offered by the Industrial Revolution. This was a time when, throughout Western Europe, many major changes were being made in economics, lifestyles, as well as in demographic structure. It was a time when humans were releasing themselves from many of the harsh environmental restrictions of the past. Yet, famine raged throughout Ireland, with hundreds of thousands dying, only a short distance from one of the wealthiest empires the world had ever seen.

CONCLUSIONS

Viewed over the last few millennia, the demographic landmarks document a series of small average gains in population. Each of these landmarks appear to be correlated with certain technological advances. Such advances may be seen either as primary contributors to human population gains or perhaps the technological achievements are the result of population pressures requiring more effective use of the environment. No matter which perspective is taken, the improvements in cultivation through irrigation, use of draft animals and plows, or the development of metallic implements can all be linked to a higher food productivity. Such achievements could then, in turn, sustain greater numbers of people, but would also lead to major economic changes and conflict. These linkages among technology, use of environmental resources, and human population are many and complex. Evidence from ancient history is too scant and selective so what we see is only a culmination of a long series of events, many of which passed unrecorded.

It is possible, however, to gain a clearer understanding of these linkages by studying a more recent time and focusing on a smaller world area, Europe, which underwent radical transitions in agriculture and industry throughout the eighteenth and nineteenth centuries while population expanded more rapidly than at any previous time in human history. England had led Europe in industrial development as it entered a new phase in human ecology and grew enormously wealthy. This phase was marked by a greater dependence on technology as well as on rapid improvements in agricultural productivity.

Chapter 4

Technology, Development, and Population Dynamics

Some Linkages

Preindustrial Europe was a period of frequent surges in population growth following crisis periods of food shortages and high death rates. Though the timing of these events and their demographic patterns varied from region to region, such cyclical gains or losses had always been major elements of human history. It was not until near the end of the seventeenth century in Europe that we began to break out of this "Malthusian trap" of people growing in such numbers that they exceeded their food supply. Slowly at first, and then with a greater acceleration, Western Europe underwent a phase of development that raised the food ceiling. Major improvements in technology and efficient use of resources led to greater environmental control that, in turn, led to increases in population. These increases could now be sustained, and this achievement marked a major turning point in history.

Such success depended on a near simultaneous advancement of economic, social, political, and cultural institutions to fully utilize technological improvements. Institutional advancement was essential to organize methods to use the resources of land and energy effectively within a given geographic area. Land tenure rights, laws governing capital flow, organized protection of shipping (military forces), and education were parts of the development complex. If any one institutional component was blocked or faltered, then the whole momentum for change (or revolution) in human–environmental relationships could be halted; if severe enough, progress could even be reversed (Braudel, 1979). Institutional developments, accompanied by rapid population growth, occurred first in Western Europe. Then these changes spread to the rest of Europe and to North America. Other parts of the world were gradually drawn into this Industrial Revolution during the nineteenth century, with colonization and trade setting off a transformation of human ecology that continues to this day.

INDUSTRIAL REVOLUTION

In the early eighteenth century, Europe and North America, led by England, began a series of technological advances that led to the establishment of an industrial economy. This radical transformation from an agricultural base involved all of the sociopolitical institutions of each nation as they developed modern economies that enabled them to exploit more and more of the world's resources. We look upon this period as an Industrial Revolution occurring between 1750 and 1900. Considering the environmental and social impact of this revolution, it is surprising that the beginning of the period was neither initiated by nor marked by any single scientific or technological achievement. Rather, it was based on numerous innovations and improvements of existing industries—a mix of household, workshop, and small factories that had been growing slowly for about 500 years (Komlos, 1989). These gradual achievements were brought together under those political regimes of Europe that were able to mobilize the technological and agricultural advances to meet the needs of growing population and environmental pressures.

Wilkinson (1988) explained that the Industrial Revolution had ecological roots that were easily defined. These "roots" consisted of a combination of resource shortages that likely provided an initial stimulus for change. By the early eighteenth century, Britain's growing population was approaching the limits of its land and energy resources. Food supplies had to be increased, which required more land for cultivation of grain or for pasture of sheep and cattle. The growth of home construction and an iron industry also added to the land burden. Further expansion had reached its limit as forests were being rapidly depleted. The high rate of wood consumption is illustrated by the fate of Ireland, which was nearly deforested between 1600 and 1700 to furnish timber for the building of large naval and merchant fleets. Much of the rest of Britain's forests were also seriously depleted, and naval timber had to be imported from the Baltic countries and then from the North American colonies. Industrialization and the use of an alternative fuel provided a way of escaping these resource and energy constraints. This escape, however, depended on a more abundant and reliable food supply to initiate the first step of industrialization.

Food Production

Agriculture played a crucial role both directly and indirectly in the industrialization of England. By the end of the seventeenth century, farming had advanced beyond its former simple subsistence level. The adoption of plants from the New World, as described in Chapter 3, helped increase food production, but advances in crop management and animal husbandry also boosted yields. Rotation of grain crops with nitrogen fixing legumes had been introduced, and fields could be planted every year. Crops were rotated instead of land, as had been the practice that left a field fallow every second or third year, reducing the productive land area by a third or more. Marshes were drained, and sandy or clay soils were chemically treated thereby increasing arable acreage. With additional acreage now available because of crop rotation, clovers and hay could be planted, improving soil fertility while also providing fodder for domestic stock. In addition to reclamation and crop rotation, improvements were made in stock breeding and selection of plant varieties. With agricultural improvements, output began to increase faster than population, a primary condition for the success of industry according to Braudel (1979). Agricultural changes, however, required increases in capital investments that in turn depended on an individual farmer's control over larger land areas.

Consolidation of many small parcels of land was achieved by a series of laws that transferred communal land to private control. These laws, called the "enclosure acts," restricted access and brought larger areas under the control of a few wealthy gentry who, rightfully or not, held some ancestral claim. Land was fenced off and divided into pasture or crop land to be intensely cultivated, providing increased yields at lower inputs of energy. No longer were the yeoman farmers allowed free access to a "commons" where they could graze a few animals to supplement the crops produced on small plots around their cottages. Without this surplus, many families were unable to survive even at a simple subsistence farming level. Demand for farm labor declined under this new system of land tenure, with its increased efficiency and with the improved management of cattle and sheep production. Though there were many benefits to be gained from these agricultural advancements—the decline of periodic subsistence crises, for one—the immediate human cost was high.

Seeking employment, displaced farm families migrated to villages and towns, where they became part of a growing labor pool for textile mills, pottery factories, coal mines, and iron foundries. In the early 1700s, such manufacturing enterprises were of small scale with low output and only a few score of workers producing labor intensive products. There was a growth potential, however, since the demand for manufactured products of all kinds grew with the establishment of the American colonies. The towns, expanding into urban centers, also created demands, as people's lifestyles changed as they shifted occupation from farmer to factory hand. The needs for housing, tools, and clothing grew as the people became less self sufficient.

Their needs could be fulfilled and a growing market satisfied because the basic mechanical devices for manufacture of most products already existed and were in use. Craftsmen continued to refine and improve these machines, but the power to drive them was still limited. Any industrial expansion required greater inputs of energy beyond the traditional, centuries-old sources of wind, water, and animal power. The waterwheel-driven grist mills and textile looms or the horse-powered carts and lifts of the coal mines were reaching their environmental limits. Factories using water power had to be located on water courses with a sufficient flow to drive the wheels to turn the machinery. Draft animals required care and feeding; the number of horses were limited by the land available for the pasture to feed them. Humans were also used to power machinery, often in ways that give us pause today. A greater input of human energy to move, carry, or dig was not an effective option, however. Factory workers were already employed at the limits of endurance in terms of time and energy expenditure. Further industrial expansion could not depend on more human energy input but required labor-saving devices and a more efficient means of powering machinery.

Energy Sources

The harnessing of energy through the use of steam power was the primary development that made industrialization possible. Though the potential power of steam had been long appreciated, a practical application was not made until 1698 when Thomas Savery patented a steam pump. It was a simple affair that involved the filling of a closed chamber with steam and then cooling it. This created an internal vacuum that could draw water upwards through a pipe connected to the chamber. The Savery pump, (called the "miner's friend"), though a simple and inefficient device without moving parts, was a major improvement. Up until the eighteenth century, mining had been limited to shallow pits because the problem of water seepage as shafts were dug below the water table. The deeper the mine, the more water had to be removed. Some mines, if located on hillsides, could be drained by small auxiliary tunnels dug parallel to the main shaft. Alternative methods were crude, inefficient horse-powered chain-linked bucket pumps, but these were only effective to about twenty feet. Also, it was more difficult to lift heavy loads of coal from deeper shafts. With the invention of steam-powered pumps and hoists, deeper seams of coal and iron ore deposits could be fully exploited (Ashton, 1986).

The first practical application of steam power in coal mines stimulated a broader interest in this energy source. Numerous craftsmen worked on steam-driven devices and, by 1712, one of them, Thomas Newcomen, a blacksmith, developed a steam-driven engine that could drive pumps capable of removing water from deeper mine shafts. It soon replaced the Savery pump, but it was still an inefficient device wasteful of heat, difficult to operate, and subject to frequent breakdowns. James Watt is credited with the invention of the first really practical steam engine in 1769. Over the next few years, there were numerous improvements contributed by many mechanics and, by 1784, the original design had evolved into an efficient rotary engine. Within a decade, 150 were being used to power machines in a variety of industries; hundreds more were soon added. The engine was in wide use to drive pumps, mills, and large mechanized looms to weave cloth (Wilkinson, 1988). Other industries benefited from steam power, and advancement in one industry led to advancements in other manufacturing processes. Several important inventions followed, resulting in improved steam-driven pumps, hoists, and power shovels. No longer were machines limited by a dependence on animal, wind, water, or human power sources. Most importantly, many of these technological improvements reduced costs of extracting coal and opened up new mining areas.

Fuel

Steam generation to drive the machines of the Industrial Revolution would have been severely limited without the availability of an abundant cheap fuel supply. Centuries before the Industrial Revolution, coal had already replaced wood as a fuel for most manufacturing processes that required boiling or heating. Coal also was an important and cheap fuel for domestic heating and cooking, as can be judged by the consumption in London of about 775 kilograms per capita in 1700. Large bulky sailing ships continually plied the waters between New Castle, Scotland and London, transporting coal from the mines near the Scottish coast. This source could meet most demands until industry began the shift to steam power. From 1750 onwards, the requirements for more and more coal caused a rapid increase in mine production. New mines were opened in several other parts of Britain. Output doubled to 6 million tons by 1800 and reached 50 million tons by mid century, exceeding the total coal mined in the rest of Western Europe by two to one.[1]

Mine shafts were sunk ever deeper and to operate effectively, mines required a greater use of machinery, especially pumps and hoists. The machinery became more dependent on steam power as various types of engines were perfected. This required fuel that was readily available at the mine site. It is not surprising that the earliest applications of steam to do useful work grew and expanded with the mining of the very fuel that was burned to generate the power. Each process was linked to and reinforced by the other, but the reason for mining the coal in the first place was for its consumption at some point distant from the mine. With industrial growth, the problem of transportation of the heavy, bulky coal cargo became more acute as tonnage consumed increased.

---

[1]For coal consumption see, J. U. Nef, *The Rise of the British Coal Industry;* London, 1932 and for production statistics, see Carlo M. Cipolla, 1972. *The Fontana Economic History of Europe: The Emergence of Industrial Societies,* Part Two, Collins/ Fontana Books.

Transportation

Just as a cheap fuel was a basic requirement of industry so was the need to transport cargoes over long distances. Shipping between seaports or along navigable rivers had long been used to move bulk cargoes of grain and coal, but this limited industrial growth to those towns located on rivers or with easy access to the sea. Grain could be carried by cart from farm villages, but deposits of coal and iron ore were more difficult to move. Horse-drawn carts over muddy roads were not sufficient to transport the tonnage needed to meet the growing demands. Not only were carts expensive in terms of the number of animals needed but their upkeep was environmentally costly as well. Water transport could provide a way of keeping costs down but most new mines were not located at sea ports. Many had access to rivers, however, so river channels could be deepened and straightened or canals dug, making waterways passable to barge traffic.[2]

An extensive system of canals was dug in the later eighteenth century, linking rivers and ports together in a network of waterways. In fact, Britain, as did the rest of Europe, underwent a frantic period of canal excavation that reached a peak in 1775. By 1800, England and Wales were crisscrossed with hundreds of miles of these waterways and construction continued well into mid-nineteenth century. Now raw materials and finished goods could be moved throughout most of the country at a third of the cost of transport by roads. The canal barges required significantly fewer horses than did road transport. In fact, justification for canal construction was often based on an argument that the fewer horses required to move barges meant less feed was needed. This would enable a diversion of farm land from the production of feed and pasture to the growth of grains for human consumption. The "releasing of 1,000 horses from employment" by the construction of the London Junction canal, according to one advocate for the construction, would free 8,000 acres of land.[3] In a nation with an expanding industry and a growing population, the change of agricultural production from animal fodder to human food was an important consideration.

Though some of the transportation problems of the early Industrial Revolution were solved by expanded waterways, all the needs were not met. Despite this extensive network, some communities still were not connected. Also, many miles of canals were too shallow and difficult to maintain and so these fell into disrepair, isolating many communities from participating in the industrial progress of the nation. Canal barges also were slow and not

---

[2]Inland waterways are still the cheapest means of moving large bulk cargo, as anyone who has viewed a string of barges moving slowly along the Mississippi or Rhine rivers can appreciate. A few crew members with a tow boat and some machinery can move hundreds of tons through the heart of the United States or Europe.

[3]The Earl of Hardwick quoted in Wilkinson, 1988.

well suited for transporting people as the public's travel needs increased. Further, though fewer horses were needed to tow barges than pull carts and wagons over roads, valuable farm land was still diverted from production of human food. By the middle of the nineteenth century, the reliance on animal power for transportation had again become an important limitation on further industrial expansion. But even as more canals were being dug, a new invention offered a way of overcoming this limitation.

An early, primitive forerunner of railroads had been used as a method of moving heavy loads around mines for years. Several miles of wooden rails were laid around the New Castle mines, for example. Loaded carts could be moved much more easily along these rails than over the rough, rutted surfaces that passed for roads. An extension of these rails transported coal to dockside for loading on the London-bound ships. The wooden rails were replaced by iron rails in 1767, and lasted longer under the weight and friction of the iron wheels of the laden carts. Ponies, horses, and sometimes humans pulled these carts, but now, with new, rapidly improving steam engine devices, it was but a short step to harness this new power to move the carts along the rails. Several versions of steam engines were already in use around mines and iron foundries. Some were merely adaptations of rotary pumps connected to cables to draw a string of loaded carts over rails from the mine entrance. Other applications mounted an engine on one of the carts to drive its wheels. These combinations of rail–steam engine applications provided models that were but a short step to the development of a "locomotive" that could pull passengers and freight over iron rails laid between cities.

Inventors were intrigued by the possibilities of using steam power to drive a "traveling engine," and several craftsmen contributed to the development of these locomotives over the next decades. George Stephensen is the one credited with starting the railroad age when his "Rocket" won a contest in 1829 for rights to use his locomotive on the newly laid tracks between Liverpool and Manchester (Douglas, 1996). From this humble beginning with a crude four horsepower steam engine, new and more powerful engines were built; the advantages of steam power were quickly realized. Rail transportation developed rapidly, and thousands of miles of track were laid in England, across Europe, and in America. There were 3,700 miles in Britain by 1840 compared to only a few hundred in all of Europe, but the rate of the addition of track over the next decade was phenomenal. It would be hard to exaggerate the impact of railroads on industrial development.

Other countries quickly adopted this new mode of transportation. By 1850, Germany had 4,000 miles and France 2,000, while Britain had increased its railway length nearly five times. The United States also started a building program during the 1830s, when three miles of track were being laid for every mile of canal dug. At first, the competition was fierce between the canal barge and railroad companies but the speed of the railroads quickly won popularity among travelers. Three thousand miles of track had been laid between the cities in the northeastern United States by 1840 (Douglas, 1996). The mileage increased rapidly as other regions were joined by rail; 9,000 miles by 1850 and 30,000 in 1860. In the next two decades transcontinental lines had been completed—the United States (1869), Canada (1885), Europe (1888), Trans-Siberia (1903). These long distance railroads, together with the hundreds of thousands of miles of track within most of the nations of the world, solved the problem of land transportation.

Adaptation of the steam engine to power ships, first river boats and then ocean-going vessels, also made a major contribution to industrialization. From Fulton's steamboat, the *Clermont,* that ran for 150 miles on the Hudson River in 1807, to the ship *Savannah,* crossing the Atlantic under steam in 1814, the use of steam power rapidly became the choice for commercial shipping. Improvements quickly followed, and by 1850 the more efficient screw propeller drive had replaced the large, clumsy paddle wheels on sea-going vessels. Though sailing ships were still in use over the next few decades, their numbers rapidly declined as they were replaced by steam ships that could move large and bulky cargoes cheaply around the world on schedules not limited by prevailing winds.

Spreading Industrialization

By the first quarter of the nineteenth century, the basic elements needed to drive industrialization had been acquired: (1) a reliable food supply; (2) cheap fuel; (3) an improved power source (steam); (4) an ample supply of raw materials; and (5) an efficient transportation system. The textile industry led the way in the integration and application of these elements producing the large scale conversion of raw material into consumer products. The power-driven looms rapidly multiplied until, in 1835, there were 120,000 operating in Britain alone (Ashton, 1986; Thomas, 1985). The iron industry likewise grew as processing of ore became more mechanized. The heating and refining steadily improved until stronger iron products and then steel could be produced to meet the demands of expanding industry. Steam boilers, rails, locomotives, and ships quickly absorbed all the iron and steel that could be produced; building and bridge construction also used increasing amounts. In all these areas of industrialization, Britain led the rest of the world.

For over a century (1750–1870), British industries outproduced those of all other nations. They produced more pig iron and steel, laid more railroad track, wove more cloth, and mined more coal then did all of Europe. During the landmark year of 1870, when Germany and France began to accelerate their industrial growth, British industry produced 32 percent of all of the world's manufactured goods. Its world trade amounted to as much as

France, Germany, and the United States combined. This British foreign trade was largely carried by British ships, which amounted to three-fourths of the world's total ship tonnage.

Britain not only led in industry but it also led in world colonization as well. In addition to its African colonies, Britain added the vast areas of India and Australia to its overseas possessions after meeting defeat in the American Revolution. Further, Britain was able to maintain a large standing army of between 250,000–350,000 men and a powerful naval force of 150,000 sailors and marines to protect its growing worldwide empire. How did this small island nation (94,000 square miles compared to France's 211,000) industrialize so early and hold a lead over other European nations for so long is a question that has been explored by many historians and economists (Braudel, 1979; North,1981).

What appears to have occurred is that the basic elements for industrialization came together earliest in a small geographic area that was under strong central political control. England had consolidated its control over the British Isles while much of Europe was still divided into independent states. Germany was only united under Bismark in 1870, for example, and France was entering a long period of social turmoil, leading to revolution and the Napoleonic wars. Further, Britain was well endowed with the raw materials (coal and iron ore) required for industrialization. There was also sufficient fertile land upon which to build a solid agricultural base and to feed its population, at least initially. This base was further expanded by institutional changes in land tenure that increased productivity, as already discussed. Equally important was the development of a large naval fleet, which enabled defense of an expanding world trade network far outpacing the early eighteenth century lead of the Dutch merchant fleet.

Britain led the way for about a half century, but the inventions and technological applications spread throughout Western Europe. Most countries, often for political reasons, were slow to join the Industrial Revolution, but join they did. Belgium is considered the second country to enter the Industrial Revolution, between 1830–1870 when it began the manufacture of heavy machinery and construction of mechanized textile mills. France, recovering from the Napoleonic wars, drew on its resource and scientific bases and rapidly became a major industrial power by 1848. Following unification of its autonomous states in 1870, Germany quickly expanded its industry, taking advantage of its vast coal and iron resources. It surpassed British production by the end of the century (Pounds, 1985). The development in Central Europe followed much the same pattern under the rule of the Hapsburg empire. The conversion to steam power, railroads, and modern manufacturing moved quickly, once started. However, Eastern Europe lagged far behind except for periodic surges of development in Russia. During these episodes, Russia made progress in iron and steel production, transportation (most notable was the trans-Siberia railroad), and some manufacturing sectors.

Across the Atlantic, America had a vast potential for rapid industrialization. It was already producing one-third of Britain's ships by the outbreak of the Revolutionary War. Its skilled craftsmen were inventing and building advanced production machinery. Eli Whitney, already famous for the invention of the cotton gin, built a factory to manufacture guns using interchangeable parts, a major innovation for 1798. The water-powered looms of New England's textile mills produced cloth as efficiently as any in Europe. However, the United States was slower in expanding this industrial base for a complex of reasons relating to its former colonial status. The small initial population at the start of the nation, a large war debt, and its basic agricultural orientation enforced a dependence on England for manufactured goods in exchange for raw materials even after the Revolutionary War.

Once started, industrialization proceeded rapidly and by 1859, the value of manufactured products exceeded agricultural production. The iron industry produced high-quality tools and railroad tracks; and the quality of American steel equaled the best of British products. The Civil War hastened the inventions and industrial developments. After the war, these developments accelerated with further railroad building and westward expansion. With its vast supplies of raw materials, large, underdeveloped territory, and an expanding population fed by increasing immigration from Europe (5 million between 1820 to 1860), the United States was set for a takeoff to become the world's industrial leader.

Conclusions

The century and a half of industrial development was a major turning point in human history, far exceeding the impact made by the agricultural revolution thousands of years before. The Industrial Revolution involved much more than expansions of technology and environmental use, however. There were socioeconomic and cultural changes of major magnitudes that included political and economic factors with the rise of the modern nation state, development of colonial empires, and the establishment of financial institutions. But the most profound of the changes were demographic, the rapid increases in size and redistribution of Europe's populations.

After many centuries of slow average growth increments, the populations throughout most of Europe began to increase at higher rates. Because of the advances in technology and improved farming methods, production increased even faster than population. Europeans began to make economic and demographic gains as no other people had before them. What is more important is that these gains became established and the people were relatively well buffered from the vicissitudes of chance and climate. A generation's increase in size was no longer easily destroyed by famine (there were fewer).[4] Also, there were fewer disease epidemics and these were of limited duration.[5] In short, even by the end of the eighteenth century peoples of Europe had become well adapted to their local environmental resources as well as those they acquired from the rest of the world. By the end of the nineteenth century, the human species had reached an even higher level of environmental adaptation and had fully developed a new niche, the urban–industrial niche.

THE POPULATION REVOLUTION

Successful adaptation to the urban–industrial niche is marked by several demographic events that led to a population revolution. Between 1680 and 1820 A.D., Western Europe increased from 71.9 million to about 116.5 million, a gain of 62 percent. The next interval, 1820–1900, was a period of even more rapid growth, with population increasing by 73 percent. Of particular interest is the population expansion of England. From its place as the second smallest country in 1680, England increased much more rapidly than any other European country, until it nearly surpassed Italy and France in population by 1900 (Table 4–1). England's most rapid increase (166 percent) came during that period encompassing the major advances of the Industrial Revolution, 1820–1900. This increase was achieved through a major reduction in death rates while maintaining high birth rates; but what really accelerated population growth was the breakthrough made earlier between 1680 and 1820. During this 140 years fertility increased as never before while mortality declined only slightly, contributing to a 133 percent increase.

A sampling of baptismal and death records from over 400 English church parishes has allowed for comparisons over broad periods of time and has documented a radical change in the demographic profile from the mid-sixteenth century to 1870 (Wrigley and Schofield, 1981). There had been a near balance of birth and death rates that resulted in close to zero population growth from 1651 to 1689 A.D. Change began to appear near the end of the seventeenth century as population gains began slowly and then quickened by the middle of the eighteenth century. During what was called the "long eighteenth century" (1680 to 1820), death rates dropped from 30.1 down to 24.5 per thousand while birth rates rose 30.7 to 39.6 per thousand (Wrigley and Schofield, 1981). This was an unprecedented net annual population increase marked by 0.48 percent in 1745, reaching a peak of 1.55 percent by

[4]There continued to be periodic crop failures, with resulting food crises, that remained a major economic problem throughout several European regions well into the mid-nineteenth century.
[5]Four great epidemics of the nineteenth century struck down thousands sometimes in a matter of days; Paris lost 7,000 to cholera in a mere 18 days. Cholera spread to many of the major population centers and accounted for tens of thousands of deaths; Russia was especially hard hit with a million dead during the epidemic of 1848–1849 (see Langer, 1963).

TABLE 4–1 Population Increases in Selected European Countries (in millions; percent interval increase)

Country	1550		1680		1820		1900	Total
England and Wales	3	64%	4.9	133%	11.5	166%	30.5	612%
France	17	29%	21.9	39%	30.5	26%	38.5	176%
Netherlands	1.2	58%	1.9	8%	2	149%	5.1	268%
Spain	9	6%	8.5	64%	14	33%	18.6	219%
Italy	11	9%	12	53%	18.4	77%	32.5	270%
Germany	12	0%	12	51%	18.1	142%	43.6	363%
W. Europe	61.1	18%	71.9	62%	116.5	73%	201.4	280%

Source: Adapted from Chesnais, 1992; Durand, 1977; Wrigley and Schofield, 1983.

1820. For the rest of the century, annual increases declined slightly but remained over 1 percent, until 1900, as plotted in Figure 4–1.

Populations of other European countries began to grow also, slowly at first but then more and more rapidly into the nineteenth century. Sweden increased its population by 45 percent from 1751 to 1820 A.D. and a further 75 percent by 1880 as death rates began to fall while birth rates remained high. Germany, with a 142 percent increase (1820–1900) came close to the level of England's growth. Russia increased even faster despite its high mortality (39.4/1000) because birth rates (49.7/1000) continued to rise over the same period. From 1725–1858, the Russian population grew by nearly 30 million, an increase of 210 percent. Ireland, long exploited economically by England, increased from 2½ million to 9 million between 1700 and 1846, when it suffered from the horrible potato famine discussed in Chapter 3 (Wrigley and Schofield, 1981).

France stands out as an exception to most of Europe's demographic experiences. While England and Germany grew 166 percent and 142 percent, respectively, France increased its population by only 26 percent between 1820 and 1900. The reasons for these differentials in growth have been a focus of much debate among demographers for years, as outlined by McKeown, et al. (1972:361). One explanation offered that the differences were founded in social customs and inheritance of property, which influenced family size (Chesnais, 1992). Such influences were far reaching and affected population growth in different ways in the various countries. England began its Industrial Revolution in the mid-eighteenth century and then a demographic revolution one hundred years later when its population tripled. By contrast, France started its demographic revolution a century before that, when its population doubled (1600 to 1700) while England and Germany each only added about 1 million during the same period.

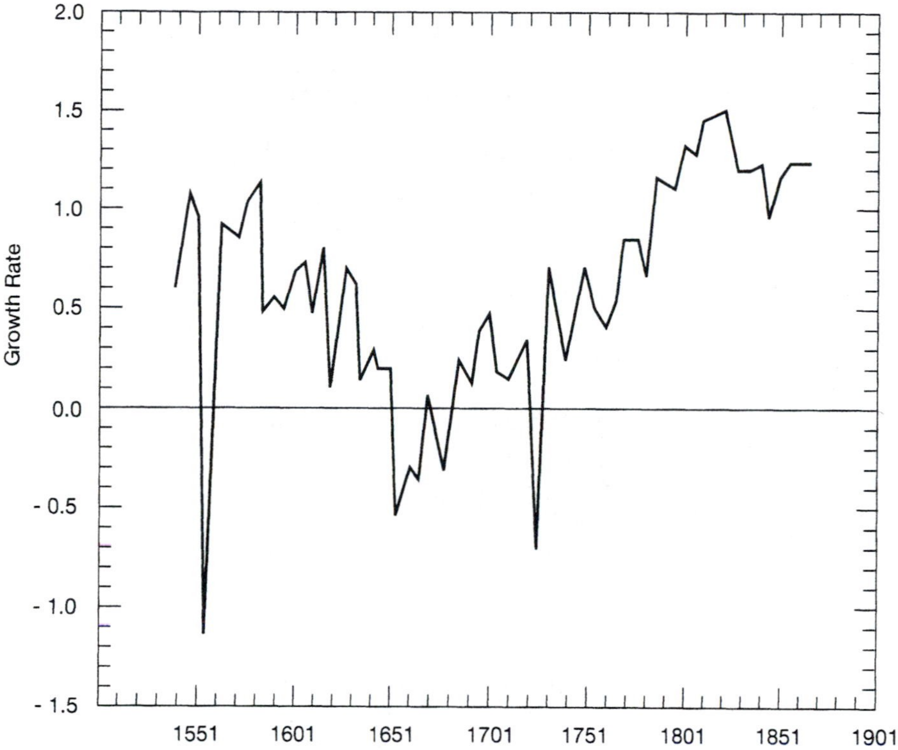

Figure 4–1 Population of England, Rate of Annual Increase, 1541–1871

From Wrigley, E. A., and R. S. Schofield, 1981. *The Population History of England, 1541-1871.* Reprinted by permission of Cambridge University Press.

Malthus

In retrospect, we can appreciate that industrialization brought forth a new era that forever changed human–environmental relationships. But people living during this era could neither fully appreciate the changes taking place nor the impact of these changes on future generations. With only the recent past to guide them at the end of the eighteenth century, there was unease about the transition from a rural–agrarian lifestyle to an urban–industrial one. As internal migration from the countryside to expanding towns and cities began, community and family influences on behavior slackened, with worrisome results. There were special concerns over increases in illegitimate births (from 2 percent to 6 percent of all births) and the decline in age at marriage, from the mid twenties down to teenage. These changes led to a rapid increase in numbers of people counted both in city and country parishes (Brown, 1991). Malthus was the most eloquent spokesman for these concerns. He not only described a "decay in morals" but warned of the dangers of overpopulation.

Malthus (1766–1834) was a well-educated clergyman who enjoyed the high rank of wealth and privilege of his day. He entered Cambridge in 1784, where he excelled in mathematics and history, an excellence that gained him an appointment as a "fellow" of Jesus College eight years later. In that same year (1793), he was appointed church curate to the parish at Okewood, Surrey, a position he held for the rest of his life. These were busy years for the young curate as he served both his parish and the university, but his dual career as scholar and cleric enabled him to broaden and interrelate academic theory and society. For as Malthus took up the duties that were to occupy him for the rest of his life, his nation and society were undergoing radical alterations. The rapid rise of population, with all of its attendant social and economic pressures, caused him to ask questions about the burden placed on future generations (Petersen, 1979). In addition, it is an interesting coincidence that Malthus's own parish enjoyed an unusually low number of deaths and a high number of births during much of the eighteenth century. A review of the parish records must have aroused Malthus's scholarly curiosity, for these records related to both his fields of expertise, mathematics and economics. Whatever the combination of influences, he was to write a long essay expressing his concerns about morals, the uncontrolled passion between the sexes, and the risk of populations growing faster than their ability to produce food. This essay was expanded into book length and became a foundation for modern demography and forever changed the way we look at human population problems.[6]

The key point of the essay was that the power of population to increase is infinitely greater than the power of the earth to provide food. With this observation, Malthus offered a mathematician's insight: "Population, when unchecked, increases geometrically while subsistence increases only in an arithmetic ratio." Malthus stressed the threat of food shortages that mankind faced unless population growth could be halted. Otherwise, humans faced the harsh balances imposed by nature: war, pestilence, and vice. How could a perfect society be achieved, let alone maintained, if population was constantly pressing against resources, Malthus asked. He urged sexual restraint and advocated marriage at later ages but, interestingly, he did not support contraception.

The essay attracted wide public attention and helped gain Malthus an appointment in 1805 as Professor of History and Political Economy at the

---

[6]*An essay on the principle of population* was first published in 1798 and went through six revisions until the last, published after Malthus's death in 1872. The essay grew from a small volume of 55,000 to 200,000 words, much of which were dedicated to explaining his original thesis in response to his critics.

East India College, founded to train colonial administrators. The professorship, the first such position in England, gave Malthus a formal academic platform from which to develop and expand his economic and population theories. These theories considered a broad range of sensitive social and political issues of the day and stimulated numerous debates between clergy and scientists. Most striking was the impact that Malthus's writing had on biology. In fact, the discussion of overpopulation is the only example of an idea developed by a social scientist that has had a profound influence on the natural sciences (Wrigley, 1986:148). Charles Darwin's acknowledgement of Malthus's influence on his theory of natural selection is a well-known example (see Mayr, 1982:478).

The Malthus essay on population established a relationship of linkages within the natural world, and its thesis inserted economics, biology, and environment into the center of human studies. It disturbed more than a few theologians because Malthus appeared to treat humans as part of the biological world. The opening statement, "...the constant tendency in all animated life to increase beyond the nourishment prepared for it," set a tone continued throughout the balance of the essay. The essay seemed to imply that humans were but another organism within nature, subject to biological laws, at least the implication was clear to those clergy who condemned it. They were disturbed by any thesis that presumed to question the divine goal of human perfection. Malthus suffered from repeated attacks for his alleged antireligious views. Both his professorship and his ordination as a minister of the Church of England helped him fend off his critics, however. In later years, he took full advantage of these professional positions and reminded readers of his clergyman's title.

Other scholars supported and praised his work, however, as an insightful thesis into man's place in the natural world. Some readers agreed with and praised the essay because they saw in it support for the popular belief that the natural order of society was threatened because the "lower classes" reproduced without restraint. Critics of the "poor laws" found scientific support in Malthus's writings. These "poor laws," a food subsidy to maintain families at or above a bare subsistence level, were widely attacked as an encouragement for the poor, the unskilled, or even the jobless to marry and have children who would then become burdens on their parishes.[7] Malthus argued that parish support might bring some immediate relief but only at

[7]The English "poor laws" date to 1531 when aged and infirm persons were licensed to beg in their neighborhoods. Several modifications over the centuries led to the Speenhamland version in 1796, which, in effect, provided supplements to families whose income was below a minimum level. This level was determined by the price of bread and subsidized the low wages of the laborer. The numerous attacks by critics led to a further modification which led to the establishment of Work Houses which provided a lower level of support than previously offered in order to discourage the poor from seeking help.

the cost of aggravating the "problem." This problem, as he defined it, was an encouragement of the poor to have children they could not support.

> "The poor-laws of England tend to depress the general condition of the poor in these two ways. Their first obvious tendencies is to increase population without increasing the food for its support. A poor man may marry with little or no prospect of being able to support a family in independence. They may be said, therefore, to create the poor which they maintain."
>
> Thomas R. Malthus, 1798

While these arguments were continued and expanded in each new revision of his original essay, world events were occurring that contradicted Malthus's assumption about food production. True, the populations of Europe continued to increase at geometric rates well into the nineteenth century, but economies expanded also. This expansion was marked by increases of manufactured products and a food supply that kept pace with and even exceeded population needs. The quantity of Britain's agricultural production, plus food imported from abroad, rose with population growth and this increase continued for a century after Malthus's death. The subsistence bottleneck of former agrarian societies had been broken, and the gloomy economic forecasts did not come to pass (Wrigley, 1986). We should emphasize here that Malthus may have missed the import of the events transpiring around him, but he was entirely accurate in his thesis of reproductive capacity and the subsistence limits of his homeland.

The "natural limits" on the English population were overcome not only through numerous improvements in food production, but mainly by changes in the use of resources through industrialization. Support of English population growth came at a great cost to others, however. Most immediately, the Irish were to suffer from English industrial and population expansion, followed by New World and then Asian peoples. By the close of the nineteenth century, the world felt the full impact of Europe's needs as countries of the continent plus America joined the Industrial Revolution. Food and raw materials were absorbed at an ever higher rate in exchange for manufactured goods.

The Malthusian Trap

Food constraints imposed limits on demography and health thereby constructing a trap that could narrow or broaden with changes in economic fortune (Komlos, 1989). When crop yields were high enough to ensure ample food supply, mortality of the young and elderly declined. Marriage rates went up, leading to increases in birth rates in the following years, and the population grew. This growth placed an added burden on local food resources whose production could not keep up with demand and nutritional status of each individual, especially children, declined. The population then entered a "Malthusian crisis," marked by a decline in health and in marriage rates. Mortality rose as births fell, easing the pressures on food production. Then the cycle started all over again with another rise in population followed by another crisis, as diagramed in Figure 4–2.

During Europe's preindustrial period, the length of the cycle from surplus to scarcity depended on the many factors of land resources, climate, food plants, and, of course, the sociopolitical systems. Hence, Northern Europe was more sensitive to seasonal fluctuations than was Southern Europe, and Central Europe's population under the Hapsburg empire varied, as did the degree of political control over the diverse ethnic groups within the empire's boundaries. Likewise, Spain, with its vast overseas colonies, varied differently than did Britain or France. The Industrial Revolution changed all of this as food constraints were gradually lifted and new political and trade boundaries were established.

Though food constraints were eased somewhat, periodic crop shortfalls continued to be a problem for certain regions well into the nineteenth century. Between 1837–1839 and again during 1846–1849, there were acute food shortages in many parts of Europe (Langer, 1963). The food bottleneck on population was finally broken with the rise of industry, modern trans-

Figure 4–2 Constraints on Population Growth

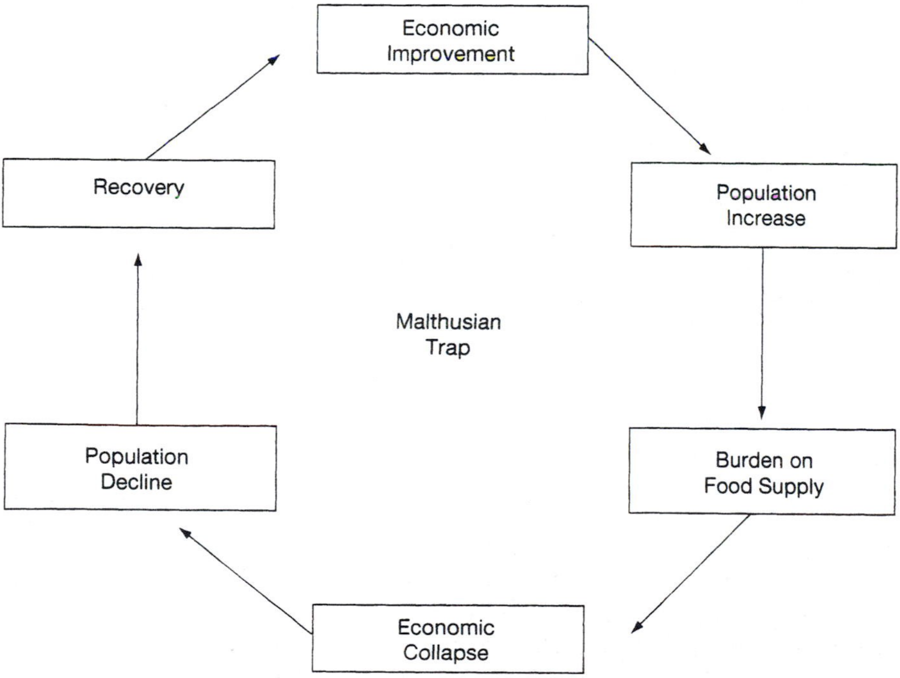

portation, migration, and increased trade. As Wrigley (1986) and Komlos (1989) have described, the Malthusian check on population (famine) was then removed from most of Europe. The human costs were high, however, as migration increased and lifestyles changed radically with the rise in population density in newly formed urban centers.

Urbanization

The social impacts of the Industrial Revolution were so numerous and broad in scope that it is still difficult to appreciate after even more than a century. One impact on society stands out among all the others—the spatial distribution of human settlements. The increased labor needs of manufacturing centers were satisfied by migration from the countryside as agriculture absorbed fewer workers from Europe's rapidly growing populations. This led to greater concentrations of people in expanding urban areas around factories and mines.

On the eve of the Industrial Revolution, less than 10 percent of Europeans lived in cities of 10,000 or more. The largest were London, Paris, and Amsterdam. The majority of people still lived on farms and in small towns or villages scattered across the countryside. But this rapidly changed with industrialization. Within little more than a generation, there was a complete turn around in settlement patterns, with larger and larger segments of the national population living in urban areas. These urban populations grew by 27 percent every decade of the nineteenth century (Brown, 1991). Figure 4–3 compares the percent of urban populations in several regions of Europe with United States and Japan and Korea. Note how Britain is distinguished by its rapid rate of change between 1760–1880. After mid-nineteenth century, the rest of Europe began to catch up as they became full participants in the Industrial Revolution. Japan began a rapid rise by the end of the century, as did Korea fifty years later, reflecting the beginnings of industrialization in Asia.

Starting from a position of the least urbanized country during the sixteenth century, Britain grew rapidly to become the most urbanized by 1800, except for the Dutch Republic (Wrigley, 1990). Between 1600–1800, urban centers had increased by 600 percent in contrast to the total British population growth of 111 percent. During this time, London became the first European city to reach 1 million. Additionally, new cities were forming from what had been small market towns; for example, Liverpool, Birmingham, and Leeds, had now entered the list of the more important urban centers (see Table 4–2).

The rapid growth within just a century was fed by increases in the numbers of young, able individuals who were eager to migrate to seek job opportunities. This rural–urban migration was not a slow steady event extending over decades but came as a deluge described as "galloping urban-

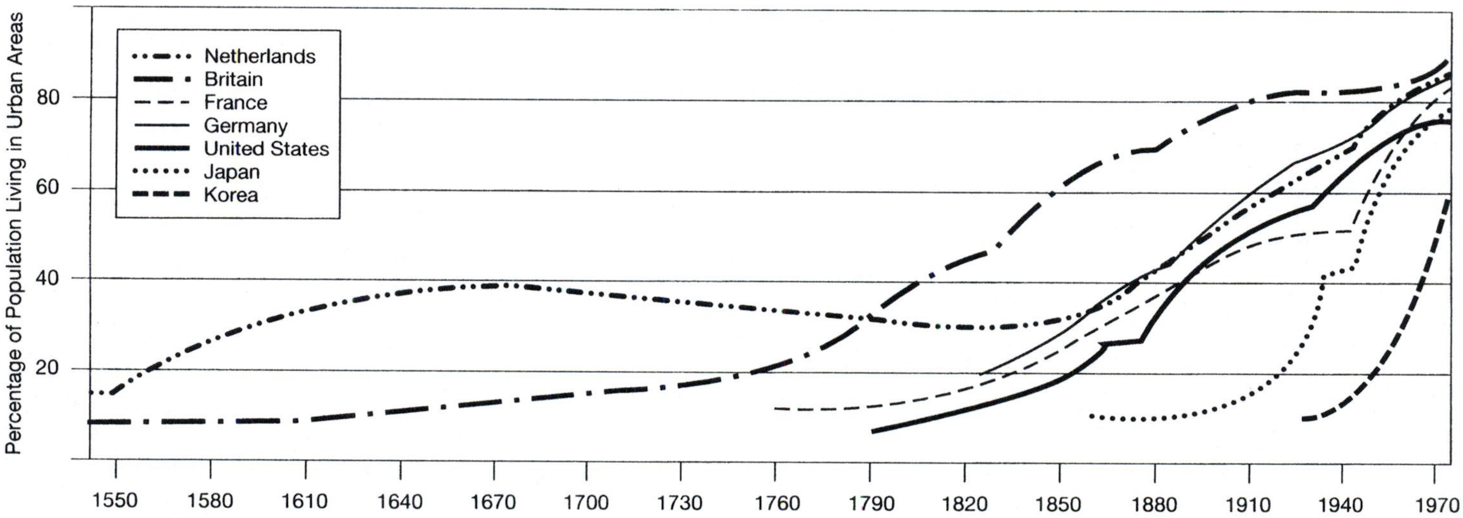

Figure 4–3 Changing Percent of Urban Populations: Select Countries, 1550–1980

From Berry, 1990. Reprinted by permission of Cambridge University Press.

TABLE 4–2 Growth of Urban Centers (in thousands)

City	1700	1750	1800	1850	1900
Britain					
London	550	657	960	2,362	6,480
Birmingham	7	23	74	233	1,248
Leeds	6	16	53	376	436
Liverpool	6	22	78	194	940
Edinburgh	35	55	82	345	386
Glasgow		21	84	346	1,072
Dublin	80	125	165	263	401
Holland-Belgium					
Amsterdam	210	219	195	224	510
Brussels	70	55	66	251	561
France					
Paris	550	560	547	1,053	3,330
Lyon	97	115	111	177	508
Marseille	75	88	83	195	410
Germany					
Berlin	24	113	172	439	2,707
Hamburg	63	90	117	132	895
Austro-Hungarian					
Vienna	105	169	231	444	2,030
Budapest	18	24	54	178	880
United States					
New York	4.5	13.3	63	682	4,242
Philadelphia	4.4	20	68	426	1,418
Boston	6.7	20	35	202	1,575
Reference Cities					
Madrid	105	123	160	281	539
Rome	149	157	153	175	438
Moscow	114	161	250	365	1,112
Peking	650	900	1,110	1,648	1,180
Cairo	175	350	186	256	595
Constantinople	700	666	570	785	900

Source: Adapted from Cipolla, 1972; Chandler, 1987.

ization" by Brown (1991). He emphasized that the increase was an average of 27 percent every decade of the first half of the nineteenth century, absorbing the excess rural populations. Such a deluge of people within two generations—by 1851 Britain had more town than city dwellers—"demanded large scale responses" (Wohl, 1983). The proper responses to meet these needs were slow in coming, however, and the human costs were high during the time of unfulfilled needs of the new urban societies. These costs were most evident in the poor health of the urban dwellers whose mortality was appallingly high. Most cities had a mortality rate nearly twice the national average (Wrigley, 1969).

CONSEQUENCES OF HIGH DENSITY POPULATIONS

The increased population densities of urbanization create many problems not faced by rural communities. Foremost among these problems are the provision of proper housing, clean water, and good sanitation—the safe disposal of human and animal wastes from the crowded urban streets. Whenever these problems are not dealt with, epidemics occur with resultant high mortality. Frequently throughout history, infectious diseases had risen to epidemic proportions, sweeping through urban populations. Also, the numerous "plagues" of the fourteenth through the seventeenth centuries suffered by the cities of Western Europe provide some of the best records, as we noted in the last chapter. Though not as deadly as the "Black Death," new epidemics became more frequent as urban centers increased during the early Industrial Revolution. The thousands of people who were concentrated in smaller spaces close to the expanding factories that generated masses of water and air pollutants, were at terrible risk for any number of a variety of infectious diseases.

Housing

The housing of families of laborers and small landowners, even in rural settings, had been seldom adequate even well into the late nineteenth century. Housing construction simply had not kept up with population increase. A British parliamentary report of 1843 described the overcrowded housing conditions found throughout rural England. Most cottages were old, with thin walls of wattle and daub,[8] dirt floors, and rotting thatch roofs that offered little protection from the elements, and there were no sanitation facilities. Whole families were crowded into one or two rooms, and at night the entire floor area would be covered from wall to wall with sleeping bodies. Children, infants, and adults would all be crowded together, the ill with the healthy. As Burnett (1991:160) described the typical rural situation: "At Stourpain in Dorset a family of eleven inhabited a two room cottage, the single bedroom of ten by ten foot square contained three beds." Though these typical country dwellings were grossly overcrowded, the buildings themselves were not densely congregated. Cottages were spaced far apart and surrounded by gardens and fields in which the people toiled. The poor urban–industrial workers and their families enjoyed no such advantage of rural space, however.

There was little or no planning to meet the needs of the deluge of workers throughout most of the industrialization period. People sought shelter

[8]Cottage walls made from twigs and branches woven together (wattle) and plastered with mud or daub was a typical construction material used throughout Europe for perhaps thousands of years.

wherever they could find it. As many as thirty people would be crammed into small two- or three-room houses that once had been home to a single family. The worst living accommodations were the so-called lodging houses, shoddily built structures meant to shelter workers temporarily but still in use decades later. Single rooms, without heat or ventilation, were covered with mattresses or rags on which people of both sexes and all ages slept. Other arrangements were made by subdividing rooms, hallways, and even cellars of existing houses whose former owners had fled to the suburbs. In these tenements, as many as twelve people would be crammed into a single room. The poorest of the tenants lived in cellars, which by 1790 accommodated one-eighth of the city of Liverpool's population. This number rose to 20 percent, or 40,000, by 1830, and conditions were just as bad in the other new industrial cities (Burnett, 1991).

As pressures for housing continued to grow, building speculators threw up cheaply constructed "back to back," houses of one room deep, sharing a common back and side wall with its neighbors. This resulted in long double rows of houses of from two to four rooms built under a single roof. One row faced on a street, usually unpaved, while the back row opened onto a narrow lane separating another block of houses. Such compact construction allowed a maximum number of family units to be crowded onto a small plot of land. These units were an improvement over the lodging houses or tenements, but they still lacked sunlight and ventilation. The water supply was minimal—a single standpipe (faucet) at the end of the street or row and two earth closets (privies), located somewhere in the lane, provided for the needs of about 150 people (Berry, 1990).

Local authorities throughout Europe were not unaware of the housing problems of their cites, and they tried to make improvements over the next decades. Building codes were established to prevent some of the worst abuses, and improvements were being made gradually. In Britain, row house construction came to be prohibited by some municipalities, but they continued to be built as late as 1909 in others. To prevent the worst of the overcrowded conditions, numerous attempts were made to regulate the "lodging houses" and tenements. But population growth and expanding urbanization, together with rising costs of construction and land, kept the pressure on housing needs. This pressure was especially acute throughout Europe where lodging houses and tenements continued to be shelters of last resort for hundreds of thousands of people, despite the known health risks of overcrowding.

London, Britain's burgeoning capital and a center of government, commerce, and industry, is one of the first cities to come to mind when housing shortages are considered. New housing construction fell far short of meeting demand, and expanding commercial development made matters even worse. By the late nineteenth century, factory, railroad, and municipal building construction, a kind of early urban renewal, destroyed many of the older buildings to make way for the new projects. Forced out of even the most minimal accommodations, people crowded into nearby tenements, raising the population density even higher. An example was Sultan street in Camberwell, described as one of the vilest slums of London. Its seventy houses sheltered 661 persons in 1871. Ten years later, the situation became more acute as over a thousand people were now packed into the same number of houses (Cannadine & Reeder, 1982). Other cities had the same problems of overcrowding; Glasgow's population increased twice as fast as its housing accommodation, for example.

Sanitation

The grossly overcrowded cities of the nineteenth century were confronted with the monumental task of waste disposal, which was far beyond the financial ability of local government councils. Typically, only the main roads were cleared of refuse and then not on a regular basis. The thousands of alleys and lanes of large cities were virtually ignored. Though throwing of rubbish onto public streets had been outlawed as early as 1600, existing laws were ignored, and household refuse and even human excreta were regularly thrown into streets or spaces between the houses. To this accumulation were added dead animal carcasses and runoff from the overflowing privies, each serving scores of families. This filth would lay in piles until rain washed it away into ditches and then flowed into nearby streams or rivers. There the wastes of thousands of households were mixed with a variety of industrial wastes flowing from tanneries, slaughterhouses, or factory mills. Some appreciation of the scope of the problem may be gained by a description of Croydon, a parish adjacent to London.

Croydon, a community of 13,000 people, was described as a "mushroom suburb" growing more crowded each year with its twisted narrow lanes and courts lined with shoddily built housing (Smith, 1979). This suburb lacked even the most rudimentary provisions for sanitation as of 1848. There were a few canals that drained rain and sewage runoff, fed by an average of one privy for every three houses. To this was added the additional privies arranged over an open ditch running through the town center. There was no organized refuse removal service since Croydon's streets and lanes were outside the jurisdiction of the Board of Highways. This meant that the daily excreta of 13,000 people (about 10,000 kilograms and 13,000 liters of urine), plus garbage and animal wastes accumulated until washed away by the next rainstorm. In the meantime, these wastes seeped into the wells from which the community drew its water.

This situation was typical of the urban environments of the Industrial Revolution, but human life and health was made even more precarious by the lack of a clean water source. Cities would take their drinking water from shallow wells contaminated by septic tank seepage, or from rivers and canals flowing with untreated sewage. London water companies, for example, had intake pipes drawing Thames water down river from streams that dumped raw sewages into the river. Sand filters had been introduced early in the nineteenth century, but the filters lacked the capacity to meet the water demands of the growing city. The system of pipes (first wooden and then metal) distributed water throughout a city into neighborhood cisterns from which water could be pumped as needed. The pipes often leaked and they, as well as the storage cisterns, often filled with seepage from nearby septic tanks or overflowing privies. People were well aware of this contamination and those that could afford it purchased drinking water from cleaner sources, supporting a profession of "water carriers." No urban areas of the British Isles or those on the continent escaped the problems related to sustaining large numbers of people in a restricted area. Inadequate housing, lack of clean water, and poor disposal of wastes were major factors influencing health risks. Given such conditions, it is not surprising that urban populations suffered a high mortality rate.

Mortality

Life expectancy was short and mortality rates were high in all of the cities. In the 1840s, infants born to mothers living in the industrial centers of Britain died at the rate of 155 per 1,000 live births. Those that survived had an average expectancy of from twenty-four to thirty-seven years, compared to forty-one years for all of England and Wales. Residents of rural areas faired much better, with an average of forty-five years. The crude death rates (deaths per thousand population) of the cities were between forty-four and fifty-three in frightening contrast to the twenty or twenty-five for populations in villages.[9] It was no wonder that cities like Liverpool, Leeds, and Manchester were known as human burial pits. London's reputation as a "devourer of souls" was well deserved when consideration is given to the "Bills of Mortality," which, for decades, listed an excess of deaths over births (Cannadine and Reeder, 1982). London and other cities could only continue to grow because of the influx of migrants from the countryside.

The ratio of urban to rural deaths was on the order of 124:100 (1851–1861), a disproportionate risk of mortality that is certainly related to environmental differences. The countryside, even with all of its difficulties of housing and heavy workload, was certainly a healthier place to reside than any of the urban slums. It did not require much thought nor a scientific study to relate living conditions to health and longevity. The facts clearly showed that death rates were higher in some neighborhoods than in others.

[9]Crude death rates of the Industrial Revolution should be viewed in comparison with the very highest today of ten to fifteen per thousand population reported for the lesser-developed countries.

TABLE 4–3 Examples of Life Expectancy of Select British Cities by Social Class (1841)

City or Region	Gentry	Tradesmen	Laborers
London	44	25	22
Liverpool	35	22	15
Manchester	38	20	17
Rutland	52	41	38
Bath	55	37	25
Leeds	44	27	19
Bethnal Green	45	26	16

Source: Adapted from Wohl, 1983; Burnett, 1991.

This was made especially clear in the case of infants and children. Infants born to mothers in the Strand district of London died at twice the rate (229 per 1,000 live births) as did infants in the middle-class section of Plumstead (115 per 1,000). Childhood mortality was also high by any standard, but here too were major differences between districts. Fifty-seven percent of the children of working class families in Manchester did not live to reach their fifth birthday. Economically better-off families had mortalities of around 20 to 30 percent (Wohl,1983).

All urban residents suffered severely from infectious diseases, but there were sharp differences in risk because lower economic status effectively established microenvironments less amenable to health. As documented by social class differences in life expectancy, people crowded into tenements were twice as likely to die. The gentry and professional classes averaged forty-four years compared to twenty-five years for tradesmen and a low of twenty-two years for laborers and their families (Table 4–3). Living space appeared to be one of the main contributing factors. The more people forced to live in one or two rooms, the higher the mortality rate. The greater a family's income, the more spacious and healthier was their living accommodations. Better clothing, a more adequate diet, and protection of children from the burdens of the heavy workloads also contributed to the differences between the social classes.

Infectious Diseases

The rapid urban growth worsened health problems and increased mortality as more people suffered from the "crowd diseases" typically found among dense populations. Three-quarters of all nineteenth-century deaths are estimated to have been caused by infectious diseases. Of these, the more significant were respiratory diseases, variously listed as consumption or *tuberculosis* and *pneumonia,* followed by water- and food-borne infections of *cholera* and *typhoid,* body-louse–transmitted *typhus,* and several types of dysenteric diseases. As vaccination became nearly universal throughout Europe, *smallpox*, the deadly disease of previous centuries, was becoming less of a threat by the 1840s, while these others continued to exact a terrible toll.

Smallpox had been responsible for between 10 and 20 percent of the deaths in eighteenth-century Europe, but by 1850 the disease accounted for less than 2 percent of total mortality. Physicians discovered that some immunity to smallpox infection could be obtained by scratching the skin of an uninfected person with pustule matter taken from an infected person. This "inoculation" had been used for centuries in Asia but only introduced into Europe in the late seventeenth century. Inoculation was increasingly used and by 1740 it was a widespread practice, but contained an element of risk and sometimes infected instead of protecting (Mercer, 1990). Most interesting was this recognition of the possibility of gaining a disease immunity more than one hundred years before the discovery of bacteria and the development of the germ theory by Pasteur and Koch.

In the latter part of the eighteenth century, a more efficient and less risky means was used to immunize—the "vaccination," or deliberate infection with cowpox. It was derived from an old folk remedy reportedly practiced for decades by English farmers to protect their families from the ravages of smallpox. The farmers had noticed that many milk maids had sores on their hands caused by contact with infected cows. These milk maids seldom contacted smallpox even though many others in the area did succumb to the disease (Hardy, 1993). A physician, Edward Jenner, studied the distribution and transmission of cowpox and described a "cross immunity," persons infected with the more benign cowpox developed a resistance to smallpox. The publication of the results of his study in 1798 convinced Jenner's medical colleagues to take this old folk practice seriously, and many vaccinated their patients—with outstanding results. Mortality rates plummeted as vaccination became a common practice. Within a decade, smallpox vaccination expanded to include most of Europe and the United States.

Several countries made vaccination compulsory and it became a universal requirement for most armies; Napoleon decreed that all of his army be vaccinated.[10] By the mid-nineteenth century, many of Europe's people had been vaccinated, and its success can be read in the major mortality reductions. The effectiveness of smallpox prevention is further emphasized by the return of epidemics whenever there were lapses in the enforcement of vaccination laws. Britain, complacent from past successes, became lax in providing vaccination for all its citizens. The epidemic of 1871–1872 came as a shock and renewed awareness that smallpox remained a danger that could

---

[10] The vaccination requirement for French army recruits lapsed after 1815, and many soldiers were unprotected for the rest of the century. During the Franco-Prussian war (1870–1871), 20,000 French soldiers were put out of action because of smallpox. This may have contributed to the French defeat (McNeill, 1977).

strike with deadly force whenever society let its guard down. This epidemic was particularly virulent, killing over 60 percent of those infected. In little more than a year, 44,500 people died of the disease, 8,000 in London alone. Such a high loss led to renewed efforts to enforce universal vaccination. In Figure 4–4 the changing death rates illustrate the effectiveness of vaccination and then the terrible return of smallpox when there was a lapse in its enforcement.

The Crowd Diseases Close and continuous interpersonal contact among people of densely populated areas provide a large host/reservoir for what we know now as disease-causing microbes. Measles, scarlet fever, diptheria, as well as smallpox, to name a few, require a certain minimal human population size be maintained for transmission between generations. For example, measles requires an estimated minimum of 300,000 persons. Other diseases, like typhus, depend on insect vectors for transmission between humans, which occurs most effectively under conditions of crowding and poor body hygiene. There is a seasonal fluctuation as conditions that influence living

Figure 4–4 Smallpox Death Rates: England and Wales, 1850–1910

From McKeown, 1979. *The Role of Medicine. Dream, Mirage, or Nemesis.* Reprinted by permission of Blackwell Scientific Publications, Ltd. and Princeton University Press.

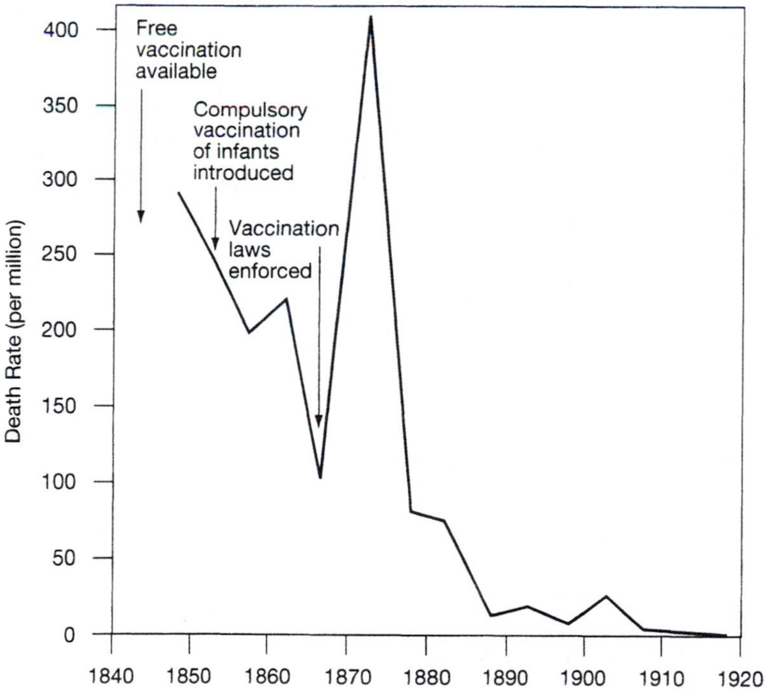

TABLE 4–4 Decline of Mortality in England and Wales (per 1,000,000 population)

Disease	1851	1861	1871	1881	1891
Smallpox	222	163	240	45	13
Measles	412	440	380	440	414
Cholera*	1,180	1,076	940 (30)	674 (15)	738 (25)
Typhoid & Typhus	908	885	490	235	182
Scarlet fever	876	971	720	334	158
Diphtheria	109	184	120	163	263
Tuberculosis (respiratory)	2,679	2,475	2,126	1,731	1,391
Whooping cough	504	528	510	450	377

*cholera and (dysentery)

Source: Adapted from Langer, 1963; McKeown and Record, 1962; Mercer, 1990.

conditions or insect multiplication vary. Typhoid, cholera, and other dysentery diseases relate to contamination of food and/or water supplies, which increase frequency and quantity of microbe contacts. This, in turn, depends on population density and how people use their environments. Air borne diseases are also density dependent and the closer and more frequent the interpersonal contact, the greater the likelihood of transmission of one of the many respiratory infections. The more significant ones for considering mortality rates of the mid and later Industrial Revolution period are respiratory: tuberculosis, pneumonia, and influenza. The recognition of the causes of these diseases came during the later nineteenth century and prevention followed a somewhat different path than that of smallpox.

There was no single vaccine or inoculation that led to the control of these most threatening of the infectious diseases. It was a rather straightforward alteration in lifestyle and use of the environment. The control of five of the eight diseases listed in Table 4–4 accounted for almost the whole of death rate reduction between 1851 and 1900 (McKeown and Record, 1962). McKeown (1979) offered convincing evidence that environmental changes were more effective in lowering mortality by the end of the nineteenth century than inoculation or by drugs (smallpox excepted). The incidence of these five major diseases were already on the decline before medical measures became effective. This is especially evident in the example of mortality from tuberculosis, which was rapidly declining nearly a century before chemotherapy was available (Figure 4–5).

Sanitation Reforms

Groups of civic-minded citizens from several professional backgrounds began to actively seek changes that were to prepare the way for the health reforms to come. Clergymen, "poor law" overseers, statisticians, scientists, and doctors were brought together by their common interest in improving

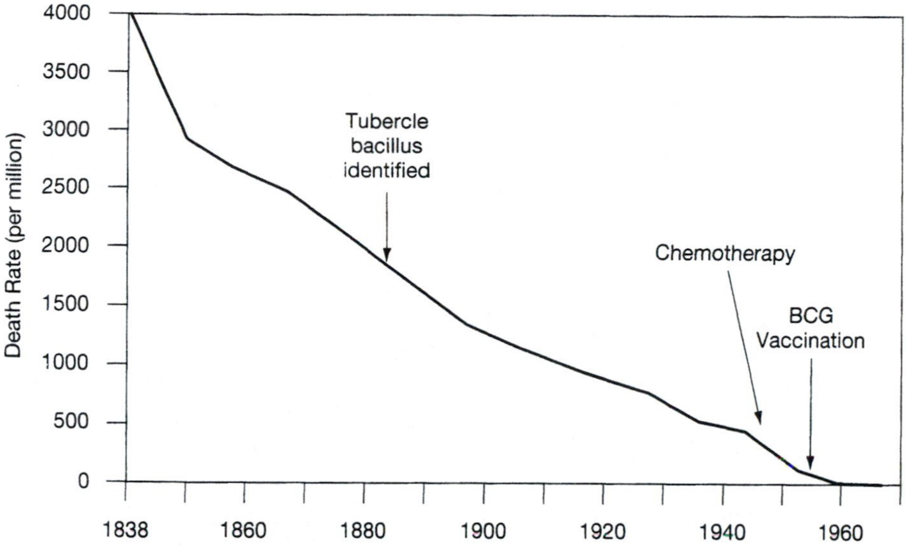

Figure 4–5 Decline of Mortality from Respiratory Tuberculosis

McKeown, 1979. *The Role of Medicine. Dream, Mirage, or Nemesis.* Reprinted by permission of Blackwell Scientific Publications, Ltd. and Princeton University Press.

urban living conditions in general and among the working classes in particular. Though direct causal connections between ill health and pollution had yet to be firmly established, civic leaders could readily associate disease with the crowded, filthy urban environments. The observation that some neighborhoods of the growing urban areas suffered more illness and death became one of the foundations of sanitary reforms.

The simple recognition that adequate provisions of life's necessities prevented illness had been made again and again at least since the time of that famous Greek physician, Hippocrates. His writings, considered a foundation of western medicine, contained acute observations of the interrelations between lifestyle and health. Men make epidemics is one way of summarizing the behavior–health interrelationships. Virchow, German physician and bacteriologist of the nineteenth century and a careful reader of Hippocrates, observed that, "Epidemics resembled great warnings from which a statesman in the grand style can read that a disturbance has taken place in the development of his people" (quoted by Nikiforuk, 1991). These observations influenced many other scientists and civic and religious leaders who were caught up in the rapidly changing world of the nineteenth century.

Local boards of health were formed and staffed by a band of elected, dedicated volunteers who served without pay, but who, unfortunately, lacked the legal authority to enforce change. These early founders of public health were practical men and women who discounted the disdainful and erroneous explanations frequently offered. A statement such as, "The epidemic victims were suffering God's wrath for their sins, for living in lust and drunkenness," may serve as one of numerous examples.[11] The reformers urging a cleanup of the cities understood that the provision of clean water, adequate food, shelter, and fresh air were life's essentials. However, urban conditions remained little changed from their eighteenth century levels and even worsened well into the next century though simple preventive measures could have been taken.

Health surveys were conducted over the years in a number of British cities, from London in 1774 to Dublin in 1806 and Manchester in 1832. Recommendations were made, local ordinances were passed and cleanups were carried out to remove some of the more offensive filth from the roads and waterways. Lacking enforcement authority and without adequate financial resources, these cleanup efforts could not be sustained nor could they be extended nationally. Main roads might be cleared and drains installed in some parts of the city but there were few improvements made in working class districts where the needs were greatest. Political opposition and the lack of funds limited early sanitation improvements, but the fact that these early efforts were made showed awareness of the problems.

Years of studies, reports, and political pressure still failed to gain national support for a public health act, but the arrival of a new disease acted as a cruel wake-up call. *Cholera* arrived in Britain in 1831 after spreading across Europe from Asia. It caused a raging epidemic, infecting hundreds of thousands of victims with tens of thousands of deaths (Wohl, 1983). Though the highest mortality was suffered in the crowded precincts of London, the rich as well as the poor became victims. The debates over environmental cleanup were renewed, but now there was some urgency. Parliament commissioned a study into the condition of Britain's cities, a study which culminated in Chadwick's "Report on the Sanitary Condition of the Laboring Population of Great Britain" published in 1842 (Flinn, 1965). The report emphasized what had already been described in dozens of regional studies: proper drainage, removal of refuse, and improvements in water supply were of primary importance to public health.

Chadwick was a capable administrator of long experience in government administration of the "poor laws" and factory reform. He also has been described as a born leader, who was able to bring together the various health and sanitarian reform groups to produce a strong document on the basic needs of Britain's cities (Boyden, 1987). Chadwick's report of 1842 was accepted, but it was put under the close scrutiny of the Royal Commission

[11] The subject of racism, social discrimination, and prejudice during Victorian times often distorted the course of scientific research. The literature is too extensive to describe here but surveys by Chase (1976), Stocking (1987), or Kevles (1995) offer a fair description of the social and scientific biases of the times.

of Towns (1844–1845), set up specifically to validate the report's findings. The commission's conclusions resulted eventually in the passage of the Public Health Act of 1848. This law, while a milestone in modern sanitary reform, was but a compromise incorporating only some of Chadwick's recommendations. It did not include any national system of health or sanitation control. Responsibilities were left to local governing bodies and boards of health were only made compulsory under the law where crude death rates were in excess of twenty-three per thousand. The Act also established a General Board of Health with three members—Chadwick, Lord Ashley and a physician, Southward-Smith.

The return of cholera in 1848 (the first cases reported just one week after the passage of the Public Health Act) generated strong support for the Board of Health. Officialdom had by now accepted the environment–health link. But with the waning of cholera within a year, support soon evaporated. The influence of the board diminished quickly and by 1854 the most vocal board members, Chadwick and Southwood-Smith were removed. Ironically, in that same year, cholera returned for a third visit.

Though several other serious infectious diseases were continually present and accounted for a higher percentage of deaths, the history of sanitary reform and the foundations for modern boards of health are intertwined with Europe's cholera epidemics. European societies were accustomed to the chronic infections and high mortalities of tuberculosis, typhus, and fevers such as typhoid, but cholera, before 1831–1832, was a different matter. It was thought of as a foreign disease, confined to Asia. With increasing world trade, however, cholera could and did spread suddenly outward, infecting and quickly killing the newly exposed populations. The arrival of cholera in Russia about 1830 was watched with dread by the rest of Europe. Borders were sealed and armies imposed a quarantine on travelers but without effect. Cholera arrived in Western Europe and Britain with a sudden impact and lethal consequences. Within months it had crossed the Atlantic by migrant ship to New York City (Rosenberg, 1962).

Infection spread rapidly through New York's crowded slums and mortality rates reached as high as 50 percent. A person could become ill one morning and die before the next dawn. Such an impact spurred New York health authorities to action clearing away refuse, isolating cholera victims, and eventually bringing clean water to the city. Such measures helped though the actual transmission of the disease was still unknown; the acceptable scientific explanation was by a miasma emanating from dead animals and rotting refuse.[12] The causal organism, *Vibrio cholerae,* would not be dis-

[12]Miasma—an early theory of disease causes; usually related to "bad air" and rotting refuse. People as early as the Greek Bronze Age would avoid living nearby marshes because of a belief in the dangers of exposure to the miasma emanating from the stagnant waters—a danger we now know to be due to disease-bearing mosquitos.

covered by Koch for another fifty years.[13] In the meantime, in both Europe and America, sewage and contaminated water supplies were being considered as probable sources of the disease.

During the reappearance of cholera in 1848, a London physician, John Snow, observed that most of his patients were concentrated within a single neighborhood. Though incomes and quality of housing varied, the families shared a dependence on the same water supply. He theorized that in some way impure drinking water was responsible and published his conclusions. His water-borne theory gained little recognition because of the popularity of the "miasma" theory of disease transmission. Also, cholera receded as quickly as it appeared and interest in its causes declined. The medical profession and public health officials returned to the more pressing concern with outbreaks of typhus and typhoid and the continued high childhood mortality.

There was a third cholera outbreak in 1854 that spread just as quickly as did the earlier epidemics, with the heaviest concentration in the same neighborhood that suffered in 1848. John Snow was now able to test his theory of transmission by contaminated water. He marked the location of the residence of each of his cholera patients. There was a discernible pattern in the distribution cases; most often his patients lived within a few blocks or even a few houses from one another. All of these households obtained their water from the same city well, which was supplied by one of the two water companies in London. This company, the Southwark and Vauxhall, drew its water supply from the Thames River, downstream from a major sewer discharge pipe. The other water company, Lamberth, collected water some distance upstream from the city's sewage discharge. As we would expect today, the consumers of the Southwark and Vauxhall water supply suffered a greater incidence of cholera than did those supplied by Lamberth. To prove his theory, Snow persuaded city officials to cap the Broad Street pump, the principle water source for the area of highest frequency of cholera cases. The area's residents were forced to get their water elsewhere and the epidemic soon subsided. These results satisfied Snow that his theory of contaminated water as cholera's cause was correct(see Morris, 1976).

Other health authorities were not as certain because, they argued, the epidemic was already past its peak and the number of cases were in decline when the Broad Street pump was shut off. Snow's data were passed over as circumstantial, a mere coincidence of infected people living in the same neighborhood. Of course, about forty years later, Snow was proven correct when the microbe that causes cholera was discovered in 1883 by the German bacteriologist, Robert Koch (McNeill, 1977). Regardless of the accuracy of his

---

[13]Koch, a German physician, is credited with the identification of the cholera organism, but recognition should be given also to Girolamo Fracastoro, an Italian physician who, in 1546, advanced a theory of contagion to support quarantine of areas of cholera outbreak.

interpretation, Snow's major contribution to science was one of the earliest applications of what we call epidemiology, an analysis of the distribution and determination of a particular disease. Though Snow's explanation of cholera transmission was not fully complete (it lacked the identification of the microbe), the publication of his results in 1855 influenced many civic leaders in both Europe and America.

One such leader was Max von Pettenkoffer, a chemist who argued that urban environments should be improved since cleanliness was the basis for good health. Snow's data on cholera epidemics provided evidence to support a campaign to persuade the Munich council to make a number of simple but very important changes. An extensive sewage system was built, rubbish was carted away, and streets were cleaned on a regular basis. Most importantly, a system of aquaducts diverted mountain streams to provide a clean water source rather than use the polluted Isar River flowing through the city. He also encouraged the planting of trees and the development of parks, believing that such esthetic improvements were an important part of a healthy environment. As these environmental changes progressed, Munich became one of the cleanest and healthiest of European cities (Dubos, 1965). Mortality rates due to cholera, typhus, and typhoid fell to levels far below that experienced by other European cities of comparable size.

Though Pettenkoffer, Snow, and Chadwick are justifiably seen as pioneers in modern sanitation, numerous others before them had advocated environmental improvements as a basis for good health. Some sanitary reforms had been started earlier in the eighteenth century but gaining acceptance was slow despite the evidence of the effectiveness of sanitation improvements. There was a reluctance to bear the cost of the civic improvements; industry and householders alike, objected to being told where and how to deposit their refuse. The regulations were viewed as impingement on individual freedom and property rights. This made it difficult, especially in Britain, to gain public cooperation and the acceptance of the necessary regulations. There was also a considerable reluctance to accept national control over what were thought of as local affairs.

In addition, there still remained a considerable confusion over the mode of contagion even after Pasteur and Koch's identification of disease-causing microbes. The germ theory was not universally accepted and had to contend with competing explanations of the cause of illness. What was more surprising was the misapplication of Darwin's theory of natural selection to social issues—the conviction that the poor had an inferior hereditary endowment, as expressed by Herbert Spencer, "The whole purpose of nature was to clear the world of the unfit and to make room for better. If they are not sufficiently complete to live they die, and its best that they do so" (cited in Wohl, 1983:413). In sum, these questions of what caused disease, as well as outright prejudice against the poor, retarded the gain of the wholehearted support of many civic leaders and medical doctors. The experiences of the military in several nineteenth-century wars, however, helped influence changes in political and scientific opinion. Most notable was the support gained for public health reform after the British army's experiences during the Crimean War(1854–1856).

During this short but bloody war with Turkey, ten times as many British soldiers died from disease as from battlefield wounds. Faced with this deplorable state of affairs and under political pressure to reduce the casualty rate, the commanding general accepted female nurses to staff the army hospitals. Florence Nightingale and thirty-eight young women sailed for the Crimea and landed in the middle of one of the worst military health crises ever recorded. Not only did the wounded have little chance of survival once they reached the hospitals, but many healthy soldiers quickly succumbed to disease once they arrived in the camps from England. Nightingale and her nurses prevailed against entrenched opposition and cared for the wounded; they also attacked the problems that were the root cause of many camp diseases.

The immediate effects of Nightingale's work in the Crimea were improvements in hospital procedures and army camp sanitation. Her work offered some very practical demonstrations of how simple changes in procedures could improve health and reduce mortality. With a hard-earned acceptance by the medical establishment and a reputation for treating the sick, Nightingale returned to England to embark on a lifetime of teaching that became the foundation for modern nursing. The short-term effects of her work are easily measured—higher recovery rates of battle casualties, reduction in camp diseases, and the acceptance of female nurses. The influence of her pioneering efforts spans generations, but is more difficult to evaluate though they touch many aspects of human health. Considering all of her teachings, perhaps what was most influential was her emphasis on disease conditions rather than specific diseases (Nightingale, 1987).

The successes of Nightingale and her nurses were much discussed in America and influenced the organization of a "Sanitary Commission" during the Civil War (1861–1865). This group of physicians, clergymen, and women nursing volunteers was established to inspect camps and hospitals and report on the living facilities for the rapidly growing Union army. Its primary goal was to lend aid to the sick and wounded. From their early beginning, the group went on to organize nursing and ambulance services, establish hospitals, and eventually to found convalescent homes after the war (Maxwell, 1956).

It would be hard to gauge the positive effects of such an effort since the disease–casualty rates in both the Union and Confederate armies were many times higher than those inflicted by battle wounds. Of the 364,000 deaths in the Union Army, only 140,400 were due to wounds; the ratio of disease-caused deaths to battle deaths were just as bad in the Confederate Army. It is safe to speculate that the disease mortality rates would have been much higher without the efforts of the Sanitary commission. The commission's work was slow in starting and not as widespread as needed, but there were improvements later in the war as nursing, ambulance services, and hospitals became better established. It took another war, the Boer War in South Africa (1899–1902), to finally prove the need for greater attention to environmental conditions. Compared to the Crimean War, the disease–casualty rate dropped to only five times the rate from battle inflicted wounds, still much higher than a decade later in World War I. It was a significant change, however, that added support to advocates of improvements in the living conditions in urban environments.

What really added momentum to social and public health programs was the declining physical quality of British males. Maintenance of a large army and navy required a continuous input of new recruits. But the manpower pool that provided the recruits seemed to be in danger of shrinking. Large numbers of adolescents and young adults were too frail and sickly to meet even the minimal physical standards of the nineteenth-century military. They seemed "a race apart" these urban dwellers—sickly, stunted in size, narrow-chested, easily wearied, and quite different from their country counterparts (Shee, 1903:quoted in Wohl,1983:336). The residents of the squalid industrial slums offered up poor candidates for military service.

The recruitment experiences of Europe's armies were similar and reveal a great deal about child growth and male health but no comparable data exists for the female population. The health of the working-class females was most likely to have been as bad as their brothers. It was probably even worse considering the heavy workload they endured, the early and frequent pregnancies, and the sharing of the same inadequate living conditions. The health of the factory girls where it has been described support this conclusion.

Since, for many youths, military service was an escape and a major step up from factory work, there was no limit to the number of volunteers. The problem was to find enough men who were physically fit. During the Crimean War, only about one-half could meet the standards and "town-bred" volunteers were rejected at twice the rate as those from the country (see Wohl, 1983:331). There were expressed concerns about race deterioration; "it is no use having an empire without an Imperial Race," stated Lord Roseberry. Clearly, the proposed health reforms offered a way of halting such deterioration, but changes came slowly during the nineteenth century. Despite all the evidence and all of the efforts to pass legislation to improve the industrial–urban environment, the health of Britain's male working class remained poor, as measured by military rejection rates.

The average nationwide rejection rate was 35 percent with the rate as high as 50 percent in Manchester and other industrial cities during the army's expansion during the Boer War (Floud et al., 1990). What was even more revealing of poor national health was that, of those accepted for military service, 10 percent were discharged for health disabilities within two years of service. A senior army general deplored the condition of the young males from which the army took its recruits and calculated that the failure rate during the first two years, added to the initial rejections, totaled close to 60 percent. He published his conclusions and raised the question, "Where to get men?" For even after lowering the minimum height requirements to 5 feet in order to expand the pool of potential recruits, the army was still hard pressed to fill its manpower needs (Solway and Lee, 1990). It continued to be a problem of grave national concern, which led to an extensive investigation by The Inter-Departmental Commission on Physical Deterioration 1903. Despite the Commission's grim conclusions regarding the poor health status of a majority of Britain's people, the problems persisted. During the First World War, the medical boards found only one-third of the males perfectly fit, another third were incapable of even a moderate degree of exertion, and the final third of young males were classified as definitely infirm or chronic invalids (Floud et al., 1990).

The lack of recruit fitness revealed broader and more serious national problems. They can be traced to the undernourishment and living conditions suffered by young children and by their mothers. The heavy workloads, poor nutrition, and polluted environments endured by women forced to work in factories resulted in poor pregnancy outcomes. For those infants that survived the first year, these conditions established a pattern of poor childhood development. Such detrimental influences on infant and childhood environments retarded growth and produced stunted, sickly adults—the development of a "race apart."

SOME MEASUREMENTS OF THE COSTS OF POVERTY

Child Growth

The height and weight of children at any age is a good measure of the quality of nutrition and the diseases suffered. Poorly nourished and sickly children grow slower and are shorter and lighter at all ages. Since social status affects childhood environment, growth is a good proxy by which to measure economic conditions, and it mirrors secular (generational) trends. Thus, years of plenty and low disease morbidity produce healthy children who grow well to become strong, tall adults in contrast to those periods of want. Times of famine and frequent disease, high mortality, and slow retarded growth resulted in small, poorly developed adults; the average height of nations are a sensitive measure of environmental and social conditions (see Fogel, 1982). These relationships have been recognized throughout history and have been used often to bolster arguments for social improvements and for the better treatment of children.

Edwin Chadwick, as secretary to the Poor Law Commission before his venture into public health reform, studied factory working conditions. His study eventually resulted in regulations that improved conditions and shortened working hours but most importantly alleviated the worst of child labor practices. From the start of the Industrial Revolution, children as young as six years old were put to work in factories, mines, and mills. They worked up to 16 hours a day without rest periods and were often beaten if they slowed in their labor or fell asleep. Chadwick and many others accepted the obvious, that such forced labor was detrimental to child health. But evidence was needed if reforms were to be accepted, and Chadwick began collecting data in what was the first growth survey ever made for the express purpose of sociological reform (Tanner, 1986). He appointed a medical health officer in each factory area who, in addition to his other duties, was instructed to collect heights of the workers. The purpose was to determine if there were any differences, at any age, between persons brought up in a factory environment and those from other, more favorable environments.

Cooperation was lax, and only a single area reported, Manchester/Stockport, but these measurements of several hundred factory boys and girls offered convincing evidence of environmental influence. Factory children were small at all ages, even below the third percentile of growth curves for British children of 1965 (Figure 4–6a). Their diminutive size, of some 3 to 9 centimeters less than that of children developing under more favorable circumstances, was sufficient evidence to influence the passage of the Factories Regulation Act. This law prohibited children under nine years of age from working in textile factories. It also stipulated that children under thirteen be allowed 1½ hours per day for rest and meals. Not much of an improvement considering the typical 16-hour work day, but it was a step forward in the recognition of the need for better treatment of children. These new regulations were seldom honored, and enforcement was weak, however. Child labor abuses remained a problem, as shown by the later measurements made in 1872; the heights of the factory children had changed little from those of forty years ago (Figure 4–6b).

This sorry state of child health was, perhaps one of the lowest points in British social history; in addition to child laborers in factories and mines, thousands of orphaned and vagrant children roamed the streets of every city. But social consciousness was awakened and reformers actively sought change. Slow improvements were made over the next decades. In addition to the factory acts limiting some of the worst child labor abuses, charitable organizations set up various shelters and hostels for orphaned children. One of these was the "Marine Society" founded to train future seamen for the navy, but mainly to provide some food and shelter for homeless vagabond boys of London. This organization is especially significant for our story because of the records kept of the boys' height throughout their

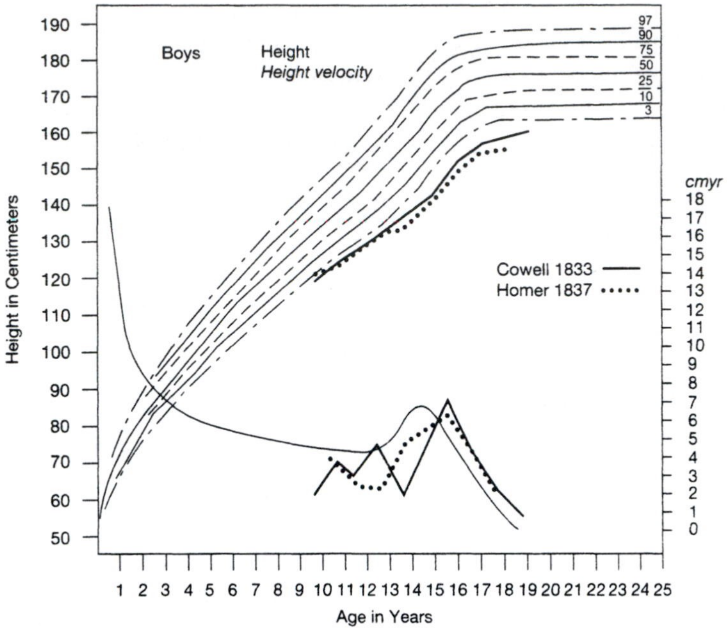

Figure 4–6a Heights of Factory Boys, England, 1833

From Tanner, J. M., 1981. Reprinted by permission of Cambridge University Press.

Figure 4–6b Heights of Factory Boys, England, 1870

From Tanner, J. M., 1981. Reprinted by permission of Cambridge University Press.

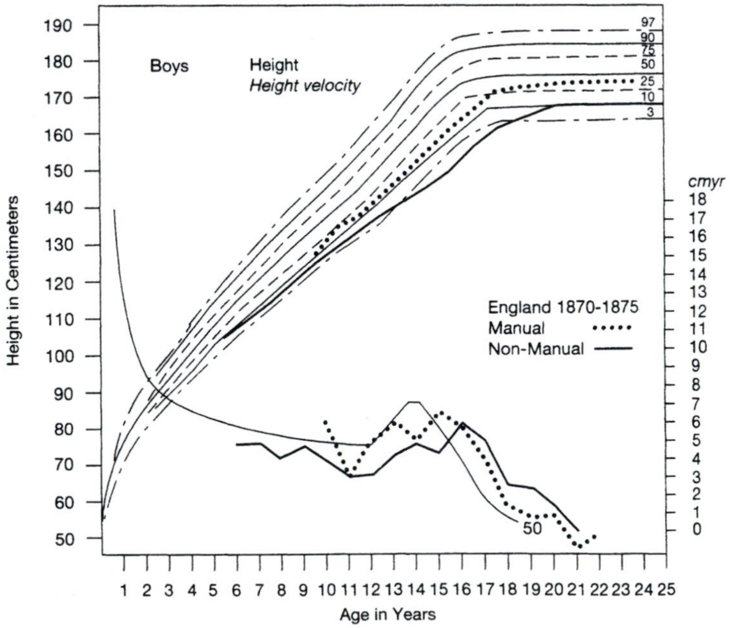

three to four years in training. These records can be read as evidence that the lot of male children improved, perhaps due to a combined effect of all the social reforms.

The heights of Marine Society recruits in the graphs in Figure 4–7 show no significant change between 1790 and 1810. Thereafter the increases in height of the fourteen- to sixteen-year-olds suggest there had been considerable improvements in growth and, by proxy, improvements in social change (Tanner, 1981). Of special note is the sharp increase in size following the end of the Napoleonic wars, when there were significant declines in food prices (Floud, et al., 1990). These improvements in social conditions apparently continued until 1850, followed by a decline over the next decade. Fifteen- and sixteen-year-olds declined in height by about 2 centimeters between 1850 and 1860. Some national change must have occurred in the preceding few years to arrest social improvements and slow down growth.

Child growth studies continued to be applied as a proxy for evaluating social conditions. Between 1878 and 1883, the heights and weights of 53,000

Figure 4–7 Heights of Marine Society Recruits, 1790–1860

From Tanner, J. M., 1981. Reprinted by permission of Cambridge University Press.

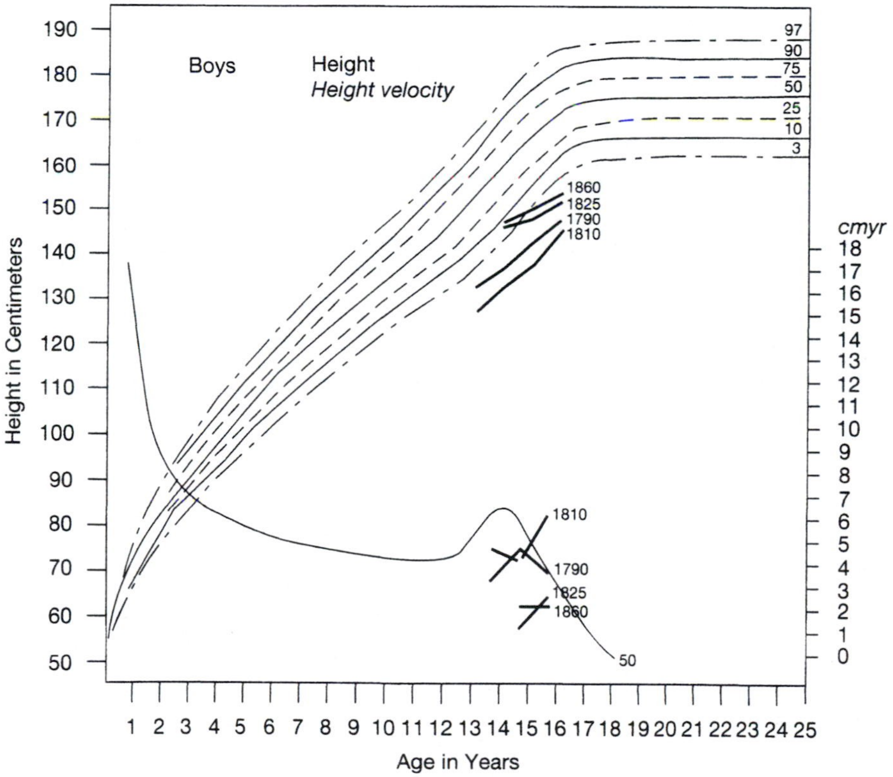

schoolchildren were taken. Their sizes differed, as expected, according to family economics. The eleven- to twelve-year-olds attending industrial schools were 12 centimeters shorter than those in public schools (a mark of higher family income). A refinement of the environmental influence question can be seen in a study twenty years later. Fourteen hundred children were measured in Edinburg, Scotland, and compared by living space the family occupied. Five-year-old boys from families living in a single room were 5 centimeters shorter than those who occupied four rooms. For thirteen-year-olds, the difference increased to 7.5 centimeters for boys and 10 centimeters for girls (Wohl,1983:58). The number of rooms provides a comparison of economic status and all its health-related factors, such as food quantity and child workload, of course. Most importantly is that the space available to a family influenced the spread of disease. The more cramped the quarters, the increased risk of disease transmission. This would affect the health of the child and retard growth.

The accumulation of these and other data from many studies of the health and welfare of children document some striking contrasts between generations and point to some significant trends. During the last half of the nineteenth century, some children were reaching maturity earlier and were larger at all ages than in previous generations. Distinct class differences in body size at all ages have been reported since at least the seventeenth century. When living conditions improved, so did the lot of children as marked by longitudinal trends depicted by the graphs in Figure 4–8. These graphs compare average heights of four groups, from age four to twenty-three and show a 15 centimeter increase in adult height since 1833. The group of boys measured in 1833 were factory hands whose growth was retarded in late childhood and adolescence. Their height at age fourteen was a full 20 centimeters less than the standard of 1965, but slow growth over a prolonged period made up for some of this deficit, as young adults continued to grow into their early twenties. This prolonged catch-up growth period suggests that depressing environmental effects are more influential on growth rate than on final size.

The welfare of children and their fate as adults has been well marked by many historical and fictional accounts. Their state of health and biological development extends the record further to establish that, while technological progress was being made, large segments of Europe's population were not benefiting from this progress. Even as living conditions declined with the rise of the industrial environment, the numbers of people increased as never before. This is somewhat of a paradox. Major diseases were being brought under control, food production and food imports increased, but the quality of the working class diet improved little. Sixty percent of their income was spent on a diet heavy in carbohydrates and fat, low in protein, few fresh vegetables, and deficient in vitamins (Tanner, 1986). Populations multiplied while not enough fit adult males could be

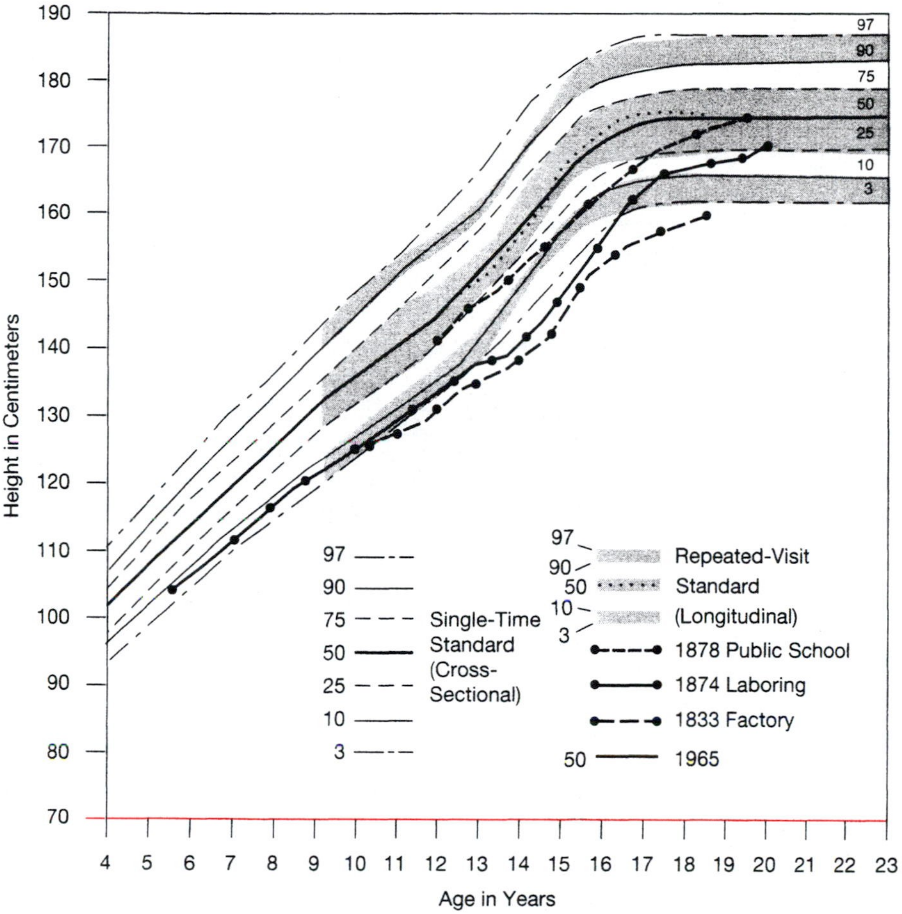

Figure 4–8 Secular Trend in Height: Class Differences

Secular trend in height is shown by surveys of the height of English boys in the years 1833, 1874, and 1965. Data are reproduced on a standard growth chart. "Single-time standard (cross sectional)" refers to the average result from cross-sectional surveys. "Repeated-visit standard (longitudinal)" refers to the average result from longitudinal surveys. The numbers 97, 90, 75, and so on indicate percent of the male population shorter than a given height.

From Tanner, J. M., "Growing Up," September 1973.

found to fill military needs. What then were the factors contributing to high fertility and low mortality that continued for at least a century in Europe?

DEMOGRAPHIC LINKAGES TO DEVELOPMENT

The period of the Industrial Revolution offers evidence that multiple linkages of complex social and technological events influenced population dynamics, environment, and, most importantly, the way in which we view the world and human ecology. The increases in food supply supported larger numbers of people, but these increases depended not just on locally grown (that is, European) food but on imports from distant lands. In the case of Britain, first Ireland and then Australia, India, and North America supplied the needs of this newly industrialized society (Table 4–5). Transportation via canal barges and then rail also allowed for wide distribution of food around Europe from key agricultural areas to industrial regions. This system worked effectively throughout most of the nineteenth century but not all areas could benefit equally. It failed to relieve the food crisis suffered in Northern Europe, for example, particularly in Norway and Sweden, who suffered a series of famines from 1867 to 1873. Relief for these populations could only be found in migration.

Emigration was an important component of the Industrial Revolution and was an essential linkage to development. It acted to relieve the strain on a nation in times of famine as in the classic case of Ireland and in the examples of other famine-struck countries. When crops failed and people had nowhere to turn in the nineteenth-century, migration, especially to the New World, was the option. Migration also acted as a safety valve to reduce the pressures of overpopulation. Between 1815 and 1914, 60 million Europeans migrated overseas, mainly to America. The largest numbers came from Germany, Ireland, and England until 1881, when the countries of origin shifted to eastern and southern Europe (Table 4–6). These immigrants were responding to pressures of home-limited economic opportunities or famine,

TABLE 4–5 Britain's Food Imports, the "Fuel" of the Industrial Revolution

Grains, Meat and Butter (value in £ 1000)		
Years	**Overseas**	**Ireland**
1814–1816	1,714	4,155
1824–1826	1,846	5,599
1834–1836	1,512	8,427
1844–1846	7,377	7,966

Source: Data adapted from Cippiolla, 1972; Thomas, B. 1985.

TABLE 4–6 Major European Migrations

Country	1821–1840	1841–1860	1861–1880	1881–1910
Austro-Hungary	—	—	80,769	3,091,692
Great Britain	100,889	691,018	1,154,939	1,604,936
Germany	159,215	1,386,299	1,506,650	2,299,620
Ireland	258,105	1,694,838	872,649	1,382,963
Norway	—	—	166,954	462,106
Russia	352	908	41,796	2,315.878
Sweden	*1,292	*34,834	153,589	867,576
Italy	2,662	11,101	67,484	3,006,079

*Norway and Sweden are combined for 1821–1840 and 1841–1860.

Source: Adapted from U.S. Census Bureau reports.

and were drawn by attractions of new lands. By 1891, 39 percent of those of Irish birth lived outside of Ireland, and during the first fifteen years of the twentieth century, migration from all of Europe was equivalent to about one-third of America's natural population increase. In this way, by changing its relation to the rest of the world and by urbanization, Europe was able to cope with its growing numbers. The population growth, migration, and increased reliance on food imports stimulated many social changes that began to affect lifestyles in the last quarter of the eighteenth century.

A DEMOGRAPHIC TRANSITION

Industrial development influenced a variety of social changes, affecting a transition from rapid to slow population growth. Europe's experience of this "demographic transition" has led to a general theory of the dynamics of population over a period of economic change. It may be described as a three-stage process: The *first* was a period of high birth and death rates typical of traditional preindustrial populations when periodic episodes of excess mortality held average growth to low levels. Societies enter a *second* stage during economic development, particularly industrial expansions, which stimulates marriage formation rates. Traditions of high fertility rates are continued, increasing crude birth rates (CBR). Improved sanitation, diet, shelter, and clothing contributed to better health and lowered mortality rates. This resulted in a net gain in people each year equal to the difference between the CBR and CDR, which averaged about 1 to 1½ percent in Western Europe. This population growth continued into the early twentieth century when both birth and death rates declined. Age at marriages rose, fertility declined (from a peak of 6.2 average births per woman living through her reproductive years down to 2.3 in Britain), and CBR fell, leading to a final stage. The *third* transition stage of slow or zero growth is one

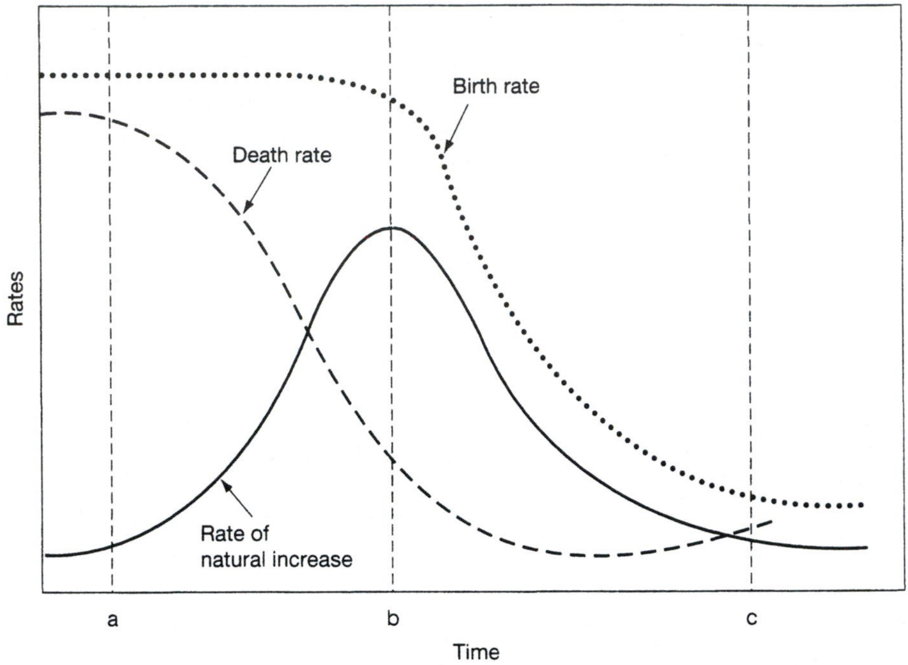

a = beginning of the transition
b = greatest difference between birth and death rates
c = end of the transition

Figure 4–9 Demographic Transition Model

From Chesnais, J., 1992. *The Demographic Transition: Stages, Patterns, and Economic Implications.* Reprinted by permission of Oxford University Press.

that most European countries have entered after a century and a half of moderate or rapid population increases. These countries have continued in this stage to this very day (Figure 4–9).

However, not all nations have followed the same schedule or pattern in their demographic transition (witness the exception of France mentioned earlier). As it industrialized in the mid-nineteenth century, France continued a fertility rate decline in parallel to death rate decline. This trend began in the previous century before industrialization for a variety of social customs and land tenure practices, a half century before it took hold elsewhere in Europe (Wrigley, 1969). France's population growth remained far below all other Western European countries for a combination of reasons—periodic acute economic pressures, slower industrialization, and smaller average family size (Clark, 1977).

Other exceptions were Sweden, Norway, and Russia, whose population growth appear to have been unrelated to industrialization. Russia's rapid increase in population occurred while there was little change in its socioeconomic structure and scant improvement in the living conditions of its people (Petersen, 1982). The rate of Russian population increase was greater than in any other European country by the middle of the nineteenth century, despite suffering the highest death rate. This high mortality was countered by an even higher birth rate, enabling the country to reach 100 million by 1900. The Scandinavian countries' population growth was propelled by improvements in agriculture, not by industrialization. When agricultural crises occurred in the nineteenth century, emigration provided relief as noted earlier.

Questions have been often raised about the reasons why populations, in general, begin to accelerate in growth at some point in their history. What were the major contributing factors? Industrialization, increase in food supply, and reduction of disease are the causes usually described but, since each nation or region has had unique demographic experiences, there are no easy answers. Russia, for example, grew nearly as rapidly as England but lagged far behind in its industrial development. Southern Europe, though a region of fertile soils and good climate, remained far outside of the mainstream of growth, as witnessed by the demographic record of Spain and Italy (Livi Bacci, 1968). While populations of Britain and Germany increased 166 percent and 142 percent, respectively, during the nineteenth century, Italy and Spain grew by only 77 percent and 33 percent over the same period. The relations of social development, cultural tradition, and economic growth to population dynamics of European regions during the nineteenth century still has not been fully explained (see Chesnais, 1992).

Britain's Population "Revolution": Why It Worked

The primary causes of Britain's population growth acceleration, begun during the "long eighteenth century," may be attributed to an overall fertility increase (Wrigley, 1983). Average age of marriage dropped from twenty-six to twenty-three years as the proportion of women who never married also fell from 15 to 7 percent. With the spread of industrialization, there were fewer barriers to marriage, and family formation rates went up. Expansion of urbanization contributed to a loosening of the social sanctions against extramarital relations: Illegitimate births tripled over the course of the nineteenth century. As a result, Wrigley and Schofield (1981) estimate that GRR (gross reproductive rate), the average number of daughters produced by women living through their reproductive years, rose from 1.98 to 2.94. Crude birth rates rose while there was a slow decline in mortality rates. This differential boosted Britain's annual population growth from less than 0.5 percent to 1.5 percent over several years, as mortality rates fell even further with the decline in frequency and severity of the major epidemics.

CONCLUSIONS

By 1900, after 150 years of rapid and dramatic technological changes, the world had become quite a different place. Oceans no longer were barriers to trade; giant ocean liners could now cross the Atlantic in a matter of days instead of weeks. Vast land distances were traversed by steam-driven trains over steel rails linking all major cities and continental areas. Raw materials, manufactured goods, and food stuffs were now transported readily between regions. Energy was cheap and plentiful in the form of coal and was soon to be supplemented, or even replaced, with petroleum. Communications between distant outposts of colonial empires could now be carried out at the speed of light by cable, telegraph, and the newly invented "wireless." Throughout the period of these developments, some of the world's peoples benefited more than others from the economic results of these technological achievements.

Starting from rural, peasant-driven agrarian societies with few cities, little industry, and a slow population growth, there was a rapid turnabout. Industrialization began and accelerated in growth from about the 1740s, and with it came radical changes in the economic and social structures of most of Europe and the United States. The major change, however, was in demography, more rapid population growth due to a number of the factors brought on by the Industrial Revolution. Not all parts of the world shared equally in these changes. Much of the New World and most of Asia continued to be sources of raw materials and food for Europe and the consumers of the manufactured goods. Most of Africa, because of its difficult climates and hostile environments, was only added to the list of European colonial conquests late in the nineteenth century. With the exception of Japan, the development of these areas of Asia, Africa, and South America was slow; most never entered into what we call industrialization; some are only starting now.

The nations of these regions make up what have been called the developing, lesser developed, or underdeveloped countries. They have continued to supply raw materials for industries elsewhere, a fact that has been the source of much debate. However, they have benefited from some of the features of industrialization, as did the rural, agrarian peoples of Europe 150 years ago. Control of epidemic diseases, provisions of basic health services, and, at times supplemental food stocks have lowered death rates and prolonged life in the nonindustrialized regions. This intervention by the Western world has contributed to rapid population growth, beginning in the twentieth century and continuing today. At the same time that the developed world has entered the final phase of the demographic transition, with balanced populations of slow or no growth, the underdeveloped world has remained in phase two of large annual increases. The results are all too clear; nations with limited or even declining resources and little prospect for industrialization are those nations with the greatest numbers of new people added each year.

This leads to a disproportionate distribution of the world's peoples, a subject of heated debate among those who view the issue in terms of nationality or ethnic identity. Some political analysts argue that the "native" ethnic groups will be overwhelmed by foreign immigrants of national origins different from the majority (the mention of "color" or "race" is usually avoided and substitute words are used instead). Other analysts, development specialists, avoid the direct confrontation of the immigration issue and advocate Third World industrial development to reduce the immigration flow and to move the regional populations into the final phase of the demographic transition. This repeatedly brings up questions of overpopulation, and family planning and medical care and interrelates them all within the sociopolitical framework. Few debates on population and development deal with the problems from an ecological perspective, however, even though a frequent comparison is made to the European experience of the Industrial Revolution.

We have become a very successful species, biologically speaking—our increase in numbers attest to this fact—but it has been achieved at great cost to world environments. Forests have been destroyed, water supplies polluted as well as the air we breathe, soils depleted, and whole regions rendered uninhabitable. A balance between humanity and its support system has not been reached. The human costs of this imbalance is the subject of this book, with the focus on the question of how to bring human needs in line with resources—the interrelationship between human needs and our environment.

Chapter 5

Population Dynamics

Some Basic Elements

In an ever-changing world, with over 227,000 new people added each day to the 5.9 billion already on this planet, the challenge is to explain not only these numbers but their distribution as well. Populations are increasing at a rate of 1 or 2 percent per year in some regions while, at the same time, there is little or no growth in other regions. The 1,178 million of the *More Developed Countries* **(MDC)**[1] had an increase of only one-tenth of a percent during 1998, while the 3,505 million people of the **LDC** (excluding China) added 70.1 million, a rate of 2 percent. The world's largest countries, China and India, must be considered separately from the other **LDC** since each follows a different demographic schedule. China's 1.242 billion people increased at a rate of just 1 percent throughout the 1990s, in contrast to India's nearly 2 percent increase of its 988 million citizens.

Contrasts are also seen in many other countries. Both Indonesia and Nigeria have large populations, with access to lands well endowed with natural resources. But differences in population dynamics could not be greater. Indonesia's 207.4 million population grew at half the annual rate of Nigeria's 121.8 million, who increased by 3 percent per year. Comparable differences are also seen between Mexico (97.5 million) and Brazil (162.1 million); both have lowered fertility and slowed their annual growth in the last decade, but Brazil has been more successful. Among the more-developed countries,

[1]The definitions of more developed and lesser developed regions follow the United Nations classification system. The MDC include all of Europe, North America, plus Australia, Japan, and New Zealand. All other regions and countries are classified as LDC.

there is less of a contrast but some population growth differences still exist; compare the United States with the United Kingdom, or Italy and Spain with France. Russia and the Ukraine, after the dissolution of the Soviet Union, are exceptional among the developed countries in their large annual net loss in population.

What may account for such diversity among nations? From a historical perspective, after more than a century of radical technological and social changes, we should be able to appreciate the impact of industrialization on population dynamics. The contrasts of demographic pattern have often been explained by reference to economic development, using the experiences of nineteenth-century Europe as a model. Complete understanding of these different demographic patterns still escape us, however.

As explained in the last chapter, increasing efficiency in agriculture and industry contributed to radical social changes affecting the dynamics of population, mainly the rising birth rates with concurrent lowering mortality. The review of these events over the past century contributed to a theory of linkage between population and development that attempted to explain rapid population growth followed by a slowing and then an equilibrium within a few generations. In other words, a transition bringing into balance the birth and death rates. Though unrecognized at the time, Western European populations experienced such a transition during the nineteenth century. Such experience has provided a foundation for a broad theory of population dynamics.

This theory of demographic transition has a long and controversial history. First introduced by Thompson in 1929 and elaborated and refined by Notestein in 1946, this explanation of population dynamics as linked to socioeconomic factors has been a popular but unproven concept with some contradictions, due in part to the variation among national patterns (see Petersen, 1982). Nevertheless, there have been continuous attempts to apply the transition theory to populations of the underdeveloped world, as if all would or could respond to socioeconomic change in the same way. The opposite, of course, has been true; there have been a variety of responses that must be studied.

The focus of such studies is, of course, the inhabitants, or population, of a certain defined region. The term *population,* however, has several meanings. To the pollster or census taker, it is a sample of a particular group of people within a geographic area, or some subdivision based on income, religion, or ethnic group. Demographers can use a similar definition; a collection of individuals that form a dynamic unit varying between generations in numbers of births and deaths, fertility rates, and divisions by age groups and by sex distribution. This use of population contrasts somewhat to that concept of the geneticist, whose concern is with kinship groups that constitute a *breeding population*—that collection of individuals forming a reproductive unit, the unit in which reproductive decisions are made.[2] The demographic population may be the same as a breeding population, but the demographic unit most often will encompass a diversity of large multiethnic communities in many nations. This requires that a demographer consider "population" in a broader sense, recognizing the social, religious, and economic, as well as biological, factors that organize people into groups or classes.

Human ecology must encompass all of these categories (political, geographic, and biological) in the study of those factors that influence variability in population size and composition between generations. If we are to consider human adaptation to environmental variables, we also must think in terms of how a population constitutes a community with its structure and institutions. Behavior and the composition of the group as a breeding population is also an important concern. The number of individuals entering or leaving a population each year or each generation is of particular interest, whether through births or deaths or through immigration or emigration. The proportion or numbers of each sex in each age interval is of significance, for these data enable projections to be made of the size and composition in the next generations. Given such projections, estimates of future needs of a population may be forecast, and resource limitations or restrictions can be predicted.

To start with, it is necessary to recognize that biological populations are ever-changing dynamic units. There may be similarities in numbers of people in different generations, but age distributions and sex ratios can vary widely because each generation is a unique composition of individuals. For example, there was a larger proportion of individuals in the 30–39 age group in the United States between 1980–1991 compared to earlier periods of the twentieth century. This proportional increase, with the large number of women in their reproductive years, was the result of the high fertility rates during the period of 1945–1964.

Europe has also undergone radical changes in population composition over the last half century. Declining birth rates have led to an aging population; the percentage of the population over sixty years of age (14 percent) is nearly equal to the proportion of those under fifteen (19 percent). By contrast, most of the less-developed countries have a young population, 36 percent or more, under the age of fifteen years reflecting the high fertility rates and rapid population growth experienced over the past two decades. But even among these nations there are numerous contrasts; some, like Thailand, have reduced birth rates by half within the last decade while others (Kenya, Nigeria, Egypt) have declined slowly.

This study of intergenerational changes may be termed population

[2] Breeding populations consist of groups that exchange mates each generation and are relatively isolated from other groups. The breeding population may be small, only a few hundred individuals, with a high inbreeding coefficient, or it may be large with hundreds of thousands of potential mates.

dynamics and applies demography in its broadest sense (see Ross, 1982; Wilson, 1985). Demography (the quantitative study of human populations) is expanded to encompass biological and social aspects, including those variables affecting change. For example, industrial development can increase population growth, as we have described, for that period of the Industrial Revolution, or it may depress fertility rates, as during development of certain Third World nations today. Differing sanitation systems affect health (measured by morbidity and mortality) and, in turn, affect population just as urbanization influences changes in class and ethnic divisions. This broader demographic approach then becomes a means of measuring degrees of successful environmental adaptation.

From a broad historical perspective, as discussed in the last chapter, populations give an impression of unity with a smooth continuity between generations. The demographic data observed over longer time spans averages out much of the short-term changes. In fact, populations appear to have a rhythm of motion, rising or falling over a human generation time length of twenty to twenty-five years. Such rhythm is even more apparent when an ecological approach is taken, defining a population in biological and social terms in relation to their subsistence base. Considering population dynamics from this perspective, an intriguing point was raised by Schofield (1986). "A crucial question is how it (a population system) can change without losing the ability to function or its capacity to adapt."

SOME BASICS OF POPULATION CHANGE

Since a great many factors influence human survival from birth to death, alterations in the social or physical environments have profound effects on population composition and size. These influences may be slight or intense or the affect on one stage of the human life cycle may be more intense than another. Infants are at greater risk of dying than are adolescents, as evinced by the comparative mortality rates of each group. After reaching adulthood, the risk of dying declines until later in life, when the mortality for the older age group increases exponentially. The mortality experience of each age group changes over time as living standards vary, so the experiences of one generation differ from another. In addition, mortality risks vary among ethnic minorities, which are generally higher than the national averages, and ethnic groups' mortality rates have declined more slowly over the decades of this century.

Birth and Death Rates

The first and most basic consideration is the rate of addition or loss of people each year, measured as a fraction of the total population. Typically, this proportion is given as a rate per thousand. The number of births is given as a crude birth rate **(CBR),** or births per thousand population. Likewise, the total number of deaths each year is converted to a crude death rate**(CDR),** or deaths per thousand population. The CBR minus CDR gives the rate of natural increase **(RNI),** a percentage of gain in population size each year (Table 5–1). In mid-1998, the United States had 270.2 million people with a CBR of fifteen and a CDR of nine, which equaled to an RNI of 0.6 percent.

TABLE 5–1 Population Increase and Doubling Time for Selected Countries

Region Country	Population (millions)	CBR[1]	CDR[2]	RNI[3]	DT[4]
World	5,926.0	23	9	1.4	49
More Developed	1,178.0	11	10	0.1	548
Less Developed	4,748.0	26	9	1.7	40
Less Developed[5]	3,505.0	29	10	2.0	35
Africa	763.0	40	15	2.5	27
Egypt	65.5	28	6	2.2	32
Ethiopia	58.4	46	21	2.5	28
Keyna	28.3	33	13	2.0	35
Nigeria	121.8	45	15	3.0	23
South Africa	38.9	27	11	1.6	43
Asia[6]	2,361.0	26	8	1.8	39
Bangladesh	123.4	27	8	1.8	38
China	1,242.5	17	7	1.0	69
India	988.7	27	9	1.9	37
Indonesia	207.4	24	8	1.5	45
Japan	126.4	10	7	0.2	330
Pakistan	141.9	39	11	2.8	25
Philippines	75.3	30	7	2.3	30
Vietnam	78.5	19	7	1.2	57
Western Europe	183.0	11	10	0.1	517
Germany	82.3	10	10	–0.1	—
France	58.8	12	9	0.3	210
U.Kingdom	59.1	13	11	0.2	433
Eastern Europe	307.0	9	13	–0.4	—
Poland	38.7	11	10	0.1	630
Russia	146.9	9	14	–0.5	—
Ukraine	50.3	9	15	–0.6	—
Latin America	500.0	25	7	1.8	38
Argentina	36.1	19	8	1.1	62
Brazil	162.1	22	8	1.4	48
Mexico	97.5	27	5	2.2	32
North America	301.0	14	8	0.6	117
United States	270.2	15	9	0.6	116

[1]Crude birth rate
[2]Crude death rate
[3]Rate of natural increase in percent
[4]Time to double population if the current RNI is continued
[5]Excluding China
[6]Excluding China

Source: Adapted from World Population Data Sheet, 1998.

In Europe, Germany's 82.3 million population in 1998 was nearly stable, with a zero or slightly negative growth due to the nation's CBR of ten balanced by a CDR of ten. Russia and the Ukraine suffered a net reduction in population. These slow to negative growth examples stand out in stark contrast to the many fast-growth nations. Mexico, with its 97.5 million people, had a rate of natural increase of 2 percent because of a lowering of death rate to five while continuing to maintain a high birth rate of twenty-seven over the same period. Indonesia's 207.4 million also showed high growth (RNI of 1.5 percent), and Pakistan's 142 million were increasing at a rate of nearly 3 percent.

These birth and death rates are referred to as "crude" since no consideration is given to age structure. An older population, one with a larger percentage of people past middle age, would have a higher number of deaths and a lower number of births in contrast to a population with a greater percentage below age twenty. The young populations of the less-developed nations have maintained high birth rates through the twentieth century, as in the examples of Mexico, Pakistan, and Indonesia. The absolute number of births are expected to be even higher in the near future as the youths under fifteen years old reach reproductive age. Though these crude birth and death rates do not take into account the age disparity between populations, they are easily derived and are useful indicators of a population status. These simple measures serve as a first step in demographic studies, providing a predictor of future growth.

Of special interest is the possibility of projection of a population's size in future generations. The number of the people estimated by the end of a given year can be calculated by multiplying RNI times the population size. If the United States continues to grow at 0.6 percent throughout 1998, then there will be 271.82 million people by year's end, not counting gains from immigration (about 800,000 at current rates). However, it is a bit more complicated to estimate size after several years of increase at this rate. The new millions must be entered into the calculation, and each year the growth of 0.6 percent results in a larger number. There will be 1.62 million added by the end of the second year (0.006 × 270.2), 1.631 by the end of the third year (0.006 × 271.82), and so on. This is an exponential growth, like the compound interest of a savings account with money accumulating according to a simple formula. This same formula enables calculation of population size after any number of years of a known rate of increase. There are actually two formulas, but the most frequently used is: $\mathbf{N_t = N_0 \times e^{rt}}$, which is a mathematical statement of population size(N) after time (t) with an increase at the rate (r), or RNI, will be N_t. This means that the U.S. population, growing at its 1998 rate (0.6 percent) for ten years, will have 286.91 million people, or 304.65 million after twenty years. A quick way to measure population growth potential given a certain RNI, especially useful for comparisons between fast- and slow-growth nations, is to calculate the doubling time (DT).

Doubling Time

The number of years it takes a country to double its size, given a certain rate of growth, is calculated by use of the same formula as above, transposed to indicate a doubling in number: $N_t/N_o = e^{rt}$. Since $N_t/N_o = 2$ (N_t is double N_o), then $2 = e^{rt}$. Taking the ln of both sides of the equation the result is $0.693 = rt$ (the natural log or ln of 2 is 0.693). Solving the equation to find t gives $t = 0.693/r$. In plain language: Dividing this number (the ln of 2) by the U.S. annual growth rate(0.6%) gives 115 years as the time needed to double its population. Since 0.693 (ln of 2) is close to 0.70, a quick way of estimating any population's doubling time is to divide 70 by a population's RNI.[3] Thus, Mexico, if it continues to grow at its current rate of 2.2 percent per year, will double in just thirty-two years (70 divided by 2.2 percent). The fifth column of Table 5–1 gives a list of examples of world regions and several select countries with varying growth rates and doubling times.

Infant Mortality

The numbers of infants dying during their first year varies among nations, social classes, and ethnic groups. This infant mortality rate **(IMR),** measured in deaths of infants under one year per thousand live births, relates to a range of environmental and social conditions influencing the health of pregnant women and their newborns. Diet, disease, living space, climate, and female workload are among the principle factors in which each society and generation differs. Further, the IMR directly affects demographic changes, influences fertility rates, and may place large demands on future resources.

Among developed nations today, we have come to expect low rates of about six to eight per thousand live births, a number that represents a major achievement of medical care, public health, and the treatment of pregnant women. It has not always been so, however. Even as nineteenth-century living conditions improved and expanding scientific knowledge forced down crude death rates, infant mortality scarcely changed. In Western Europe, 15 percent, or 150 per thousand infants, died before their first birthday, most during the first four weeks of life **(neonatal period).** This rate remained fairly constant well into the twentieth century. England, for example, continued to suffer with an IMR of around 150 from 1841 until 1914, when a gradual decline brought infant death rates down to modern levels. IMR in the United States was also high during this period and remained so until about 1918 when the rate began its modern decline nearly in parallel with England (UK) and other Western European nations. By 1922, the IMR was down to seventy-seven and decreased sharply each decade until it was

[3]This is a most widely used formulation using the natural log **e** or ln. Another formula may be used with the common log (log), and the results will be nearly the same. The U.S. doubling time is given as 115.86 years instead of 115.5 years, as calculated by the natural log formula.

reduced to eighteen by 1975. Other developed countries of the world followed this pattern, and in 1998, most IMR clusters around eight or nine per thousand live births while Sweden, and Japan dipped below five (Table 5–2a). This dramatic reduction, especially during the last fifty years, suggests that there were major social changes and improvements in health care. Unfortunately, many of the lesser-developed countries have not fared as well and have retained the high levels typical of the more-developed countries decades ago. Table 5–2b lists two groups of twenty countries by the highest and by the lowest infant mortality rates, as of 1998.

Grouping together all Lesser Developed Countries (LDC), their infant mortality rates average out to sixty-four. If China, with its low rate of thirty-one, is removed from the equation, then the LDC average jumps to seventy per thousand, which is a reflection of the wide range among those countries classified as lesser developed (LDC) by the United Nations. Afghanistan ranks the highest with 150, and Mexico at 28 is one of the lowest of the lesser-

TABLE 5–2a Infant Mortality Reduction Since 1900 (select countries)

Regions	1900	1920	1975	1998
More Developed	—	—	—	8.0
Less Developed	—	—	—	64.0
Europe	—	—	24.0	10.0
Germany	229	90	18.0	4.9
France	160	90	16.0	5.1
Russia	252	198	26.0	17.0
Sweden	99	63	10.0	3.9
United Kingdom	154	77	18.0	6.1
Africa	—	—	156.0	91.0
Egypt	—	—	103.0	63.0
Kenya	—	—	135.0	62.0
Nigeria	—	—	180.0	84.0
Asia	—	—	102.0	57.0
China	—	—	55.0	31.0
India	200	212	139.0	72.0
Indonesia	—	—	125.0	66.0
Japan	155	172	12.0	3.8
Philippines	—	—	78.0	34.0
Latin America	—	—	79.0	36.0
Argentina	—	—	60.0	22.2
Brazil	—	—	94.0	43.0
Peru	—	—	110.0	43.0
Mexico	—	—	61.0	28.0
United States	162	85	18.0	7.0

Source: Data adapted from World Prospects, UN, 1986, Population Data Sheet; Langer, 1975.

TABLE 5–2b Infant Mortality Rates, Countries by Rank

Rank	Lowest Country		Highest Country	
1.	Finland	3.5	Afghanistan	150
2.	Japan	3.8	Mozambique	134
3.	Sweden	3.9	Ethiopia	128
4.	Norway	4.0	Iraq	127
5.	Switzerland	4.7	Angola	124
6.	Spain	4.7	Somalia	122
7.	Austria	4.8	Cambodia	116
8.	Germany	4.9	Rwanda	114
9.	France	5.1	Zambia	109
10.	Australia	5.3	Congo (Zaire)	106
11.	Ireland	5.5	Brundi	105
12.	Netherlands	5.7	Laos	97
13.	Italy	5.8	Pakistan	91
14.	Denmark	5.8	Nigeria	84
15.	Belgium	5.8	Myanmar (Burma)	83
16.	Czech Republic	5.9	Bangladesh	82
17.	United Kingdom	6.1	Uganda	81
18.	Canada	6.3	Nepal	79
19.	Portugal	6.9	Yemen	77
20.	United States	7.0	Hati	74

Source: Data adapted from Population Bulletin data sheet, 1998.

developed nations. Within this broad range are countries of the African continent with an average of 91 (for a range of 55 to 104), Southeast Asia with 57 (for a range of 14 to 112)[4], and Latin America and the Caribbean with an average of 36 (6 to 75). The numbers change from year to year as conditions improve or deteriorate.

Averages can divert attention from real differences even in the best documented surveys. Minority groups may suffer two or three times a national rate, and there are significant differences between rural and urban areas, reflecting a harshness of life that is greater in some areas than in others. The vast nation of India, with its 988 million, may serve as an example of the diversity in quality of life and the resultant effects on infant mortality rates. The Population Reference Bureau reports an IMR of 72 for India, mid-1998, down from 122 a decade before. This is among the highest rates in the world, but an examination of data from urban centers and individual states offer a clearer perspective for this demographic marker.

India's urban populations record an IMR of forty-five while the rural areas are listed at eighty-two (mid-1998). The Indian state of Kerala, with its 26+ million in 1988, lost 27 infants for every 1,000 born alive, a low figure, comparing favorably to several European countries at the time. By contrast,

[4]The small states of Brunei, population 300,000 and Singapore, population 3.9 million, actually have rates and economies that place them in the MDC category but are counted in the SE Asian average.

the highest rate was found among the 132 million of Uttar Pradesh. Seven of the other states also record figures in the 100+ range. None of the remaining twelve Indian states come close to the low infant mortality rate seen in Kerala. Such differences raise several questions about the divergence in environmental and social conditions found in each region.[5]

Within many of the more-developed countries, there are also divergent demographic factors including widely differing infant mortality rates between national regions and among sub-population units. The Soviet Union, before and following its breakup into the several republics, can serve as an example.[6] An infant mortality rate of eighty was reported in 1950 for the entire USSR, a figure two to three times as high as that for countries of Western Europe. Within a decade, the rate was brought down to thirty-five, and the decline continued into the 1970s and hovered at about twenty-four. Then there was a turnaround, and the IMR began to climb again, passing a peak of thirty-six in 1982, then a decline to seventeen where it remains today—even after the separation of the republics (see Table 5–3). The status of infant health and mortality rates among the several regions and republics is quite different and covers a broad range, from twelve in European Belarus to forty-two in the Central Asian republic of Turkmenistan.[7]

Indigenous peoples diverge considerably from national averages, and they have suffered a high rate of infant loss through much of the twentieth century, while their nation's mortality declined. Table 5–4 lists a selection of populations along with comparisons to the national rates. Note the contrasts in several cases. The gaps are widest in the developed countries of United States, Canada, and Australia, where indigenous people remained well above national rates even as they declined from a reported high in the recent past. The Canadian Inuit (Eskimo) had an infant mortality rate of 150–180 by midcentury and rose to a peak of 250 in 1956, a time when they began to congregate around radar construction sites for most of the year.[8] From this frighteningly high peak of infant mortality, the rate began to decline rapidly to ninety-four by 1962 and then eighty-four by 1967. Though still high com-

---

[5]Data on individual Indian states is taken from The India Population Data sheet, 1988, S. B Manti, Slippery Rock University, Penn.

[6]Because of the inconsistent reporting and secrecy imposed by the former Soviet bureaucracy, demographic data has been hard to obtain. Some of the best interpretations have been offered by Murray Feshbach, a specialist on Russian population. His work over the past decades on Soviet population and environmental conditions is summarized in *Ecocide in the USSR* (see Feshbach and Friendly, 1992).

[7]For a discussion of the rising infant mortality rate of the USSR prior to the breakup, see Davis and Feshbach, 1980. See also the *Statistical Handbook of Former USSR*, 1992.

[8]During the 1950s, the U.S. and Canada cooperated in the construction of a network of radar stations stretching across the continent above the Arctic Circle—the DEW line. The purpose was to detect incoming aircraft or missiles that might be launched from the Soviet Union. The food and shelter, and later jobs, offered by these facilities attracted many Inuit. The drastic shift from their traditional diet and sustained contact with microbes exerted a heavy toll.

TABLE 5–3 Russia and Former Soviet Republics: Some Demographic Markers, 1998

Region	Population (millions)	CBR	CDR	RNI	IMR	TFR	GNP
Eastern Europe							
Russia	146.9	9	14	–0.5	17	1.2	2,410
Belarus	10.2	9	13	–0.4	12	1.3	2,070
Moldova	4.2	12	12	0.1	20	1.8	590
Ukraine	50.3	9	15	–0.6	14	1.3	1,200
Northern Europe							
Estonia	1.4	9	13	–0.4	10	1.3	3,080
Latvia	2.4	8	14	–0.6	16	1.2	2,300
Lithuania	3.7	11	12	–0.1	10	1.4	2,280
Western Asia							
Armenia	3.8	13	7	0.6	14	1.6	630
Azerbaijan	7.7	17	6	1.1	19	2.1	480
Georgia	5.4	11	7	0.4	17	1.6	850
South Central Asia							
Kazakstan	15.6	15	10	0.5	25	1.9	1,350
Kyrgyzstan	4.7	22	8	1.5	28	2.8	550
Tajikistan	6.1	22	5	1.7	32	2.9	340
Turkmenistan	4.7	24	7	1.7	42	2.9	940
Uzbekistan	24.1	26	6	2.0	26	3.2	1,010

Note: Crude birth rate (CBR), Crude death rate (CDR), Rate of Natural Increase (RNI), Infant Mortality Rate (IMR), Fertility Rate (TFR), Per Capita (GNP).

Source: Adapted from World Population Data Sheet, 1998.

pared to Canadian or U.S. rates of twenty-seven, it was a vast improvement (Lum et al., 1986). Similar experiences have been seen among native Australians, whose infant death rates once exceeded 168 and have since declined to twenty-six, three times the Euro-Australian average (Kenen, 1987).

Reductions of infant mortality rates for these indigenous people were the result of many factors. A shift to a more sedentary life, reduced female workloads, improved diets, cleaner water, and an access to medical services are among them. But experiences of these populations have varied so widely that no one group of factors may explain all of the reductions; the Arctic peoples (Inuit) experiences were quite different than those of the hunting nomads of Southern Africa (the San). In some cases, access to contraception has allowed wider birth spacing and thus improved the survival chances of each newborn. In other examples, an increased supply of nutritious weaning foods contributed to early weight gain of the infant, improving survival chances. Greater access to prenatal and neonatal medical care also has become an important factor in the health of indigenous populations as they shifted away from their traditional lifestyle.

TABLE 5–4 Infant Mortality Rates, Indigenous People and Other Minorities

Population	Rate	Year
Africa		
San	120.0	1960s
Turkana	109.0	1967–76
Kenya(all)	62.0	1998
Australia		
Aboriginal	138.0	1965
Aboriginal	51.6	1976
Aboriginal	26.4	1981
European	18.5	1965
Papua New Guinea		
Murapin	85.0	1966
National	77.0	1998
South America		
Yanomama	131.0	1959–69
Yanomama	78.0	1970–79
Yanomama	209.0	1980–86
Peru (national)	43.0	1998
Brazil (national)	43.0	1998
Venezuela (national)	20.9	1998
Canada		
Inuit	150–180.0	1950s
Inuit	84.0	1967
Inuit	58.2	1980
Canada (national)	27.0	1967
Canada (national)	6.3	1998
United States		
Inuit (SW Alaska)	102.6	1960s
Inuit (SW Alaska)	17.1	1980
Native American (all)	36.6	1965
Native American (all)	16.1	1977
United States (natl.)	24.7	1965
United States (natl.)	14.1	1977
United States (natl.)	7.0	1998
United States (Black)	16.84	1992
United States (White)	6.92	1992

Sources: Wadsworth, 1984; Sindiga, 1985; Population Reference Bureau,1998; Kenen, 1987; Thomson, 1984; Sinnett et al., 1981; Early and Peters, 1990; Condon, 1991; Thouez et al., 1989; Lum et al., 1986; National Center for Health Statistics, 1992.

Understanding the multiplicity of factors requires careful review of well-recorded data and, for this, we must turn to the more-developed countries. The nations of Western Europe, the United States, and Japan have made great strides in delivery of health services and in the care of pregnant women and of newborns. Fewer than eight of every thousand infants are lost before their first birthday. But among this select group of low IMR countries, the largest and wealthiest, the United States, ranks twenty-second; that is, twenty-one other countries have lower IMRs. This represents a decline from seventh place in the 1950s, as the United States reduced their infant mortality rate more slowly than did most other industrialized countries.

The national IMR for the United States is seven but the distribution is quite broad among the states. The highest IMR is recorded in the District of Columbia (16.2), Mississippi (9.9), and Louisiana (9.7) and the lowest rates are found in Hawaii, California, and New York and also in the smaller western states of Montana, North Dakota, and Idaho. What may account for these differences? Is it economics, religion, or that category so often applied to explain patterns of sociocultural differences—race and ethnicity—responsible? The degree of urbanization is also a consideration since residence patterns and population density influence access to health care. Reviewing these possibilities and seeking answers to the question of why should some regions of the United States be so different from others leads to consideration of some of the basics of infant and maternal health.[9]

One factor that has been mentioned often is the frequency of teenage pregnancies. Even though the rate has been falling (Figure 5–1), the United States still has the highest among the developed countries, 58.1 per thousand women ages fifteen to nineteen, compared to only 11.1 for Germany (Ahlburg and de Vita, 1992). Also, as teen pregnancies have declined, the percent of births to unmarried mothers is on the rise. It was 33 percent of all births in 1995, and the number is even higher among minority women, up to 72 percent (Bianchi and Spain, 1996).

The relationships among maternal age, marital status, and infant mortality form a complex web of biological, medical, and social factors that are only just becoming appreciated. We can start with the age factor and note that the lack of biological maturity of an adolescent mother (seventeen years or younger) predisposes her to giving birth to an underweight infant. That is, the subadult female will more frequently give birth to a infant whose weight is below 2,500 grams(5.5 lbs). Birth weight is a critical marker of fetal development, since low birth weight infants are at greater risk of dying during the first twelve months, especially during the first four-week (neonatal)

[9]The demographic data reported by state or region is now more frequently divided by race (African American, white, etc.) and by ethnic groups (Hispanic, Native American, Pacific Islander, etc.). These classifications are not consistent nor are they meaningful in regards to genetic composition or degrees of ancestry, since it is a matter of self-identification. Even then, the divisions do show significant differences in mortality and morbidity rates.

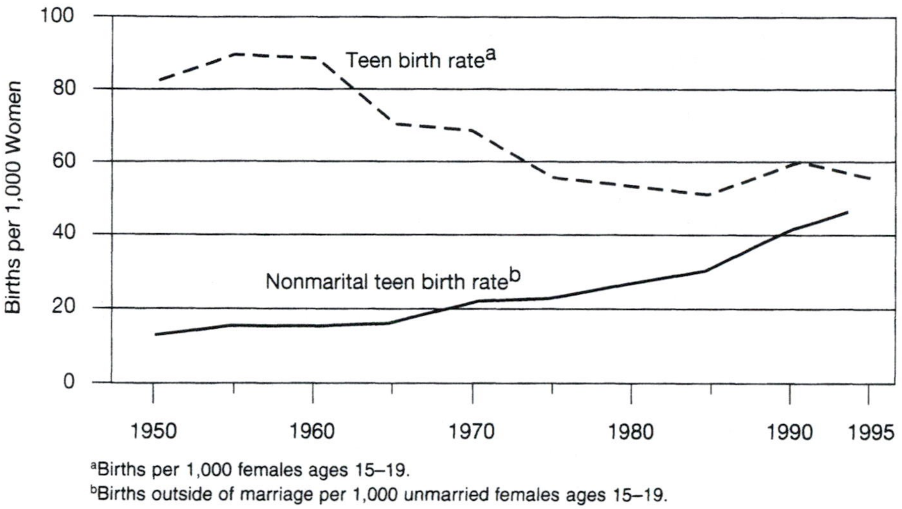

Figure 5–1 Birth Rates for Teenage Mothers

From Bianchi, S. M. et al., 1996. Reprinted by permission of Population Reference Bureau, Inc.

period. For comparison, less than 0.5 percent of infants greater than 2,500 grams die during their first year; 10.2 percent of those weighing between 1,500 and 2,500 grams, and 45.3 percent of the infants of very low birth weight (under 1,500 grams) are lost (Luke et al., 1993). The United States produces a larger percent of infants in these low birth weight ranges than other developed countries (Miller, 1985). Higher rates of teenage pregnancies is but one of the contributing factors, and the mother's race is believed to be another. In a large complex society such as the United States, race is too often used for identification and too carelessly applied to questions of health or habits. As a result, race becomes a kind of a code word for socioeconomic status and is, by default, synonymous with underclass. The same usage generally applies to ethnic or minority group labels.

Maternal health, prenatal care, and race (or socioeconomic class) are often cited as affecting newborn health. Poor diet, smoking, and alcohol and drug abuse are listed, among other more serious influences, on maternal health. Teenagers as a group are less likely to be watchful of their health and, especially if unmarried and with little family support, are less likely to seek prenatal care. The net result is: The higher the rate of unmarried adolescent pregnancies, the higher the rate of high risk births. In fact, those states with the highest percentage of low birth weight infants are those with the greatest number of teenage pregnancies, the lowest incomes, and the highest infant mortality.

Encompassing all of these considerations are two closely interrelated factors—maternal ethnicity and socioeconomic position. Studies of maternal health and infant mortality rates often emphasize the "racial" differences, noting the higher rates among African Americans, Hispanic and Native American groups. Low birth weight infants are twice as frequent among African Americans as among Whites, just as is the rate of teenage pregnancies. These two conditions contribute to the higher infant mortality rate among this minority group. Seldom compared, however, are economics, education, household size, and place of residence. When these socioeconomic conditions are factored into the infant health equation, the differences between "White" and "non-White" groups diminish. That is, if income levels, place of residence, and access to prenatal care are considered, than the ethnicity factor diminishes to insignificant levels. The differences among race/ethnic groups are frequently those of education and poverty. As emphasized by a large study in Los Angeles County, the rise in the numbers of high risk teenage mothers and the increase in low birth weight infants was a response to socioeconomic deterioration (Gould and LeRoy, 1988).

Infant health relates not to ethnicity and poverty as much as to the delivery of quality health care. This has been made clear by the example of Sweden, the world's leader in prenatal care and one of the first countries to decrease infant mortality to below ten per thousand. Sweden has admitted many immigrants from high IMR countries of Eastern Europe and the Middle East over the last few decades. These people fill the many menial jobs in an advanced industrial society, and they occupy the lowest socioeconomic status. Yet, their health, especially that of infants and children, is excellent, and there has been no lowering of the national averages (Miller, 1985). Sweden's experience has demonstrated the importance of health care delivery, and it counters those arguments that have emphasized race and ethnicity as causal factors influencing infant health.

A similar example is provided by the reduction of infant mortality rates achieved in several low income countries because of their attention to provision of health care. Low levels of infant deaths have been achieved by Costa Rica where IMR fell to 11.8 in 1998 from 18.9 a decade ago. Sri Lanka likewise has been able to reduce infant mortality (16.5 down from 30.5), even with a low economic level, bitter political divisions, and civil war between the two dominant ethnic groups. Cuba has also made gains in infant and maternal health despite an economic decline after the loss of foreign aid from Russia.[10] On the other hand, a rich economy is no guarantee of good health and low mortality. Saudi Arabia, despite its oil wealth and vast public expenditures, still has a comparatively high IMR of twenty-nine. The infant mortality differences between these and other countries are more than a matter of per capita income; female education and health care delivery seem to be the critical factors.

---

[10]See Chesnais, 1992; World Population Data Sheet, 1998.

FERTILITY AND FERTILITY RATES

Critical to any population study is the consideration of fertility rates. The use of crude birth rate is helpful as an initial step but for more accurate depiction of growth or growth potential, a measure of a population's fertility and female age composition is necessary. This measure is taken as the average number of live births to females in their reproductive years. Since almost all births are to mothers between fifteen and forty-nine years of age, this is considered as a standard age range for calculating fertility rates.

The total number of children born during the year to women in this age range is a relatively easy measure to obtain and is called the *General Fertility Rate* (GFR) and is calculated as the total number of births per thousand women ages fifteen to forty nine. This ratio considers the age factor and allows for comparisons between populations so predictions of sizes of future generations may be made. The greater number of women within this age group, the greater the reproductive potential compared to those populations with higher proportions of females of age groups above or below the reproductive life span.

Whenever a census has recorded the numbers of births by age of the mother, an *Age Specific Birth Rate* (ASFR) may be calculated. To facilitate the calculations, reproductive age span is divided into five-year intervals, and the births per thousand women in each interval is listed. Typically, female fecundity (biological ability to conceive) is low for the first few years following menarche and then rises during young adulthood. A peak is reached somewhere between ages twenty to twenty-nine. It is during this middle period of reproductive life span when conception is most likely and when the highest fertility rates (marked by live births) occur in any population. After age twenty-nine, these rates decline rapidly as women approach menopause, but there are wide ranges of variation recorded among the several diverse populations listed in Table 5–5. Some of the "natural" fertility rates are higher in the adolescent age group and continue at a high rate past the thirty-five to thirty-nine interval. Note the fertility listed for Mexico and for the Mormons and Hutterites.

"Natural Fertility"

Human fecundity is high though seldom fully realized except in the most extraordinary cases. Because the human gestation period is nine months (the duration from conception through the growth and development of the embryo and fetus), a woman could theoretically give birth every year. This would mean that given a reproductive life span of thirty-four years and regular intercourse throughout this time, a single birth each year would result in thirty-four children. Such a record never has been documented, though there are many instances where women have had twenty or even more chil-

TABLE 5–5 Natural Fertility Rates

	Age Intervals							
Groups	**15–19**	**20–24**	**25–29**	**30–34**	**35–39**	**40–44**	**45–49**	**TFR**
Botswana	0.127	0.213	0.203	0.187	0.146	0.082	0.037	5.00
Hutterites	0.300	0.550	0.502	0.447	0.357	0.222	0.061	12.20
Japan	0.214	0.326	0.304	0.300	0.221	0.122	0.034	5.00
Kenya	0.153	0.315	0.295	0.246	0.183	0.099	0.034	6.60
Mormons	0.461	0.453	0.405	0.363	0.314	0.182	0.025	11.02
Nigeria	0.144	0.267	0.274	0.222	0.162	0.095	0.067	6.20
Zhu	0.179	0.263	0.325	0.290	0.280	0.000	0.000	6.70
Mexico	0.099	0.296	0.299	0.236	0.189	0.079	0.016	6.02
Comparison Groups								
Africa	0.143	0.276	0.274	0.228	0.156	0.088	0.035	6.00
Asia	0.044	0.192	0.189	0.119	0.064	0.027	0.007	3.20
L. Amer.	0.068	0.173	0.161	0.113	0.068	0.025	0.040	3.10
N. Amer.	0.055	0.111	0.124	0.079	0.027	0.005	0.000	1.93
Europe	0.024	0.099	0.117	0.071	0.025	0.005	0.000	1.70

Sources: Zhu Women (San) of Southern Africa, 1976–80 see Wilmsen p. 313, 1989. Botswana, Kenya, and Nigeria see Cohen, 1995. Hutterites in the mid-19th century see: Coale and Watkins, 1979. Mormons during 1890–94 see Mineau et al., 1979. Nakahara, Japan, 1717–1830 see Eng and Smith, 1976. Mexico, 1975, U. S. Census Bureau, 1979. Comparison groups: See World Population Prospects, United Nations, 1992.

dren as single births. The *Guiness Book of Records* lists a nineteenth-century Russian woman as a mother of sixty-nine children from twenty-seven pregnancies (see McFalls, 1991:3). Considering that the reproductive organs require recovery and a newborn must be nursed for a period of months, it takes some time to regain fecundity. The highest theoretical average number of births that could be expected for a population given the best of living conditions would be from fifteen to seventeen.[11]

Since individual female fecundity varies widely, population fertility falls far below this theoretical average. No matter the human biological capacity to reproduce, couples make decisions about family size to conform to their economic situation, individual preferences, and their society's norms or religion. These decisions, together with basic biological factors that reduce fecundity (for example, breast feeding), lengthen the interval between births. The longer the intervals, the fewer the total number of births to a women during her lifetime. The result is a fertility that is "natural" in the sense that large families are the norm for the populations in the list in Table 5–5, and

[11] Natural fertility is that reproductive level reached by a population with a norm of unlimited family size. The theoretical "natural" fertility rate of human populations is 17 per woman (see Merrick 1986; also, Petersen, 1975).

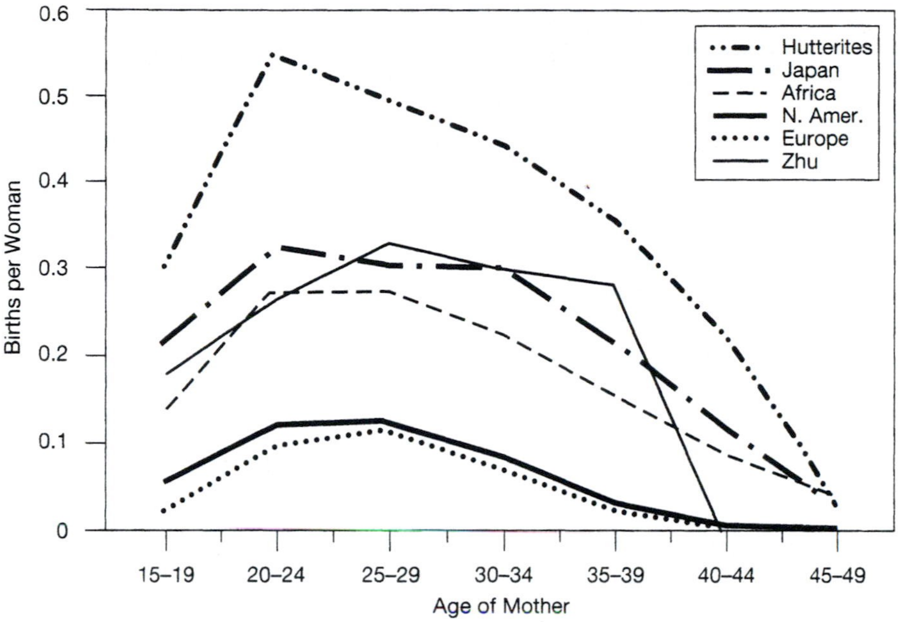

Figure 5–2 "Natural" Fertility Rates

Data selected and adapted from Coale, 1979 (Hutterites); Eng and Smith, 1976 (Japan, 1717–1830); Wilmsen, 1989 (Zhu); United Nations, World Population Prospects, 1992 (Africa, North America, and Europe).

married couples do not practice contraception. The highest fertility is recorded for the women of the Hutterite religious colony who continue to bear children through most of their reproductive years. Another example of "natural fertility" is provided by the Japanese that lived in Nakahara, Japan from 1717 to 1830. This population had an age specific fertility schedule comparable to the several African groups listed in the table. These all differ significantly from the several comparison groups.

In contrast to these high fertility groups, populations in less-developed countries in the comparison group have reproductive rates far below any theoretical potential, around three to four births per woman by completion of her reproductive life. In the more-developed societies, the number is nearer two to three, with most at two or less as in the case of Europe. What is interesting is that a majority of populations conform closely to the age specific fertility, higher in the early twenties and quickly declining after thirty (Figure 5–2).

This *total fertility rate*, or the number of lifetime births per woman living through her reproductive period and reproducing at the average rate, can be easily calculated if the number of women in each age interval is known. The number of births in that interval is divided by the number of women. For example, there were 503,000 live births to 9,043,000 females,

TABLE 5–6 Total Fertility Rate Calculation Ilustration (U.S., 1996)

Age	Females[1] (1000s)	Births[2] (1000s)	Age Specific[3] Birth Rate
15–19	9,043	503	0.056
20–24	8,561	945	0.110
25–29	9,469	1,071	0.113
30–34	10,708	898	0.084
35–39	11,318	400	0.035
40–44	10,506	75	0.007
45–49	—	—	—
Totals	59,605	3,892	0.405

(Sum of Intervals × years of interval) = Total Fertility Rate

$0.405 \times 5 = 2.03$[4]

[1]Female population in age interval.
[2]Total number of births to women of that interval.
[3]Age specific rate for five years of time interval.
[4]This TFR is most likely to change as women in any of the age intervals alter their reproduction rate, or the number of women increase or decrease.

Source: Adapted from Monthly Vital Statistics Report, 1998; Haput and Kane, 1991.

ages fifteen and nineteen, in the United States during 1996. The fertility rate for that age interval is calculated as fifty-five per thousand females (or 0.056). The intervals for all of the reproductive periods are totaled, and an average lifetime rate of 2.03 or TFR is obtained, as illustrated in Table 5–6. Comparisons of fertility, taking into account the number and age distribution of women, can readily be made between populations by using this TFR, a sum of the age specific rates.

Fertility Transitions

Many nations in this century and especially within the last few decades have undergone dramatic changes in their demographic patterns. Japan and China stand out as examples of those who experienced the most rapid change. Following World War II, Japan was confronted with the problem of absorbing millions of returning military and civilian personnel into a war-ravaged economy and a drastically reduced land area. With the loss of their overseas colonies, Japanese citizens had to be repatriated and a place had to be found for them on the home islands. To cope with the present and anticipated population pressures, a number of measures were instituted to reduce births. Contraceptives were made widely available, and the Eugenics Protection Law of 1948 permitted abortions for economic reasons; abortions rose from 246,104 in 1949 to 1.17 million by 1955 (Appleyard, 1980). There was a rapid fall in fertility after an initial rise in the late 1940s. Japan went from one of the world's highest fertility rates in the developed world to one of the lowest within just a decade. Declines continued, and fertility fell from a peak of 4.5 in 1949 to 1.9 by 1991. Then, slowly, TFR descended to a TFR of 1.4 by 1998 (Ogawa and Retherford, 1993).

China's demographics are a bit more difficult to track because of its political regime, its vast size, and the sketchiness of census data prior to 1981. Since then, there has been a reported decline of TFR from 2.8 in 1981 to 1.8 in 1998, largely due to an aggressive (some say draconian) family planning program with strong community and central government coercion to restrict family size. The attempt to enforce the one-child family edict of the central government attracted international criticism and much local resistance. In response, the regulation has been relaxed somewhat. The rate of natural increase rebounded slightly through 1986 to 1988 (TFR of 2.4). This rebound added millions to world population growth during those years as noted earlier. The family planning decisions taken in China have demonstrated the powerful influences that even slight changes in family size may have far-reaching effects on the world community.

In examples of most of the less-developed countries, especially Latin America, there has been a downward trend in fertility since the 1950s, which had slowed somewhat by the 1970s. The decline resumed as progress has been made in family planning, as illustrated in Figure 5–3, which plots

Figure 5–3 Contraceptive Use and Total Fertility Rate Reported for Select Countries, 1998

Data selected and adapted from World Population Data Sheet, 1998, (Population Reference Bureau).

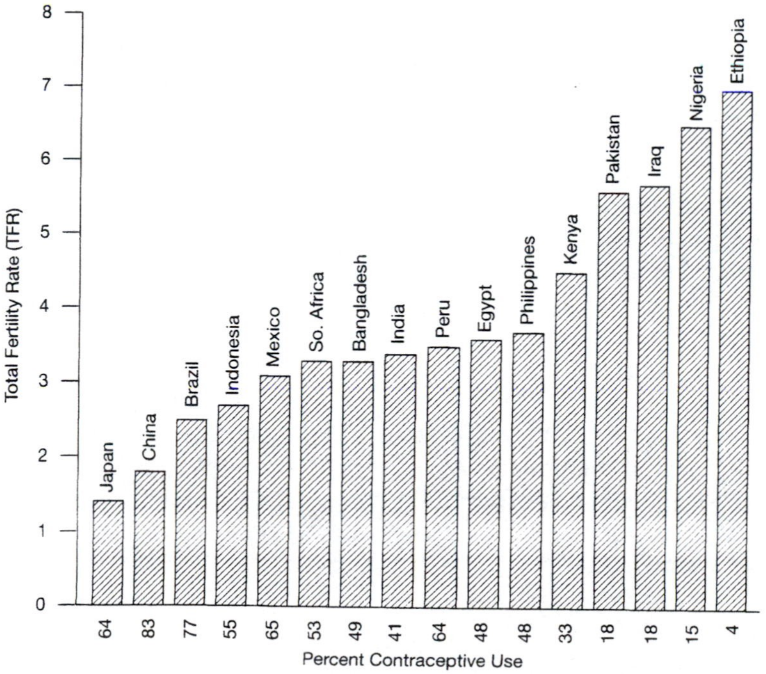

national fertility against contraceptive use. In just this decade there has been a decline from 4.3 to 3.0 TFR. Brazil, one of the largest developing countries, has made major advances in reducing fertility rates, from over 6.2 down to 2.5 by 1998. Because of its young population, however, Brazil still maintains a 1.4 percent rate of natural increase. Several of the smaller nations, Peru (TFR 3.5), Bolivia (TFR 4.8), and Ecuador (TFR 3.6), for example, have retained high fertility rates, and their populations continue to grow at over 2 percent per year.

Family planning for most African nations has not been as successful during this period of fertility transition. The rate has hardly changed at all from a high TFR of over 6.5. This contributes to continued population growth. Egypt (3.6 TFR) and Kenya (4.5 TFR) maintain high fertility despite some successes in family planning. Though both governments are sensitive to the socioeconomic and demographic problems related to high fertility rates, they continue to grow because of their young populations. The largest of the subSaharan countries, Nigeria, Ethiopia, and the Congo, accounting for about a third of all of African peoples, have changed little from their high fertility rates of a decade ago. These three large African nations will be the major contributors to the continent's population, doubling by about the year 2025 A.D. if current trends continue.

Muslim countries, with the exception of Indonesia, have maintained high fertility while lowering mortality rates; the result has been large annual increases in population. Syria, Iraq, and Saudi Arabia, to select three examples, have maintained fertility rates of from 6.6 to 7.0 over the past decade. The Central Asian Republics of the former USSR also continue their high fertility. By contrast, Turkey and Indonesia have reduced their rates to 2.6 and 2.7, respectively. These differences by region, national religion, political orientation, plus the dramatic declines seen at certain periods raise the question of the primary causes of fertility rate variability among populations.

In addition to the biological variables affecting female fertility (discussed in the next chapter), religious and socioeconomic factors weigh heavily in the fertility transition of any nation. The strength of a nation's family planning program and the female's role in society are the principle influences, however. As traditional roles of women alter and their status improves, there have been changes in reproductive rates. This is reflected by the fertility declines in nations as diverse as Brazil, Thailand, Jordan, and India. We have already mentioned certain of these factors in relation to infant mortality; similar relationships exist for fertility rates.

A special example is again provided by Kerala, the Indian state with the lowest infant mortality rate of the nation. In this predominantly agricultural economy, women enjoy a high status of property ownership, voting rights, and an equal access to education. One of the results has been India's highest female literacy rate (86 percent compared to the national rate of only

39 percent). Kerala is distinguished also by a lower fertility rate, 2.0 versus the national average of 3.9 in 1993 (see Visaria and Visaria, 1995).

The expansion of female education and their increased entry into the work force outside of the home has significantly delayed age of marriage. This delay has contributed to the reduced births seen in several developing countries. South Korea declined from a TFR of 6.1 to 4.0 between 1960 to 1970 and then it declined further to 1.6 as average age of females at marriage rose from eighteen to twenty-four. The differences between Bangladesh and Sri Lanka are likewise attributable to an increased average age at marriage, sixteen versus twenty-five (Merrick, 1986). Kerala also has, for Asia in general, a later age at marriage, 22, in contrast to the average of eighteen years for India as a whole. Education and participation in the cash economy serves the additional function of communication and awareness of the alternatives offered by family planning. In sum, where females enjoy greater economic freedom, there is a lower infant mortality, delay in marriage, lower fertility, and an increase in the proportion of unmarried women.

The developed world has undergone an even more striking change over the last fifty years. Women are spending more time in school than did their grandmothers, and more are entering the labor force (as of 1995, 46 percent of the U.S. labor force were women, compared to only 18 percent in 1900). They are marrying later and choose to have fewer children or none at all. Sometimes the decisions are based on economic or social considerations, as in the examples of the depressed economies of Eastern Europe and Russia. Societies enjoying favorable economic conditions may also elect to have fewer children, as in the examples of dramatic declines in Italy and Spain. Delays in marriage, greater use of contraceptives, and increases of legalized abortions have played important roles in bringing down birth rates to replacement levels or even below. In other words the fertility rates have dropped in many European nations to the point where growth has ceased or there is a net loss of population.

Replacement level is generally considered to be at a TFR of 2.1, but this depends on several factors of population age composition, mortality rates, and social customs, for example, age at first sexual union. Germany, with its late age at marriage, a high unmarried rate, and low fertility over several decades, has a very small proportion of its population under age fifteen (16 percent compared to 22 percent in the United States, or the 37 percent average for much of the less-developed world). For Germany, a TFR greater than 2.1 will be necessary to sustain population size. Replacement level also depends on average life expectancy. A TFR slightly greater than 2.0 is required to compensate for deaths of infants and children, and also to allow for the fact that not all women will live through their reproductive years. In populations with higher mortality rates, a TFR greater than 2.1 is needed. For example, Kenya, with a life expectancy of 49, would require an estimated replacement level of 2.25 in contrast to 2.06 for the United States with a life expectancy at birth of 72 (male) and 79 (female) years.

POPULATION STRUCTURES

Because we pass through a series of stages in our life cycle from birth to death and because we fulfill different biological and social roles at each stage, a population is not simply a matter of numbers of individuals. It is a matter of composition or of proportions of individuals by age and by gender; how many children, adolescents, young adults, etc. are there in each age grouping. Demographers usually divide population into five-year groupings, arranged in a vertical structure from birth to the oldest surviving members. The horizontal axis represents the percentage of each sex in that age division or cohort.[12] Most importantly, the sizes of these cohorts reflect a population's fertility and mortality experiences.

The graphic representations in Figures 5–4 a-h give the appearance of pyramid structures since the bottom layers, representing the youngest individuals, are generally larger than each of the succeeding age divisions above it. The pyramid for the U.S. population in 1900 is nearly symmetrical in shape with a gradual reduction in each succeeding age cohort. This distribution is reflective of the high fertility (TFR of 3.8) around the turn of the century, which caused a broader base (a higher proportion of population in the 0–5 year cohort). The next two levels are smaller because of the high infant and childhood mortality of the time.

Forty years later, a constriction appears at the base of the 1940 pyramid due to the fertility decline of the 1930s when the rate came down to a low of 2.2. This reduction in the sizes of the two age cohorts born between 1930 and 1940, the "depression babies," is reflected throughout the succeeding decades. Marriages were delayed, and the number of never married women was higher than in any previous decade. The Great Depression and World War II had major socioeconomic and demographic impacts, with repercussions that are still being felt. By the end of World War II, however, there was a return to the higher fertility rates of pre-depression times.

During the late 1940s, there was an increase in marriages, and a higher percentage had children within the first few years. Further, couples who had delayed starting a family because of hard times or because of wartime separation began to have children; a higher percentage of women were bearing children after age thirty. These trends contributed to an unprecedented pop-

[12]A cohort is that group of people sharing a demographic event; e.g. a birth cohort is that group born during a specified period of time.

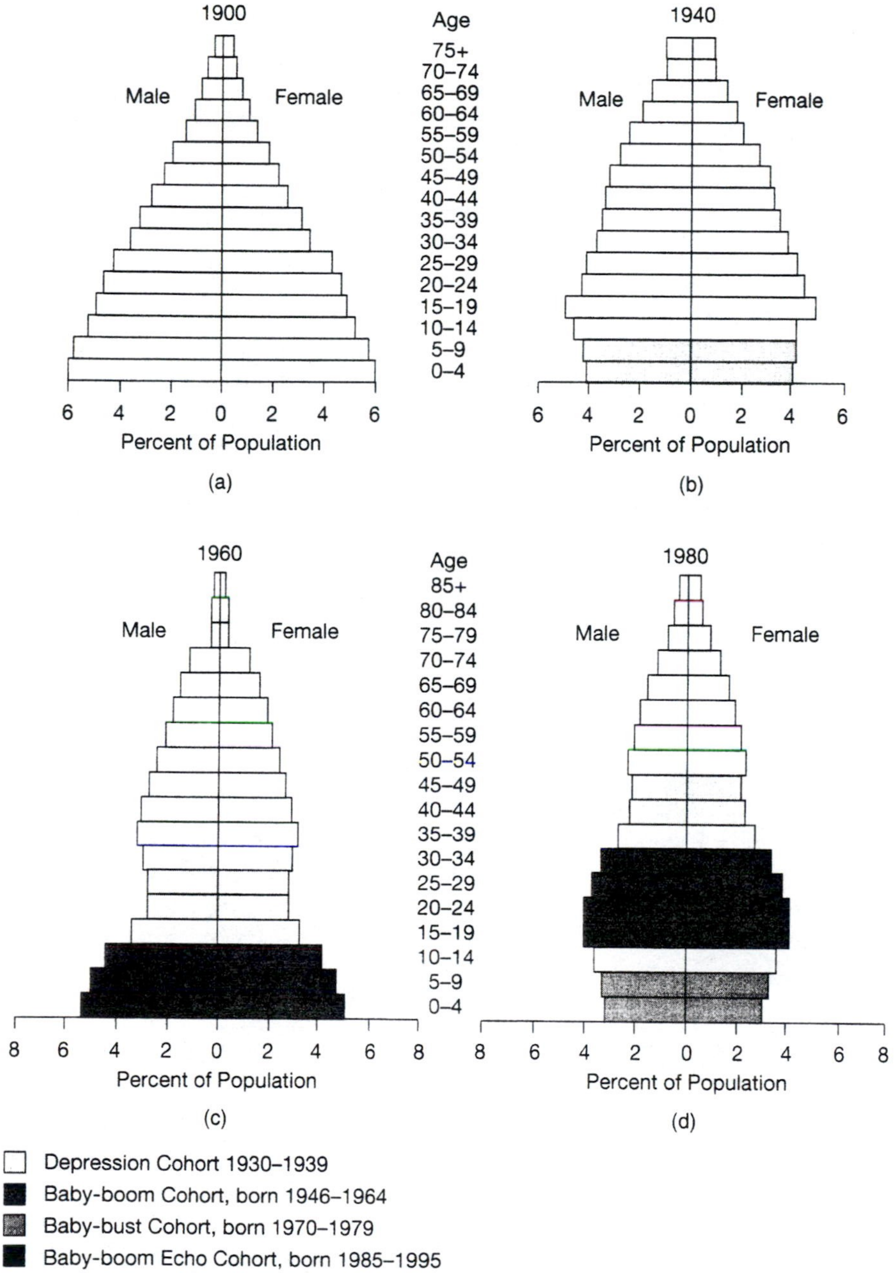

Figure 5–4 a-d U.S. Population Pyramids, 1900–1980

From Bouvier, F. et al., 1991. Reprinted by permission of Population Reference Bureau, Inc.

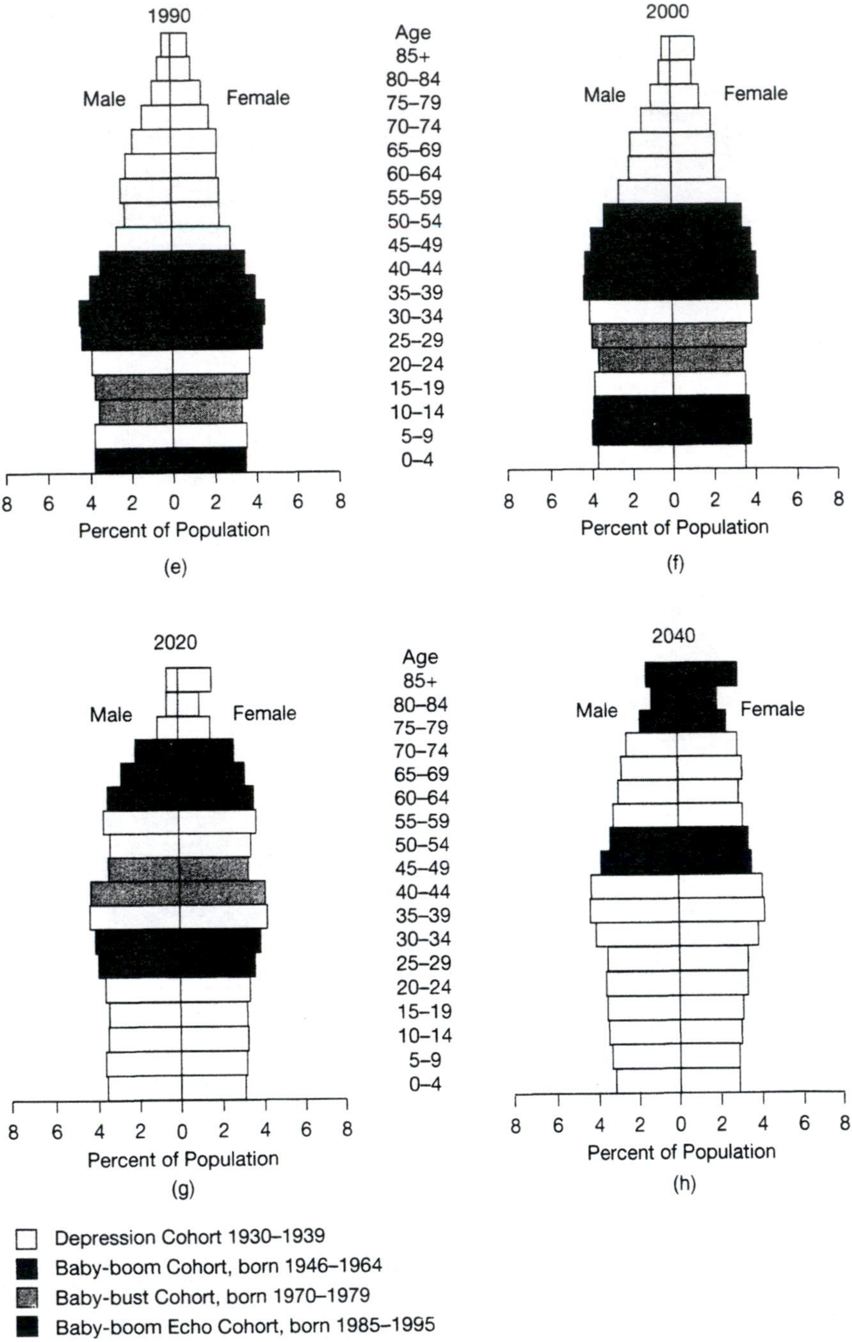

Figure 5–4 e-h U.S. Population Pyramids, 1990–2040

From Bouvier, F. et al., 1991. Reprinted by permission of Population Reference Bureau, Inc.

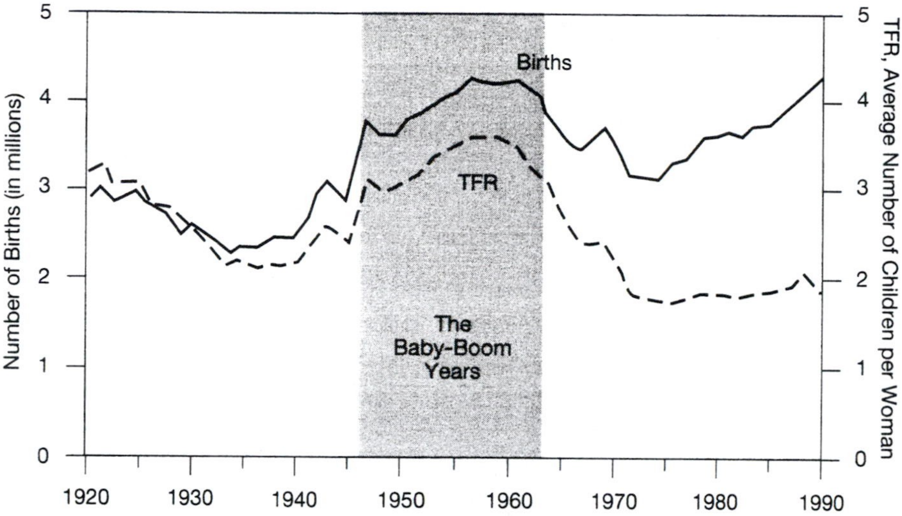

Figure 5–5 Annual Births and Total Fertility Rate (TFR) in the United States, 1920–1990

From Bouvier, F. et al., 1991. Reprinted by permission of Population Reference Bureau, Inc.

ulation growth, or what has been called the "baby boom," resulting in one of the largest birth cohorts in U.S. history (Weller and Bouvier, 1981).[13]

Fertility rates increased during the later 1940s to a peak of 3.7 during the 1950s and continued above 3.0 over the next decade. Even though there were fewer women in their reproductive years (the depression babies), the number of births rose because of the higher average fertility, as shown in Figure 5–5. The results of this prolonged period (two decades) is represented by a broader base of the U.S. population pyramid, the 1950–1954, and 1955–1960 cohorts. The shear size of these cohorts (80 million people) has had major demographic consequences. One is a high crude birth rate despite a drop of fertility below replacement level as these cohorts have reached reproductive age.

Fertility reached a low of 1.7 by 1978 where it remained for a decade and then slowly increased to 2.0 by 1998. Despite averaging less than half the number of births per woman compared to the peak baby boom period, crude birth rates declined very slowly and settled at a plateau of sixteen per thousand, which, in a population of 246.1 million people, resulted in over

[13] The baby boom is generally defined as the rise of birth rates during the postwar era, generally set between 1946 and 1964. The peak was reached in 1957 and began to decline after 1960, continuing to drop through a "baby bust" period (1964–1975), as delays in family starts by the now adult baby boomers reduced birth rates. After 1975 and through present times, an echo effect began to appear as the number of births rose, despite a lower fertility rate.

3,938,000 births in 1988. The 270.2 million population of 1998 produced 4,053,000 children, compared to 4,090,000 in 1960 when the TFR was twice as high. This has been referred to as an "echo" effect, which was due to the large number of women in their reproductive years. The women of the 1990s have continued to add to population growth, but at somewhat different rates than their mothers. This growth is reflected in the sizes of the two cohorts below the baby boom (see the Figures 5–4e-f). Increased marriage age, delays in having children, and a wide use of contraceptives and elective abortions have effected significant changes in the population age structure (Bouvier and De Vita, 1991).

While the United States, Canada, Australia, and New Zealand had experienced similar declines in births followed by baby booms, most of Europe has steadily reduced fertility since the 1900s. The population pyramid of Denmark in Figure 5–6c is typical of European countries at the end of the twentieth century. Several European nations, in fact, now have such low birth rates that the populations have ceased to grow or have even posted negative growth. Given the small size of the reproductive age cohorts, we can assume significant declines for future generations. If present trends continue, in Germany, for example, where TFR is 1.3, then 40 percent of the population will be sixty-five years or older in about thirty years. Though certain demographic features differ among other European countries, the trends are very similar. Populations of the future will have fewer young adults, more delayed marriages, and lower birth rates. Such countries have reached that stage of zero growth with stable and aging populations, as compared to rapid growth and slow growth countries, shown in Figure 5–6a,b,c.

Countries of the less-developed world have quite a different population structure. They may be described as young populations since from 35 to 45 percent are under fifteen years of age. Population pyramids of these nations conform to the shape of Kenya, illustrated in Figure 5–6a. The large percentage of the young is illustrated by a broad based pyramid and indicates a great potential for population growth. As this bulge moves upward through the age levels, Kenya as well as other countries with young populations will experience increasing pressures on their sociopolitical systems to meet the needs of this fateful population bulge.

Population Momentum

These young, fast-growing populations will continue to increase for decades even after replacement levels have been reached because of what might be termed a reproductive momentum. Just as the U.S. population did not stop growing when its fertility rate dropped below replacement level, the lesser-developed nations will continue to grow well past the middle of

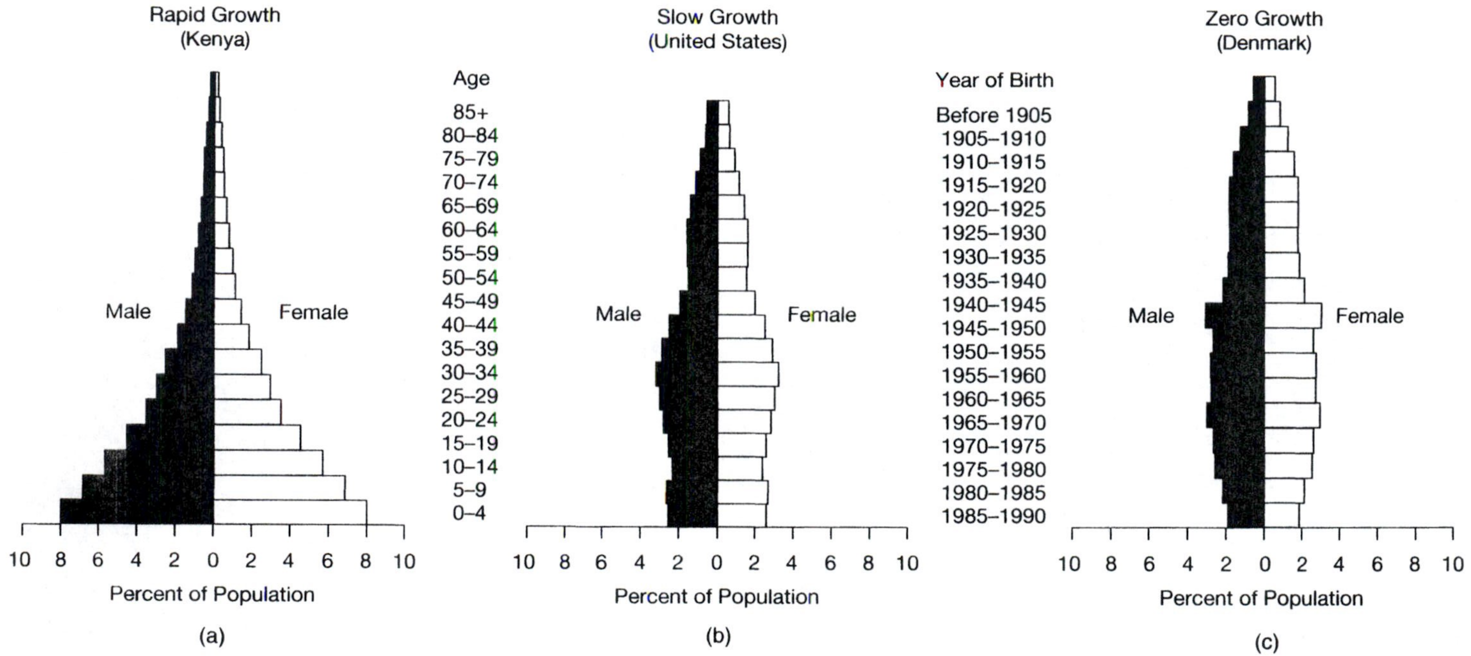

Figure 5–6 Age Patterns of Population

From McFalls, Jr., J. A., 1991. Reprinted by permission of Population Reference Bureau, Inc.

the twenty-first century. Mexico had nearly as many births in 1998 as it did twenty years ago, even though there had been a significant decline in TFR. Given the assumption that CBR and CDR remain near present levels, Mexico will likely reach 140 million within twenty-five years. Significant population increases are also probable for several other countries, like Brazil and Indonesia, who will continue to grow because of the shear size of their reproductive age groups, a size that is a result of the last generation's high fertility.

India, with its continued high fertility, will approach China in population size and probably surpass it within thirty years. Bangladesh's remarkable achievement in the reduction of its TFR within a single decade has brought down the number of births despite its young population and demonstrates what can be achieved. Countries like Nigeria, Ethiopia, and Pakistan continue on a rapid growth path with both high fertility and a young population. Each will add 50 percent or more to its population within two decades. Table 5–7 offers comparisons of the world's largest nations accounting for about two-thirds of the world's total population (1998). The absolute number of births will remain nearly the same or even increase despite fertility declines.

The rapid transition to low fertility can bring about other problems for future generations, as in the case of China. The enforcement of a rigorous one-child family policy since 1979 has worked, and this policy, plus large-scale family planning efforts, has effectively slowed growth. But its long-term effects are just becoming recognized, the critical disruption of age distribution. The large cohort of citizens sixty-five and older, those born during times of rapid population growth, will face an old age with only a small number of productive citizens, the children born during the family reduction stage. With an age top-heavy pyramid, China is facing what can be called a demographic dilemma—how to control population without a major dislocation of its age structure (Yuan Tien et al., 1992).

A similar experience is already being confronted in the slow-growth nations of Europe. Also, Japan, after a generation of near or below replacement level fertility, will soon have the problems caused by an imbalance of age distribution. Only 15 percent of Japan's population is below age fifteen, the lowest rate in the world. The United States likewise anticipates problems as its baby boom cohorts pass through middle age (see Bouvier and De Vita, 1991). Simply put, in the developed world there will be too many pensioners supported by too few wage earners, a prospect that continues to arouse arguments about pension fund solvency over the next twenty-five years. The hypothetically ideal population would be one neither overwhelmed with too many young or too many old, nor an imbalance at any one of the age intervals. Members leaving an age cohort would be replaced by an equivalent number of those maturing from the younger cohort.

TABLE 5–7 Population Growth Momentum

Region, Country	Population (millions)	<15 (%)	Women(1000s) (15–49)	CBR-CDR (/1000)	RNI (%)	DT (years)	IMR (/1000)	TFR	Births (1000)
World									
1998	5,926	32	1,566,686	23–9	1.4	49	58	2.9	136,298
1988	5,128	33	1,265,371	28–10	1.7	40	77	3.6	143,584
1978	4,219	36	na	29–12	1.7	41	99	na	122,351
Ethiopia									
1998	58.4	46	14,108	46–21	2.5	28	128	7.0	2,686
1988	48.3	51	10,799	46–15	3.0	23	118	7.0	2,222
1978	30.2	44	na	49–25	2.4	29	162		1,480
Nigeria									
1998	121.8	46	25,939	45–15	3.0	23	84	6.5	5,481
1988	111.9	45	18,939	46–17	2.9	23	122	6.6	5,469
1978	68.4	45	na	49–21	2.8	25	157		3,352
China									
1998	1,242	26	348,874	17–7	1.0	69	31	1.8	21,114
1988	1,087	29	311,905	21–7	1.4	49	44	2.4	22,827
1978	930	33	na	22–8	1.4	50	65	3.3	20,460
India									
1998	988.7	36	258,915	27–9	1.9	37	72	3.4	26,695
1988	816.8	38	209,231	33–13	2.0	35	104	4.3	26,954
1978	634.7	40	na	34–14	2.0	35	129	4.8	21,580

(continued)

TABLE 5–7 Population Growth Momentum (continued)

Region, Country	Population (millions)	<15 (%)	Women(1000s) (15–49)	CBR-CDR (/1000)	RNI (%)	DT (years)	IMR (/1000)	TFR	Births (1000)
Indonesia									
1998	207.4	34	61,535	24–8	1.5	45	66	2.7	4,978
1988	177.4	38	48,926	27–10	1.7	40	88	3.3	4,790
1978	140.2	44	na	35–15	2.0	29	91	4.1	5,051
Bangladesh									
1998	123.4	43	34,185	27–8	1.8	38	82	3.3	3,332
1988	109.5	46	25,287	43–17	2.7	26	135	5.8	4,709
1978	85.0	43	na	47–20	2.7	26	153		3,995
Mexico									
1998	97.5	36	27,450	27–5	2.2	32	28	3.1	2,633
1988	83.5	42	21,559	30–6	2.4	29	50	4.0	2,505
1978	66.9	46	na	42–8	3.4	20	66		2,810
United States									
1998	270.2	22	70,350	15–9	0.6	116	7	2.0	4,053
1988	246.1	22	65,806	16–9	0.6	116	15		3,276
1978	218.4	24	na	15–9	0.6	116	15		3,276

Source: Adapted from World Population DAta Sheets, 1978, 1988, 1998.

LIFE EXPECTANCY

Statements are frequently made regarding the average number of years one can expect to live, and many social, medical, and financial decisions are based on these expectations. For example, when pension systems were founded in the late 1930s, future funding requirements are presumed to have been calculated on a shorter life span than a sixty-five-year-old enjoys today. But, in fact, there are only four years' difference in the average life expectancy at that age. Today, a sixty-five-year-old male may look forward to another sixteen years, while in 1939 his grandfather could expect another twelve years, on average. What has upset many calculations has been the fact that more people are surviving to age sixty and beyond despite the slow gains for adults over forty. In the United States, only a few years has been added in the twentieth century. True, life expectancy at birth has expanded by about twenty-five years, but most of this advance has been due to the dramatic reductions of infant mortality. One writer emphasized that increases in life expectancy has been the exclusive result of the elimination of mortality in the young age groups (DuBos, 1965).

This statement still merits consideration, even though medical advances over the last thirty years have helped extend the life span of the elderly. The true meaning of life expectancy is the chance of reaching a given age because of the lowering of mortality rates of the previous age cohort.[14] The reality of health and mortality risks for adults is given by comparisons of the average number of years of life remaining at different adult age groups. Table 5–8 lists life expectancy at four age intervals for males and females from 1900 to 1992; comparisons are also given between Black (African Americans) and White racial classifications.

Note the gender and race differences. Male mortality is higher than females from birth on, increasing the gap after middle age. Greater differences are seen among ethnic minorities and especially indigenous people. Most minorities have life expectancies that are far below the national average, and the mortality rates at each age interval are lower also. Infant mortality is nearly two times as great among African Americans and Native Americans as the average of the European American majority. Likewise, infectious disease rates are higher. African Americans and Hispanics have made some gains over the last half century but still lag behind the other groups. These distinctions suggest subenvironments with different, and probably a lower, quality of life.

---

[14]Calculation of life expectancy is made by use of "life tables" that are constructed from the demographic experiences of the current or recent population. These are then converted into a table of calculations for a hypothetical cohort of 100,000 who pass through the age cohorts of five-year intervals dying at those rates established by current experience. Refer to Vital Statistics of the United States, 1992.

TABLE 5–8 Life Expectancy at Four Ages (United States)

		White		Black	
	All	Male	Female	Male	Female
	(average number of remaining years)				
at birth					
1992	75.8	73.2	79.8	65.0	73.9
1900	49.2	48.2	51.1	32.5	35.0
Age one year					
1992	75.4	72.8	79.3	65.2	74.1
1900	55.2	56.6	56.4	42.5	43.5
Age twenty					
1992	56.9	54.3	60.6	47.2	55.6
1900	42.8	42.2	43.7	35.1	36.9
Age sixty-five					
1992	17.5	15.5	19.3	13.5	17.4
1900	11.9	11.5	12.2	10.4	11.4

Source: Adapted from National Center for Health Statistics, 1996.

The contrasts between the more-developed and lesser-developed countries are much broader. The lowest life expectancies are in sub-Saharan Africa, with a range of fifty for males and fifty-three for females in contrast to sixty-six (males) and seventy-two years for females in Latin American and Caribbean countries. Table 5–9 illustrates these differences by regions of the lesser-developed world. In the more-developed countries, the longest lived people are in Europe where life expectancies are seventy-five and even older. Japan and China must be added to the list of long lived countries, with sixty-nine (male) and seventy-three (female) in China compared to life expectancy of seventy-seven (male) and eighty-four(females) in Japan.

There are many causes for these differences. The higher rate of infectious and parasitic diseases in the tropics, especially during infancy and childhood, account for many of the contrasts. Populations with histories of long-term exposures to malaria are particularly at risk of lowered life expectancy. The appearance and spread of HIV infection (AIDS) since the 1980s is becoming evermore threatening. Diet is perhaps another one of the key factors distinguishing between East Asian populations and the United States. The fat-rich diets high in animal proteins of the more-developed countries of the Western world are a likely cause of shorter life span, as will be discussed in Chapter 7. Also, there are significant variations in some of the chronic diseases that relate to the lack of access to medical care, marginal diets, and harsh work environments.

TABLE 5–9 Comparative Life Expectancy of Selected Countries

	IMR		e_x(birth)[1]	
Region, Country	**1988**	**1998**	**1988**	**1998**
World				
MDC[2]	15	8	73	75
LDC[3]	86	64	60	63
LDC[4]	96	70	57	61
Africa	110	91	52	52
Egypt	93	63	59	67
Ethiopia	118	128	50	42
Kenya	76	62	54	49
Nigeria	122	84	47	50
South Africa	66	52	60	58
Asia[5]	82	57	50	63
Bangladesh	135	82	50	59
China	44	31	66	71
India	164	72	54	59
Indonesia	88	66	58	62
Japan	5.2	3.8	78	80
Pakistan	121	91	54	58
Philippines	51	34	66	66
Vietnam	53	38	63	67
Northern Europe	9.0	6.0	75	76
Sweden	5.9	3.9	77	79
U. Kingdom	9.5	6.1	75	77
Western Europe	8.0	5.0	75	77
Germany	8.6	4.9	75	77
France	8.0	5.1	75	78
Eastern Europe	18	15	71	68
Poland	17.5	12.2	71	72
Russia	25	17	69	67
Hungary	19.0	10.0	70	70
Latin America	57	36	66	69
Argentina	45.6	22.2	70	72
Brazil	63	67	65	67
Mexico	50	28	66	72

[1]Life expectancy at birth.
[2]More Developed Countries.
[3]Less Developed Countries.
[4]Excluding China.
[5]Excluding China.

Source: Adapted from Population Data Sheets, 1988 and 1998.

CONCLUSIONS

Demographic processes that influence the dynamics of population are not simply a matter of number of births minus the number of deaths over each time span. The structure, sex and age ratios, and how they fit into some socially defined category affect population composition each generation. The key to understanding these effects is to recall that demography consists of a merging of biological needs with social events to provide for each individual who, in turn, contributes to the whole population unit. Recall the influence of female education on fertility. The better educated women were no different biologically than their sisters throughout their nation. They just lived under a different social regime that had important influences on their reproductive potential. The more mature, educated women were in a better position to control their reproductive health.

Other correlations between society and biology are seen in the cases of infant mortality rates and life expectancy differentials among ethnic groups. We have noted a range of differences for these measures, but there also are significant variables for fertility. The majority of U.S. women, those classified as "non-Hispanic White" had a TFR of 1.9 in contrast to Mexican American women whose TFR was 3.2. Can we explain these differences of population dynamics by religious or cultural traditions, or does the answer lie elsewhere? Consider that population dynamics are intrinsically bound up with economic and social welfare, and fertility (fecundity realized) is an allied phenomenon (Rajan, 1991). This, plus the variants of health (discussed in Chapter 7), all point to the interactions between social and physical environments. These interactions, or linkages, must be considered in any study of human population dynamics.

Sociopolitical events of the recent past are often reflected in the population pyramids, and a study of these schematics of population structure can aid in the analysis of biosocial interactions. Note Germany's detailed pyramid of 1989, shown in Figure 5–7. The tragic effects of two world wars and an economic collapse are well marked. The higher number of women in the over age sixty group reflects more than just female longevity. This lopsided part of the pyramid records the effects of military losses during two world wars. The economic depressions following these wars are indicated by the sharp indentations over several years when birth rates were low. The other parts of this year-by-year structure reflects the boom and bust cycles that we have seen in other populations of the developed world, including baby busts and echo effects. Analysis of such proportionate changes within populations where vital statistics are well recorded enable projection of future trends.

The declines and increases have, in the past, followed patterns or trends set by socioeconomic events. One in particular has been industrial development that supposedly has had a major impact on population dynamics. The recent history of population dynamics in Western European

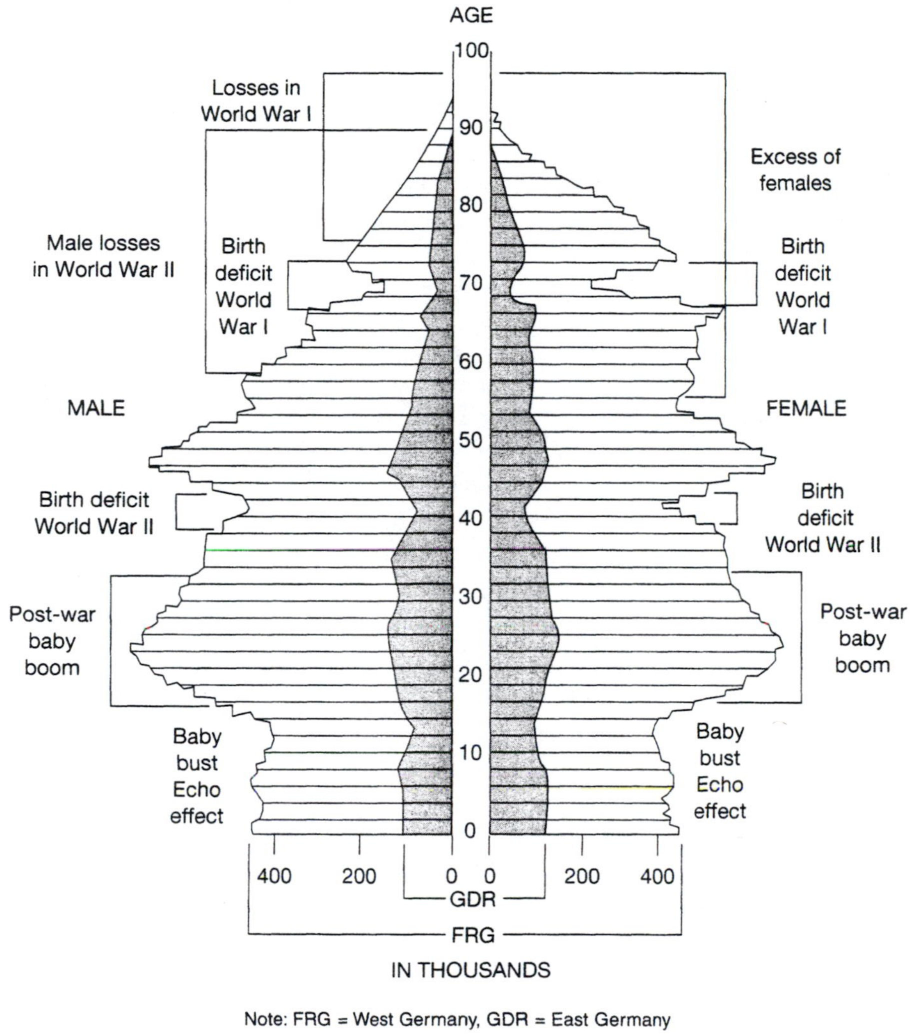

Figure 5–7 Germany's Population by Age and Sex, 1989
From McFalls, Jr., J. A., 1991. Reprinted by permission of Population Reference Bureau, Inc.

countries is often used as an example. These countries, after a time of rapid growth, successfully lowered birth rates in parallel with declining death rates. These changes followed a pattern referred to as a *demographic transition,* described in the last chapter. Basically, the industrializing nations increased population rapidly as development progressed and than, after a point, births began a decline.

The economics of development and the social advantages accompanying a rise of income were supposedly influential on family size. These certainly are important factors of socioeconomic and demographic change as we have described. A number of writers have argued that the less-developed countries will experience a similar transition as their economies evolve with industrial development. They point to the experiences of Europe and the United States to bolster their predictions. But there are two critical differences. Changes in Europe occurred because of internal forces, a home grown industry was driving development. Secondly, the demographic transition occurred over a long time period. It took nearly one hundred years to reduce mortality rates to ten per thousand population, a century during which industrialization was rapid and major migrations acted as a relief valve for population pressures. The world no longer has the space for expansion nor is there such a time frame available for the less-developed countries. Further, most countries with rapidly growing populations do not have the release of population pressures from migration. This leads to the question of what is the relation of development to population, as we shall examine in the following chapters.

Chapter 6

Diet, Adaptation, and Development

Human subsistence has undergone a considerable transition since our earliest existence as hunters and collectors of wild plants. From a stock of over 3,000 plant species potentially useful as food, farmers have cultivated about 150 of them over the centuries and have supplemented their dietary needs by collecting. Gradually, the bulk of our diet has been provided for by an increasingly narrower selection. The more productive plants have been selected as human population grew, especially during the past two centuries. For the major portion of our food today, we depend upon only twenty crops, and of these, three cereals—rice, wheat, and maize—provide over 50 percent of the world's food energy. Three groups of animals—pig, cow, and poultry—are sources of 80 percent of our animal protein (Scrimshaw, 1983; Bender and Smith, 1997).

Many less-developed countries (LDC) rely almost entirely upon grains and tubers for their basic subsistence. Because of the expense, food from animal sources make up but a small part of the LDC diet. By contrast, the more-developed countries (MDC), supplied by factory farms, have access to a greater variety of food from both plant and animal products. Specific food items are not a nutritional concern, however, as long as sufficient amounts can be provided economically. The important factor is that the quality and quantity of dietary nutrients meet the human organism's biochemical requirements for normal physiological functioning. These nutrients are divided into three broad categories: carbohydrates, fats, and proteins. Added to these are the several classes of vitamins and chemical elements that we require in either large or micro amounts (the trace elements).

FOOD CATEGORIES

Proteins

The tissues of the body, the hemoglobin and plasma of the blood, as well as enzymes and most hormones, to name just a few substances, are made up of proteins. Throughout our lives, these must be formed, rebuilt, or replaced as our bodies grow, age, and repair damaged tissues. The turnover rate is about 2½ grams per kilogram of body weight per day, or about 175 grams for the average adult male. Thus, there is a continuous need for new protein, which requires basic components—amino acids—so synthesis may proceed. There are twenty different amino acids that are the basic building blocks of a protein complex. Linked together in a particular variety, number, and order, the amino acids determine a protein's specific identity and function. Some proteins are short strands of only a few amino acids (insulin with only fifty-one, for example) while others consist of long complex chains of hundreds (skin collagen or hemoglobin, for example). During synthesis, these amino acids have to be taken up and arranged in their proper order under genetic control. All but eight of the twenty amino acids can be synthesized in the body from other products. These eight indispensable (essential) amino acids must be available in the foods we eat (Table 6–1). Two additional dietary amino acids (histidine and arginine) are considered essential during childhood since children are unable to synthesize them in sufficient quantities to meet the demands of their rapidly growing tissues.

Most animal proteins provide the best sources of these essential amino acids and are classified as a Grade I since all eight are present. By contrast, vegetable proteins (Grade II) are lacking in one or more of these essential eight. Maize (corn) is deficient in lysine, rice lacks lysine and tryptophan, and most varieties of beans are deficient in methionine. But combinations of

TABLE 6–1 Required Dietary Amino Acids (Essential)

Amino Acids	Children (0–4 years)	Adults
arginine	++	—
histidine	++	—
isoleucine	++	++
leucine	++	++
lysine	++	++
methionine	++	++
phenyalanine	++	++
threonine	++	++
tryptophan	++	++
valine	++	++

Source: Adapted from Ganong, 1993.

vegetables can complement each other in vegetarian diets. A combination of rice and beans is one favorite and maize and beans another.

When sufficient amino acids are ingested and proteins are synthesized to compensate for the "wear and tear" quotient of tissue breakdown and repair, then a person is said to be in *nitrogen balance*. As proteins are broken down, a quantity of amino acids are *catabolized*—they are separated into the basic elemental units of their composition. Some of these elements, principally nitrogen, are excreted in the urine. When nitrogen intake (as part of dietary amino acids) is equal to the amount excreted, then a balance is obtained. Where more tissue is lost than is replenished, as in starvation, or if there is an increase in hormones such as cortisone or insulin, then there is a negative balance. More nitrogen is lost than can be replaced by the ingested food components.

In addition to providing for the basic protein synthesis, it is necessary to replace the "obligatory loss"; there is about 10 percent of protein turnover per day that is lost, mostly through excretion. Any diet should contain proteins beyond a basic level to compensate for this loss, as well as provide for new tissue building and to allow a safety margin. Though recommended daily allowances have changed over the years, amounts of between 0.8 and 1 gram per kilogram of body weight are recommended at this time. Increased amounts are necessary for children and pregnant or nursing women. The diets of many populations around the world appear to fall far below these protein levels, however.

Fats

Energy, in excess of daily requirements, is stored in the form of molecular compounds called lipids, or fatty acids. Most lipids are contained in adipose cells congregated into fat layers at several locations throughout the body. This fat tissue, as differentiated from muscle and bone, is a significant part of total body weight that varies with the balance between energy intake and expenditure. Normal, nonobese adult males have 10 to 12 percent of their body weight as fat, and females have around 20 or 25 percent.[1] When food intake increases beyond energy needs of the basal metabolism and exercise, body fat content rises; it declines when the reverse is true.

There are numerous other functions of lipids in addition to energy storage. They are a major constituent of cell membranes, they coat nerve fibers, and provide chemical precursors for steroids and cholesterol. Lipids are also important for the absorption and transport of several nutrients, like calcium and the fat soluble vitamins, A and D. In addition, of major biological importance is the energy supplied by the fatty acids (triglycerides) to muscle tis-

[1] Obesity is defined arbitrarily as body weight greater than 20 percent of the standard weight for height, age, and sex.

sue at resting or at low levels of exercise. As exercise increases energy expenditure, the muscle contraction needs are provided by carbohydrates (Ganong, 1993).

Dietary fat is a rich concentration of energy since it supplies over twice the amount per gram provided by either carbohydrate or protein. It is then relatively easy to exceed one's energy needs on a diet high in fat content. Diet fats are grouped into saturated and polyunsaturated, according to molecular structure. The type of fat has received a great deal of attention because of concerns with health problems associated with diet, obesity, and heart disease. We can get along on very little fat in our diets (less than 6 percent of total caloric intake) as long as the animal fat or vegetable oils we consume contain the three essential polyunstaturated fatty acids (linolenic, linoleic, and arachidonic).

Carbohydrates

This class of foods vary from a simple compound, such as glucose, to complex starches like glycogen. We are most familiar with carbohydrates as starches in potatoes, wheat products, and rice, or as sugar, in candies and ice creams or in the sugar bowl. The major physiological role of this class of compounds is to provide energy within the cells (glucose) or to store it in the liver and muscle tissue as glycogen, where it is readily available for quick conversion to glucose. The excess glucose in circulation is converted to triglycerides and stored in adipose cells.

Our carbohydrate requirements are not of the same order as either the essential fatty acids or amino acids. There seems to be no specific type of carbohydrate that our metabolism requires. Most food plants contain carbohydrate starches consisting of long chains of glucose molecules (amylose and amylopectin). These are digestible but plants also have fibrous structural materials made of cellulose, which are not. The ratio of cellulose to digestible starches makes some plants more or less desirable as human food. Many of the tubers that have high starch concentrations can be produced cheaply, and the nutrients are easily obtained. By contrast, grains that contain starches wrapped in an indigestible fibrous sheath are costly in time and labor to remove. Nevertheless, grains are a plentiful source of carbohydrates and provide, in various processed forms, the bulk of caloric intake for a majority of humans today.

Micronutrients

To enable metabolic processes to proceed within normal body temperature ranges, two groups of micronutrients—*vitamins* and *minerals*—must be present as essential dietary components to act as catalysts. The *vitamins* serve many vital functions in chemical processes throughout the metabolism, functioning individually or as cofactors with enzymes. One of the earliest demonstrations of vitamin needs was the frequent occurrence of scurvy among sailors on long sea voyages. Lacking access to fresh foods for extended periods of time, the early voyagers would slowly weaken and many died as the soft tissues throughout their bodies slowly degenerated; ligaments lost elasticity and walls of smaller blood vessels ruptured (Carpenter, 1986). The collagenous fibers of these structures could not be maintained or rebuilt in the absence of vitamin C. The first sign of this problem is bleeding of the gums and loosening of the teeth as the supporting ligaments degenerated. These seafarers expected to suffer from this disease as one of the costs of months at sea without fresh foods. Eventually, they learned that supplements of pickled vegetables or small amounts of citrus juice could maintain health and prevent scurvy. Centuries later, the antiscurvy compound in fresh foods (vitamin C) was identified, and many other essential vitamins have been discovered since.

Other examples are found in the cases of poorly formed and distorted bones (rickets) of malnourished children, described in Chapter 4. Rickets was eventually related to vitamin D deficiency, a vitamin plentiful in fish oils. Certain types of visual impairment is another example. The lack of vitamin A or its precursors(the carotenes) in many fresh vegetables causes various forms of visual impairment, especially xerophthalmia and night blindness. Xerophthalmia is the major cause of blindness in young children of developing countries, especially where rice is their dietary staple, with few fresh vegetables. Pellegra, a generalized disorder affecting skin, mucous membranes, and the central nervous system has long been associated with overdependence on maize as described in Chapter 3. Such a diet, largely devoid of other foods, is niacin deficient, which is a key vitamin for the normal functioning of most cells. Thiamin deficiency is another of the vitamins related to a poor diet. Where polished white rice is the diet staple, people are at risk for beriberi, a malfunctioning of the neurological system and of the heart. These are but a few examples of the earliest and best-known disorders related to vitamin deficiencies.

Mineral elements, as components of our diet, also serve numerous vital functions. Calcium and phosphorus provide the mineral structure of bone; iron is responsible for the transport of essential substances. Bound with a globin protein, iron is the key element in the transport of oxygen. Hormonal functions of trace elements are also important, as in the example of iodine combining with molecules of the amino acid tyrosine in the thyroid gland to produce thyroglobins. These thyroglobins, principally thyroxine and thyronine, control metabolic processes mainly by regulating cells' oxygen consumption. They influence growth and development, increase absorption of carbohydrates through the gut wall, and help regulate lipid metabolism. These functions ultimately depend upon only a small daily supply of iodine (about 40 micrograms) to stimulate the function of a healthy thyroid gland.

Perhaps the first trace element deficiency disease to be identified was goiter, the hyperactivity and swelling of a thyroid gland that produced too little thyroxine because of iodine insufficiency. Goiter is typically found among those populations subsisting on foods grown on the iodine poor soils found in many parts of the world. Peoples throughout much of Asia and Europe have a long history of this disease. People living in the New Guinea highlands have especially high goiter rates because their low iodine intake is made worse by diets high in substances that inhibit thyroid function. The Yanomama of South America also have low iodine intake but they rarely exhibit goiter symptoms, probably because of a unique ability to absorb and retain the element (Neel, 1994).

These mineral elements of iron, calcium, phosphorus, and several others must be present in fairly large quantities in the body, and they need to be replenished at a high rate. Several other required elements are needed in varying amounts—from only a few micrograms to several milligrams. Cobalt, selenium, and magnesium are some examples of this group of elements, which function in the body as essential components of certain metabolic processes. Zinc, for example, is necessary for normal growth and for tissue repair, as in wound healing. The element cobalt is a key component of vitamin B12, selenium is needed in but a few parts per million for skeletal mineralization and muscle development, as is magnesium, though it is needed in much larger quantities (Fowden et al., 1981). The list is quite extensive and a real appreciation of the role of trace elements in human nutrition has just begun.

The final nutritional component, *water*, is one we seldom consider as one of the dietary essentials. This universal solvent is the fluid that moves cells, nutrients, and wastes; body water accounts for approximately 60 percent of our total weight. Average daily intake is about 1 liter with upward adjustments to compensate for fluid losses under hot, arid conditions. In addition, drinking water also serves to bring many dissolved minerals into the body from the surrounding environment, as in the case of fluoride, iodine, or calcium. Pollutants, toxins, and microbes enter by this route as well, depending upon the water source. If the source is a stagnant pond, the chance of microbial intoxication is greater than from a swift running stream. The bacteria and parasites can and do interfere with the absorption of nutrients through the intestinal tract, and many will cause severe gastric upsets, like cholera or dysentery, or chronic anemia, as in the example of a snail-borne parasitic disease, schistosomiasis. Many nomadic populations living in arid lands suffer not only a water shortage but they are at serious risk from the high concentration of microbes in stagnant ponds and water holes they are forced to use, especially during dry seasons.

Considering the multitude of our nutritional needs and the variety of ways that we have found to fulfill them, the quantitative and qualitative requirements of the human diet are difficult to standardize. What is the optimum diet needed for good health is a question that has been often asked and is still debated. We know about some deficiencies that cause pathological responses but are unsure of what others may exist. Measurements have been made of the energy needs of the growing child or the working adult, pregnant women, or the elderly. So many exceptions have been recorded, however, that reference to any single standard or average is of limited value since guidelines have been developed mainly from studies of populations of a people of the more-developed countries.

Comparative Diets

The three food categories collectively fulfill our need for energy and tissue rebuilding. Which ratio of carbohydrate to protein or fat to protein is correct continues to be the subject of much debate. There is evidence that a fat-free diet is unhealthy and even lethal; beyond the need for the essential fatty acids, lipids are needed to aid the digestion of animal protein. But the optimum amount of fat needed is not known. Recommended protein levels have changed over the last few decades. From a high of 2 grams per kilogram, it has been lowered to 0.57 grams and then increased to 0.8 to compensate for a lower digestive efficiency of certain protein types. A relatively small amount is sufficient as long as the essential amino acids are provided. No advantage is derived from increasing protein intake. The level of carbohydrates, that cheapest of food sources, is likewise uncertain. A good deal depends upon family income, though. In most countries, the lower the income and the larger the family, the higher the carbohydrate proportion.

Diet is a matter of available food varieties, custom, income, and taste. Table 6–2 offers some examples of diets reported for several groups. The weight of each category is given in grams and from this the number of kilocalories is calculated. Then its percent of the total energy intake is determined. Hence, the British male daily caloric intake was listed as 3,016 Kcal and, of this, carbohydrates contributed 53.6 percent, fat 32.9 percent, and protein only 13.3 percent of the total. Note that in all the groups, protein contributes the lowest energy proportion, fat the second, and carbohydrate the highest. Note also the range in proportions of the fat energy contribution. Though it is difficult to recommend an optimum ratio, nutritionists describe a 50–35–15 proportion of carbohydrates, fats, and protein as desirable. As customs change and income rises, so does diet composition; usually it is the proportion of animal fat that increases. But humans have always managed to use a diversity of foods to satisfy hunger, if not their physiological needs.

A more revealing approach to a study of human nutrition may be offered by a review of the subsistence of small-scale societies during their ecological transition from their traditional lifestyles. Comparisons of different groups at several stages of change from their traditional diets should shed light on basic human nutritional needs. The key question is what foods

TABLE 6–2 Comparative Diets

Ethnic Group	Total Calories	CHO			Fat			Protein		
		cal	%	gm	cal	%	gm	cal	%	gm
United States[1]	2860	1110	37	270	1628	57	179	308	10.8	75
British[2]	3016	1619	53.6	400	995	32.9	110	401	13.3	100
African[2] (Kikuyu)	2182	1579	72.3	390	198	9.0	22	405	18.5	100
Pacific[2] (Tokelauans)	2350	818	34.8	202	1258	53.5	139	275	11.7	68
Inuit[3] (Canada)	2290	41	2	10	1720	66	185	530	32	200
RDA (male)[4]	2800	1400	50	341	980	35	105	420	15	102

Caloric values per gram:
Fat 9.3 Kcal
Carbohydrate(CHO) 4.1 kcal
Protein 4.1 kcal

[1]National Academy of Science, 1982.
[2]Harrison et al., 1988.
[3]Schaefer, 1981.
[4]Recommended daily allowances (RDA), National Academy of Sciences, 1989.

are used, their seasonal availability, and the effects of introduced foods as they supplement or replace traditional diets.

TRADITIONAL SOCIETIES AND NUTRITIONAL ADAPTATION

Diet composition is determined by many factors but environment, suitable plants, and animal products are the primary ones. Food selection, though, is complicated by culture; to taste good a food must "sound good" to the palate or stomach. One society will relish a variety of grubs, caterpillars, and other insects while another avoids insects with repulsion. Hunting and foraging nomads of arid lands can find an ample food supply while most of us from developed societies would be blind to the food around us. We would view the same area as a barren desert devoid of life and water. Likewise, arctic dwellers survive only because of their specialized knowledge, where nearly all others would perish from lack of skill to hunt the marine and land mammals of the region. It is more than a matter of taste, experience, and local knowledge. Certain inherited factors of the digestion may be involved in the acceptance or rejection of certain food items, as we will consider further along. Whatever the reasons, humans gain sufficient nutrients, as they must, from their environments by a variety of special skills of the hunter and forager, or by horticulture and pastoralism. Adaptation to the nutritional environment may be illustrated by dietary transitions.

Examples of Traditional, Indigenous Societies[2]

Small semi-isolated populations, varying in size from a band of only a few families to villages containing several scores of individuals, were once more numerous and widespread throughout the world. Most of these indigenous small-scale societies have become extinct, dying out from disease, warfare, and starvation upon contact with Europeans. Others, in recent history, have survived by adapting to a dependency on dominant communities, or sometimes living on reservations, or in encampments near towns, or laboring on farms. A few groups, however, because of their geographical isolation, have continued to follow some form of their aboriginal lifestyle throughout much of this century, retaining their language and cultural traditions despite the hardships they confronted.

Such populations, found in Africa, Australia, New Guinea, the Arctic, and South America, offer evidence of contrasting forms of adaptations to a diversity of environmental resources. Each can provide examples of alternative methods of exploiting environments to gain a living, but most important is the record of their responses to the impact of change brought on by contact with more technologically developed societies. Fortunately, for the record, some of these populations have been studied over extended periods of time. Their cultural traditions, diet, health, and demography under various environmental and social conditions have been recorded as their aboriginal world changed with increased contact and interdependence with other communities. Such people offer examples of the transitions in lifestyles, subsistence, and environments made by societies caught up in the throes of change. Sometimes change was gradual but more often it occurred within less than a generation as trade or colonization absorbed them into a wider, sometimes worldwide network of linkages.

Homeland areas became more restricted with fewer of their traditional resources and less social and family control. Their diet, social setting, and settlement patterns radically altered with numerous attendant biological and social consequences. For these people, whose world has been "turned upside down," the old familiar ways of coping with the demands of the environment no longer worked to provide for their survival. Direction and regulation now came from outside forces and, faced with these changes, they became "players" in a new ecology.

---

[2] Indigenous society is used here to mean original, or aboriginal, a native to the area. Formerly, the word *primitive*, or preliterate societies, had been used to designate an indigenous (aboriginal) people, but this term falsely implied a lower or less evolved state of mind, as we discussed earlier in Chapter 3.

Each of the groups to be discussed inhabit environments with extraordinarily different resources, exploitable by the simple technologies of traditional indigenous societies. These resources were frequently limited and seasonal restricting population size and movement. The periods of rainfall, the migrations of animals, or differing plant growth rates have influenced variations in human survival. Some people have been more sensitive to these seasonal factors because of resource scarcity.

Australians, living and hunting throughout some of the most arid regions of the world's driest continent, followed the availability of water preserved in a few soaks or pools in otherwise dry river beds. Their migrations were more limited by these water sources than by the wild plant foods that provided a majority of their food. Though there is an enormous variety of plants that had been used, the quantity is reduced as one proceeds from the coastal regions into the arid center. Here, food collection depended more on tubers, seeds, and numerous small fruits, which provided well over two-thirds of their calories; hunting of marsupial mammals and goanas (lizards) added but a small portion to their diet. By contrast, the tropical North of Australia offered a greater variety and quantity of food sources to be exploited. An abundant supply of wild yams could be found and were a major part of the subsistence base along with numerous marine organisms (Kirk, 1981; Saggers and Gray 1991).

Similar restrictions applied to hunters of Southern Africa, the San.[3] Their arid homeland, mainly the Kalahari, also restricts their migrations to accessibility to water sources, especially during the dry season. However, herds of a variety of grazing herbivores offered more hunting opportunities than were available to the Australians. Still, collection of wild plants—the roots, seeds, and nuts—provided for the bulk of their diet. (Lee, 1969; Wilmsen, 1989)

The close pastoral neighbors of the San, as well as the pastoralists of East Africa, rely on domesticated cattle herds and were somewhat less restricted. In the recent past, they were able to move their herds following the seasonal rainfall to take advantage of the new grasses. Over 200,000 Turkana distributed over the remote bushland of northwestern Kenya best exemplify this dependence on mixed herds of cattle, goats, and a few camels, but mainly cattle. Like the Maasi, another pastoral people of Kenya, milk, blood, and meat were the major sources, with milk providing over 60 percent of their calories during the wet season. Dependence shifts to a more frequent use of blood during the dry season. As drought progresses, meat from

[3] The term *San* is a linguistic classification that refers to numerous related groups of people previously called by the pejorative term, Bushman. They were once spread over Southern Africa, but now are generally limited to the more isolated western regions. The better known of the San groups include the !Kung, Cae Cae, and Zhu who have been the subjects of many anthropological and medical studies.

their few goats kept for the purpose, is more frequently consumed. For those who can afford to sell some animals, there is a greater dependence on a purchase of grain (Galvin, 1992).

A radical contrast in human subsistence is provided by Arctic populations of Saami herders (Lapps) near the Arctic circle in Scandinavia and the Inuit (Eskimo) of North America and Greenland. These people survive by exploiting the treeless Arctic Tundra, coastal regions, or adjacent ice floes, and they are outstanding examples of human adaptability. The "complete" hunters, the Inuit, were most subject to the "whims" of nature and the luck of the hunt as they sustained small populations over vast areas of Arctic wastes even in recent decades. The Saami or Siberian Evenki (another herding people), by contrast, have relied on their skills as herdsmen, moving seasonally, seeking the most favorable grazing opportunities for their reindeer herds (So, 1980; Leonard et al., 1994).

Differing even more than hunters and herders of desert and arctic lands are the many cultivators within tropical areas. These people have practiced simple forms of agriculture to exploit the tropical rain forests by shifting from one plot of land to another. Trees were cut down and burned with a garden planted in the ashes and then in a year or two the plot was abandoned and another acquired. This process was repeated continuously with long fallow periods of up to thirty years. In some areas, the fallow period was shorter or longer depending on soil and rainfall. More recently, because of environmental disruptions from road building, mining, and lumbering, less land is available to enable a continuation of traditional horticultural practices. In nearly all examples of tropical peoples, cultivation was limited to a few high yielding plants, and diet was supplemented by gathering of a variety of wild plants and some hunting.

The 20,000 Yanomama of a remote area adjoining Venezuela and Brazil provide an example of a forest people of the vast Amazon basin who make their living exploiting the tropical rain forest by simple horticulture, supplemented by hunting and gathering. Various tubers, papaya, and bananas are the principal food plants. Since European contact with South America and the introduction of "old world" plants, the African cooking banana has become a dietary staple, providing over 60 percent of the calories. By shifting their gardens frequently, the Yanomama had been able to sustain large populations scattered in small villages of fifty to a hundred in one of the most isolated areas of South America (Early and Peters, 1990; Smole, 1976). They remained isolated, that is until road and airfield construction opened the Yanomama territory to gold mining during the last three decades.

Adaptations of the people of New Guinea differ in a number of ways from the agriculturists in South America, but their basic strategy has been much the same. In their tropical rain forests they practiced a shifting agriculture, but also supported large numbers of domestic pigs. Their diet, however, was dependent largely upon one or two root crops, the native yam or the sweet potato, introduced some 400 years ago. Collections of some wild plants add small, but essential supplements. People living around swamps and along the sea coasts rely heavily on collection of a native palm (the sago) for its eatable pith, which is scrapped out, dried, and made into a flour (Ohtsuka, 1983). What makes most New Guinea people so unique for dietary studies was their high degree of isolation maintained until nearly the middle of the twentieth century. There were more than a million people living in the central highlands of the island who were unknown to Europeans until 1936 when they were first contacted by government patrols exploring the region. This isolation enabled a preservation of traditional diets, health, and growth patterns (Sinnett, 1977; Bayliss-Smith, 1985).

Both of these tropical rain forest horticulturists contrasted to farmers in the Andes where high altitude and cold restricted not only agricultural choices but reduced the availability of wild plants as well. Nevertheless, several million people have been farming the Altaplano(3,000 to 5,000 meters elevation) for thousands of years. The ancient domesticated plants are still being used today despite the inroads made by imported, refined foods, mostly flour and its products, and rice. The resident Quechua farm the thin rocky soils much as their ancestors did, producing several varieties of potatoes and a hardy grain, quinoa, adapted to high altitudes. This grain and fresh or dried potatoes made up the majority of their diet and still serves today. Sheep are pastured at higher altitudes where plants cannot grow. Given the longivity of agriculture in this region, its accessibility, and the persistence of traditional foods there have been a good many studies of Quechua diet, growth and adaptation to life at altitude (Baker and Little, 1976; Little and Haas, 1989).

Some comparisons of subsistence bases of these groups can demonstrate the many skillful ways humans may adapt to even the most rigorous of environments. The cold of the Arctic made special demands on humans in contrast to the tropics, which presented other challenges to be met. A second component, rarified atmosphere at higher elevation, exerted an entirely different stress on the people. These diverse resources in the different zones of human habitation presented problems but opportunities as well, and large populations have been maintained throughout human history through skillful use of the available resources. Whatever their environmental adaptations, a prime consideration is how they gained all of the nutrients required to satisfy human dietary needs.

Satisfaction of Nutritional Needs the Traditional Way

As we described, *carbohydrates* are obtained from a variety of tubers and grains that today are obtained from highly refined foods. The desert Aboriginals of Australia and the San of southern Africa gained most of their carbohydrates from a collection of roots, nuts, wild fruits, and the seeds of several grasses. By contrast, Arctic hunters like the Inuit(Eskimo) had limited access to plants and, over the course of a year, would consume only small amounts of carbohydrates. What little these hunters would obtain was in the form of glycogen from muscle and organ tissue. At the opposite end of the human subsistence scale are tropical horticulturists cultivating several root crops for their dietary staple; yams and sweet potatoes in New Guinea or cassava (manioc) in South America. Formerly dependent on cassava and a collection of wild plants, the Yanomama have come to rely heavily on plantains (African cooking banana). Pastoral peoples like the Maasi and Turkana of East Africa ingest a large quantity of milk or milk products, rich in lactose sugar, which supplies most of their carbohydrates. The intensive farming by the Quechua of Peru provide several varieties of potatoes and some grains as primary sources of carbohydrates.

The oils of plant seeds, insects, and animal tissues provide another vital nutritional category, *fat*. The Arctic hunter consumes fat directly from the marine mammal tissues. Most other hunters, by contrast, have a less plentiful supply available since many of their animal prey are often very lean, nearly devoid of fat except during certain seasons. Since the intake of some fat is essential for digestion and absorption of muscle tissue, hunters often will abandon a carcass if it is too lean (Speth and Spielmann, 1983). Since there is a wide seasonal variation of weight gain and fat storage of the important game animals, hunting and gathering groups in the more arid regions depend upon collection of wild seeds and nuts for the major portion of their diet including fat from the seed oils. The mongongo nuts, a dietary staple of the southern African San, are a rich source of polyunsaturated fat. In addition, certain insect species, like bogong moths, are highly prized for their fat content. Australians would trek hundreds of miles each year to cliffside nesting places to collect this insect (Flood, 1980). The animal herds of the Maasi and Turkana amply supply this nutrient through milk, milk products, and blood.

For many indigenous people, *protein* is a bit more difficult to obtain. Plant sources are very diverse in their amino acid content, but combinations of vegetable foods can meet human needs. The supply of various proteins found in wild food plants can usually supply the eight essential amino acids and supplement the poor quality root plants. Yams, sweet potatoes, and cassava are especially deficient in protein, for example. Likewise, bananas and plantains are low in protein content, 1 percent or less. The richest and most complete supply is found in animal tissue, and here the Arctic hunter's diet exceeds that of the tropical horticulturist. The pastoral nomads' use of milk, blood, and occasional flesh of their domestic animals puts them near the top in terms of quality and quantity of protein intake. The Turkana of Kenya, for example, consume between 150–400 percent of the recommended amounts.

By contrast, many hunter–forager groups, heavily dependent upon wild plants for a majority of their food, gain the necessary protein quantity less easily. If they are able to consume a variety of different plant species, then the chance of a complete amino acid combination is increased. Some groups, like the San of southern Africa, have access to certain plant foods with high protein content. The mogongo nut staple is as rich in protein as it is in fat. Others, like the Australians living along the northern coastal areas, enjoy access to marine organisms rich in protein.

Many tropical horticulturists, whose food staples are roots or herbaceous plants, must depend upon wild plant, animal, or insect supplements. The tropical horticultural Yanomama have access to fruit-bearing palms and several other wild fruits that are protein sources, making up for the deficiency of their basic plantain diets. Animal tissues, though small in the total calories of the diet, can be another important protein source at certain times of the year. Where game animals are scarce or when they are deemed too thin to be of use nutritionally, the people apparently make do with small supplements from a variety of insects, leaves, and fruits.

The horticulturists of the New Guinea highlands seemingly are protein malnourished, subsisting on a diet far below recommended standards. Though many villagers raise pigs, pork is rarely eaten and then only at special events. The New Guinean's near total reliance on sweet potatoes, high in calories, but low in protein, has perplexed nutritionists for years. The people seldom showed signs of deficiency and appeared able to thrive on such a skewed diet. One explanation that has been offered was that the people had developed intestinal bacterial colonies that were able to fix nitrogen, making up for the dietary deficit (Oomen, 1970). Another, more plausible explanation points to the use of the leaves of certain wild plants that added a small but essential amount of protein. In contrast, the Andean farmers who also rely on a root as a staple (potatoes, with about 1 percent protein) use quantities of grains that have between 10 and 12 percent protein content. This combination of grain and potato adds up to a very favorable balance.

Micronutrients

Most traditional diets contain sufficient food variety to adequately provide quantities of vitamins and minerals. This has been especially true for tropical peoples, who made their living through foraging or horticulture. Even the agriculturists of the Andes, with a more limited range of food sources, have been able to acquire adequate micronutrients. Collections of plants or insects may supplement the diet in some populations, even the use of small amounts of earth taken with the food as a "seasoning" has helped balance certain mineral needs. For hunters of the Arctic, it has not been as easy.

A diet heavily weighted towards consumption of animal flesh and lacking in fresh vegetables and fruits might be expected to be deficient in some vitamins. The Inuit, however, are able to obtain most if not all of the necessary vitamins from their natural diet. Vitamins A and D are in plentiful supply in the fish and marine mammal fats; most of the B complex is also offered in the quantities of animal tissues consumed, especially the organs.

Even vitamin E, once thought to be low in Inuit diets because of the lack of cereals and vegetable oils, has been found at high blood levels of those Inuit living on traditional diets. This is explained by the fact that vitamin E is present in marine mammal fat. In fact, the vitamin found in marine mammals is in a more active biochemical form than that found in a modern American diet rich in grain carbohydrates (Draper and Wo, 1978).

The dietary sources for some vitamins were easily appreciated but how the Inuit were protected from scurvy was, for a long time, difficult to comprehend. European explorers cut off from fresh foods for months at a time suffered from scurvy just as did seamen on long voyages. Several of the early Arctic and Antarctic expeditions, in fact, failed because of the ill health of the personnel due to malnutrition, especially scurvy. While seafarers turned to the use of citrus juice or pickled vegetables, Arctic explorers looked to the native peoples of the polar region for guidance on how to survive in an Arctic niche.

The puzzle was why the Inuit appeared to be so healthy despite what appeared to be a grossly unbalanced diet, at least compared to European experience. A particular question was how did the Inuit escape the ravages of scurvy. True, they ate the few wild berries found during the short summer season and relished eating the vegetation in the stomach contents of caribou but for most of the year meat or fish were their diet staples. The European explorers who had tried could not maintain their health on such a diet until one of them took a closer look at Inuit food preparation. Stefansson required his men to condition themselves to the native dietary regimen, a practice that preserved their health during the long expedition. The practice of eating fresh, lightly cooked meat seemed to be the answer. This was later confirmed by experiment when Stefansson and Andersen consumed nothing but fresh meat and some fat for one full year. Their continued good health proved that one could ingest sufficient vitamin C to remain free of scurvy if fresh meat was not overcooked, a method that followed the Inuit practice of eating nearly raw meat (Draper, 1977:310).

Nutritional Needs and Traditional Diets: An Overview

These illustrations offer some evidence of human ingenuity in extracting a living from even the most restricted environments. Whether the environments are desert, tropical rain forests, semiarid grasslands, or arctic, indigenous peoples have been able to survive on locally derived resources. Tables 6-3a and b list the prime foods used as dietary staples by two groups living in southern Africa; note the predominance of plant over animal sources. There may be seasonal scarcity when certain of these are in short supply and total caloric intake of proteins or fats fall below average population needs. In time of scarcity, there are responses, behavioral or physiological, that enable survival. People continue to work, to reproduce, and children to grow.

TABLE 6–3a Foragers: Dietary Contribution of Food Groups per Person by Month, 1975–1976[1] (Kilocalories)

	J	F	M	A	M	J	J	A	S	O	N	D	Daily Kcal	%	Average
Plant foods	994	918	1,838	2,718	2,572	2,370	2,183	1,845	1,738	1,564	1,653	1,146	21,539	85	1,795
Meat	502	462	336	396	4	207	111	253	79	286	108	126	2,926	12	244
Milk	165	165			40								370	1	31
Meal			136						29	29	29	136	359	2	30
Total	1,661	1,545	2,310	3,114	2,616	2,577	2,294	2,098	1,846	1,879	1,790	1,408	25,194		2,100
Kc/kg	40	37	55	74	62	61	55	50	44	45	43	36			42

[1]The contribution of these major food groups is listed as the average kilocalories per day for each month.

Source: Data adapted from Wilmsen, 1989.

TABLE 6–3b Pastoralists: Dietary Contribution of Food Groups per Person by Month, 1975–1976[1] (Kilocalories)

	J	F	M	A	M	J	J	A	S	O	N	D	Daily Kcal	%	Average
Plant foods	559	675	1,450	1,888	1,799	2,183	2,134	1,814	1,701	1,601	1,341	971	18,125	65	1,510
Meat	398	280	259	448	1,291	49	20	38	40	21	46	52	2,942	11	245
Milk	660	660	660	495	495	330	330	330	165	165	165	330	4,785	17	399
Meal	350	350					175	175	175	175	175	350	1,925	7	160
Total	1,967	1,965	2,369	2,831	3,573	2,560	2,659	2,357	2,081	1,971	1,727	1,703	27,777		2,314
Kc/kg	43	43	52	62	78	56	58	51	45	43	38	37			46

[1]The contribution of these major food groups is listed as the average kilocalories per day for each month.

Source: Data adapted from Wilmsen, 1989.

Upon impact with Western society, there have been radical alterations in the subsistence base of all indigenous groups. New foods were introduced, replacing traditional ones and changing dietary balances. Inuit added refined carbohydrate products in good quantity while decreasing their intake of fats and protein, and Australians were supplied with flour, sugar, and tea as a basic ration from missions or cattle stations. No longer did they have to forage for seeds and roots, but their diets were skewed away from its former protein–fat balance. The San of the Kalahari have been settling around farms and ranches for most of this century to work as laborers and have been receiving their pay in kind, mainly rations of maize meal and milk. The homeland of the New Guinea farmers has been progressively opening up to outside contact until many families are now dependent on a cash economy. The people have increased their consumption of store-bought foods, mostly rice, canned meats, and sugar. The expansion of mining has hastened this westernization process. Even in the Andes where much traditional farming is still practiced, diets of the Quechua include more purchased foods. Overall, remarkable changes have occured in traditional diets, as outlined in Table 6–4. These changes have affected health, growth, and

TABLE 6–4 Some Dietary Transitions

Ethnic Groups	Total Calories	CHO[1]			Fat[2]			Protein[3]		
		Cal	%	gm	Cal	%	gm	Cal	%	gm
New Guinea(a) (Traditional)	1361	1200	88.2	292	30	2.2	3	131	9.6	32
New Guinea(b) (Mixed diet)	2236	1865	83	454	207	9	22.3	164	7	40
San(a) (Traditional)	2140		n/a			n/a		381	17.8	93.1
Inuit(a) (Traditional)	2290	41	2	41	1720	60	185	530	32	100
Inuit(b) (Mixed diet)	2770	820	32	200	1120	43	120	830	25	156
United States (Standard)[4]	3000	1066	35.5	260	1627.5	54.2	175	307.5	10.2	75
British (Standard)	3016	1619	53.6	400	995	32.9	110	401	13.3	100
RDA(male)[5]	2800	1400	50	341	980	35	105	420	102	56

[1]Carbohydrates calculated as calories, percent of total intake, and grams.
[2]Lipid compounds from all sources; animal, vegetable or seeds.
[3]Proteins from all sources.
[4]Standard refers to an estimate of food consumption of the average adult male.
[5]RDA; recommended daily allowances.

Source: Data from Schaefer, 1981; Ulijaszek et al., 1987; National Academy of Science, 1989.

reproduction. It is in the record of these processes that we are able to measure human adaptation to their environments and to calculate resource limitations.

CHILD GROWTH AS ADAPTATION

Children are more affected than adults by changes in living conditions since their growing bodies are sensitive to even mild fluctuations of the environment. The status of a population's children, then, is one of the significant measures of a people's successful exploitation of their environment, as we noted in Chapter 4. Specifically, the mortality and morbidity rates from infancy through adolescence say a lot about adaptation when comparisons are made between generations or to other populations. Additionally, since diet deficiencies and disease are closely linked and influence an individual's progress through childhood's stages, growth (the proportionate change in size) can offer an excellent record of a population's adaptation. Simply, if conditions are good and there is adequate food, shelter, and protection, childhood disease and mortality rates will be low. Children will respond by achieving a rate of growth that will enable them to reach a certain size and weight range at each age. Comparatively, then, child growth followed by measures of final adult size become markers of adaptive success.

Humans grow in a pattern that is specified by their genes interacting with an environment until they achieve a size and shape relative to their chronological age. That is, at each age a child is expected to have reached a certain size and will have obtained a level of development of organ and physiological systems. For example, by about six years of age the first permanent molar teeth have erupted. The skeletal system, as illustrated by radiographic standards, will have developed to specific points of calcification beyond that achieved during infancy and early childhood. The glandular and central nervous system will have reached a certain level of size and function; the brain will have grown to approximately 85 percent of its ultimate adult size by the fourth year. The body size of six-year-olds will be between 109 and 118 cm in height, weighing between 15 and 21 kilograms with little difference between boys and girls. A divergence in body size and shape will begin to appear later in childhood and will be fully expressed by the time of adolescence. However, there can be broad individual size variation within families, as well as among populations. Children may, and often do, fall above or below the means. Such variation is a reflection of both environment and genetic influences, but mainly environmental factors are responsible for differences among populations and between generations.

Starting with simple observations of human growth patterns, that is, a child is so large and so heavy at a certain chronological age, we may use these values to compare populations. Tables 6–5a and b lists height and

TABLE 6–5a Heights (cm) and Weights (kg) of Select Populations (Children and Adults—Males)

	3 years		6 years		9 years		12 years		15 years		18 years	
Groups	**Ht.**	**Wt.**	**Ht.**	**Wt.**	**Ht.**	**Wt.**	**Ht.**	**Wt.**	**Ht.**	**Wt.**	**Ht.**	**Wt.**
United States												
NCHS-Ia[1]	95.0	14.5	115.4	21.1	133.2	30.2	148.4	41.6	169.2	58.8	176.8	69.1
NCHS-IIb[1]	94.6	14.4	116.2	20.5	134.4	29.9	147.6	40.0	171.2	64.2	176.7	72.2
Africa												
San[2]	—	—	111.2	18.33	—	—	132.5	27.5	—	—	160.6	48.7
Hutu[3]	—	—	111.4	18.2	122.9	22.3	137.0	20.2	154.7	41.5	167.1	57.5
Tutsi[3]	—	—	115.2	18.65	128.9	23.4	142.7	30.3	162.4	42.8	176.5	57.4
Turkana[1]	89.2	11.3	106.2	15.1	122.9	20.2	139.4	26.9	148.1	34.8	162.1	47.0
Asia												
Japan[1]	92.0	14.0	113.0	20.0	130.0	28.0	147.0	40.0	166.0	56.0	170.0	61.1
China(PRC)[1]	95.1	14.0	114.7	19.2	130.6	25.3	144.2	33.0	162.0	46.9	167.7	53.2
Evenki[4]	92.8	14.2	110.5	19.0	123.3	23.6	133.0	27.9	157.1	47.3	160.6	57.3
Amerind												
Inuit[5]	91.2	15.3	110.4	21.0	125.3	27.3	137.1	35.0	154.1	48.1	165.5	63.9
Inuit[6]	98.6	17.7	112.7	21.4	128.7	29.1	142.8	39.4	159.7	54.7	171.1	70.5
Quechua[7]	88.2	14.0	107.8	19.7	121.6	25.3	133.0	31.7	149.4	44.5	160.0	57.2
Quechua[8]	84.5	11.0	104.2	18.7	118.5	24.2	129.5	29.8	144.0	38.0	153.7	48.2
Pacific												
Australia[9]	90.2	12.7	114.3	18.2	128.6	24.1	143.1	31.4	163.3	48.1	173.0	60.0
PNG[10]	85.2	11.5	97.0	15.2	110.6	20.4	123.0	25.6	136.7	32.9	149.8	52.0
PNG	84.1	11.5	103.3	16.8	116.1	21.3	124.8	36.4	144.1	40.1	152.1	50.0
Fijian[1]	92.0	14.6	112.8	20.1	128.7	26.2	140.0	33.0	157.3	45.0	169.0	62.8

Sources: [1]Eveleth and Tanner, 1990; NCHS-Ia: National Center of Health Statistics-White; NCHS-Ib: African American. [2]Hausman and Wilmsen, 1985; Heights and weights reported for ranges of ages, 2–4, 5–9, and 10–16 so a midpoint age is recorded in this table. [3]Hiernaux, 1964. [4]Leonard et al., 1990. [5]Rode and Sheppard, 1994. [6]Auger et al., 1980. [7]Leatherman et al., 1995. [8]Frisancho and Baker, 1970. [9]Brown and Townsend, 1982. [10]Heywood, 1983.

TABLE 6–5b Heights (cm) and Weights (kg) of Select Populations (Children and Adults—Females)

	3 years		6 years		9 years		12 years		15 years		18 years	
Groups	Ht.	Wt.	Ht.	Wt.	Ht.	Wt.	Ht.	Wt.	Ht.	Wt.	Ht.	Wt.
United States												
NCHS-Ia[1]	93.6	14.0	114.4	20.2	132.0	29.3	150.2	42.1	161.7	55.1	163.8	
NCHS-IIb[1]	93.8	13.9	115.8	20.8	133.1	29.9	154.1	50.1	162.2	57.1	—	—
Africa												
San[2]			110.0	16.2	—	—	133.7	26.6	—	—	—	—
Hutu[3]		—	—	—	122.4	22.3	135.1	28.8	149.2	37.6	155.0	—
Tutsi[3]	—	—	—	—	126.4	22.5	138.0	27.9	155.0	39.4	162.3	—
Turkana[1]	91.2	12.2	105.7	14.4	125.7	21.7	140.1	29.3	152.4	34.8	164.4	—
Asia												
Japan[1]	92.0	14.40	112.0	19.0	130.0	23.0	149.0	41.0	156.0	51.0	—	—
China(PRC)[1]	91.5	12.8	110.0	18.4	123.4	22.9	138.7	31.4	142.9	40.2	151.1	—
Amerind												
Inuit[5]	92.0	16.0	106.0	19.6	119.7	25.5	139.3	39.0	150.8	50.7	149.4	—
Inuit[6]	94.2	16.1	112.2	21.3	128.5	30.3	147.2	45.3	156.8	56.8	158.0	—
Quechua[7]	88.4	13.6	104.8	18.8	120.1	24.8	137.9	35.7	147.0	46.5	148.9	—
Quechua[8]	85.5	11.3	103.9	17.0	119.0	22.4	131.3	30.0	141.6	42.9	147.8	—
Pacific												
Australia[9]	—	—	112.0	18.0	130.0	26.0	148.0	37.5	156.0	47.5	—	—
PNG[1]	85.0	11.6	99.2	15.9	114.9	20.6	123.0	26.8	140.7	37.7	147.5	—
PNG[10]	—	—	106.2	18.1	—	—	138.1	34.4	141.6	39.8	146.6	—
Fijian[1]	89.5	13.5	112.0	20.0	128.0	26.0	143.6	35.2	155.5	49.3	161.5	—

Sources: [1]Eveleth and Tanner, 1990; NCHS-Ia: National Center of Health Statistics-White; NCHS-Ib: African American. [2]Hausman and Wilmsen, 1985; Heights and weights reported for ranges of ages, 2–4, 5–9, and 10–16 so a midpoint age is recorded in this table. [3]Hiernaux, 1964. [4]Leonard et al., 1990. [5]Rode and Sheppard, 1994. [6]Auger et al., 1980. [7]Leatherman et al., 1995. [8]Frisancho and Baker, 1970. [9]Brown and Townsend, 1982. [10]Heywood, 1983.

weight means for male and female children, ages three to eighteen years, from a sample of populations compared to National Center for Health Statistics (NCHS) norms.[4] These populations are representative of a wide range of ethnic groups at different economic levels living in diverse environments. Children in the United States are larger and heavier at all ages, with their growth slowing as they near their final adult height at about age sixteen (females) or eighteen (males). Children of the several indigenous groups lag behind in the attainment of size at each age. Their growth is slower and prolonged, sometimes into early adulthood. Most achieve an adult height significantly lower than the U.S. mean except for the Turkana, whose males continue to grow beyond age twenty, eventually reaching a final adult height slightly exceeding the U.S. standard.

Though patterns of growth are clearly differentiated among groups, most are comparable until about three years. After this age, some children grow more rapidly than others, gaining weight and height increments at rates near the level of the NCHS standards. However, there may be a growth faltering at certain ages. Note the divergence of weight and height below the NCHS norms among the Quechua and PNG children after age three. These and other ethnic groups may fall further behind during adolescence when growth normally accelerates. Metabolic energy demands of growth and work increase about this time in the life cycle, and the dietary requirements may be difficult to fulfill. Colder climates and high altitude environments can further retard growth rates. In the Arctic, most food energy is expended merely to maintain body temperature, which helps to explain the growth faltering of Inuit children, seen even among those on a Western diet. Lower atmospheric oxygen as well as the cold contribute to slower growth, as in the case of the Quechua. Generally, children in populations who subsist on limited diets enter adolescence later grow slower, mature later, and attain a smaller adult size.

Comparisons of male height for age of the indigenous groups illustrated in Figure 6–1 show that all groups fall below the NCHS standards from the third year on, with the gap becoming wider at each age interval. Several populations converge with or come close to the NCHS norm by age twenty. The Turkana and Australian children, for example, continue their growth beyond age eighteen and reach a final adult height comparable to U.S. adults. The other groups remain at a lower level throughout the age range, though they continue to grow slowly beyond late adolescence; the

[4] The NCHS is used as a reference standard in the evaluation of the children of many ethnic groups. Though recognizing that genetic influences are important and are responsible for many factors of growth diversity, the NCHS standards of both European Americans and African Americans offer a benchmark for evaluation of children and the quality of their environments in many nations because the environmental influence vastly outweighs the genetic in most cases (see Eveleth and Tanner, 1990).

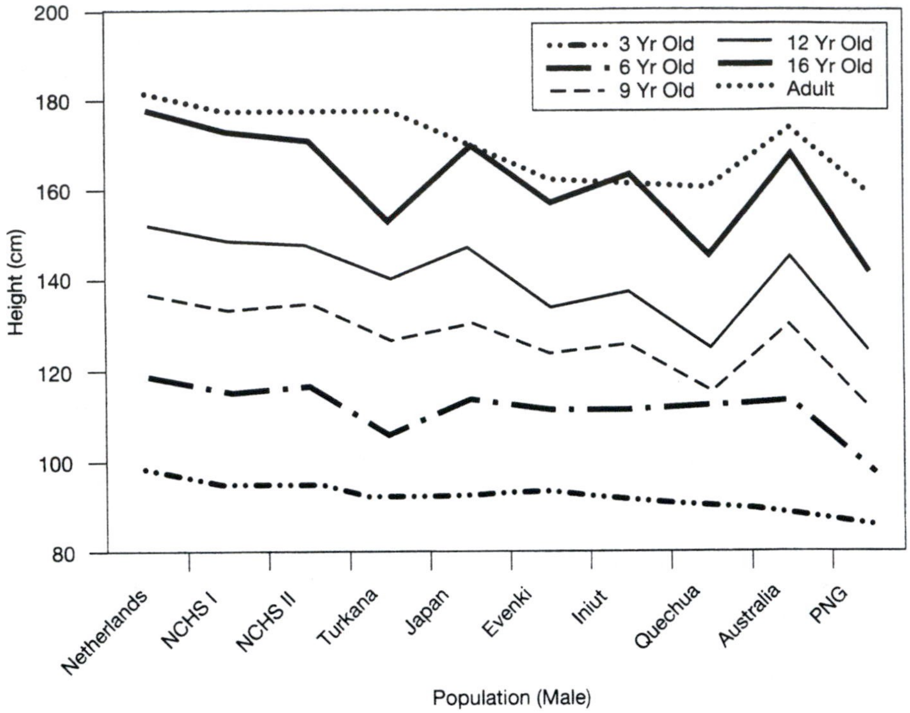

Figure 6–1 Stature for Age

From data selected and adapted from sources listed in Table 6–5 and Table 6–6.

New Guinea groups (PNG) are the smallest, followed by the Quechua Andean populations and then the Arctic Inuit. The children of both groups, living on traditional diets, have maintained a pattern distinct from American or European children, as illustrated.

How much these differences are due to an annual average of undernutrition or simply to seasonal food shortages is hard to determine. But there are some clues offered from comparisons of groups before and after nutritional changes. Food supply fluctuation and resultant growth or health changes have been followed more closely in the San and Turkana of Africa than in any group. When a more stable food supply becomes available, however, size and weight increase to near the norms for other, more sedentary societies. Though among the smallest and lightest people in the world, adult San have gained 6.6 cm for males and 3.4 cm for females over the last seventy-five years. This increase is attributed to an improvement in the lot of a "disadvantaged people," especially a supplement of foods gained from their pastoral neighbors (see Tobias, 1978).

Among the San, such supplements to their traditional diet tend to level out seasonal effects that, in the past, have caused fluctuation in adult weights, but have especially affected children. This observation is supported by the improved growth response of children in villages where their families work as farm laborers. These children were taller and heavier and fewer fall below the 5th percentile for their age group when compared to NCHS standards. Only 23 percent of one- to four-year-olds and 24 percent of five- to nine-year-olds fell below the 5th percentile in 1970 compared to 65 percent who did so in 1967. Fewer differences were seen in the older age groups (Hausman and Wilmsen, 1985). Further contrasts were shown in a study of children from another settlement, some of whom attended school and some who did not. The children not attending school did not differ significantly from the same age groups measured twenty years before; a majority of both groups were below the 3rd percentile. Benefiting from a supplemental feeding program, only 29 percent of the schoolchildren fell below this level. They were taller and heavier with greater fat stores, approaching that of other ethnic groups in the same village, the pastoral Tswana and Herero (Hansen et al., 1993). The transition to sedentary life and a regular food supply increased energy intake and resultant body fat stores, hence their improved rate of growth.

The children of the Turkana pastoralist society have responded in the same way to diet changes. Growth was slow, as noted, and is illustrated by both males and females who remain below the NCHS 5th percentile for African Americans until after age nineteen and sixteen, respectively, when they begin to approach African American standards. A lack of dietary calories depresses weights far below standards but the high protein intake sustains a linear growth. With the establishment of a settlement complete with crop irrigation to encourage sedentary agriculture, the growth profile is changing. Children in the five- to ten-year-old range are taller and heavier than their nomadic counterparts, though infants in the nomadic community are heavier, probably due to a greater milk intake. The advance in growth of settlement children have been ascribed to the supplemental feeding at nursery and primary schools (Little et al., 1983).

On the other side of the world, in extremely different environments, the native Australians and peoples of Papua New Guinea (PNG) have shared much the same experiences as their African counterparts. Children have an accelerated growth pattern, in contrast to previous generations, as diets have shifted more towards the Western type. The Australian Aboriginal child, however, still lags behind the non-Aboriginal Australian. Growth improvements have been noted among Aboriginal children in towns and urban areas who received supplemental feeding, in contrast to remote outstations where quantity and quality of diet is more limited. Of the one hundred children surveyed in "fringe camps" near the town of Cunnamulla, Queensland, only ten children were at or above the 50th percentile for their ages. In contrast, thirty-four of the ninety-eight "town" children had attained this growth level (Copeman et al., 1975).

Comparisons of Aboriginals who grew up during the 1930s with their children and grandchildren some thirty years later showed an increase of as much as 6 centimeters in adult height for both sexes. This secular increase over about a thirty-five-year period may be described as "due to improvements in nutrition, health, and general living conditions." The living conditions certainly changed as more Aboriginal Australians became sedentary occupants of government-run settlements or living in "fringe camps" around towns, but the improvements in diet and lifestyle may be questioned. There has been a steady increase of refined European foods, mainly flour and sugar, in their diets while "bush foods" of their traditional diets have declined. This near total reliance on a few refined foods has reduced the variety of nutrients while increasing diet energy intake. It may be that this increased energy intake is the primary cause of the secular growth increase (Barrett and Brown, 1971).

Not too distant in miles, but environmentally a world away, are the wet tropics of the mountainous island of New Guinea. The occupants of these rugged highland valleys are among the smallest people in the world (see Table 6–5). They are smaller at all ages than their Australian neighbors, and their children are the slowest growing of any population. This may be considered as an adaptation to the rigors of the wet tropical environment and their high carbohydrate, low protein diets (Heywood, 1983). However, over the last few decades, with mining developments, the sale of timber, and cash crop agriculture, Papua New Guinea populations are rapidly moving more into the cash economy of the modern world. Among the many affects of this shifting economy is a greater dependence on imported foods with a concomitant increase in protein and in refined carbohydrates.

Such dietary shifts have resulted in greater weight gains at all ages throughout those New Guinea populations participating in this transition. The Bundi, for example, gain more of their subsistence from western, store-bought foods than they did twenty years ago. As a result, there has been a significant influence on growth. Adolescents of both sexes grow more rapidly and are heavier than their counterparts of two decades earlier. Despite this increase of growth rate, adults remain short and lightweight compared to U.S. standards (Zemel and Jenkins, 1989).

Response to changing diets has been most apparent among children of urban areas or in boarding schools where their diets departed significantly from the traditional. The major differences were in the protein content, and an experiment with diet supplements demonstrated the importance of this food component for New Guinea child growth. Over eleven years, one group was given a supplement of 10 grams of protein a day while a second group received 20 grams. The height and weight gain of both groups exceeded that of children on traditional diets. Bone density and maturation rates also were significantly improved in the supplemented groups. Beneficial growth effects of protein were further demonstrated by the differences between the two supplemented groups; those receiving 20 grams per day excelled over those receiving only 10 grams (Lampl et al., 1978).

The health impact of an increased cash economy is clearly underscored by the weight and height gains of people in the OK Tedi region of western Papua New Guinea. Since 1975 when gold and copper mining began providing employment, greater height gains (156.8 vs. 154.3) are evidenced by a larger stature of the younger adult males in 1984 who had consumed more "western foods" during their growth stage. In addition to increased consumption of imported foods (mainly rice and canned fish), improvements in subsistence farming were made with the shift to a fast-growing variety of sweet potato displacing the taro root as a major food crop of the region. This improvement alone may account for at least some of the growth gains over the decade.

The influence of economic change due to mining operations is further documented when working and nonworking families are compared. Males employed at the mines are taller and heavier than their nonworking counterparts living a traditional lifestyle (158.1 vs. 155.4 cm; 58.6 vs. 51.9 kg), and females of working spouses are also taller and heavier (149.2 cm vs. 147.4; 51.1 vs. 44.6 kg). Interestingly, there is even a difference seen between those living closer to the mines and those living further away; individuals living within a days' walk are taller and heavier. Though the children remain below standards for height and weight at all ages, some improvements were seen; food availability due to the mine employment was a likely cause(Lourie and Taufa, 1986; Ulijaszek et al., 1987).

In contrast to the high temperatures and heavy rainfall of New Guinea, the Quechua of the Andes have to cope with the cold and a rarified atmosphere in addition to the seasonal variation of yields from subsistence farming. Where the Papuans of New Guinea are confronted with malaria and other tropical diseases, the Quechua have to endure low oxygen pressure of the higher elevations. In the district of Nuñoa in southern Peru, most people are living between 3,800 and 4,000 meters elevation. The reduced atmospheric oxygen at these elevations affects both growth and work performance and requires special adaptation. The children grow slower and mature later than their co-ethnics at lower elevations. Even small altitude differences within the district have effected a difference in adolescence growth (Frisancho and Baker, 1970). The exception is a larger rib cage, which allows expanded lung volumes. But dietary deficiencies exacerbate these growth differences under the stress of altitude (Guppta and Basu, 1991).

Children at Nuñoa lag far behind standards for their ages for both height and weight, as depicted in Tables 6–5a and b. But there have been some improvements, as seen in the comparisons of weights of children measured in 1983 with those measured in 1964 (Quech.1 and Quech.2 in Figure 6–2). The children of the 1983 group are heavier but with less difference noted in adults. The size of the Nuñoans, the smallest of any Andean population, is effected also by seasonal food scarcity exacerbated by socioeconomic differences (Leatherman et al., 1995). Lower income groups rely more on a traditional diet of locally produced foods whose quantity changes over

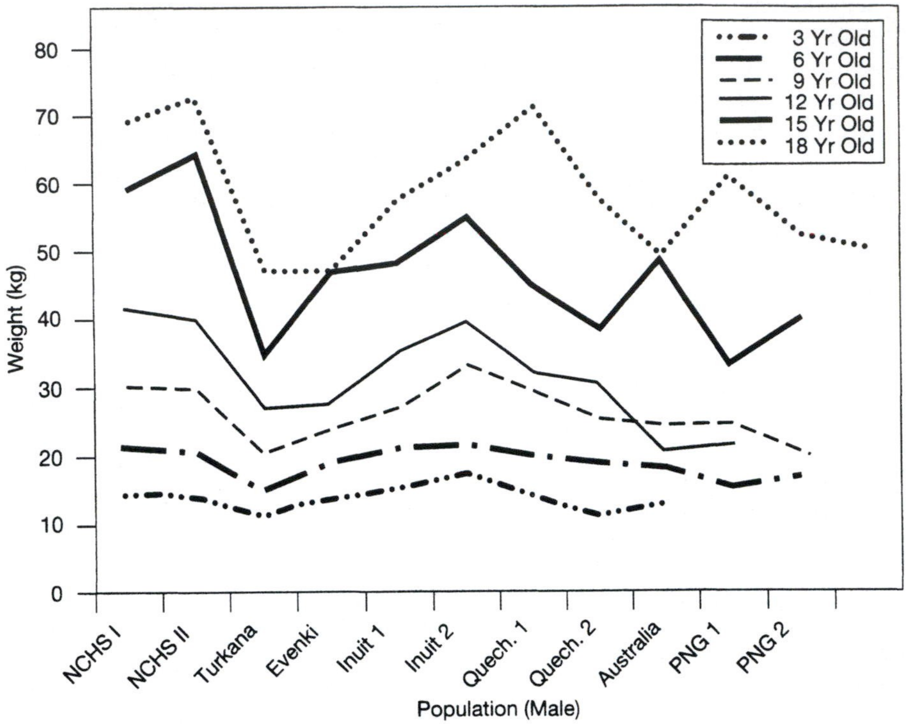

Figure 6–2 Weight for Age

From data selected and adapted from sources listed in Table 6–5 and Table 6–6.

the course of a year and these people suffer greater seasonal variation. As costs rise, they are able to purchase less of the high energy processed foods, so their caloric intake varies. In contrast, upper-income families make use of a wider variety of nontraditional foods purchased at the markets, and they are able to maintain higher energy intakes throughout the year. The results are seen in the growth patterns of their children, who excel over those of the lower-income groups (Leonard et al., 1990).

There is evidence that low environmental temperatures also influence growth, and there are apparent "stunting" effects of the Arctic climate. Among the Evenki, a pastoral people in Siberia, adults fall below the 5th percentile for height and weight. Limited food supply is probably not the problem. The Evenki control large reindeer herds, which provide meat and milk, more than an adequate supply of protein and energy. In addition, their diet is supplemented with imported foods, mainly sugar and white flour. Nevertheless, these people are shorter and lighter in weight than Alaskan Inuit and even Finnish Saami reindeer herders (Leonard et al., 1994).

Leonard and his colleagues noted that, though dietary consumption may be more restricted during the winter when there is a decrease in food imports, seasonal reductions in food supply does not seem to be limiting growth and body size of the Evenki. However, their elevated metabolic rate, required to maintain body temperature in an extremely cold climate, probably utilizes more of the food energy needed to support growth. This hypothesis—elevated metabolism of cold-adapted people limits their growth—is supported by the experiences of several other Arctic peoples, as will be discussed later in this chapter (Energy Requirements).

Though several of the Inuit (Eskimo) groups are taller than many other Arctic peoples, they still fall significantly below NCHS standards. Their growth status appears to have improved over that of their parents and grandparents a half century ago. Comparisons of Cumberland Sound populations in 1938 and 1968 showed children heavier at all ages and a height gain of 9 cm in males and 7 cm in females over the thirty-year period (Table 6–6). This gain was closely correlated with an increase in Western food consumption, an increase which, interestingly enough, coincided with a decline in protein(from 300 grams/day to 100 grams/day per capita). As the people shifted away from their native diet and depended more on imported Western foods, there has been an overall caloric increase (Schaefer, 1970). Similar, but less dramatic changes have been seen among the people living at Igloolik, Canada, on the shores of the Hudson Bay above the Arctic circle, throughout the 1970s and 1980s. Children under eighteen approached the Canadian and NCHS standards (Rode and Shephard, 1994). This relationship of growth pattern to diet adaptation is comparable to that experienced by the western Alaskan Inuit. These Inuit were among the earliest to make trade contacts and they have achieved growth patterns, comparable to NCHS standards, several decades ago.

Secular Trends[5]

The children of the indigenous populations, already discussed, have all outgained their parents in weight and height, especially after three years of age. This has come about as the people have undergone a transition from their traditional lifestyles and is most apparent in the examples of hunters and gatherers who have shifted to a sedentary life. The Australians and Inuits have responded in a dramatic way to high inputs of refined carbohydrates, mainly sugar and flour, or their pastry products. Children of both groups

[5] Secular trend in this context refers to long term, or generational, changes in body size that have been observed in many populations over this century. The majority of studies have been made on populations of developed countries where final adult height has increased from 1 to 1.5 cm per decade, especially noted in the USA, Western Europe, and Japan. In addition, many indigenous peoples also have undergone an increase in stature following a change in diet and living conditions as noted.

TABLE 6–6 Comparisons of Heights (cm) and Weights (kg) of Select Asian and Arctic Populations (Males)

	3 years		6 years		9 years		12 years		15 years		18 years	
Groups	Ht.	Wt.	Ht.	Wt.	Ht.	Wt.	Ht.	Wt.	Ht.	Wt.	Ht.	Wt.
United States[1]												
NCHS-I	95.0	14.5	115.4	21.1	133.2	30.2	148.4	41.6	169.2	58.8	176.8	69.1
Asia[2]												
Japan	92.0	14.0	113.0	20.0	130.0	28.0	147.0	40.0	166.0	56.0	157.3	61.0
China(PRC)	95.1	14.0	114.7	19.2	130.6	25.3	144.2	33.0	162.0	46.9	167.7	53.2
Arctic												
Evenki[3]	92.8	14.2	110.5	19.0	123.3	23.6	133.0	27.9	157.1	47.3	160.6	57.3
Inuit(1938)[4]	87.6	15.3	108.7	22.2	123.3	27.7	132.3	34.5	145.3	43.7	158.5	63.6
Inuit(1968)[5]	96.0	16.5	111.5	20.0	128.5	28.6	140.7	36.4	153.2	44.8	163.1	62.3
Inuit(1970)[6]	98.6	17.7	112.7	21.4	128.7	29.1	142.8	39.4	159.7	54.7	171.1	70.5
Inuit(1970)[7]	91.2	15.3	110.4	21.0	125.3	27.3	137.1	35.0	154.1	48.1	158.5	63.6
Inuit(1980)[8]	—	—	—	—	137.0	33.1	143.5	39.1	162.5	57.4	163.5	63.0
Saami(1970)[9]	92.7	14.3	112.5	19.6	128.8	27.0	140.4	36.9	160.2	43.0	168.7	58.5
High Altitude												
Quechua[10]	88.2	14.0	107.8	19.7	121.6	25.3	133.0	31.7	149.4	44.5	160.0	57.2
Quechua[11]	84.5	11.0	104.2	18.7	118.5	24.2	129.5	29.8	144.0	38.0	153.7	48.2

[1]Reference Populations (USA) (I) White. [2]Asian reference populations reported in Eveleth and Tanner, 1990 [3]Siberia, 1990; Leonard et al.,1994. [4]Cumberland Sound, Alaska; 1938; Schaefer, 1970. [5]Cumberland Sound, Alaska; 1968; Schaefer, 1970. [6]Western Alaska; 1970; Auger et al., 1980. [7]Igloolik, Canada; 1970; Rode and Shepard, 1994. [8]Igloolik, Canada; 1980; Rode and Shepard, 1994. [9]Saami(Lapps); 1970: Auger et al., 1980. [10]Nunuoa, Peru; 1986; Leatherman et al., 1995. [11]Nunuoa, Peru; 1968; Frisancho and Baker, 1970.

have accelerated their growth and gained earlier maturation, but at some cost to their health in later years.

The San and Turkana of Africa have also undergone significant changes but in somewhat different ways. The San are becoming taller, while the Turkana are gaining in fat stores as exhibited by the village children of both groups on supplemental feeding programs. There is a more consistent level of nutrients available throughout the year. Growth and work requirements are met without broad variations in food availability, in contrast to the seasonal fluctuations of previous times. But, again, improvements and changes in the diets of these former nomads are not without costs to their health, and there have been influences on female fertility.

The agriculturists in both New Guinea and the Andes are experiencing changes because they are more integrated into a cash economy as their nations become involved with the developed world. Social class stratification is becoming a new and major factor differentiating among subgroups within each of these populations. Those families with the means to purchase store foods tend to thrive as reflected by their children's growth. The seasonal effects related to dependence on traditional foods is lessened in the case of the Quechua. Also the greater participation in a cash economy by the Papua New Guinea peoples has improved their protein intake together with the addition of refined carbohydrates and fats.

Considering the examples of these indigenous populations in relationship to their subsistence levels, their responses are very similar in that they grow slowly on their traditional diets. Their growth adaptations have resulted in a secular change in size, regardless of the degree differences between the new and traditional diets. Of course, there are many factors influencing height and weight at each age but one common factor seems to tie all of these populations together in their experiences and that is the increased provision of food energy for both work and growth.

ENERGY REQUIREMENTS OF GROWTH, WORK, AND REPRODUCTION

Considering human survival, the major factor is the fulfillment of nutritional needs, which vary among individuals due to age, gender, and workload. Hence, a population with a large proportion of young adults and high work expenditures will have greater energy requirements than more sedentary groups with a higher proportion of individuals under fifteen years of age. Larger average body sizes also will increase food energy needs, particularly in relationship to mean annual temperatures; the lower the temperature the greater are the metabolic needs to compensate for heat loss to the cooler air. These needs may be understood by a consideration of energy balance. In addition to energy required for human growth, the available quantity of energy to satisfy other needs depends upon a certain level of efficiency of the population in the capture of energy from the food chain. As a measure of these various needs we can start with a consideration of basal metabolism rate (BMR).

At a resting state, after 24 hours of fasting, the lowest rate of biochemical activity consonant with life is called the basal metabolic rate (BMR). The total energy expenditure of these biochemical processes is measured in kilocalories (kcal).[6] Another way of viewing these processes is to consider that a nude body in a room at about 25–27^{0}C (77–80^{0}F), will generate enough metabolic heat while at rest to replace body heat lost to the cooler air. This basal or steady state, enables all biochemical reactions to continue with minimal energy expenditure while normal body temperature of 37^{0}C.(98.6^{0}F) is maintained. Any activity that requires muscular exertion will elevate the metabolic activity and thus can be measured in reference to the BMR.[7]

The measurement of metabolic rates is made by recording the volume of oxygen consumed per minute, which is then converted to an energy measure since 4.82 kcal are generated for each liter of oxygen. Hence, a person consuming 250 ml of oxygen per minute will have consumed 360 liters over the course of a 24-hour period, which is equal to 1,735 kcal (360 × 4.82). Since heat is lost through the body surface area, the rate considers not only energy over time but body size as well. In practice then, BMR or metabolic rates are given in terms of kilocalories per square meter of body surface per hour. An average-sized male (176 cm tall, weighing 75 Kg) has a surface area of 1.91 square meters. His BMR would then be 1,735 divided by 1.91 M^2 divided by 24 hours, which equals 37.85 kilocalories per square meter of surface area per hour of energy expended by this individual.[8]

This amount varies over a wide range of individuals, depending on their age. The BMR of a six-year-old child is 50–53 kcal/M^2/hr compared to 36 to 41 kcal at age twenty. There are also gender differences in metabolism; female BMR is normally 10 to 20 percent lower than males. Standard tables

[6]A calorie is a unit of heat needed to raise the temperature of 1 gram of water 1 degree Celcius. In measures of metabolic or of food energy, the unit is in terms of a thousand calories, or *kilocalories*.

[7]For comparisons of activities, a *physical activity ratio*, or PAR, is used to record the metabolic rate elevated above one of the base references (BMR or RMR).

[8]A temperature-rate relationship may be seen by comparison of oxygen consumption of an individual at different room temperatures:

Room Temp. (degrees celcius)	*Oxygen (ml/min)*
0	330
10	290
20	240
30	250
40	255
45	260

typically list 40 kcal/M^2 for males to 32 for females (Ganong, 1993). This difference is largely due to body composition.

If lean body mass is used in the calculation (total weight minus the percent of weight due to fat), then rates of energy consumption are about equal since females have over twice the percent of total mass as body fat (Durnin and Passmore, 1967:36). It becomes a more accurate description if estimates of lean body mass are made.[9] Recorded as energy per unit of mass aids comparisons between individuals by taking into account their energy requirements relative to their body weights. A simple way of estimating energy requirements for various work tasks, especially when comparing indigenous peoples, is to compare energy needs for each task in proportion to body weight.

Because body heat loss is proportional to surface area, climate also influences BMR differences among populations, even with the traditional variation in clothing use. The higher the mean annual temperature, the lower the average metabolic rates of a population. Tropical populations average lower rates than do temperate or arctic peoples since less body heat is lost in warmer environments. Some ethnic variation has been reported that suggests genetic influences, but these comparisons are doubtful since few allowances have been made for dietary differences. Europeans, even after they have acclimatized to an arctic-type diet, still record a lower metabolic rate than do Inuit, however. Disease states as well as hormonal balances also play a role in varying the metabolism; hypothyroid conditions reduce metabolism, for example, while increases in thyroid activity (hyperthyroid) or disease infections elevate the metabolic rate and body temperature.

Resting metabolic rate (RMR) is more frequently used as a measure of energy consumed over a period of time because of the rigor required in measuring BMR (measurement at rest taken after 24 hours of fasting). Measurement of the amount of oxygen consumed by an individual only 3 or 4 hours after a meal is more practical, and the results do not differ significantly from the basal rate. The RMR enables the measurements of more individuals when studies are carried on under field conditions. It is especially helpful as a reference data point for determining the metabolic needs of numerous indigenous people(see Leslie et al., 1984).

Energy and Work Effort

Energy expended to breathe, continue metabolic processes, and to keep warm obviously is not sufficient for survival. Some work effort must be expended to gain food, shelter, and other needs of living. This work effort

[9] Lean body mass is the total body weight less the percent of body fat. The percent of weight due to fat can be calculated in several ways: weight of submerged body divided by weight in air with corrections for lung volume, x-ray densiometry, and most frequently, estimates are made for skinfold thicknesses (see Slaughter et al., 1988).

has been measured by numerous physiologists to provide a record of the necessary occupational energy expenditures. These expenditures of people in developed societies are listed in detail by Durnin and Passmore (1967). The energy required to carry out tasks typical of many populations—industrial, horticultural or hunting and gathering of food—will vary from a few kilocalories per hour as in walking (120–150 kcal/hr), classified as very light to a high of 450 kcal/hour (as in logging or mining).

The energy costs of various tasks carried out by a traditional agricultural group in West Africa are listed for each sex (Table 6-7a,b). Note that the

TABLE 6–7a Work Energy in a Small Scale Agricultural Community[1] (Females; average of 54.1 kg, 156.2 cm)

Activity	PAR[2]	Cal/hr[3]	Cal/Kg/hr[4]
RMR	1.02	55	1.01
Walking	2.6	138	2.55
with a 30 kg load	3.56	188	3.47
Weeding	3.9	204	3.77
Chopping wood	3.52	186	3.44
Planting[5]	3.81	199	3.67
Hoeing	3.78	199	3.68
Harvesting	3.51	181	3.34
Pounding	2.57	138	2.55
Peeling	1.86	97	1.78
Sieving	2.19	116	2.14

[1]The subjects of this study were taken from a marginal agricultural community in the Cameroons, W. Africa.
[2]Physical Activity Ratio.
[3]Energy expenditure in kilocalories per hour.
[4]Energy expended by body weight per hour.
[5]A majority of the planting, harvesting, and preparation was of the root cassava (manioc), a hardy tropical forest plant of New World origin and widely used throughout much of Central Africa since its introduction by the Portugese, 500 years ago.

Source: Data adapted from Pasquet and Koppert, 1993.

TABLE 6–7b Work Energy in a Small Scale Agricultural Community (Males; average of 60.3 kg, 164.2 cm)

Activity	PAR	Cal/hr	Cal/Kg/hr
RMR	1	66	1.089
Walking	2.62	168	2.78
with a 30kg load	(assume 26% increase over female)		
Bush clearing	4.36	280	4.64
Paddling a canoe	3.52	210	3.49
High intensive labor	4.3	281	4.65
Building a canoe	4.77	307	5.09
Fish net pulling	3.54	230	3.81

Source: Data adapted from Pasquet and Koppert, 1993.

rates are higher for males since total weight and not lean body mass is used in the equation. Considering these rates it is easy to see the increased energy needs beyond the daily RMR (Pasquet and Koppert, 1993). Various occupational activities increase energy expenditure from 500 kcal per day above the RMR, about the amount used by an office worker (or sedentary professor), to 3,000 additional kcal per day for persons doing heavy manual labor. This can be calculated from the tables by adding the work effort (hours of work times the energy) to the RMR for the worker's age, sex, and size. These records have been used as standards for comparisons of nonindustrial populations, many living their aboriginal lifestyle. These provide some guidelines but it should be kept in mind that metabolism declines with age, differs due to lean body mass, and will even vary with the season. Whatever the workload, it must be balanced against other energy needs to bring into balance the total with the food energy available.

Growth Rates and Energy Requirements

At birth and for the first year, gain in body length is very high, on the order of about 24 cm for the first twelve months for both sexes, then the annual increments of growth fall to less than a third of that rate for the next ten to twelve years. Then growth accelerates by about 50 percent near the age of twelve in girls and fourteen in boys in what is called the adolescent growth spurt. This is the beginning of a complex maturation process lasting several years during which time the individual passes through adolescence, developing from child to adult. The growth spurt may be delayed two or more years in many populations due to undernutrition, as described for the San, Turkana, and the Papua New Guinea populations in particular. Also, the "spurt" with its accelerated growth is less well defined when food is scarce and growth rates are slow and prolonged into the early twenties as was seen in the Turkana and Quechua.

In well-nourished populations, growth is completed at about age eighteen, and sexual maturity is gradually achieved in the male during adolescence with no single dramatic change. There is the gradual appearance of secondary sexual characteristics of beard, heavier musculature, pubic hair, and maturity of sexual organs. However, the onset of sexual maturity in females is marked by menarche (the first menstrual period) between twelve and fifteen years of age. At this point a girl may conceive and bear children. Her growth continues slowly for several more years, and with each year the probability of conception increases. A great deal of attention has been paid to the age of menarche because it is a marker of the beginning of potential conception (fecundity) and delay or advancement in age has a significant effect on fertility.

Table 6–8 shows examples of age at menarche of a sample of populations. The age range is broad, from eleven or twelve to a delay of eighteen

TABLE 6–8 Ages at Menarche

Population	Age	Date Reported	Ref.
Norway	15.6	1860	1
Finland	17.0	1880	1
Hungary	12.7	1983	1
United States	12.8	1973	1
San	14–15	1976	2
Tutsi	16.5	1958	1
Japan	12.5	1988	1
Inuit	13.4–15	1977	4
Yanomama	13–14	1970	3
PNG	18.0	1967	1
Fijian	13.6	1985	1

Sources:
1. Eveleth & Tanner, 1990.
2. Howell, 1979.
3. Neel & Weiss, 1975
4. Schaefer et al., 1980.

years among the Bundi of New Guinea's Eastern Highlands. Such a large delay in menarche has not been known since the last century in Northwestern Europe as recorded by the data from Norway and Finland. Near comparable delays have been reported in the case of food shortages during war time or major famines. In fact, famine or "war amenorrhea" was first described by a Polish gynecologist in 1916 who argued that the near starvation diet of poor women was the primary cause for interruption of menstruation. Following this observation, other publications described similar delays in menarche related to periods of food deprivation; Leningrad in 1920, Spain in 1936, and France in 1942 all recorded menarcheal age delays of from one to three years (Menken et al., 1981). In addition, there are numerous descriptions of amenorrhea occurring in Europe during times of famine in earlier centuries (Ladurie, 1975).

These observations of the relation between nutrition and female growth and fecundity reinforce the logic that well-nourished women have a potential for reproduction at higher rates than malnourished women. There is a biological explanation offered for these correlations, and it is referred to as the "critical fat hypothesis" (Frisch, 1988). Simply stated, an adolescent girl, nearing the end of her growth spurt will have to obtain a certain level of body fat before menarche. The level of body fat is about 17 percent of total body weight in a 165 cm girl weighing 44 kg and is believed to be the minimum needed to initiate menstruation. This fat level represents stored energy and increases with maturity until reaching a level of 28 percent, which is maintained throughout their reproductive years. These quantities are only averages, of course, and subject to wide individual variation. Thinner girls (low weight for height) do show a delay in menarche in contrast to girls who are heavier and begin menstruating earlier. A body composition effect is also seen among ballet dancers and athletes whose fat/lean body ratios fall below a critical level during their more intense training, causing amenorrhea. This condition is corrected when diet increases and/or the exercise regime changes.

The question of female maturity among indigenous populations has been raised many times, and there has been some reports on age at menarche and the effects of traditional living conditions and diet. As an example, Howell(1979) described the San women as very slender—a description borne out by other reports (Truswell and Hansen, 1976; Lee, 1979). These women have a late age at menarche, about sixteen or seventeen, but the age declines in those groups who become sedentary, increase caloric intake as they change from their traditional foods, and gain body fat. Similar experiences have been reported for Inuit who have undergone major nutritional changes during their lifestyle transition. The increased intake of refined carbohydrates probably contributed to a year and half decrease in menarcheal age (Schaefer et al., 1980). Those groups with the longest history of acculturation—contact with the developed world—had undergone the greatest change. The females of the New Guinea highlands, marked by a late age at menarche (sixteen to eighteen years), also have been maturing more rapidly in recent years as growth rate accelerates with dietary changes (Wood, 1992).

Other factors, in addition to dietary adequacy, are likely to be involved in female sexual maturity and fecundity. The variability of energy expended through mobility searching for food, the carrying of children, and the work of various household tasks are important considerations when calculating the degree of fat storage possible with a given diet. Additionally, the energy costs of pregnancy, breast feeding, and child care are important in calculating the environmental influences on a population's well being.

Energy Costs of Reproduction

The needs of the growing fetus are estimated to be about 300 kilocalories per day or 80,000 kcal of energy are needed to bring the pregnancy to term. Another 500 kilocalories daily are required to support breast feeding. These requirements are in addition to those needed for a mother's own metabolism and any work energy expenditure. Since work load, diet, and energy expended in care of other children vary considerably among the women of different populations, these energy estimates are set at a high, optimum level. The values are calculated to ensure a successful pregnancy and to provide energy for the coming lactation period without endangering the mother's health or depleting her body reserves (Food and Nutritional Board, 1980).

Only modest energy increases have been observed in many pregnant women, and this has caused a downward adjustment of energy needs. An additional 100 kcal per day would probably cover the increase, but would be scaled upward with physical activity; the moderately active would require 200 kcal and the active 280 kcal (see James and Schofield, 1990). Some direct measurements of eleven normal, healthy women established energy requirements of reproduction at 27,120 kcal to meet the metabolic needs of the fetus, or about 100 kcal/day (Emerson et al., 1972). The extra energy for lactation was also calculated at a lower level. Given the efficiency of lactation of about 80 percent and the fecal losses in the infant, the mother must add 135 kcal to sustain each 100 kcal provided for her infant through breast milk (see Leslie et al., 1984). These lower calculations were based on controlled clinical studies of women from developed societies as opposed to the higher, more conservative estimates of the FAO/WHO, however. For comparisons of women of indigenous societies in calculations of their dietary needs, we shall take the more conservative and higher estimates (300 kcal/day for pregnancy and 500 kcal/day for lactation).[10]

In addition to child bearing, the major burden on the females of any indigenous society is the energy they expend in growing or collecting of food for their families. The San females, for example, provide upwards of 60 percent of the family's food energy. This amount increases during times of wild animal scarcity when the proceeds from hunting decline. A great deal of energy is expended in search of food. Women may walk between 3 and 20 kilometers during their gathering trips, usually three or four days per week, for an average of 2400km per year as they trek to the sources of vegetable foods to be collected. The distance increases to 10 or 12 kilometers as the dry season progresses. The food, in the form of nuts, must be gathered or, if roots, must be dug out of the ground, activities that require several hours of walking, stooping, and digging. Then the gathered foods (weighing 7 to 15 kg) must be carried back to camp together with any child under four years of age, adding another 5 to 15 kg (Lee, 1979). This load, plus personal belongings, all add up to quite a burden, as described by Blurton-Jones and Silbey (1978).

Upon her return to camp, her work continues. The roots must be cleaned, scraped, and cooked. The nuts must be cracked and the edible portion extracted; five hours of cracking and pounding are required to produce 1 kilogram of nut meat or about 1,300 kcal of food energy per hour of work. This provides a net yield of about 8 or 10:1 since about 140 kcal are expended in the preparation process. This time-energy commitment limits the number of food collection days and becomes more restrictive with the approach of the dry season. The family's choice of camp sites is then limited to a few per-

[10]Arguments may be offered over the acceptance of the higher or lower amounts given in various publications by different health agencies without resolution of the question. What dietary energy level is to be maintained if the female is not put at health risk by pregnancy and the following months of lactation. Given the arduous conditions encountered by so many indigenous women in their daily lives, a more conservative estimate is taken as the minimum to support reproduction and health.

TABLE 6–9 Southern African San Energy Expenditure[1] (Female; weight of 41kg, height of 150cm)

Activity	Time(hrs)	Kcal/kg/hr	Total Kcal expended
RMR	8	1	328
Walking			
no load	2	2.5	205
14kg load[2]	3	3.6	443
Collection	3	3.8	467
Light work[3]	8	1.6	524
	24	2.13 (average)	1967

[1]Estimates of physical activities and energy expenditure during a daily round of activities.
[2]Loads will vary considerably and will include infant, firewood, roots, and nuts collected on daily round of food gathering. At certain times of year, the load and distance traversed may increase substantially.
[3]Miscellaneous camp activities; tending children, food preparation, cooking, resting, etc.

Source: Data adapted from Lee, 1979; Wilmsen, 1989; Durnin and Passmore, 1967.

manent water holes and the nearer food collecting areas soon become exhausted. Foraging must range further and further from the camp area. Collecting of water, other chores, as well as child care add to the work load of the females. Estimated daily energy expenditures for females of reproductive age are illustrated in Table 6–9. Satisfaction of all the average daily energy requirements is close to 2,000 kcal per day, and over the year this amounts to 720,000 kcal. Though not as well documented, women of other indigenous populations probably bear similar burdens of work.

In many of these populations—hunters, herders, as well as small agriculturists—work demands increase as readily available food supply is diminished. The women gathering the family's food must search further afield, the pastoralist spends more time moving or digging for water, and the farmer enters into the most arduous part of the agricultural cycle, clearing the field and planting. The Turkana females likewise are stressed during periods of water shortages; wells must be dug deeper in dry river beds and water must be hauled upwards of 30 feet and then carried long distances. The dry season forces pastoral people to move more frequently, and most of the burden of shifting a family's possessions and the building of new shelters falls on the women. The effects of these workload increases is reflected by seasonal body weight reductions. West African farmers also show wide-ranging seasonal fluctuations in body weight, being the lowest at the beginning of the rainy seasons, the time of planting when labor demands are the greatest (Thomson, 1977). Cyclical changes are noted in other groups and are well documented for the Quechua in Nuñoa, Peru, where weight changes follow the seasonal food stress experienced among the lower-income groups of the population who are dependent on locally grown food (Leonard, 1989).

The simple addition of all daily energy needs listed in Table 6–9 added to the requirements for successful pregnancy and breast feeding of up to three years suggest that females exist on a narrow margin of stored body energy. Even during the best of times, this energy reserve is borderline between a sufficiency or deficiency. Women can be and often are pushed over the edge seasonally or by an extended drought and unusual food shortage. The net energy deficit is reflected by a number of biological factors in all segments of the population, male and female, but especially by a periodic loss of weight and a decline in female fertility.

Seasonality of Births

There are a number of reports of marked birth seasonality among groups following a traditional or near traditional lifestyle: some of these are listed in Table 6–10 with data from Korean National birth records, which have been examined for seasonality.. The rate differences range up to 100 percent between the months of high and low births. Oaxacan farmers of Mexico differ from their national average, as do Turkana, Maasai, and Kenya. Indigenous peoples especially show that female fertility is effected to a large degree by environmental variables.

In many cases it is the extreme variation in rainfall, and hence fluctuation in food supply, that influences significant differences of birth rates over the year. The San showed a marked seasonality in births among those populations who were largely dependent upon traditional foods. A maximum birth rate of 14.5 percent of the total annual births was reached in March and April, the result of high rates of conceptions in June and July. These cool dry winter months in the Southern Hemisphere followed an interval of plant growth during the preceding summer rainy season. Hence, food supply had reached a maximum supporting a peak in average individual body weight. Thirty six percent of their children are born nine months after the women had reached a peak in their body weight (Wilmsen, 1989). Table 6–11 illustrates the birth rate variation over the year among the San and notes the months of

TABLE 6–10 Birth Seasonality

Population	High(%)[1]	Low(%)[2]	Sources
Turkana(pastoral)	12.8	3.3	Leslie&Fry,1989
Fulani(agro-past.)	19.0	5.7	van den Eerembeemt,1985
San (Hunters)	14.5	5.5	Wilmsen, 1989
Uganda (Farmers)	11.5	6.0	Thompson & Robbins,1973
Oaxaca (Farmers)	14.5	4.4	Malina & Himes, 1977
Matlab, Bangladesh (Farmers)	24.8	10.8	Becker & Sardar, 1981
Korea(National)	12.3	5.5	Cowgill, 1966

[1]Month of highest percentage of total annual births.
[2]Month of lowest percentage of total annual births.

TABLE 6–11 Birth Seasonality (San)

Percent of Births by Month[1]					Month of Conception		
January	9.2[2]	10[4]	6.6[5]	→	April[3]	2.5 /5cm	
February	9.2	10	7	→	May	0/1cm	
March	14.5	8	7.5	→	June	2.5cm/0	Winter (cool&dry)
April	14.5	8	8	→	July	0/0	
May	5.5	8	8.5	→	August	1cm/0	
June	5.5	8	8	→	September	4cm/0	Spring (hot&dry)
July	5.5	8	5.5	→	October	1/2.5cm	
August	5.5	8	10	→	November	4/7cm	
September	5	6	10	→	December	12/5cm	
October	5	6	9	→	January	4/25/13cm	Summer (rainy season)
November	9.2	9.2	7	→	February	8/15/3cm	
December	9.2	10.2	8	→	March	1/2.5/14cm	

[1]Data adapted from Wilmsen, 1989.
[2]Traditional foraging economy (total of 127 births).
[3]Rainfall measured monthly in the Central Kalahari during 1966–68, respectively; Botswana Weather Research Bureau reported in Tanaka, 1980.
[4]Agro-pastoral economy (140).
[5]Maun hospital records, 1953–80 (7,113 births).

conception grouped by season. By comparison, the neighboring sedentary agro-pastoral groups of Herero differed little over the year. Likewise, there was little birth rate fluctuation over the three decades recorded at the regional hospital in Maun township, Botswana. It is interesting to note that the San identify an infertility period that comes with the harsh conditions of drought when food intake falls below energy needs (Wadsworth, 1984).

The Turkana of northwest Kenya have the most highly seasonal distribution of births ever reported. Conceptions are highest during the early dry season, a time that follows a period of maximum food supply and when the population has reached its highest nutritional status (Leslie and Fry, 1989). Births reach a peak nine months later (13 percent of the annual total) at the start of the new rainy season. Not only is there an extreme seasonality among this group, but it is clearly linked to rainfall. This is exemplified by a lag of three and half months after the best of the annual rainfall, the time needed for pasture growth and for the cattle to recover from the seasonal drought. Table 6–12 records birth rates over the annual cycle related to month of conception and the rainfall that month. The cyclical biological changes (growth, weight gain, and conception rates) observed in these pastoral people follow closely that of the food gained from their cattle and hence the independent environmental factor of rainfall.

There are other factors that affect conception and birth intervals besides nutrition and body composition. Seasonality, to a small degree, even effects modern industrial societies. There appears to be certain months with a significantly greater number of births even among peoples in developed countries. In the United States there is between 10 and 20 percent variation; births reach a peak in late summer and early fall and then decline to a low in midwinter(Seiver, 1985).

TABLE 6–12 Birth Seasonality (Turkana)

	Births	%	Conception	Rainfall(cm)
January	18	3.9	April	4.1
February	4	0.8	May	4.0
March	56	12.4	June	3.1
April	59	13.0	July	3.3
May	59	13.0	August	1.1
June	56	12.4	September	2.3
July	21	4.6	October	1.8
August	46	10.2	November	1.9
September	33	7.3	December	1.0
October	34	7.5	January	1.0
November	43	9.5	February	2.3
December	23	5.0	March	4.2
Totals	452			29.3 (cm)

Source: Data adapted from Leslie and Fry, 1989.

These differences appear to relate to sociocultural factors of economics, availability of housing, and career choices that influence decisions of when to marry and when to start a family. Economic and housing conditions have been major influences in Eastern European countries since World War II and have had the effect of keeping fertility rates low. Similar problems occurred during the Great Depression in the United States. Western Europe was also influenced by cyclical changes in population growth rates when a delay in age at marriage increased during times of economic crisis or during wartime, as discussed earlier.

In addition to the social choices available, there are other important environmental considerations besides rainfall that influence conception. One is the extreme seasonality of sunlight in the Arctic and far northern temperate zones. Demographic data from a Canadian Inuit population at Holman, on the west coast of Victoria Island, in the 1970s showed that many women planned births for late winter or early spring, but a majority of unplanned births also occurred during this time (Condon, 1991). These results are comparable to those obtained from church records of 3,700 Inuit births in the community of Nain, Labrador, dating from 1778 to 1940. There was a peak of births in March, falling by 50 percent to a minimum during the summer months of June, July, and August. The births rose again in September and then fell by 30 percent in December and January. Counting back nine months from each of these dates identifies that the months of conception with the highest or lowest rates were seasonally related and or influenced by socioeconomic events (Ehrenkranz, 1983).

The hypothesis offered to explain seasonal influence on rates of conception relates to the incidence of sunlight and the activity of the pineal body, a gland deep in the base of the brain. As winter progresses, the hours of daylight grow shorter, limiting the photo period thus reducing stimulus to the pineal gland. This reduced production of certain neurotransmitters and thereby reduced sexual interest. This lowered the conception rates during those months with the least amounts of daylight.[11] It is plausible and explains, to some degree, the monthly variations in births seen in many populations of the far north. Humans, with their elaborate and complex social systems, often overcome this and other environmental stimuli, however.

The weather conditions of the arctic winters introduce additional harshness and challenges to survival, a time of food shortages and a time of intense cold affecting metabolic processes. Also, winter is a time of change in subsistence activities that takes males away from their families at more frequent intervals as they hunt or run their trap lines. Another factor is that in recent decades, infant feeding practices have altered birth spacing, increased

[11]In the region of Holman, 300 miles north of the Arctic circle, for example, there is no direct sunlight from mid-November to mid-January. By contrast, there is continuous sunlight from mid-May through mid-July.

birth rates, and reduced seasonal effects. Economic factors have also been important. The changes in housing, from traditional to modern heated cabins with artificial lighting, for example, and the increases in wage labor and government subsidy payments have contributed to a lessening of seasonal influences (Condon, 1991).

DEVELOPMENT, FERTILITY, AND POPULATION GROWTH

As just outlined, health, diet, and workload influence the growth and rate of sexual maturity of female children. Generally speaking, nomadic women living a traditional life produce fewer children than the average women of sedentary societies. Comparative studies of several groups of indigenous people who have undergone a lifestyle transition in the twentieth century document this difference.

On average, San women bear their first child about age nineteen and breast feed for up to four or five years. The prolonged period of nursing and the high work energy expenditure have served to keep fertility lower than expected for noncontraceptive-practicing populations.[12] The composition and quantity of their diet has changed in the last three decades, however, when they came to live and work on farms or tend cattle. There were suitable weaning foods for babies, and this led to a reduction in the duration of breast feeding. In addition, more calories provided by milk, meat, and grain, plus a lessened work energy expenditure, enabled women to add body fat stores. Birth intervals were shortened by several months, and between 1963 and 1973, the total fertility rate rose from 4.3 to 6.7 (Wilmsen, 1989). There are several reasons for the rise in TFR and the shortening of birth intervals by several months (see Howell, 1979). The improvement in female nutrition is the most likely cause since the "bush foods," or traditional diets, are invariably associated with low body fat.

Some of the best evidence for diet influence on birth intervals has been provided by Nancy Howell(1979) who reported that the thinner women living a traditional lifestyle average an interval of 42.5 months between births, compared to a 32.3 months for their counterparts living on cattle stations where diets of milk products and grains have boosted their body fat stores. The thinner women living at the cattle posts had a longer birth interval (38.7 months) than the fatter, traditional-living women (36.7 months). The dividing line in body weights for resumption of menstruation and fecundity seemed to be about 42 kg (or 23.7% body fat).

These data are comparable to that derived from Australian studies that also noted the low average number of births per woman in nomadic bands.

---

[12]Suckling stimulates the secretion of prolactin, a hormone that inhibits ovulation (Ganong, 1993).

Genealogies of bands in western Australia, where they had continued to follow a nomadic life with little contact with European Australians until the 1960s, record that women completing their reproductive years had between two or three surviving adult offspring. This number is close to the estimate for precolonial Aboriginal Australians, according to Cowlishaw (1981, 1982). Cowlishaw argued that fertility was low in those groups following traditional lifestyles, contrary to the view that aboriginal women everywhere had suffered from high fertility. She explained, "Low physiological fertility rather than high infanticide and high infant mortality accounted for the low birth rates that have been reported for precontact Aboriginal populations." These low rates are in marked contrast to the increased birth rates seen among populations living on mission or government reserves.

The people on the Yuendumu station in Central Australia, a reserve established by the government in 1946, provide an example. Women have their first child at age nineteen and continue for twenty years with a mean birth interval of thirty-three months. The reproductive histories of twenty-eight women, from 1953–1969, showed a mean of 5.6 children with 4.8 surviving to adulthood, or about double the rate reported among nomadic groups (see Middleton and Francis, 1976). From the 1960s onward, Australian Aboriginal women on this and other reserves conceived earlier; girls as young as fourteen were having babies, an unheard of event within living memory of many older women. Birth intervals had become shorter and reproductive life spans extended, probably due to changes in mobility, dietary energy, and a reduction of the length of breast feeding (White, 1977).

The fertility rates of arctic populations following traditional lifestyles are hard to identify accurately. Fertility rates were likely to have been low, given the harshness of the environment, the heavy work burden, and the small family sizes reported at early European contact. This quickly changed during and following World War II, with construction of military installations, mining, and oil exploration throughout the Inuit's homeland above the Arctic Circle. The people began to work at these sites as hunters and guides for cash wages. As employment increased, they were drawn more into a modern economy. This led to radical changes in diet and a more sedentary existence—easing the workload, especially on the females. There was a sharp rise in fertility during this period of transition until, by 1961, the Canadian Inuit population had reached a TFR of 9.2. The continued modernization over the next twenty years, including a consciousness of family planning, contributed to a decline to a TFR of 4.5 by 1983. This rate is still above the Canadian national rate of 2.5 and probably higher than before European contact (Norris, 1990; Shephard and Rode, 1996).

Sedentary horticulturists like the Yanomama and Quechua agriculturists in South America have had much higher reproductive rates, up to two or three times higher, than nomadic hunters. Studies of the Yanomama between 1960 and 1985 report a TFR of between seven and eight, rates among the highest ever reported for any people. However, only about 35 percent of those females who reach their fifteenth birthday live to age fifty. This mortality, plus a high infant mortality rate and infanticide, keep the net reproductive rate at 1.25; that is, for every female living to age of reproduction, 1.25 daughters will be produced (see Early and Peters, 1990).

The Quechua of Peru also show a high fertility rate, about 6.5 among those living at elevations above 3,000 meters. This is in contrast to a TFR of 8.6 among Quechua living at lower, less stressful elevations. Both groups share a recent common ancestry and live under similar conditions, except for the contrast in oxygen pressure. The fertility difference is probably due to the effects of altitude hypoxia on pregnancy outcomes. Women at altitude give birth to smaller infants, and there is a greater frequency of low birth weight infants (those below 2,500 gm) (McClung, 1969).

Some New Guinea populations may have had high TFRs since the earliest times even before the impact of European influence, as evidenced by the dense settlements in the central highlands of the island. Fertility rates of between 4.6 and 7 have been reported for New Guinea populations between 1959 and 1978, and it is probable that there were similar rates during precontact times (Bentley et al., 1993). In other areas, high infant and childhood mortalities likely kept increases to low levels until the time of contact. The low completed family size (two to three children) reported among the Oriomo, a coastal group who were living with relatively little input from the national economy as recently as 1975, is an example (see Ohtsuka, 1983). Likewise, the Murapin of the Western highlands show a low of 2.7 children per woman surviving to adulthood, though women, by the completion of their reproductive life span, averaged 4.1 children (Sinnet, 1973).

Rate of Natural Increase

The widening of the gap between CBR and CDR have resulted in a high rate of natural increase (RNI) in many of the indigenous populations. This has been best illustrated by the Australian Aboriginal studies, which show RNIs of from 2–2.5 percent over the second half of the twentieth century. The result is a young population, where 46 percent are under the age of fifteen years, compared to the 27 percent for European Australians (see Saggers and Gray, 1991). Comparable RNIs with a large percentage of younger people are reported for several of the more recently contacted groups in New Guinea and South America. The Yanomama were reported as growing at the rate of 0.5–1.0 percent annually in the 1970s (Neel et al., 1977), a rate that increased to an estimated 2.4 percent by 1986 (see Early and Peters, 1990).

Several groups in the New Guinea highlands experienced rates of greater than 1 percent over the decades after contact. This rate has since risen above the 2 percent level. The Murapin, for example, living in one of New Guinea's areas under the earliest European control, were increasing at 2.7

percent per year as early as 1966. Female reproductive life span has increased by at least ten years in some areas, and mortality rates at all ages have been brought down (Scragg, 1972). At the same time, there has been an increase in concern for family planning and the use of contraceptive methods, first in the urban areas and later in the more rural areas since the 1960s. This has contributed to fertility declines in several major highland regions. The Gende people of the Bundi highland area showed a drop from a TFR of 7.4, during the decade of 1964–1974, to a low of 5.75 in the following decade (Jenkins, 1993). However, with the establishment of more frequent contact between regions and with movement into urban areas, sexually transmitted diseases were probably a factor in lowered fertility since these diseases have increased from 4.8 percent (1976) to 28.2 percent (1984) and were still rising into the 1990s.

Obviously, such high rates of natural increase could not have existed over a long period nor can they be sustained much longer. Consider, for example, South America, which has been populated for at least 20,000 years. If the Yanomama had been increasing at the rate of 1 percent over a millennia, then a small band of one hundred original settlers would have produced 14,841 descendants within just a thousand years. If they continued to maintain the same RNI, then over the next 1,000 years they would have increased to 660,793 people, and in 2,000 more years there would be over 14 billion Yanomama. Impossible numbers, to be sure, but an example of the effect of a high RNI maintained over long periods.[13] So numbers alone do not tell the full story of human adaptation; consider that the currently recorded RNI for the several indigenous people, mentioned above, may be of recent origin coinciding with introduction and adoption of certain foods and changes in lifestyles. Demographic measures must be taken in a context of time and environment.

DIET, ADAPTATION, AND DEVELOPMENT: SOME CONCLUSIONS

Differing adaptations and food sources have been used and indigenous peoples apparently have been able to maintain relatively stable populations. But with the impact of development, as increasing contacts were made with the Western world, this stability was radically altered. Colonization and the development of land and resources have either worsened or improved the nutritional state of indigenous peoples everywhere. The dietary status of Australians, for example, declined rapidly as they were cut

[13]Consider a band of thirty people crossing the Bering Straits about 15,000 years ago, the approximate entry of Native American ancestors into the New World. Should they and their descendants increase at the rate of only 0.2% per year, then they would number in the billions by the time Columbus claimed the Americas for Spain.

off from their traditional food resources. Collected into mission stations, they had to subsist on rations of flour, sugar, and tea. When supplies ran out, as they would from time to time, the expectation of the European staff that the Australians could collect food in the old way was unrealistic (Kamien, 1980). The several hundred men, women, and children living at a settlement just could not be sustained on wild plants in the immediate vicinity. When the supplies were exhausted, severe nutritional diseases would appear, from scurvy to beriberi, diseases seldom seen in the twentieth century but occurring as late as the 1930s in some locations.

Likewise, the Inuit's diet declined as they shifted to one of lower protein and more refined food. On the other hand, the New Guinean's have improved their nutritional status with a greater access to store foods; the rice that many have come to rely on more than their native taro or sweet potato provides nearly three times the calories and protein. Also, the steady supply of government rations of a mixed supplement meal has leveled out the seasonal deficiencies suffered formerly by the San of southern Africa. By contrast, the Yanomama of South America are being overrun by gold seekers, and their homeland reduced, and resources depleted. Though their subsistence base was markedly improved by contact a few centuries earlier when some native African plants were introduced, the Yanomama will be hard pressed to survive this new contact and intrusion into their native habitat.

These changes have been reflected in the patterns of child growth and by certain demographic markers. Growth acceleration has been notable in some of these societies for a long period (Australian and Inuit). Others, more recently impacted, are showing evidence of improved growth as they increase participation in a cash economy, New Guinea in particular. Though there has been some disputes over the benefits of shifting from a horticultural subsistence to cash cropping, for the people of New Guinea, at least, it has been an improvement (Bogan and Crittenden, 1987). As the Quechua increase participation in the national economy, their dietary intakes have been changing, with some improvement, but more division along socioeconomic lines. Children of parents who can afford to purchase foods during seasonal shortages are fairing better in their growth pattern. Generally, most of the children of indigenous people have shown significant increases in their growth and earlier maturity.

Female fertility has, on average, increased, and birth spacing has declined. For the former, hunter–gatherer groups like the San, Inuit, and Australian birth rates have gone up as death rates have declined. For some, fertility has decreased from a former high, especially in the case of urban populations (Papua New Guinea). After the high mortality and low population growth rates suffered upon initial impact, many indigenous people have recovered and are increasing rapidly. This recent and rapid growth has caused another problem, one of space. Land is being taken up by mining or timber operation, and large plantations or cattle grazing has cut more indigenous people off from their traditional homelands. The San living on cattle stations, peoples of the New Guinea highlands, and urban-dwelling Aborigines in Australia are facing an overpopulation problem. Their societies have radically changed and are becoming socially stratified as arable land becomes scarce and dependence on wage labor increases; the mine or plantation workers live by wages and occupy an economic level above that of their relatives living in a traditional way.

Chapter 7

Health, Disease, and Development

"Health is a state of complete physical, mental, and social well-being and not merely the absence of disease."

World Health Organization

Health status may be one of the clearest measures of the impact of environmental change on a population. Yet, it is difficult to agree on a simple definition because the mere fact of survival is not a sufficient measure. Health is not simply the absence of disease, but it is a particular condition or state of being that varies between environments and among the differing populations occupying them. When an environment is altered, then people must adapt by altering some component of their behavior. In other words, people must be prepared with adaptive responses to the changing conditions confronting them. A simple point, perhaps, but often overlooked in the study of human ecology. In the previous chapter we described several responses to changing subsistence bases. The growth of children, workloads, and female maturity and fertility are examples. Here we will examine changes in the health–disease state of populations confronted with transitions of their environments, living conditions, and diets.

The definition of health offered by the World Health Organization may be used as a guide, with some modification. Since humans occupy a range of environments and subsist on diverse diets, it is more helpful to consider health status relative to a point along a continuum that encompasses a broad range, from low to high morbidity.[1] For example, some people have survived

[1]Morbidity, the relative incidence of disease, may refer to a single or combination of disease entities.

under conditions of malnutrition and disease stresses while others have not. The health of the survivors, enduring these stresses, would be located on the lower end of the continuum. Their life expectancy would be short, morbidity would be high, and the children would not achieve full growth potential. These measures would improve or decline with environmental changes.

EPIDEMIOLOGICAL TRANSITIONS

Epidemiology is more than the term implies—a study of epidemics. It is a study of the geographical *distribution* of a disease or its frequency among divisions within a population (age, gender, ethnic, or economic). For example, most cancers occur more frequently among older age groups, and some appear to have a geographic distribution. Yellow fever, a deadly viral disease, transmitted by a certain mosquito species, has a tropical and subtropical distribution. The bacterial diseases typhoid and cholera, distributed by contaminated food or water, are seasonal, rising to a peak during the summer. Typhus, a bacterial disease carried by lice from human to human, is rare today but was common among the poor in their crowded living quarters a century ago. Adult onset diabetes strikes hardest among certain ethnic groups, like many Native Americans, Polynesians, and Australians.

The epidemiologist records the incidence or frequencies of these diseases and their distribution. In other words, what makes people ill or causes less than optimum health; the answer involves the consideration of a pattern of time, place, and economics. An explanation of this pattern utilizes the second major component of epidemiology, *determination,* which must apply many of the diverse elements of human ecology. This is clearly illustrated by the numerous epidemiological transitions from one group of major diseases to another, which have occurred in the past and still continue among some populations today.

Towards the end of the eighteenth century, we were leaving an era of pestilence where a large percentage of children died before their fifth birthday. As this *Stage I* of the epidemiological transition receded, we entered a period during the nineteenth century when there were fewer mortality peaks spaced further apart in time. It was a transition in many ways resulting in higher survival rates and a lower average mortality from fewer infectious diseases. This was *Stage II* of the epidemiological transition (Omran, 1982). It was marked by periodic episodes of high mortality caused by outbreaks of infectious diseases like smallpox, cholera, typhoid, plague, and a variety of acute respiratory diseases. Such diseases, singularly or in combination, would spread throughout the poorly housed, poorly fed populations, crowded into the growing cities of Western Europe. Mortality was highest among infants and young children, holding average life expectancy down to thirty or forty years. Then gradual improvements in sanitation, housing, and living conditions in general reduced the impact of many of these infectious diseases and shifted mortality rates to older age groups; children were now more likely to survive to adulthood.

This second stage persisted for several decades into the twentieth century. Infectious diseases of childhood were brought under control as more vaccines were developed and nutrition improved. In many countries, food, water, and airborne diseases continued to be a problem, but the probability of dying was again shifting to older age groups as childhood mortality declined. Life expectancy at birth in the United States rose to sixty-eight years by 1950, a gain of ten years since the beginning of the century. For adults over forty years old, life expectancy changed little, however. There were significant differences in morbidity and mortality rates between ethnic and socioeconomic levels, and some of these differences continue to this day.

Recent Epidemiological Transitions

Transitions in the health status of populations continue as development and environmental changes proceed. Now the range of differences among societies are much broader than at any time in history. In the more developed industrialized world, the principle illness and major causes of death have shifted to several chronic diseases, like cancer, diabetes, and diseases of the cardiovascular system. These are probably human-caused, a result of significant changes in diet, lifestyle, and environmental pollution. By contrast, most populations of the less-developed world have continued at a middle level of transition, where they are still subject to mortality from infectious and parasitic diseases and enjoy only a moderate life expectancy. The death rates at Stage II are still high, but declining towards the lows reached at Stage III, where they have stabilized at 10 for the more-developed countries and around 15 to 20 for many of the lesser-developed countries.

This third stage of transition began early in the twentieth century in Europe and the United States. Because of preventive measures and vaccines, several infectious diseases were no longer significant problems. The incidence of gastrointestinal diseases, several childhood diseases, tuberculosis, and pneumonia, all with a high morbidity and once the leading causes of death, have been reduced to insignificant levels in developed countries. The major causes of death are now the chronic, degenerative types of disease, with cardiovascular disease, cancer, and obstructive respiratory diseases leading the list (Table 7–1). Several kinds of cancers and cardiovascular disease have steadily increased to replace tuberculosis and pneumonia as leading causes of death. By 1950, the longer life expectancy increased the risk of dying from one of several of the chronic, degenerative type diseases. In the past decade, new health threats have begun to appear in the form of chronic respiratory diseases, like emphysema and bronchitis, and are becoming more significant factors in the death rates of an aging population. Medical

TABLE 7–1 Average Annual Death Rates per 100,000 from 15 Leading Causes, United States—1900, 1950, and 1995

	1900		1950		1995	
	All Causes	1,755.0	All Causes	963.8	All causes	880.00
1.	Tuberculosis	201.9	Heart disease	356.8	Heart	362.5
2.	Influenza & pneumonia	181.5	Malignant neoplasms	139.8	Malignant neoplasms	204.7
3.	Diarrhea & enteritis	133.2	Cerebrovascular	104.0	Cerebrovascular diseases	60.2
4.	Heart	132.1	All accidents	60.6	All accidents	34.1
5.	Congenital	91.8	Perinatal diseases	40.5	Pulmonary disease	39.9
6.	Acute & chronic	89.0	Influenza & pneumonia	31.3	Pneumonia & influenza	31.8
7.	Stroke	75.0	Tuberculosis	22.5	Diabetes	22.5
8.	Bron-pneumonia	67.6	Atherosclerosis	20.4	Suicide	11.8
9.	Cancer	63.0	Kidney	18.7	Cirrhosis	9.5
10.	Diphtheria	43.3	Diabetes	16.2	Infection & Parasitic	18.9
11.	Thyphoid	35.9	Congenital abnormal	12.2	Kidney	9.1
12.	Liver cirrhosis	12.9	Suicide	11.4	Homicide	8.1
13.	Measles	12.5	Cirrhosis of liver	9.2	Septicemia	8.0
14.	Whooping Cough	12.1	Hypertension	8.3	Perinatal diseases	5.2
15.	Diabetes	9.7	Intestinal obstr.	5.9	HIV	16.2

Sources: *Statistical Abstract of the United States*, U.S. Government Printing Office, Washington, D.C.: 1930; *Monthly Vital Statistics Report*, vol. 38, no. 5, Supplement, 1995; U. S. Dept. of Health and Human Services; U. S. Department of Commerce, *Statistical Abstract of the United States*, 1976, *Statistical Abstract of the United States*, 1997. 117th ed., U. S. Dept. of Commerce.

intervention is increasingly successful in delaying fatalities from such diseases, and a fourth stage of transition has been established, a stage of delayed dengerative diseases.

The health problems confronted now relate to overnutrition and its consequences of obesity, diabetes, and cardiovascular problems. Overeating, especially of animal fats, coupled with limited physical exercise, are believed to be contributing factors to cardiovascular diseases. For years, the American Heart Association has recommended that Americans reduce total caloric intake and limit fat consumption. Its recommendations are supported with statistics that have established the links of high cholesterol and obesity to heart disease. There are also many linkages among these diseases, environment, socioeconomic status, as well as diet. In sum, changing lifestyle accompanying urbanization, the rise of industrialization with its pollution, coupled with tobacco smoking and overnutrition have contributed to this modern epidemiological transition.

Cardiovascular Diseases (CVD)

In the United States, diseases of the heart account for 33 percent of all deaths, and in Western Europe these causes of fatality are nearly as high. Certain developing countries have been reporting increases in coronary disease among the wealthier classes who are adopting Western lifestyles. This trend has been noted among males of Indian origin in Malaysia and Fiji. The business classes in China's burgeoning urban centers are undergoing this experience as well. As their incomes rose, so did their food consumption.

Dietary influences were underscored by the experiences of several European populations during World War II. The incidence of coronary heart disease dropped to one-third of the prewar incidence in Finland and the Netherlands, but after the war, as nutrition rose back up to prewar levels, so did coronary heart disease. A realization of the importance of proper diet and exercise began to influence health, and several countries showed a dramatic decrease. The United States reduced the rate from 470 in 1975 to 362 per 100,000 population in 1995.

Mortality rates from all types of cardiovascular diseases showed a broad difference among a ranking of fifty-two nations.[2] They varied from a low of 119.4 per 100,000 in Guatemala to a high of 449.7 in Romania (54 percent of all deaths were due to heart disease). Other high rates are found throughout Eastern Europe. By contrast, Finland, New Zealand, northern Ireland, and Denmark are in the midrange of all types of cardiovascular diseases (ranks of 36, 33, 39, and 18, respectively), but rank at the top for deaths due to coronary heart disease (peaks of 47, 46, 52, and 42). Considering only the highly developed industrialized countries, Japan has the lowest mortal-

[2]Ranks range from one, the lowest mortality, to fifty-two, the highest.

ity rate, whereas France is the next lowest for all types of cardiovascular diseases (World Health Organization, 1987; see also Polednak, 1989). These differences have stimulated numerous questions regarding behaviors that relate to health, as well as possible genetic influences. Significant variation between ethnic groups has been recorded in those nations reporting health statistics by such classification.[3]

In Finland, for example, a country with one of the higher coronary heart disease rates, the Saami (Lapps) have a significantly lower rate than the national average. Finns living in a region of northern Norway have higher coronary heart disease rates than Norwegians and Saami living in the same area. Careful studies of populations in another high-rate country, New Zealand, also reveal considerable ethnic group differences. Maori, the aboriginal inhabitants, had a higher rate than those of European descent; there was even a significant difference between Maori who followed the Mormon religion and those who did not. The Mormon Maori, adhering to their religion's sanctions against tobacco and alcohol, had the lower incidence. An interesting aspect of the study was the finding that Maori women were at higher risk from coronary heart disease, the reverse of results from so many other studies that showed males at a higher risk (Prior, 1987).

In a majority of the more-developed societies, the incidence of cardiovascular diseases have been declining for the past two decades. The decline has been unevenly distributed across social and ethnic boundaries, however. Rates have remained higher and have declined less among the urban poor, who subsist on diets higher in fat, with more refined carbohydrates and fewer fresh fruit and vegetables. Accordingly, they suffer CVD rates well above the national average. Though in the past, CVD had been more of a problem for the upper socioeconomic classes as it is today in the developing nations, the reverse is now true. Those groups at the lower-income levels in the more-developed nations are at greater risk. From childhood on, blood cholesterol exceeds recommended levels, and obesity is near universal. Such a reversal has been reported for nations from the United States and Canada to Australia, Britain, and Holland (Cavalli-Sforza, et al, 1996).

Hypertension

On average, blood pressure tends to rise with age, with excess body weight, and is higher in males than females, at least among populations of the developed world. Though the division between normal and high blood pressure is rather broad, significant differences exist in developing countries and between social and ethnic groups. Hypertension is becoming a major prob-

[3]Though a considerable discussion is offered over racial and ethnic differences in mortality and morbidity, few nations divide their populations into these classifications. Further, there is little consistency in those that do record data by race and/or ethnic groups.

lem in China, for example. Increases over the past two decades have been reported and probably account for about 50 percent of all deaths. There are significant differences between populations in the northern and southern regions and between rural and urban. In the north, the incidence of hypertension is higher, and the rate among urban populations exceed that of the rural. Various explanations have been offered, including the higher use of salt and a lower intake of calcium in Northern China, for example. In fact, the increases of dietary calcium while lowering salt intake has been an effective treatment. Diet changes as well as the stresses of city life must be considered together as factors when comparing urban–rural differences (Cavalli-Sforza et al., 1996).

The ethnic factor has been frequently reported in the United States; African Americans—both males and females—have consistently higher pressures than Whites. These differences have been attributed to dietary habits, the frequent and heavy use of common table salt (sodium chloride), and possibly genetic factors as well. It has been hypothesized that African Americans may be highly sensitive to sodium and less able to manage even moderate intakes. The hypothesis assumes genetic adaptation to low sodium diets because their reputed original homeland, West Central Africa, is a region low in available salt supplies (Wilson, 1986). This may be questioned on the grounds that there is a variation in hypertension throughout populations in Africa today and that large salt supplies existed and were an important part of precolonial trade. Most importantly, African Americans are a heterogeneous population containing a diverse combination of European and African genes. It is highly unlikely that any particular trait of African origin would persist evenly throughout the entire population after four centuries of interbreeding with peoples of European and Native American origins (see Molnar, 1998).

A more likely explanation for hypertension in ethnic minorities may be found in social differences. The frustration and tensions encountered in the daily lives of persons of lower socioeconomic status can add to anxiety and increased blood pressure. Attempts to link skin color (assumed to be a crude measure of African admixture) with blood pressure have met with little success when corrections were made for socioeconomic level. Persons with darker skin did tend to have higher blood pressure but only if those measured were persons in the lower economic and educational levels (Klag et al., 1991). African Americans, as well as other minority groups around the world, encounter many stressful situations in their daily lives, and there is ample physiological evidence that anxiety and tension brought about by many causes can quickly elevate blood pressure. Even the measurement procedure itself is often a sufficient cause of anxiety.

Native Australians offer another example of the effects of environments and ethnicity. On Western diets they are at high risk for heart disease, diabetes, and especially for hypertension. The incidence of hypertension is especially high among urban Aboriginals. When small family groups have left the poverty and poor living conditions of towns or on reservations and revert to at least part of their traditional life, their health and spirits have improved markedly (Saggers and Gray, 1991).

The stresses of modern living certainly influence us all to some degree. Populations living in isolated rural communities frequently show lower average blood pressures than their relatives living in urban areas. When aboriginal peoples move to towns and cities where they adopt Western diets and lifestyles, one of the earliest detectable physiological responses is increased blood pressure. This relocation affect has been measured in peoples as diverse as the Inuit, New Guineans, Solomon Islanders, and Australian Aboriginals. In their native environments, not only are there few people with hypertension, but there is no significant increase in blood pressure with age, as has been typically recorded for Europeans and persons of European ancestry.

In addition, nomadic tribes of East Africa, normally with low pressure patterns, increase blood pressure when they adopt a sedentary lifestyle. The same experience is shared by numerous other tribal groups throughout Africa (Hutt and Burkitt, 1986). A feature common among these low blood pressure communities is a low salt intake, while diverse ethnic groups on high salt diets show a similar history of rising blood pressure with age. The salt intake level and blood pressure relationship is not as simple as once thought, however. Other factors, such as the intake of potassium or calcium, are influential; an increase in these elements in proportion to sodium lowers the salt risk factor. Regardless of the causes, hypertension is a serious factor in the incidence of cardiovascular diseases (CVD).

Cancer

Cancers or malignant neoplasms are formed when a collection of cells radically change their normal functions and begin to multiply rapidly in uncontrolled growth, which eventually leads to a spreading and an overwhelming of healthy tissues in other parts of the body. There are one hundred varieties of this disease, classified according to the site or organ in which it originates (lung, skin, breast, prostate, colon, and so on). Certain cancers are more lethal than others, and approximately 50 percent of malignancies may prove to be fatal. The fatality rate depends a great deal on the type of neoplasm, the length of time it has grown before detection, and, of course, the medical treatment. The cure rate of skin cancers (basal and squamous types) is close to 100 percent, whereas it is less than 50 percent for lung cancer and the third type of skin cancer, melanoma.

Though heart disease-related deaths leveled off and have begun a decline two decades ago, deaths from cancers have continued to climb in many countries. Cancer has replaced heart disease as the leading cause of death in some industrial countries, Japan for example. The U.S. cancer mortality rate increased by 6.3 percent between 1973 and 1992. There has been some success in bringing down rates of most types of cancer and, if lung cancer is excluded, the overall rate has dropped by 3 percent. Despite this decline, about 24 percent of the deaths in the United States are due to malignant neoplasms compared with the 40 percent caused by cardiovascular disease.

In the developing world, cancer mortality is growing rapidly as urbanization and industrialization increases. One estimate is that as many die from cancer in the developing world as do in all of the developed countries combined. This amounts to 1 million in China and about 400,000 in India. These rates are certain to go higher, replacing infectious diseases as the leading cause of death (Lopez, 1993). Ironically, the decline of infectious diseases in the young has extended their life span, which has increased the risk of the chronic diseases. As this large cohort, born during periods of rapid population growth, reach old age, the leading causes of mortality will radically change.

Causes of many cancers are still obscure—that is, the mechanisms that cause cells to become malignant are not known for certain, though there are several studies that point to a mutation in the somatic cells' DNA that energizes growth stimulation and receptor systems (Ames and Gold, 1995). Ionizing radiation from x-rays, nuclear power, or cosmic rays has long been known to have such mutagenic effects. In addition, persons who have been exposed to fallout from atomic testing have two to three times the national average for leukemia. Another source, ultraviolet rays from the sun, causes skin cancers, which occur most frequently in fairer-skinned persons and usually on the backs of the hands and parts of the face. Skin cancer is more likely in such persons whose occupations keep them outdoors a good part of the day. The rates are higher among fair-skinned farmers and fishermen in tropical areas, for example.

In addition to these mutagens, a number of environmental risk factors have been listed for different types of malignancies. Close correlations are seen between certain diets and cancers of the stomach and colon; between alcohol and esophagus, throat, and mouth cancer; and between tobacco smoke and lung cancer. A long list of organic chemicals and substances like asbestos fibers are also implicated as causes of cancers of the lung, liver, and bladder, especially because workers exposed to them through their occupations have an extremely high incidence of certain types of cancer (lung cancer among asbestos plant workers, for example). Cancers of the lung, large intestine, and breast cause over half of all cancer deaths.

Lung cancer, described by Cairns (1975:69) as "a disease of the twentieth century" is closely correlated with cigarette smoking; the risk of contracting lung cancer is 50 times greater in smokers than in nonsmokers. Further evidence of tobacco's influence was provided by the rising incidence of lung cancer among females who began to adopt the smoking habit some twenty to thirty years after males. The rate among women was more than three times as great in 1985 as in 1950, whereas the male rate increased 2.7 times during this period. From 1973 to 1992, lung cancer mortality for women rose 136.5 percent, compared to only 16.5 percent for men, again reflecting their later adoption of the habit (Rennie and Rusting, 1996).

Though tobacco use in much of the developed world has declined significantly this past decade, it is on the increase in many Third World countries, especially throughout Asia. China now consumes one-fourth of the world's cigarette production. Lung diseases of all types are expected to increase in the developing world in contrast to the decline that is already evident among the developed countries. About 30 percent of tobacco-related deaths in 1995 were in the developing countries, and this rate is expected to rise to 70 percent by 2025 (Lopez, 1990a,b; McGinn, 1997). Many health officials have pointed out that if tobacco smoking were abolished, this form of cancer would be nearly eliminated. Air pollution, though a contributing cause of lung disease, has been given less attention, however. In many of the Third World countries, rushing to industrialize, emission control has not been a high priority. Factory furnaces and electric generating plants belching unfiltered smoke add to an atmosphere already burdened with exhausts from auto and truck traffic. Added to these pollution sources is the wide use of low grade, high sulfur coal which emits thousands of tons of sulfates into the air each year.

Food habits are another likely cause of certain types of cancers. A diet high in meat and fat but low in cereals appears to be closely linked to cancer of the large intestine; a significant factor appears to be the low amount of dietary fibers found in a highly refined carbohydrate diet plus the abundance of meat and animal fat. The distribution of colon cancer corresponds closely with dietary quality, and this form of cancer varies considerably among countries; the MDC have the highest incidence (Burkitt, 1971). Males and females in the United States have a rate of between 30.1 and 26.1 per 100,000 population, in contrast to Japan, India, and Nigeria where the incidence is less than 5.4/100,000 (Hutt and Burkitt, 1986).

The Inuit stand out as an exception to this correlation described by Burkitt. The critical dietary differences are the types of fatty acids found in the flesh of marine mammals and fish—these fats do not promote tumor growth as do the fatty acids from beef or pork. Such critical differences in chemical structure allow the Inuit to escape bowel cancers that would be expected otherwise on a low-fiber, high-fat diet (Cohen, 1987). Because of this relationship to diet types, a great deal of attention has been directed to the fat and fiber content of Western diets.[4]

[4]Western-type diet refers to the typical high fat, protein, and refined carbohydrates of the more-developed countries.

The most frequent cancer of women, breast cancer, has a world distribution similar to that of colon cancer. Women on Western-type diets have the world's highest rate of breast cancer. Women in Canada and the United States have an incidence of about 80/100,000, compared to women in Japan and India with less than twenty. Because this distribution closely follows dietary quality, it is possible that a high-fat diet encourages tumor growth. Also, the highly refined nature of the carbohydrates may be another factor. The low-fiber quality of the Western diet suggests that some component(s) are lost during the refining of cereal grains.

Though the evidence is not complete, it seems that the element selenium and vitamin E may be some of the factors involved. These substances are found in abundance on the outer surfaces of many whole grains but most is lost during the refining processes. Test results have demonstrated the antioxidant properties of selenium and vitamin E, which work to protect cell membranes from oxidation by products of cell metabolism (Combs and Scott, 1977). The general functions of selenium in human nutrition are becoming better understood as well as its influence on certain cancer sites (Levander, 1987). The environmental influence (dietary), rather than genetics, is supported by the examples of Japanese women who migrated to Hawaii. Here, within two generations, their breast cancer rates were nearer those of Hawaiian women (80 per 100,000) than in Japan (11 per 100,000). However, there is an increasing number of genes that have been implicated in the susceptibility for the growth of certain types of tumors, but environment plays a major role.

The preceding examples, plus others, suggest that many cancers, perhaps 70 to 90 percent of the cases, are environmentally determined (Mayer, 1983; Trichopoulos et al., 1996). The data on diet, the concentration of environmental pollutants, alcohol use, and smoking all point to this likelihood. Additional evidence is provided by a comparison of ethnic groups that have migrated and adopted the food habits of their new homeland. Japan's populations have very high rates of stomach cancer (from 76.9 to 82.0 per 100,000), but Japanese immigrants living in California and Hawaii have significantly lower incidences (25 to 28 per 100,000), declining further with each generation. The high incidence of stomach cancer in Japan probably relates to a diet that contains large quantities of salt fish and pickled vegetables. Other groups with comparable diets that include large quantities of dried, salted fish also have high rates of this disease: Iceland, Finland, and Norway.

Further evidence of the environmental effects on the course of the disease is offered by the increase of cancer incidence with age. Cairns (1975) described that the over-sixty age group was at greatest risk. He reasoned that the longer one is exposed to carcinogens, the greater the chance of the disease; the effects of many carcinogenic substances may not show up until twenty to forty years after exposure. With an increased number of persons living into their eighties, a higher cancer rate is to be expected. Japanese people, with the world's highest longevity in addition to a shift in diet proportions from carbohydrates to higher animal fats and proteins, would expect to experience a further increase of cancers in the years to come.

This increase was predicted ten years ago for many of the developing countries. According to Maurice (1991), the number of new cases were likely to double from 5 to 10 million, and this is exactly what is happening. With aging, the probability of contracting cancer increases, and it follows that as the average age of a developing country's population increases with declines in mortality from infectious diseases, cancers will be more frequent.

Diabetes

This disease, diabetes mellitus(DM), is a complex syndrome principally characterized by an inability to maintain blood sugar levels within a normal range. The condition of "glucose intolerance" has a variety of causes. These include insufficiency of insulin (a pancreatic hormone regulating glucose levels), cellular insensitivity to the action of insulin, an excess of glucagon (another hormone of the pancreas), and a host of other factors—some caused by rare genetic defects of the carbohydrate metabolism. The most frequent expressions of the disease are classified into two categories: Type I, juvenile or insulin dependent (IDDM), and Type II, an adult-onset form or noninsulin dependent (NIDDM).

The juvenile or IDDM type is least frequent, has a significant genetic influence for susceptibility to certain pancreatic viruses, and the symptoms appear by adolescence or young adult age. It may be controlled, principally by insulin injection. Type II, NIDDM is ten times as frequent as Type I and is the most common form of diabetes afflicting world populations. High blood glucose levels with related symptoms usually appear after forty years of age. Family and twin studies show a strong familial component and suggest genetic factors, but there are significant environmental influences, principally dietary and physical activity.

With major dietary and lifestyle changes in many populations, Type II diabetes has increased dramatically over the past decades and continues to rise (Harris, 1990). Once only the twenty-seventh cause of death, Type II diabetes has now reached near-epidemic proportions and has risen to the seventh most frequent cause of death in the United States. Today, there are approximately 10 million cases reported in the United States, with 500,000 new cases added each year.

Perhaps no disease that afflicts humans has been so thoroughly studied and its environment and behavioral links so well explored as diabetes. Though there is an unspecified hereditary influence, this disease is closely related to overnutrition; diabetes distribution has followed the spread of an affluent diet and one high in refined carbohydrates. In developing countries, diabetes is found mainly among the wealthier classes in urban areas. For example, among the rich urban residents of India, diabetes is twice as likely to develop as among the rural poor. Further, though rare among Japanese women before the end of World War II, diabetes is now the eighth most frequent cause of death. In Puerto Rico, though the general health of the population improved during the economic boom of the 1960s, diabetes rose from twelfth place to become the eighth most frequent cause of death (Eckholm, 1977).

Further evidence of the influence of Western-type diets is provided by the experiences of populations like Australian Aboriginals, Polynesians, Melanesians, and several groups of Native Americans (Figure 7–1). The Pima and Papago of southern Arizona are especially predisposed to diabetes by middle age; more than 60 percent of the adults aged forty-five to sixty-five were diagnosed as diabetic, which was a 50 percent increase since the epidemiological survey of 1965. Several other Native American groups also have significantly higher rates than the United States, on average up to nineteen times higher. In addition, urban Hispanics also show a high incidence of diabetes, about 6 percent in the United States and Puerto Rico (Knowler et al., 1990; de Herrera, 1999). Other ethnic group differences are seen among African Americans who had twice the diabetic rate as that found among Whites, with females of both groups higher than the males (Harris, 1990). Among Australian Aboriginals subsisting on Western diets (especially high in sugar and white flour), the incidence of diabetes has been diagnosed in 10 percent of the adults compared with only 2.3 percent among a European population living near the Aboriginal reserve where the study was carried out (Kirk et al., 1985).

Throughout the Pacific, high diabetic rates have been reported for numerous Polynesians and Melanesians who have "urbanized" and have adopted a diet of canned fish, rice, sugar, and flour. They have reduced their work energy expenditure as their caloric intake has increased far beyond their needs. With excess dietary energy, average body weights have increased significantly for all ages (King, 1992). People on the island of Nauru are a classic example of detrimental health effects of a changing lifestyle.

This small Pacific island of only 8.2 square miles is populated by 10,000 people who suffer one of the world's highest diabetic rates, about 42.2 percent. The disease was unknown before 1945 but, following the transfer of royalties from the sale of the island's rich phosphate deposits, the population's income rose to $34,000 per capita. With such wealth, their living habits were radically changed. They ceased fishing or gardening and imported all of their food from Melbourne, Australia. Contract laborers were imported to work the phosphate mines, build roads, houses, and carry on the day-to-day work of the community (Schooneveldt et al., 1988).

The Nauruans have used their wealth to purchase all of the manufactured goods of the developed world, from airplanes to motorcycles. They

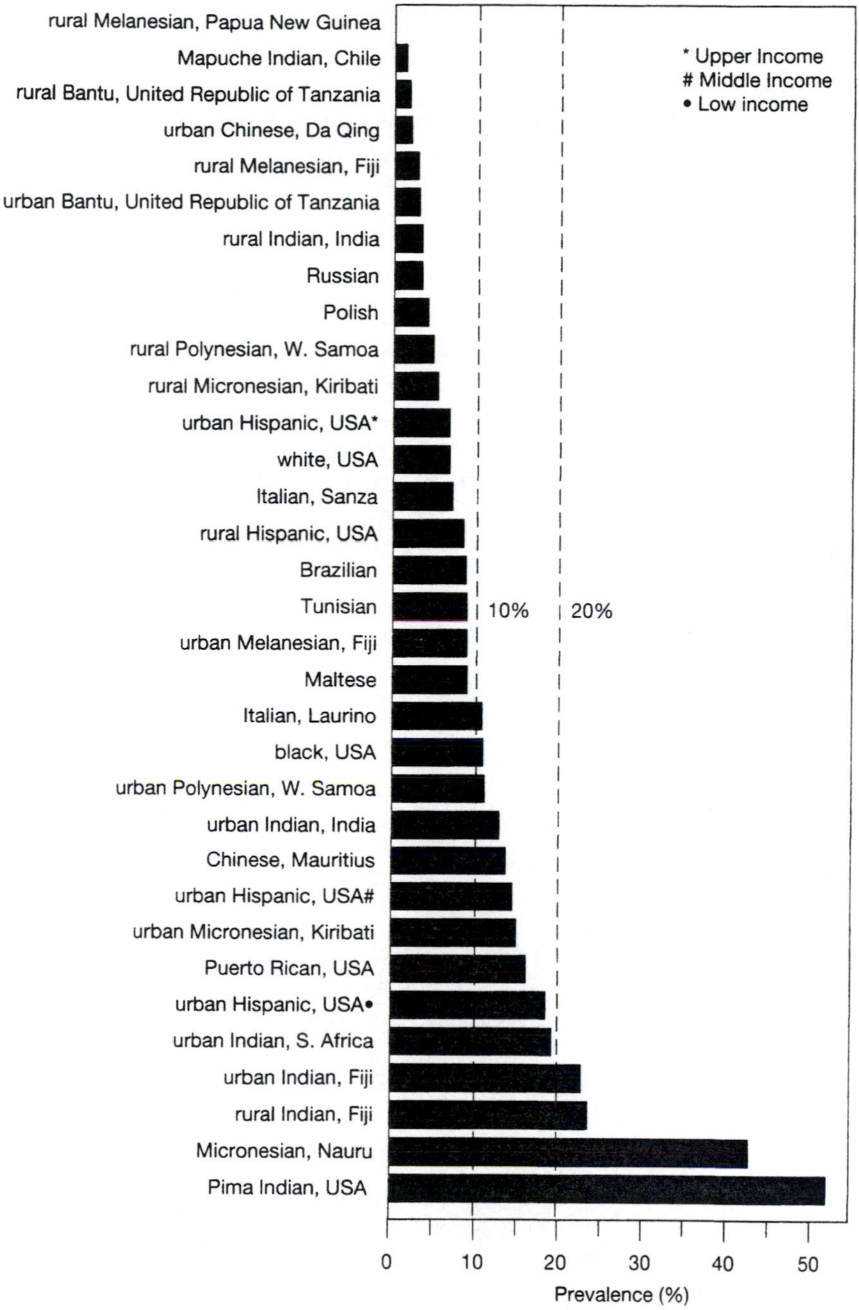

Figure 7–1 Prevalence of Non-Insulin Dependent Diabetes among Selected Populations

From World Health Report No. 844. Reprinted by permission of World Health Organization.

especially enjoy an overabundance of imported processed foods high in fat, salt, and sugar content. Their caloric intake averages 7,200 kcal per day and, as a result, the Nauruan health has suffered with near universal obesity, hypertension, cardiovascular disease, and a record incidence of diabetes (Pollock, 1992; Zimmet, 1982). Mortality rates are from six to eight times that of European Australians. Their life expectancy is short; at age fifteen, expectancy is 39.5 years for males and 48.5 for females, in stark contrast to the sixty plus years of most of the developed world.

Other Pacific peoples have suffered increases in Type II diabetes as they have "urbanized" and altered diets and work habits. The New Zealand Maori incidence is five times the rate of New Zealanders of European ancestry. Where highland peoples of New Guinea have continued traditional diets, diabetes is zero, but the disease reaches 16 percent in the country's capital, Port Moresby. The rate is down to about half among residents of coastal towns near the capital. Fijians living in urban communities of their islands, especially Nandi and Suva, have an increased diabetic rate. The wealthier people of Indian descent in Fiji have twice this incidence, probably reflecting a difference in diet and work habits(King, 1992).

There is no single or simple explanation for these dramatic increases in diabetes for Nauruans or other indigenous peoples. Diet quantity and composition, to be sure, are likely factors, but Europeans and Americans have been altering diets and lifestyles for most of this century without the explosive development of the diabetic syndrome. True, the disease has increased in this century and is occurring at an earlier age, but the pattern of change has been slower than that of Native Americans and Pacific peoples. The Inuit and other arctic peoples could be added to this list; as their diets and lifestyles have changed so has their health (Schaefer, 1981).

There is a probability that certain ethnic groups are genetically better adapted to their traditional diets. Their work energy expenditure and food energy intake has been in some balance on the average. Also, consider that humans had, for 99 percent of the species' existence, consumed a diet highly variable in quantity from day to day and with a large mixture of complex carbohydrates. Attempts to explain this in genetic terms has been a "genetic nightmare" since the disease is widespread and is probably due to multiple genes (Turner et al., 1995). One geneticist, with broad experience studying ethnic group diversity and adaptation, has tried.

Neel (1962, 1982) offered a hypothesis he called the "thrifty genotype" to explain the excess food energy assimilation and storage capacity possessed by certain peoples. He noted that hunter-and-gatherers' diets had ranged between "feast to famine," times of scarcity alternated by plenty, when the people gorge themselves. During these times, persons with the physiological ability to convert and store the excess energy as body fat are at an advantage. This body fat would be a source of energy that enabled them to survive those periodic episodes of shortages or starvation.

During times of plenty, their insulin-producing beta cells of the pancreas are more sensitive to stimulus, or a quick trigger response. The rapid rise of insulin levels aided in energy storage.[5] If such persons, with their sensitive insulin-producing cells, ingested large quantities of refined carbohydrates daily over a long period, as in the case of so many people today, they would exhaust the cells' insulin-secreting potential by middle age. Then they would become unable to regulate their blood-glucose levels within physiologically acceptable limits. This hypothesis of an adaptation to a "stuff or starve" mode of existence applies to all humans and does not locate ethnic groups along any evolutionary scale. Europeans, or persons of European descent, are at risk of acquiring non-insulin dependent diabetes just as are the Pacific islanders. The incidence varies, though, and appears to relate to dietary habits and workloads. What genetic combinations and what degree of genetic influence is a puzzle that has yet to be unraveled. Comparisons of ethnic groups is a source of data that can be applied, and the thrifty genotype hypothesis is a useful guide that needs to be tested further.

Another advantage of efficient food energy storage to early populations was described by Prior (1971). He hypothesized that Polynesians, famous for their long sea voyages in open canoes, had an advantage because of their body form. On a food surplus, they could gain weight and rapidly become obese with a high body mass index. This ability served them well in ancient times while navigating on the open ocean. Even in the tropical climate of the South Pacific, cold can be a problem. The temperature drops rapidly when the sun goes down, and people in small outrigger canoes are exposed to cold winds, causing a rapid loss of body heat. Persons with thicker fatty layers and a higher body mass ratio would be better insulated (Houghton, 1996). Metabolic heat loss would be reduced, preserving stored energy and enabling survival for longer periods on a minimal diet. Today, this predisposition for rapid weight gain, once an advantage, may now contribute to a high incidence of Type II diabetes.

THE DEVELOPING WORLD AND EPIDEMIOLOGICAL TRANSITIONS

The rise of these several chronic diseases in the more-developed countries has marked a new epidemiological stage. It offered one illustration of the impact of environment and social change on human survival through the twentieth century. In the less-developed countries (LDC) where the young, growing populations are participants in economic development, the epidemiological transition is not complete. Most countries are stalled in a Stage two, with infectious and parasitic diseases still important causes of morbid-

[5]Insulin hormone facilitates the transport of glucose through cell membranes and is essential in glucose conversion and storage in the liver.

ity and mortality. Nearly one-third of the 53 million world deaths in 1998 were due to infectious and parasitic diseases(IPD), and 96 percent of these occurred in the LDC. Most deaths from IPD were caused by the "big four": acute respiratory infections, diarrheal diseases (the leading cause of deaths among children under five), tuberculosis, and malaria. Figure 7–2 lists mortalities by world region and relative proportion by disease category, IPD, and other causes. "Other causes" would include, in addition to suicide and accidents, deaths from all of the chronic disease types.

The relative proportions suggest the lesser-developed regions entered Stage two later and remained longer at a level comparable to epidemiological conditions typical of early nineteenth-century Europe. These nations have developed more slowly because of a combination of political, economic, and demographic pressures. Within many, though, there are socioeconomic distinctions that have marked boundaries of health status and life expectancy. Because of a more nutritious diet, better housing, and a greater access to medical care, the upper classes will likely suffer less from infectious and parasitic diseases. They will have a greater longivity but will suffer more from the diseases of affluence, however (Table 7–2).

Figure 7–2 Percent Mortality from Infectious and Parasitic Diseases for Major World Regions, 1990

From Olshansky et al., 1997. Reprinted by permission of Population Reference Bureau, Inc.

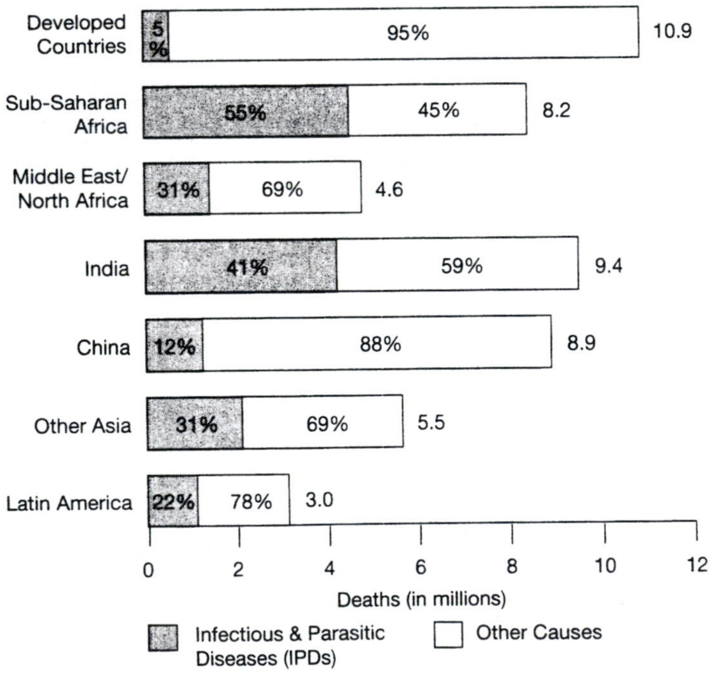

TABLE 7–2 Diseases of Affluence[1]

Atherosclerosis
Cardiovascular disease
Diabetes
Gall bladder disease
Hypertension

[1]These diseases are most frequent among those people who have recently changed their lifestyle and are consuming a Western-type diet.

Source: From Hutt and Burkitt, 1986; Schaefer, 1981.

Cholera

Since the beginning of the nineteenth century there have been seven pandemics spreading outward from a reservoir of infection among populations in southern India and Southeast Asia. When conditions favored the multiplication and transmission of cholera bacteria, it would sweep through populations infecting a majority and, in the early days, killing a large percent of the victims. The first cholera pandemic (1817–1823) was of limited scope and confined to the Middle East. The second (1829–1851) spread from Russia across Europe to Britain and then by crowded immigrant ships to New York City. This and the third pandemic, which followed closely a year later, served to alert concerned officials to the need for improvements in living conditions and sanitation practices as described in chapter four. The actions taken by Snow, Pettenkoffer, Chadwick, and Virchow are well recorded and document the rise of modern epidemiology. Their efforts to understand and control the spread of cholera and other infectious diseases among the rising urban centers in Europe clearly illustrate the interactions of the linkages of development with diet, disease, and demography.

Despite the increased knowledge of public health and of the bacterial causes, cholera proved to be too powerful a force; as world transportation increased towards the end of the nineteenth century, a fourth (1863–1879) and a fifth pandemic (1881–1896) spread again. Mortalities among the infected were lower as authorities became more efficient at dealing with outbreaks and the duration of each epidemic was shorter, By the end of the sixth pandemic (1899–1923), it was thought that mankind had seen the last of this periodic scourge, except in those areas of dense urban populations in south Asia. Improved sewage disposal and clean water would prevent a repeat of past epidemics. In fact, most of the world was free of cholera for nearly forty years until the eruption of the seventh pandemic in the 1960s.

A new strain of bacteria began to spread out of Indonesia in 1961, infecting populations throughout the region and into southern India. Within a short time it began to appear in East Africa. In the past, cholera would rise into acute, local outbreaks and then decline only to rise again. Continent-wide transportation had expanded since the last pandemic eighty years ago, however. Previously cholera would spread along the traditional trade routes on rivers and the few primitive roads, but the distribution of the bacteria from population to population was much more rapid now. Extensive road networks had been constructed, carrying heavy truck and bus traffic and within a few years, the bacteria had spread to the interior. Most significant, for the distribution of cholera and other diseases was air travel. In fact, cholera's 1971 appearance in West Africa has been traced to an infected passenger arriving by plane in Conakry, Guinea. By 1980, twenty-five African countries were reporting nearly 100,000 cases. Despite control efforts and treatment, the number of cases remained high, and new outbreaks were being reported throughout the decade, but cholera still had not jumped the Atlantic to South America (Garenne, 1994).

North and South America remained untouched by this most widespread and persistent of the pandemics; that is, until 1991. In February 1991, cholera appeared in coastal communities a short distance to the north of Lima, Peru. It spread with intensity along a 2,000 kilometer stretch of coastline in just two weeks, infecting 80,000 people within a month. Health authorities quickly responded with medical treatment and kept the mortality down to about 1 percent. Despite their efforts, the epidemic continued to spread. Travelers carried the bacteria to the Andean highlands (Alto Plano) and over into the Amazon starting a spread of the disease into Brazil, Venezuela, and Ecuador. Cholera continued its march through the Americas and thousands of cases have been reported throughout Central America and Mexico. By the end of 1991, there were over 0.5 million cases reported by the WHO member states, and South America far exceeded those reported for Asia or Africa (Weekly Epidemiological Record, 1994). By the end of 1995, new cases were still being reported in the Americas, a total of 85,802 with 8,471 fatalities (Epstein, 1996).

Questions about the direction and rapid spread of the cholera pandemic involves examination of the nature of the disease itself and the interactions among world communities. First, though the seventh pandemic was well established in West Africa since the 1970s, it did not spread into South America through Brazil. Cholera arrived from Asia and entered communities along the Peruvian coast by way of the food chain linked to marine organisms. Ships often discharge seawater, carried as ballast, into coastal and harbor waters, and some ship arriving from Southeast Asia probably had bilge water contaminated with cholera bacteria. This deposited bacteria then found its way into the local plankton colonies of the coastal waters. Fish feeding on these marine organisms became carriers of the bacteria that were then transmitted to the human victims who ate the infected fish.

This offers an explanation for the transoceanic contact from regions of high cholera incidence (Indonesia, India, and Bangladesh) to uninfected regions. The continued transmission, contact, and persistent reinfection of the human population may be due to the local plankton colonies acting as reservoirs, maintaining a high concentration of the cholera bacteria. According to one interpretation, the plankton "bloom," or rapid multiplication under certain weather conditions, encouraged the seasonal outbreak of the disease (Colwell, 1996). If this correlation of plankton bloom and cholera outbreak is correct, then it would partially explain the rapid spread along the west coast of South America, where within days, thousands of people were infected.

The next stage or link in the cholera distribution among populations depends upon living conditions that, in turn, relate to socioeconomic levels. Consumption of infected fish quickly spread bacteria through the people living in crowded shantytown slums. These shantytowns existed partly as a result of economic depression forcing migration from the countryside, fueling an explosive urban growth typical of many developing countries. Without sanitation facilities and lacking clean water, the communities were at a high risk of infection, and the organism spread through the populace as it had for centuries, by fecal-contaminated water and food.

The transmission was hastened by the local food tradition of eating fish raw, marinated with lime juice (ceviche). Not only was the uncooked fish a danger to the consumer, but the act of washing the pieces in contaminated water added to the risk of passing on the bacteria. Shellfish had been identified as a source in Ecuador and the outbreak in Santiago, Chile was traced to fresh vegetables. This illustrates that even where there is water treatment (Santiago's water is 80 percent chlorinated), cholera can still be a threat. Cholera was probably spread because of the practice of using untreated sewer water to irrigate crops during time of drought (Glass et al., 1992).

Cholera is dispersed along routes of communication as it always has, roadways, waterways, and by sea, but now we must add air travel to this list. The few cases that appeared in Europe and North America have been traced to air travelers returning from cholera-infected areas. Medical treatment was quickly applied and there was no further spread of the disease. In Peru, the application of medical treatment and the transport of patients to treatment centers kept mortality low. This same transportation of patients, however, may have aided in the spread of cholera into the Andean highlands and over into the Amazon basin.

These experiences of the last decade illustrate how cholera may crop up unexpectedly in locations previously free of the disease. The increases of international shipping carrying organisms in contaminated ballast water is one major modern addition to lines of disease transmission. This world redistribution of a variety of organisms by way of a ship's ballast water has been described as a kind of "ecological roulette" (Carlton and Geller, 1993). Jet planes cannot match cargo ships for volume but they certainly exceed the ships for speed and for a greater number of contact points. Modern airliners frequently touch down on all continents, and many islands where large ocean going vessels cannot. Air transportation is now a very significant addition to causes of disease contacts, as the experience in the Pacific illustrates.

Cholera had never been identified in the South Pacific until it was introduced onto the island of Tarawa, probably carried by an infected aircraft passenger. Once introduced, the bacteria spread quickly in an environment that had limited sewage disposal facilities; privies built to empty into lagoon waters from which fish and mollusc were harvested within a few hundred yards distance. The local population picked up the bacteria and passed it on throughout many of the other islands in the Gilbert chain (Maung, 1979). Between September and December 1977, the first cholera epidemic in South Pacific history claimed twenty-one victims. A total of 1,102 cases was reported, but the death toll was kept to a minimum by early diagnosis and the ready availability of modern treatment. This mini-epidemic, plus the spread of cholera from Peru throughout the Americas twenty years later, further illustrates the ever-present threat, as the seventh pandemic continues. Small events, like the arrival of a ship with contaminated bilges, an infected traveler, or infected shellfish can escalate into a potentially catastrophic epidemic under certain conditions.

Malaria

This mosquito-borne parasitic disease has been responsible for untold millions of deaths throughout human history. It was widespread throughout the tropics and subtropics and even into the more temperate regions of Europe and North America (probably introduced by colonists). Major efforts, dating back to the eighteenth century, were made to control mosquitos. Swamps were drained and stagnant water pools were coated with a light oil to kill the mosquito larvi. With the invention of effective insecticides, especially DDT, there was wholesale spraying wherever the insect accumulated. These efforts appeared to work and, for a time, malaria subsided as a problem. In some areas, Europe and North America for example, the disease disappeared altogether.

Today, even with all of our scientific knowledge, malaria is on the increase and infects 500 million people each year, resulting in about 2 million fatalities. It is the leading cause of death of all the infectious diseases, and 40 percent of humanity are at risk. Most of those at risk live in the lesser-developed countries of the tropics. Throughout Africa, India, and Southeast Asia, malaria continues to be the scourge it had been before major attempts had been made to control it. Therein lies a story of interactions among science, epidemiology, development, and environment directed towards the control of a single disease.

The beginnings of modern control efforts were quite promising. The insecticide DDT was widely used during the 1940s around the Mediterranean area to eradicate body lice and thus prevent typhus. It also worked well with other insects and eliminated most of the Anopheles mosquitos, the vector that transmits the malarial parasite to humans. In Egypt, new malaria cases dropped to near zero and in Southern Italy and Greece malaria was eliminated; 16 percent of Greek children carried the parasite in their blood in 1946 but less than 1 percent did so two years later (Harrison, 1978). This success of the major malarial eradication campaign, started as part of a wartime disease control program, encouraged a broader worldwide effort.

A global program was underway by the mid-1950s, and DDT was applied widely, reducing the mosquito population and malarial cases rapidly dropped. North Africa, India, and Southeast Asia began to enjoy a malaria-free era. The large island nation of Sri Lanka, where the control program started earliest, showed one of the most dramatic successes. The 1 million cases in 1955 plummeted and only eighteen were recorded by 1963. Other South Asian nations also benefited, but the most accurate account of the malarial control came from India. Seventy million cases were reported for 1947 but, as the program began to take hold, the case load declined to just over 100,000 by 1965. This decline is even more remarkable since it occurred at a time that India's population was growing rapidly. The changes wrought by massive uses of insecticides during the decade from 1955 to 1965 were pointed to with pride by health authorities. Malaria, that ancient scourge responsible for so many deaths, was finally being controlled and perhaps even eradicated from the planet.[6]

The optimism was short lived, however, as India's case load began a gradual increase in the late 1960s and then accelerated. The disease carried by migrants spread outward from the few isolated areas, or residual endemic foci in forested areas of middle and eastern India (Learmonth, 1988). Within ten years, 5 million cases were reported (Table 7–3). Though somewhat of a disappointment, the 5 million people infected with malaria in a population of 613 million still represented a remarkable achievement compared to the 70 million cases out of 350 million three decades before. But what caused the turnaround when total control seemed so possible? The reasons involve the nature of the disease itself and relate to a complex of events, both biological and social.

With malaria eradicated from 88 percent of India, continued spraying of interior walls of houses, and destruction of mosquito larvi breeding places, complete eradication appeared technically feasible. The regular indoor spraying was proving to be a less successful means of insect control, however, than during the early days of the control program. Insecticide

[6]Lesions found on some skeletal remains from Greece suggest that malaria had been afflicting humans since the Bronze Age (Angel, 1966).

TABLE 7–3 Incidence of Malaria in India, 1965–1976, 1987, 1988

Year	Total Malaria Cases
1947	c. 70,000,000
1965	100,185
1966	148,136
1967	278,621
1969	348,647
1970	694,647
1971	1,323,118
1972	1,362,806
1973	1,934,485
1974	3,167,658
1975	5,166,142
1976	5,082,467
1987	1,611,189
1988	1,780,906

Source: Data adapted from Learmonth, 1988; WHO, 1990.

resistant mosquitos had begun to appear, and this became a major problem that required the change from DDT to different insecticides. Control programs both for spraying and treatment of stagnant water faltered as operation costs rose and funds declined. There were simply not enough personnel or equipment to continue to cover the vast areas that needed treatment. Further, the malarial parasites began to spread out of residual areas and reinfected populations who had been disease-free for decades. It was difficult to deal with new outbreaks because of costs, DDT shortages, and new resistant strains of the mosquitos (Sharma and Mehrotra, 1986). Containment, not eradication, became the national goal.

The rise of urban malaria added to the problem. Disease control was the responsibility of local authorities, which resulted in a scattered distribution of malaria-infected populations. The increase of migrant laborers from such areas could and did spread the disease over the country. A region might have been declared malaria free then an infected individual would arrive. The person would be bitten by local female Anopheles mosquitos picking up parasites with their blood meal from the victim. The parasites, multiplying in the mosquito's digestive tract, then would be passed on to an uninfected human bitten by mosquitos, now carriers of the malarial parasites. Within days the parasites could be spread through a disease-free population. So a seemingly simple chain of events, starting with a traveler leaving his village to seek work, could initiate a sequence of human-mosquito-human contacts that could result in over a thousand malarial cases.

World economics of the 1970s made matters worse. The soaring oil prices drove up the costs of fuel and all petroleum products, of which the

DDT spray was one. India and other developing nations were especially hard hit. Fuel costs made it more difficult to transport field control teams and the insecticide and larvicidal oil prices exceeded most budgets. Added to this economic-epidemiological dislocation was the now rapid increase in the density of DDT-resistant mosquito strains, forcing the use of more expensive insecticide substitutes. Malarial control faltered until around 2 million cases were reported annually throughout India in the 1990s—certainly not eradication but an impressive achievement none the less given the large population size, the amount of travel, and the increased urbanization of India's population.

Other world areas have had similar experiences with malaria resurgence. Brazil's reported cases have climbed from 50,000 in 1971 to around 600,000 per year by 1990. It seems to have stabilized at this level, but the caseload could be much higher since underreporting is likely, particularly in the Amazon frontier areas. The expansion of road building and an increase in mining, logging, and oil exploration have brought tens of thousands of workers into areas seldom penetrated except by indigenous people. This migration has spread malaria into areas previously free of the parasite. Increased outbreaks have also been reported in Bolivia, and in the tropical valleys of eastern Peru for many of the same reasons. The additional factors noted by authorities are declines in surveillance and control, long periods of warmer temperatures, and higher rainfall due to the El Nino phenomenon. In fact, throughout tropical America, the number of malarial cases is rising.[7]

New Guinea with its high rainfall, tropical climate, and dense population has always suffered a high malarial incidence along its coastal areas. Over the past few decades, however, the disease has been spreading into the central highlands, which were formerly free of the parasite. Increases in movements of peoples between the rural highland villages and urban centers have been stimulated by shifts to a cash economy over the past twenty years. The extensive mining operations also have brought on many structural economic changes that have contributed to malarial increases, the concentrations of families in roadside hamlets, for example (Ulijaszek et al., 1987; Inaoka, 1995). Malaria, as well as other parasitic and infectious diseases, are certain to increase over the island as road systems expand and mining, logging, and plantation agriculture further disrupt the landscape.

The countries of the temperate zone have not escaped the resurgence of malaria. South Korea, which had been free of malaria for fifteen years, registered a few cases in 1993. The number has grown slowly each year, reaching 1,000 by 1997. Europe, likewise, is registering more cases each year. France reported 5,000 in 1996, most were traced to contacts in Africa and

[7]The rise in malarial caseloads have been reported on the ProMed network, 1–9 Sept, 1997.

were of the *Plasmodium falciparum* type, the most lethal of the malarial parasites. Italy too, has seen a rise in malaria brought in by African immigrants or by returning vacationers who had visited malarious areas. One to two thousand cases are reported in the United States each year, again brought home by some of the more than seven million tourists. With the vast movement of people today—vacationers, business travellers, or migrants—the exchange of parasites from human to mosquito vector and back again is increasing. Also, a new type of malaria has been defined, "airport malaria." It seems that many species of insects, including mosquitos can survive for hours in the wheel wells of jet aircraft. Numerous cases of malaria have been reported among people living near international airports in Europe and in the United States (Shell, 1997).

In sum, the threat of malaria provided the impetus for an international program to eradicate the mosquito vectors. Despite immediate successes during the early days of the program, the diversity of the Anopheles mosquito's environments and the insect's adaptability made total control difficult in some areas and impossible in others. The insect vectors have responded to chemical agents (principally DDT) by adapting to them. A second factor is that the parasites responsible for malaria, especially the falciparum species, have evolved strains that are resistant to most of the antimalarial drugs. Added to these biological basics is the rapid multiplication of humans who use the environment evermore intensely, and one may appreciate how an ecological balance tips in favor of the disease. All of these factors interrelate because of the very nature of the parasite's life cycle and the environmental effects on transmission between human and insect host, as diagramed in Figure 7–3. Climate, housing, human use of the environment, and the mosquito species are all correlated in maintaining malaria.

While control efforts are continuing, roads are being built through tropical rain forests opening up land for denser human occupation. Trees are cut down and stagnant pools of water form in the denuded soil providing a breeding place for mosquitos. The walls of farmers' homes offer a resting place for the insects who may feed on the family members at will. These same roads that have encouraged a bloom of mosquito populations provide a distribution network for the parasites as infected humans travel between areas. Multiply this small scenario many times with modern transport and massive refugee and immigration movements and it becomes clear that almost no country or region is insulated. It is simply that some are better prepared than others to cope with the disease. Economics and politics are important considerations above and beyond the technical aspects of DDT immune mosquitos and drug resistant parasites. The story of a near eradication and then a resurgence of malaria is one of a victory followed by defeat, or at best, a close tie. Today there is a near standoff, a fragile balancing act maintained between control efforts and outbreaks.

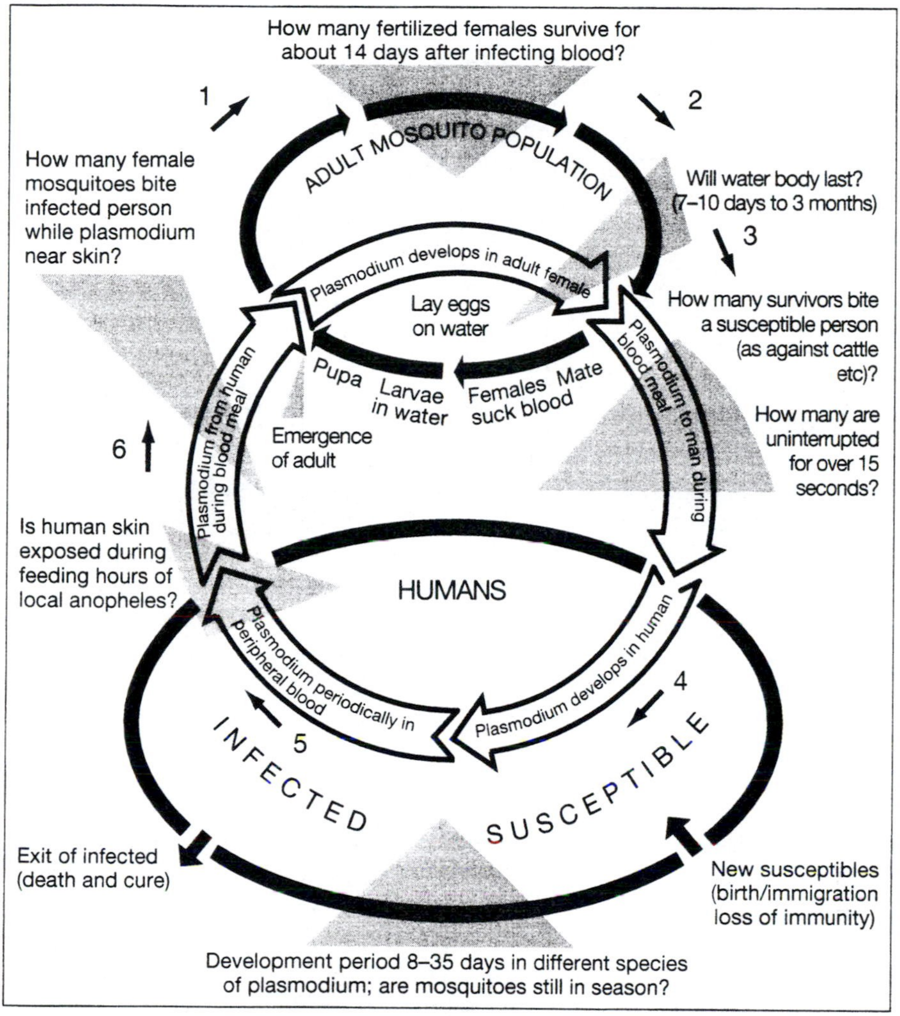

Figure 7–3 Interlocking Life Cycles of Mosquito and Plasmodium Parasite

From Learmonth, 1988. *Disease Ecology: An Introduction.* Reprinted by permission of Blackwell Publishers, Ltd.

SOME NEW VIRUSES AND ECOLOGICAL LINKAGES

Hundreds of viruses can infect humans and cause mild to severe illness or even death. Some are transmitted by insect vectors, animal matter, or they may be airborne, carried from person to person by a single sneeze (as one of a variety of cold/influenza viruses). How regular or how widespread the transmission depends upon a number factors of the environment. Environmental conditions and the host reservoir form a system of interaction that leads to periodic outbreaks, such as the "flu season" we all know about. Some viruses are carried by animal hosts, rodents, for example, that seldom trouble humans except under specific conditions, as when there may be a change in rodent–human contacts. Then the virus appears in the human population, sometimes causing great harm, especially if it is a virus new to humans.

The Hanta Virus

In the summer of 1993, there were several people who were struck with a mysterious illness in the Four Corners area of the American Southwest. They started with flulike symptoms, fever, muscle and headaches then quickly progressed to what is a called acute respiratory distress syndrome (ARDS). Their lungs filled with fluid making breathing difficult, and none of the standard treatments seemed to work. Tests ruled out the most likely causes including plague, a suspect since this bacteria is endemic among many rodent species in the area. What puzzled physicians was the rapid decline and sometimes death of their patients; a normally young healthy person could become ill with these symptoms and then die within a few days. Between May 14 and June 7 there were twenty-four cases, with twelve fatalities.

The Centers for Disease Control began an active investigation and, once plague was ruled out, turned their search to a viral cause. Within just seven days, the hanta virus was isolated in tissue and blood samples of the victims. This type of virus was first discovered in Korea, where it had caused a hemorrhagic fever among 2,500 army troops with 121 deaths.[8] But the illness of the Four Corners outbreak was somewhat different. It affected the lungs of the victims with pneumonialike symptoms, which raised the possibility of person-to-person contact. Even more problematic was the discovery of this new strain of rodent-borne virus and its likelihood of existing in several rodent species in other regions of the United States.

Within six months, this was realized when there were fifty-five confirmed cases of ARDS due to Hanta virus in sixteen states, with thirty-two fatalities. The geographic range had extended from New Mexico and Texas to Mississippi and Florida. Trapped rodents in these case areas showed that many were hanta virus carriers. Now that the relationship between a type of respiratory failure and hanta virus had been established, the investigators

---

[8]Hemorrhagic fever is characterized by episodes of high fever, leakage of fluids through capillary walls, kidney inflammation, and sometimes kidney failure. The mortality can be high, especially among those without early medical treatment.

did a retrospective analysis. They checked for the virus in tissue and blood samples saved from victims of ARDS. The hanta virus was found in several, and this retrospective analysis traced the virus back to a victim in New Mexico who died in the summer of 1991.

The victims all had one thing in common: they had been working or living in close contact within spaces contaminated by infected rodents. The virus is spread in the environment by the animals droppings and urine. This matter contaminates surrounding objects, the brush, soil, or nesting materials; it also is picked up by the wind after it dries, and its particles are blown about. People living in arid regions especially would be at risk, as would individuals working around structures where there were rodent nests, or gardeners who spent time in their plant-potting sheds. Soldiers, living under field conditions as during the Korean War, were at special risk, as were UN troops in Bosnia. All of these factors of transmission from animal to humans were well known to disease control experts. What was not known at the time, however, was the reason for the cluster of these 24 ARDS cases in the Four Corners. The answer was to be found by a study of the area's rodent populations.

There was unusually high snowfall followed by a moist spring over the usually arid area during the 1992 season and this moisture resulted in an exuberant plant growth throughout. Grasses and bushes of all types were thicker than they had been in many years, and the hardy pinon pine trees bore a heavier load of nuts. The Navaho tribal elders said that they could not recall when the pinon nut crop had been so plentiful or the mice so numerous. This abundance of food enabled the local population of rodents, the species commonly called deer mice who feed upon nuts, seeds, plants, and insects, to rapidly multiply. Beginning in the spring of 1992, their numbers increased tenfold, and the overcrowding spread the mice populations outward from their normal ranges closer to human habitation. As Garret (1994) relates, the deer mice population explosion was reaching its peak about the time of the hanta fever outbreak and when the Centers for Disease Control was beginning their investigation.

During the early months of the investigation, there were doubts about the connection between rainfall, the "bloom" of the rodent population, and the hanta epidemic. Later, after studying trapped rodents of several species, the virus was isolated to the deer mouse, the majority rodent of the area and the species known to have undergone a population explosion. The weather–rodent–disease linkage now looked stronger, and, as the old tribal shaman had always warned, illness increased during times of heavy pinon nuts harvests.

Since the earliest cases, sporadic outbreaks of what is now called the hanta virus pulmonary syndrome (HPS) have been reported from the United States to Argentina. There have been over 500 confirmed cases with most reported in these two countries. The experiences of the hanta virus distribution in the Argentine Pampas and parts of Chile validate the climate–rodent–disease experience just described. The El Niño oceanic conditions altered the climate throughout much of South America as elsewhere. Heavier rainfall (in the late 1990s) contributed to plant growth and one plant in particular, the flowering bamboo, is mentioned. This plant is one of the basic food supplies of a pygmy mouse species whose population had undergone a radical increase like that of the the deer mouse in the Four Corners area. Outbreaks in other South American areas have also been related to "blooms" in the local rodent populations. The possibility that some hanta infections in Argentina may have been spread by person-to-person contact adds a note of caution when dealing with this new source(hanta virus) of acute respiratory infection (Yates, 1997). Considering the spread of confirmed cases, health ministers of all of the American countries have increased surveillance and have warned about rodent contacts.

The hanta virus is but one of the examples of a new virus that seem to suddenly appear when environments are disrupted due to natural or human causes. In 1967, a very lethal form of hemorrhagic fever occurred in a biological lab in Marburg, Germany. The laboratory used African monkeys in their experiments and one of the animal handlers became infected with a strange disease and suddenly died. Before the contagion was contained, thirty-one people became infected and seven died from an acute form of hemorrhagic fever. Medical science had been introduced to a new virus, now called the Marburg. The probable origin of the virus has been traced to green (vervet) monkeys imported from an area of Uganda, around the western shores of Lake Victoria. Whether these primates are the reservoir for the Marburg virus is uncertain, but greater care is now taken in the selection of imported primates, and no further European outbreaks have been reported.

Two years later, another fever made its appearance in Nigeria. The first patient to succumb was a mission nurse who died from massive hemorrhaging. Several of the hospital personnel who had treated her also contracted the disease and died. The cause of this fever was a virus called Lassa for the region where the first case originated. The Lassa virus is transmitted easily to persons who came into contact with blood or body fluids of the infected patient, and for a time it seemed to have a preference for hospital personnel. Eventually, the virus was traced to rodents in an area of northeastern Nigeria. Since the original infections in the 1960s, the Lassa virus reappears and spreads causing epidemics from time to time. In West Africa, several hundred patients had been diagnosed with the disease and up to 29 percent had died, by 1996. The fatalities had been largely confined to Sierre Leone, where civil war has prevented many patients from getting to one of the treatment centers established by the Medical Emergency Relief International organization. The crowded conditions in the refugee camps are exposing more people to this virus.

Another of the hemorrhagic viruses that has attracted world attention lately is the Ebola, one of the deadliest infectious agents known. It was first identified in 1976 as the cause of an epidemic in Zaire and Sudan, claiming 90 percent of the 600 persons infected. Ebola strikes so suddenly and spreads with such speed that often panic sets in and hospital personnel and patients alike flee the area. How many may carry the virus during their flight is hard to estimate. A more recent epidemic in 1995 killed 244 people, and only rapid action prevented its spread to Zaire's capital 100 miles away. Sanitary precautions, quick burial of the victims, and area isolation, which is now common practice, can stop the spread. When and where Ebola will strike next is hard to predict.

These viruses appear to be maintained in a reservoir in Central Africa where periodic outbreaks occur with high mortality, but their source is not actually known. What is documented is that the viruses have been carried by infected travelers, tissue samples from patients and by monkeys imported for lab experiments. A readable, but very alarming book, *The Hot Zone,* by Richard Preston, gives a brief history and fictionalized account of some of the episodes of the transmission of these dangerous virus. He points to the region around Lake Victoria in East Africa as a possible "hot" virus homeland. While the earliest outbreaks of these hot viruses attracted our fearful attention in the 1970s, another deadly organism had already spread around the world and was about to announce its presence as a new disease syndrome, AIDS.

AIDS: A New Pandemic

Sometime during the 1970s, a new disease syndrome began to appear among homosexuals and intravenous drug users in Europe and the United States. There was a failure of the natural immune systems of patients from these groups and, as a result, they suffered from a series of what are described as "opportunistic infections," mostly rare respiratory forms. In general, the victims suffered from repeated rounds of infections that would not respond to treatment because of their suppressed immune systems. The T cells of the lymphocytes (our natural line of defense), instead of increasing as expected when challenged by infectious agents, declined by as much as 50 percent. About a third of these patients also had a rare form of cancer, Kaposi's sarcoma. As the number of cases began to climb by 1981, the disease was recognized as *acquired immune deficiency syndrome,* or AIDS. An extensive search was made to isolate the agent that infected and gradually destroyed a major set of cells of the immune system. By this time, the recognition of related illness among the general population in Africa added to the evidence that mankind was confronted with a new disease (Jamison and Hobbs, 1994).

The cause of AIDS was identified as a retrovirus and labeled human immunodeficiency virus (HIV) in 1983.[9] The virus inserted itself into the lymph tissue cells and disrupted the synthesis of the lymphocytic cells needed for immune responses to invading microbes. HIV viruses have a long latency period, from seven to ten years, before the symptoms of immunodeficiency appear. In other words, a human can be a carrier for years without any outward signs. This enabled a near silent spread of the HIV throughout the 1980s, but it probably has been around much longer, probably since the 1950s. Once the virus was discovered, suspected carriers could be tested.

The discovery of the cause did not retard the speculation and venomous comments about AIDS sufferers. It was "God's punishment" brought down on the homosexual sinners and drug addicts, or it was "The curse of King Tut" on those who defiled his tomb, are but a couple of examples. The fact that HIV was being discovered in heterosexuals and nonaddicts in Europe, Africa, and Asia, as well as in North America, did not slow down the mindless rumors and speculations. A classic example of ignorance of the medical facts and genetics was given by the editors for Burke's Peerage, a compilation of aristocratic family lineages in Britain. The editors announced that to preserve the "purity of the human race" the publication would omit all families in which somebody was known to have AIDS. Their reasoning was that AIDS may have a genetic cause and was not due to an infectious agent, no matter how transmitted (Chandavarkar, 1992). Evidence of the spread of AIDS through blood transfusions or by the blood clotting products used by hemophiliacs, as well as by heterosexual contact, did little to slow such rumors. That is, the speculation continued into the 1990s as the world was confronted with this newly recognized infectious disease now present in pandemic proportions.

There were over 600,000 AIDS cases reported to the World Health Organization in 1992, though the actual figure was believed to be nearer 2.5 million, since there was an underreporting of cases by many nations. Even this higher number turned out to be much too low an estimate. As surveillance methods improved, the number of HIV carriers for 1992 was listed at 4.2 million in the United States and 18.8 million worldwide (see Jamison and Hobbs, 1994). In the United States, AIDS became the ninth leading cause of death and the number one killer of males, ages 25–44. Females of this age group are but one-sixth of this rate but are increasing fast (Statistical Abstracts, 1997).

While the number of cases have begun to stabilize in the industrialized

---

[9] A virus that inserts itself into a segment of a cell's DNA.

countries, the worldwide cumulative AIDS cases and HIV-infected persons are increasing rapidly each year. By 1997, there were over 42 million HIV-infected persons and 15 million with AIDS. One-third of those infected with HIV since the later 1970s have died of AIDS. The toll will likely increase as the pandemic continues, especially among the poorer nations, as the spread of HIV has divided into two epidemics; the one in the more-developed nations is being attacked with state of the art medicine and expensive drugs, while the poorer nations are hard pressed to even test for HIV and control the disease transmission, and they are ill equipped to treat the AIDS victims.

Sub-Saharan Africa, home to only 10 percent of the world's population, has over 63 percent of the HIV infected people in the world. As of 1997, an estimated 7 percent of African adults in rural areas were infected, rising to 20 or even 30 percent in urban areas like Nairobi, Kenya and Harare, Zimbabwe. This adds up to 20 million adults in sub-Saharan Africa infected with HIV. Most of the AIDS deaths occur in this region, and, according to UN reports, nearly 12 million have died of AIDS since the beginning of the epidemic sometime in the 1970s (UN Report, 1997). Given the frequency of HIV and the continuing transmission of the virus, there is a projection that the high AIDS death rates in the near future will have significant impacts on African populations well into the middle of the twenty-first century. Figure 7–4 (page 242) lists projected population growth with and without the estimated AIDS mortality. Not only is the rate of natural increase expected to decline to half or less by 2010, but life expectancy will be shortened among the several countries listed. The twenty-one countries in Africa plus Brazil and Thailand (where AIDS increases are projected) will have a total of 2.8 million deaths attributable to AIDS by the year 2000 (U.S. Bureau of Census, 1997).

These mortality rates, though alarming, are small by comparison to what the future may hold, given the increasing number of infected people. From a seemingly slow start, no world region has escaped the spread of this virus. Africa leads at present with about a million new people infected each year, but Asia is catching up fast, with a projected 1.2 million HIV carriers by 1999. China and India, where the infection is still mostly confined to drug addicts and prostitutes, will likely see a dramatic surge of the virus in their dense populations. Given these large numbers and the probability that 50 percent of those with HIV will develop AIDS, mortality will skyrocket well into the next century.

Though its origins are obscure, HIV is believed to have spread undetected through countries around Lake Victoria in Eastern Africa. It could have been carried by a nonhuman primate host, probably the numerous vervet monkeys who live in close contact with humans; in fact, a simian form of the virus (SIV) has been isolated. The virus may have mutated and then "jumped" species to infect humans. Alternately, HIV, which has a long

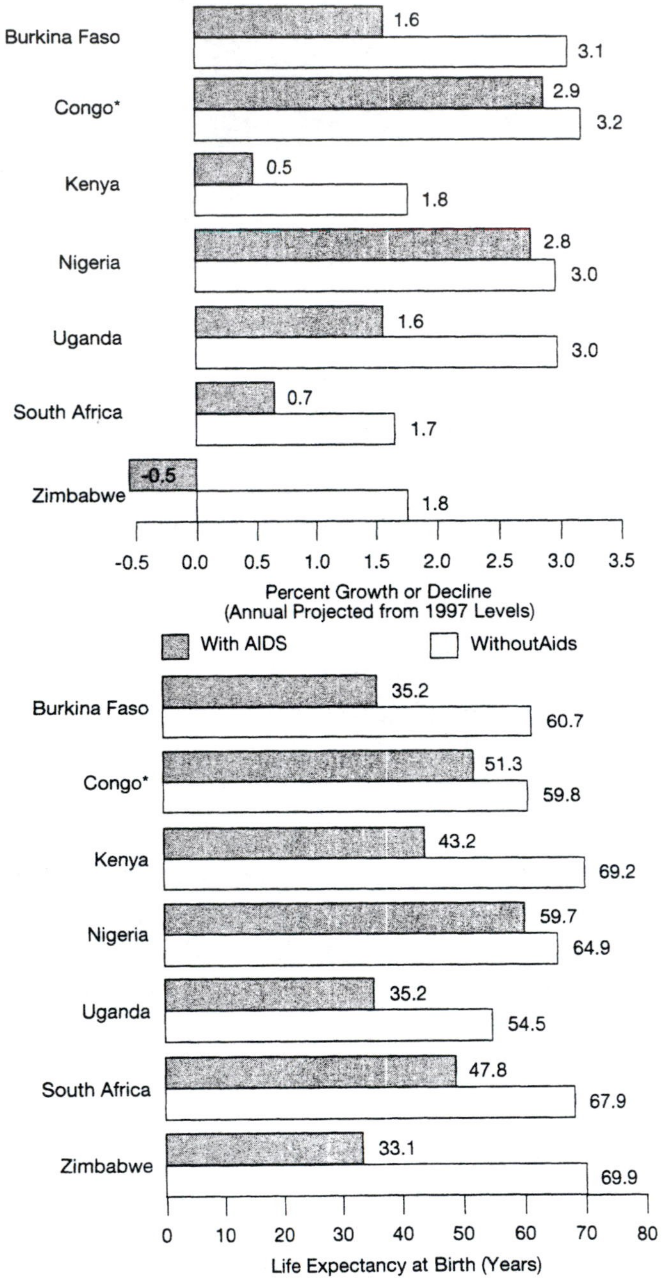

*Formerly Zaire.

Figure 7–4 Effect of AIDS on Population Growth and Life Expectancy in Sub-Saharan Africa, 2010

From Olshansky et al., 1997. Reprinted by permission of Population Reference Bureau, Inc.

dormant period, could have been around for many years, existing only in small isolated populations. Considering the rapid African population increase in the last twenty years, this is an attractive hypothesis. For as the population increase occurred, people spread into previously sparsely occupied areas, removed the forests, and planted their crops. Another factor was the development of a network of road systems throughout East Africa to connect the highland areas to the port cities. This added to the disruptive effect that agriculture had on the environments around Lake Victoria, destroying plants and scattering wildlife. Given the nature of HIV—its long dormant period—the virus spread easily between seemingly healthy people. Since HIV is spread among adults in Africa mainly by heterosexual unions, the road network played an especially important role.[10]

The movement of traffic along these roads eventually extended as a transcontinental highway all the way into West Africa, passed through small villages built roadside to service the traffic. At these roadside rest stops a driver or passengers could get a meal, a beer, and a bed, sometimes shared with a woman (most likely infected with an STD and HIV). Given the unstable political condition of the Lake Victoria region, with several ongoing wars over the past few years, there were mass refugee movements. Tens of thousands of people have taken to the roads and there was no lack for women who have turned to prostitution, after losing family and home. This combination of population explosion, environmental disruption, increasing commerce, and the bloody ethnic wars that gripped the region for decades led to the formation of what one novelist called the "AIDS highway" (Preston, 1994). This model of linkages leaves a number of questions unanswered but it does help explain why African AIDS is a phenomenon of urban areas and transport routes (Goliber, 1997).

From a probable African origin, HIV may have spread into Europe and the Western Hemisphere, carried by the occasional traveler assisted by modern air transportation. Once introduced into the industrial societies, the infection was passed on through the drug culture and homosexual networks. Eventually, perhaps decades after its introduction, the virus appeared in a cluster of cases among these groups. Before the nature of transmission could be identified, the virus was passed on into national blood banks and from there it began to infect people who were neither drug addicts nor members of the gay community. Unfortunately, the misunderstanding about virus transmission delayed action by public health authorities and contributed to the virus spread. But then this is another story well told by Garret (1994). It is sufficient to add that social and political bias can easily distract from the basic scientific issues that affect a people's health.

[10]Because of shortages of supplies, the reuse of hypodermic needles is also considered an important source of HIV contraction; mother-fetus and blood transfusions appear to be the main means by which children contract the disease.

OLD DISEASES IN A NEW WORLD: SOME CONCLUSIONS

There have been some radical changes in world environments and human population size, and these changes are proceeding at an accelerated rate. Starting from a technological base established during the Industrial Revolution, all of our systems of manufacturing, communications, and transportation have risen to ever higher levels of efficiency. Accompanying these changes are transformations of sociopolitical systems so that nations are being divided into separate worlds of demographic and economic strengths or weaknesses. In the process, mass movements of people have been encouraged in all parts of the globe. Migrants, either fleeing war zones, political persecution, or seeking employment, flood across national borders, either on foot or by every means of modern transportation.

The results are seen in the radical changes in human use of space and an increase in the exploitation of environmental resources. The impact of these migrations, especially the nearly 1 million people per week moving into urban areas, is being felt throughout the world. A lack of adequate shelter, safe drinking water, or sanitation for a third or more of the urban populations means that the health and very survival of hundreds of millions are threatened. Crowded conditions, poor diet, and a lack of basic city services place the urban poor at risk of epidemic diseases, both old and new. Incidence of diarrheal diseases and the other "big four," already high, will probably rise given the increased population densities and the polluted environments.

Old diseases like typhoid, diptheria, and even typhus are already reappearing, as is cholera, arising in another world pandemic as new bacterial strains appear. Plague also is still part of our disease threat as the 1994 outbreak in India demonstrated. Six thousand people, 80 percent of them residents of urban shantytowns, were infected. Early diagnosis and fast action by public health officials, aided by antibiotics and insecticides, fortunately contained the epidemic and kept mortality to low levels. The outbreak served, though, as a reminder that infectious diseases can still be a problem as we disrupt environments. Another reminder of our vulnerability are the insect vectors that are developing insecticide immunity and the many antibiotics that no longer are effective in treatment of several types of infections.

Like the turning of the tide, as one writer described it, microbes that were once easily controlled by antibiotics have returned in newer, more virulent forms. Despite the announcement of the U.S. Surgeon General in 1969 that, "we can close the book on infectious diseases," several major microbes have persisted and are now an even greater threat to human health. Staphylococcus bacteria, the cause of a variety of infections of skin, internal organs and bone have mutated to several drug resistant strains, likewise for Streptococcus, the cause of skin eruptions, rheumatic fever, and scarlet fever. Gonorrheal bacteria also have developed resistance to penicillin, and even malarial parasites have evolved varieties that resist the standard drugs used to treat the disease. These mutant strains of bacteria and parasites all present problems for medical treatment, but the greatest threat appears to be from an old disease enemy, tuberculosis, which has returned in a more virulent form.

Tuberculosis (TB)

This disease scourge of the Industrial Revolution had never really left us, its prevalence merely declined to lower and lower levels in the twentieth century. In 1900, TB was the number one cause of mortality in the United States, and then began a decline to seventh place by 1947. Deaths from TB were only one-sixth of what they had been, and this reduction is attributed to improvements in housing, diet, and general health (McKeown, 1979). Antibiotic treatment reduced the active cases even more rapidly and by the 1950s tuberculosis was eliminated as a leading cause of death. The number of active TB cases reported continued to decline until 1985 when the numbers of infected persons began to increase. These cases have been increasing each year since, mainly among inner city residents, and about one-half of the cases appeared among those people classified as "non-whites,, mainly African American. Further, a substantial number of the new TB infections were caused by a new drug resistant strain of bacteria.

Many of us harbor the tuberculin bacteria in our systems but seldom suffer from the active disease. As long as our general state of health is good and our immune system functions efficiently, we are able to resist the growth and spread of the tuberculin organism. If our health declines and we are repeatedly exposed to infection, our immune system will be overchallenged and then the bacteria seizes the opportunity and multiplies rapidly. This has happened in AIDS patients and other groups of individuals who, because of economic circumstances or drug abuse, suffer from failing health and an impaired immune system. When treatment is sought, one or a combination of drugs are given but a significant number of patients have failed to respond; and physicians soon recognized that there was a new TB bacteria loose in the urban population. The drugs that had been used successfully since 1948 now frequently fail to halt the progress of the disease. How widespread this multiple drug resistant (MDR) bacteria has become is not known, but its presence in many patients has alerted health officials who are gravely concerned about this new wave of tuberculosis. The caseload in the United States was 26,673 reported cases in 1992, about a 20 percent increase since 1985 the year with the lowest number since case reports have been recorded (Weekly Epidemiological record. no. 9, 1994). A significant number of the TB patients have the MDR type infection; up to 20 percent of the cases reported in New York are of this type.

The United States is not unique, among the developed nations, for its TB resurgence. London has seen a 100 percent increase in the last few years, and Britain is predicting over 6,000 new cases for 1999. France, Germany, and, particularly Eastern Europe are undergoing alarming increases, just as they are experiencing the rise of HIV infections. What adds to the threat of a resurgence of tuberculosis is the fact that persons carrying the HIV virus are at a higher risk. Forty-seven percent of the new TB cases were HIV positive and, because of the long dormancy period of HIV, are likely to be a source of a rising caseload of tuberculosis in the coming decades.

If the tuberculin bacteria can overcome modern medical treatment in the United States and Western Europe, then the situation can be expected to be much worse among Third World populations, and it is. Two-thirds of the world's TB cases are among Asian populations. According to World Health Organization's reports, tuberculosis is the cause of 1,000 to 2,000 deaths each day in India, where about one-half of the adult population is infected. This number is expected to rise as HIV infections spread and economic conditions worsen, forcing more and more people into crowded urban slums. These processes that encourage the spread of TB are well underway from Latin America, Africa, and throughout Asia (see Olshansky et al., 1997).

The World Health Organization is putting its resources, already stretched thin, behind an international control effort. Sixteen national trouble spots have been identified, partly because of population size, large urban centers, and poverty. But surprisingly, one-half are classed as "middle-income" nations that have the financial and technical resources to attack the tuberculosis threat. Brazil, South Africa, and Russia have been singled out for comment because of their slow progress. Indonesia, Iran, and Mexico should be added to this list of those nations able to deal with the threat but have yet to give their efforts a high priority. The reader will note that in each case of these middle-income countries, political and demographic issues may be more involved than economic resources. Nations like Pakistan, India, and Ethiopia lack many of the resources; their populations are too large, communications inadequate, and their finances too slim (WHO, 1998).

Russia provides a special example of tuberculosis epidemics for many reasons. There has been the worse resurgence of the disease of any European country. In fact, throughout the countries that were part of the Soviet sphere of influence before 1989, there is an uncontrollable spread of the disease. Cases are appearing faster than health officials can record them. The urban poor, which are a growing majority of the once highly industrialized nation, have been especially hard hit. Nothing occurring among the populations of the major cities can compare with the inmates of the still large Gulag of the Russian penal system, however.

Hundreds of thousands of convicts, their guards, and support personnel still maintain large colonies in Russia's far eastern regions. They are ill fed, poorly housed, and malnourished. Medical care is rudimentary at best.

The crowded conditions and climate add to the problems that furnish a near perfect setting for the incubation of diseases that the developed world had long since conquered. These diseases, typhoid, typhus, and diptheria, are breaking out again in this isolated corner of the world. The worst has been tuberculosis with an estimated 100,000 inmates infected and about 20,000 deaths in the last two years. Incomplete treatment, partly because of a shortage of antibiotics, has increased the frequency of the highly contagious, drug-resistant type. Guard personnel are not immune, nor are their families, and it is only a matter of time before the multiple drug resistant strain is passed along to the general population.

The decline and near total disruption of the basic institutions and infrastructures of a society following the breakup of the Soviet Union in 1989 have created a situation not seen in the developed world since the last century. There are large population segments without means of support who are migrating to urban areas, while, at the same time, these urban centers are in economic collapse. The social services, especially those that relate to a population's health and well being, have declined even more rapidly. These radical changes have not been due to natural catastrophes. The land and resources are still there, and the personnel to take advantage of them are available but what is lacking is an organization of effort. Political events have overcome a modern, First-World society and turned it completely around to an earlier time.

Similar examples could be drawn from other middle-income countries and their efforts to control disease and maintain the health of their people. Brazil, Indonesia, Mexico, and South Africa offer examples. Resources are there, and a population willing and able to use them exists. What has occurred, and what still exists after a long chain of events, is a situation of sociopolitical problems that stand in the way of development. This is development in its broadest sense in providing for and maintaining a population. No longer may the nations of the world be divided between less or more developed, but another more complex scaling method must be applied. Where are emerging countries to be placed or how does Russia fit in the classification by economics or development?

Chapter 8

Development, Populations, and Linkages

The Impacts on Planet Earth

Support of our growing population depends on development methods of increased complexity. There are numerous linkages and feedbacks among resource extraction, food production, and the provision of space for 6 billion people. These feedbacks between effort and response touches on every aspect of our planet. From soil to atmosphere and from ground water to ocean, no corner of the world remains unchanged. But this has always been so, or at least since the modern era of industrialization. Now change and its effects come more rapidly than ever, but there are no new frontiers to cross and exploit. We must make do with substitutions and the use of alternative materials and methods. In doing so there are feedbacks that cause unintended consequences that are often counterproductive. We pollute, extract, destroy, and displace people from adaptations that had sustained them for hundreds or thousands of years. The quest for a means to expand the earth's human-carrying capacity has been costly, with many casualties along the way.

DEVELOPMENT

The concept of development during earlier centuries can be understood as obtaining resources needed for survival, and when a local area became depleted, our ancestors would move on and repeat the cycle. If surpluses were ever obtained, then trade networks were formed and goods would be exchanged, allowing substitutions to be made for those items in short supply. As skills and tools improved, development was expanded to meet the needs of growing populations that were rapidly depleting local resources. The trade networks were extended ever wider, or people moved into undeveloped regions and began the extractive, destructive process all over again. Populations grew, forcing further development, that in turn led to further expansion fueled by more effective technologies with greater extractive powers.

This cycle appears to have a momentum all of its own and seems destined to go on forever. But we can no longer treat resources as if they were unlimited. Our vast industrial expansion throughout the twentieth century with its wars and conflicts has seen to that. We are confined to the same old planet of finite size that is now supporting 6 billion people. Some are living under conditions that would make life in the nineteenth-century Manchester, England slums seem luxurious by comparison, while others enjoy material benefits unimagined but a few decades ago. The extract, use, discard, move-on style is gone forever, and limits have been reached. Now we and future generations must cope with the reality of development and its impacts.

The most common use of the development concept is the conversion of some resource into a profitable product for some benefit, real or imagined. The concept has been synonymous with industrialization, which equated progress with the improvement of the quality of life. This has been a remarkable success for about 20 percent of the world's people. But the process got out of hand and the many hidden costs of environmental degradation have now become visible. What was worse was that depletion of resources and the polluting effects of industrialization were shared unequally around the world. In Europe, industrialization altered most of the continent and then moved on to other world areas, mostly those colonies of the European governments. This process of expansion and progress spread the methods of the Industrial Revolution globally but unevenly. In fact, post–World War II development divided our planet and its people into different "worlds."

Worlds of Differences

Following the end of World War II, several nations, most of them former European colonies, came together at a conference in 1955 to declare their solidarity as newly independent states. What was especially important for the time was their stance of nonalignment with either the capitalist or the communist bloc of countries that had organized following the war. This group of former colonies, some, like India, under European control for centuries, had high expectations for their futures. The freedom to develop on their own pathways would bring wealth and stability to their citizens. But these expectations were not to be fulfilled, at least not for a majority. This Third World of nonaligned nations, as it came to be called, never reached the level of industrial development that its founders envisioned. They struggled along for decades with burgeoning populations and unstable political systems and continued as sources of raw materials for the industrialized countries. Some improvements were made, usually with the help of international aid organizations, but the quality of life for a majority remained so low that the term *Third World* became, rightly or wrongly, synonymous with overpopulated, impoverished nations.

Then some countries in the 1960s and 1970s began to break out of this trap and began to pull ahead. Their agricultural production went up, industrialization began to advance, and the several markers of human well-being improved (diet, health, mortality rates, income, etc.). Two or more lines of development began to emerge from the Third World until there were several national groupings that could be classified. The United Nations declared the establishment of a new world order and began to discuss developing nations, or less-developed nations, in contrast to the more-developed nations of the industrialized world. By this time, several "worlds" could be described. Those with resources were undergoing development that opened many opportunities, nations with some problems getting started, and those that lacked the resources or the management to develop. Despite their size, geography, or political system differences, they all shared an enormous problem with rapid population increase.

This is an oversimplification of a complex of world nations that are hard to judge, evaluate, or classify because of differing geography, history, and politics. These distinctions among the former Third World nations are mentioned to show that changes in development, progress, and population growth take very different pathways, often divergent from those that had been predicted. The countries of the developing world, or less-developed world, might be located along an axis according to a human development index and a human poverty index proposed by the United Nations (Human Development Report, 1997). These indexes take into account education, life expectancy, and real gross domestic product. Using these measures, comparisons can now be made of a nation's progress relative to any other single or group of nations. What is shown is the wide gulf between nations within any grouping (Table 8–1). Some small, but poor nations are improving the lot of their citizens while others with more resources and wealth are not. Reference is now made to developing countries and least developed countries.

Some writers have been looking at a global picture of development and are fond of describing a "North-South axis" or a global south, implying that world communities divided along such hemispheric boundaries form a meaningful division of development stages. However, recent events over the last decade have added another level of complexity. The world political changes moved quickly in the 1990s and the old Third World alliances divided into many separate lines as the communist bloc fractured into several interdependent parts. The Eastern European countries, now free from Soviet dominance, are described as economies in transit. The development

TABLE 8–1 Ten Most Populous Countries and Their Human Development Ranking

Country	Population (1998)	HDI[1]	HPI[2]
China	1,242.5	108	17.5
India	988.7	138	36.7
United States	270.2	4	na
Indonesia	207.4	99	20.8
Brazil	162.1	68	na
Russia	146.9	67	na
Pakistan	141.9	139	46.8
Japan	126.4	7	na
Bangladesh	123.4	144	48.3
Nigeria	121.8	141	41.6

[1] *Human Development Index* for 1994 is a comnposite index of life expectancy, educational attainment, and real GDP per capita for 175 countries.
[2] *Human Poverety Index* describes the rankings of 75 developing countries. It is a composite of percentage of people dying before age 40, of adult illiteracy, of underweight children under age 5; it also includes persons deprived of safe water and health care and who are malnourished.

Source: Adapted from United Nations World Development Report, 1997; Population Data Sheet, 1998.

of each has proceeded along a different pathway. Some towards improvement of their human development index while others have descended into ethnic divisions or outright warfare, as has occurred among the republics of Yugoslavia.

The dissolution of the Soviet Union also resulted in several Soviet Republics declaring independence, but they soon formed a loose confederation, the Commonwealth of Independent States (CIS). This CIS brought together nations as diverse as Belarus, Russia, and the Ukraine of Europe with Uzbekistan, Tajikistan, and Kazakstan of Central Asia to name but six of the twelve members of the confederation. Among them they control most of the industrial capacity, the best of the agricultural land, and the oil fields of southern Russia and around the Caspian Sea. They hold the resources and have a potential for great influence on future world development. Their very diversity of political interests and history make management of resources a major political challenge, to say the least. Just listing these few and some of the other world groupings should illustrate that the complexity of alliances and resources negate the simple application of a North-South axis, or developed–less-developed worlds, but we are stuck with the labels. As we shall explain, it is the political process that dictates human environmental impacts now that development has become more global than ever before.

Sustainable Development

Several of the founding countries of the Third World alliance have continued to be suppliers of raw materials with the help of government aid and various subsidies. These foreign aid programs were intended to stimulate growth, the buzz word for development throughout the 1960s. Agriculture was to be modernized, land to be reclaimed, roads built, and rivers were to be brought under control for irrigation and the generation of electric power. According to the development plans of the time, modernization and growth would improve the lives of millions of people. But it did not work out quite that way. The commercial crops of cotton, peanuts, tobacco, or sugar cane brought profits for a few, but reduced the amount of land used for growth of traditional food crops. The dams impounded and conserved millions of acre feet of water, but prevented silts from being deposited during flood seasons and, thus, soil fertility was lowered and productivity declined. The large networks of irrigation canals distributed snail-borne parasites, and the reliance on irrigation caused erosion and salinization of the soils. In sum, the development/growth plans brought about major changes but any improvements were not equally shared.

After nearly twenty years of major development projects throughout the world, there was more of a concern with equity and sharing. There was also a growing consciousness of the environmental impact of development projects, and there were growing concerns over how local populations would be affected. Too often it seemed that the number deprived of their homes and livelihoods exceeded those who would benefit (Scudder, 1973). The human costs in many areas of South America, Africa, and Southeast Asia were much greater than expected. There were many unanticipated side effects of even the most modest of development ventures. Also, rather than obtaining equitable benefits from industrialization or exploitation of natural resources, the opposite result was achieved. Fewer and fewer people have benefited while their environment was degraded. Such costs were not entered in the equation measuring the gain from development, just as a market value of biodiversity, clean water, or conservation for future generations has not been counted (Tolba, 1995).

There has been a growing awareness, however, of these hidden problems and the realization that development costs could not continue to accumulate and be passed on to future generations. The concept of sustainable development was introduced by Gro Brundtland, prime minister of Norway, at a conference on development (The World Commission on Environment and Development, 1987, commonly known as the Brundtland Commission). She described sustainable development as that development that meets present needs without compromising the ability of future generations to meet their needs. With the Brundtland Commission report, "sustainability" became the new buzz word of development. Without being negative about such an important statement regarding the state of our planet, nor to distract from the concern that it expresses, we should point out that such sentiments have been repeated many times since George Marsh wrote about human environmental impact in 1864 (see Chapter 1). It may be summarized by a statement made just thirty years ago. "Every source from which man has increased his power on the earth has been used to diminish the prospects of his successors," as Darlington (1969:673) described human damage to the environment impairing the survival of future generations.

Expressed more along the lines of contemporary economic productivity, Clarke expressed the interconnection within the human ecosystem, "all production results in the destruction of something else" (Clarke, 1977). This issue of production and destruction was taken up some five years earlier and expressed most eloquently by Barbara Ward and Rene Dubos in *Only One Earth* (1972). After considering the issues faced by humanity at the beginning of the decade (1960s), and after consulting with world experts, they carefully laid out the several problems. The key to our understanding of environmental problems is given in their assertion that humans actually inhabit two worlds: "There is the biosphere we inherit and a technosphere of our creation." These two spheres, they argued, are out of balance and potentially in deep conflict. The conflict arises from the extraction from a biosphere at a greater rate than can be sustained as population growth continues. Their observation, made nearly thirty years ago when we numbered less than 4 billion, is now being recalled as we become more cautious with development plans.

Sustainability has four themes that define it (Ohtsuka, 1995). The first is the relationship between population and food; quite simply, the more people, the more food required. However, the quality and quantities define the means of production and this is influenced by the land. Industrial resource management is listed as a second theme and can mean how energy is employed and work directed with a maximum gain and minimum of environmental disturbance (for example, pollution). The third, and perhaps the key to sustainable development, is the recognition and/or reaction of people whose lands will be affected in some way by development. There are already too many cases where local peoples have been simply pushed aside, relocated, ignored, or worse. Gaining local participation and sharing benefits is essential but a seldom realized goal. Finally are the health issues that are involved in development. As we shall outline, there may be many health affects or few, depending on climate, geography, and type of development scheme.

All of these themes are but an extension of rational planning before resources are extracted from one environment to be used to benefit a distant place or people. As a colleague once observed, "The pressing problems of the world today are scarcely technical." We agree, at least in part. The technology exists to solve many problems, but the will and the motivation to apply technological solutions is often lacking. Thus far we are in agreement. Where we may depart is in the faith in technological/scientific solutions. The side effects or unanticipated results are often unknown. The diversion of water, the narrowing of a nutritional base, an overreliance on fewer varieties of food plants, the cutting of a road through virgin wilderness, or urbanization can be beneficial, but new problems are created. So technology must move cautiously with a watchful eye for the surprise of unanticipated consequences. A balance of the spheres (bio and techno) must be maintained.

FOOD PRODUCTION AND POPULATION

The nearly 2 billion tons of food grains (rice, wheat, and corn), together with the soybean and root crop production of 1998, is sufficient to feed 10 billion people, about the number projected for the year 2050 A.D. This could provide an adequate diet if, and there are two big ifs, everyone was a vegetarian and if the food was equitably distributed. But food today is not fairly distributed between countries, or even within a single nation (Bender and Smith, 1997). People die in famines because they are too poor to buy food or it cannot be delivered due to lack of transportation. There are an estimated 43 percent of Africans who are malnourished and 22 percent in Asia, many for the reasons of poor economics planning or because of armed conflicts.

Norman Borlaug, the agronomist credited with starting the "green revolution" with the development of a high yielding variety of wheat, described the food-population situation that the world faced. He had already emphasized in his Nobel acceptance speech (1970) that the phenomenal successes of increased crop yields allowed some breathing space, or time for the world to gain control of population growth, which was then increasing at a rate of 2 percent per year. Several years later he noted that the 3.3 billion tons of world food production that fed 3.9 billion people in 1975 would have to double by 2015 if population continued its current growth rate of 1.9 percent (Borlaug, 1981).

Fortunately, population growth had slowed to 1.4 percent per year by 1998, but we have not yet reached the stage of food production doubling. Agriculture has continued to make gains, however, thanks to Borlaug and other agronomists like him. Grain production has increased one and one-half times since 1975 but increases are becoming harder to achieve, even with greater inputs of water, chemical fertilizers, and a more liberal use of pesticides. Also, per capita production has remained about level at 300 kilograms per person per year; the gains in grain production are balanced out by more mouths to feed. These numbers seem to indicate a balance and in that a measure of success except for two things. First, there is little grain surplus, only a fifty-seven day supply in 1997 compared to a surplus equivalent to 104 days in 1984 (Brown, 1998). Second, there is an uneven distribution and consumption of world grain stocks. The developed countries consume an average 958 kilograms per person, most of which went to feed livestock, while the developing world consumed 200 kilograms, most of it directly.

The costs of feeding at different levels of the energy pyramid (see Chapter 2) are shown in Table 8–2. It takes 7 kilograms of grain to produce 1 kilogram of beef, nearly 3 to produce the same weight in poultry and so on.

TABLE 8–2 Feed Grains Needed to Produce Meat and Milk

Product	Kg of Feed to Produce1 Kg of Product	Feed Grain Kcal per Kcal of Product
Beef	7.0	9.8
Poultry	2.7	5.7
Pork	6.0	7.1
Milk	1.0	4.9

Source: Data adapted from Bender and Smith, 1997; Brown, 1997.

What is more revealing for agricultural costs are the amounts of water needed, a critical consideration in arid lands where water must be pumped from ever-greater depths as aquifer levels fall. As pumping increases, fuel costs rise. The probability that a certain production level can satisfy our needs depends not only on water but on how farm output is used. Of equal significance is the wastage factor, the amounts lost in harvest, thrashing, or transport. These all add to the costs and may erase many of the food production gains.

The possession of large quantities of arable land, rainfall, and skilled farmers is no assurance of food self-sufficiency. Over a third of Nigeria's 350,000 square miles is rich arable land. Yet despite a favorable agricultural position and rich oil exports, this most populous country in Africa has had to import millions of tons of grain to feed its rapidly growing population. Two million tons were imported in 1990, and this rose to 15 million tons by 1996 (Sobowale, 1997). Population growth over the decades since independence in 1960 has forced a more intense use of cropland, mostly by traditional methods. There has been less rotation with shorter fallow periods, leading to erosion and desertification. To make matters worse, there has been a steady stream of younger migrants into urban areas where already 40 percent of Nigeria's population live. This leaves an aging group of knowledgeable farmers in the countryside with few replacements. All add to a decline of local production and crop shortfalls that must be made up by increasing food imports.

There are many such examples throughout the developing world and most relate to internal migrations influenced by changes in farm price structure, expansions of cash crops, and a growing scarcity of land for traditional crops. In the 1960s high yielding varieties of wheat and rice were introduced in several areas and the success has been measured by the phenomenal rises in productivity. But there were costs that have been reluctantly entered into the ledger of progress. These new varieties require large inputs of fertilizer, water, and insecticides and, because of costs can only be profitably used by large-scale farming operations. The net result was a kind of "rural removal," a pressure for migration building an ever larger and larger urban sprawl.

India may serve as an example. After its near disastrous crop failures of the early 1960s when only shipments of millions of tons of wheat from the

United States prevented a major famine, India had to modernize its agriculture and turn to existing technology to increase food production. It could not continue to view grain storage elevators in Kansas as India's food reserves. Production had to increase in order to meet the needs of over 500 million people, increasing at the rate of 2.5 percent per year.

The new hybrid wheat from Mexico was introduced and proved to be well adapted to the hot, dry Indian climate. Grain harvests doubled in just seven years (Brown and Kane, 1994). Construction of fertilizer plants and insecticide plants increased proportionately to supply the new agricultural needs. Extraction of ground water doubled in volume also, and deeper wells had to be sunk to reach the receding aquifer levels. Irrigation works also expanded to distribute water through the more arid regions.

With these technical advances, India has been keeping up with its population growth, but just barely. Its 990 million of 1998 were still growing by nearly 2 percent annually while its urban population was increasing at a rate of 3 percent. Bombay and Calcutta, already among the top ten of the world's largest urban agglomerations in 1995, will grow even larger. This urban growth has been principally due to displacement of small landowners who move to urban fringes in search of work. Other displaced small farmers have remained in their villages and marginally survive as casual day laborers on the expanding commercial farms.

Similar experiences from other world regions should remind us that the agricultural revolution that began 10,000 years ago is never ending. More people require more food, which means more land when there was new land to move onto. As land scarcity grew and production declined, new technologies were developed to meet the needs of a rising human population. In a way, Boserup was correct: The growing population pressure forced a search for and development of new technologies to increase food production (Boserup, 1965). But, as with everything else in the human–environment equation, there are exceptions and limits to human resourcefulness. We may have reached a limit with the amounts of chemicals we can apply to improve crop output, though plant genetics may again come to our aid. Climate is still a problem as it always has been. The rains come at the wrong time or place, and seasonal temperatures vary, as in the "Little Ice Ages," and erosion and salinization still impose limits on irrigation. Today, climatic conditions are made worse by the buildup of "greenhouse" gases from the burning of fossil fuels causing global warming.[1]

[1]Global warming is occurring and vast volumes have been lost from the ice shelves around Antarctica coastline, Alaskan glaciers are retreating, and Greenland's ice cap is reducing by about an inch in thickness per year. Temperatures are likely to increase with the buildup of carbon dioxide and other gases. The scientific disagreements are over how much and how soon will this increase in ice melt affect sea levels, not over the existence of such a global warming phenomenon (O'Meara, 1997).

All of the above impose some degree of limits on food production but the available water is by far the determining factor. Every country has had to increase its water supply for industry, which uses 70 percent, and agriculture, which uses 20 percent. Many countries have come up against limits, especially as climates gyrate through droughts or floods. The great plains area of the United States suffered a prolonged heat wave and drought through the summer of 1998. The relief, when it did come, brought torrential rains and wide spread flooding over the plains and much of the Southeast. Droughts occurred also that summer in the South Pacific, and sugar cane and other crops dried up for lack of rainfall. Central, America likewise dried out and forest fires raged throughout the area. The arrival of late season hurricane, "Mitch," put an end to the fires but also devastated much of Central America, wiping out most of the coffee and banana plantations and about 50 percent of the nation's infrastructure. The roads, bridges, power distribution networks were almost totally destroyed in Honduras and Nicaragua.

Among the most graphic examples of sudden climatic shifts and their aftermaths are the droughts in China that inspired concerned articles on the severe water shortages in China's northern plain (Brown and Halwell, 1998). The 1990s had been especially dry years, and China was suffering water shortages throughout the country. The lower reaches of major rivers, one of them the Yellow River, dried up before reaching the sea for as long as 226 days in 1997. Most of 1998 was as dry until heavier than normal rains began in the early fall, and a disastrous flood struck South China. The Yangtze and its tributaries overflowed, forcing millions to evacuate their homes. China went from being extremely dry to wet within a matter of weeks, but the rains have not improved its water resource for the long term.

The delay in the monsoonal rains that caused droughts in China, India, and throughout Southeast Asia and the Pacific in 1997 and 1998 dried out vast areas of forest. This drying was especially severe throughout Malaysia, Indonesia, and even New Guinea (noted for its high rainfalls) suffered. Then the fires bagan as the region's indigenous peoples followed their tradition of burning off small sections of brush and trees to clear a plot for their gardens. They choose the time and place to be most effective, and the widely dispersed areas burned has been of little consequence in the past. Now with more people, less space between them, and large sections of forests already cleared by commerical logging leaving behind mounds of inflammable debris, the stage was set for a major burn when the monsoonal rains were delayed. The small fires, normally started this time of the year just before the monsoon rains, quickly spread into major conflagrations, putting up a pall of smoke over most of the entire region.

On the island of Sumatra alone, there were an estimated two hundred square miles of forests burning, and up to six hundred fires at one time. Other large fires raged through Malaysia and Borneo. At their peak, the fires covered 14,000 square miles and the smoke cloud extended from Thailand to the Philippines and to Australia. The smoke became so thick in some areas that flights in or out of major airports had to be canceled and thousands of people were forced to seek hospital treatment. The rains finally came, but then fires flared up again in early 1998. These few examples show some of the results from a collision between traditional land use, modern exploitation, and a change in weather patterns.

Blame it on El Niño, as erratic weather patterns have been blamed throughout most of the 1990s, but the floods and fires were, in a large part, due to human action. The excessively reduced river flows during low rainfall years and then the raging floods when rains finally come are due to the deforestation and erosion of the mountain uplands where the streams that feed the rivers originate. Such poor hydrological management has been seen in every part of the world. The results of alternate floods and droughts place not only lives, property, and crops in jeopardy, but raise the risk of uncontrolled wild fires as well.

Water Resource Developments

Good agricultural land is not always in areas where there is sufficient rainfall, so wells must be sunk or irrigation canals dug. Both endeavors require large inputs of energy and are a major part of food production expense. An estimated 60 gallons of water is required to produce 1 pound of wheat and four times that for rice, so as costs go up so will food prices. Irrigated farmland supplies 36 percent of world food production and most crops grown in Asia depend on this method. Since the diversion of river water for irrigation (the methods of early agriculture) has its limits, water is increasingly obtained from deeper underground aquifers. Costs continue to increase as water levels of underground aquifers fall and pumps have to work harder to raise the water.

It is not just rising fuel costs but the depletion of water that places limits on food production. Water is being withdrawn faster than it can be replenished by rainfall. In arid areas of the world, it has taken many centuries to form these pools of ground water, and it is being extracted at higher and higher rates. China is already facing serious water shortages as annual withdrawals increase to meet demands of industrial and agricultural growth. Figure 8–1 puts these water needs in a world perspective in terms of freshwater available per person for China and select countries. Note that China and India, the two largest countries, have the least available water. Pumping more water is not a solution. China's aquifer levels have been dropping up to one meter per year in nearly all of its major water basins and some tables are down by three meters per year. In coastal regions infusion of salt water has become a major problem (Brown and Halwell, 1998).

India, as well, is faced with water shortages. The green revolution that quadrupled India's food production has required more and more water,

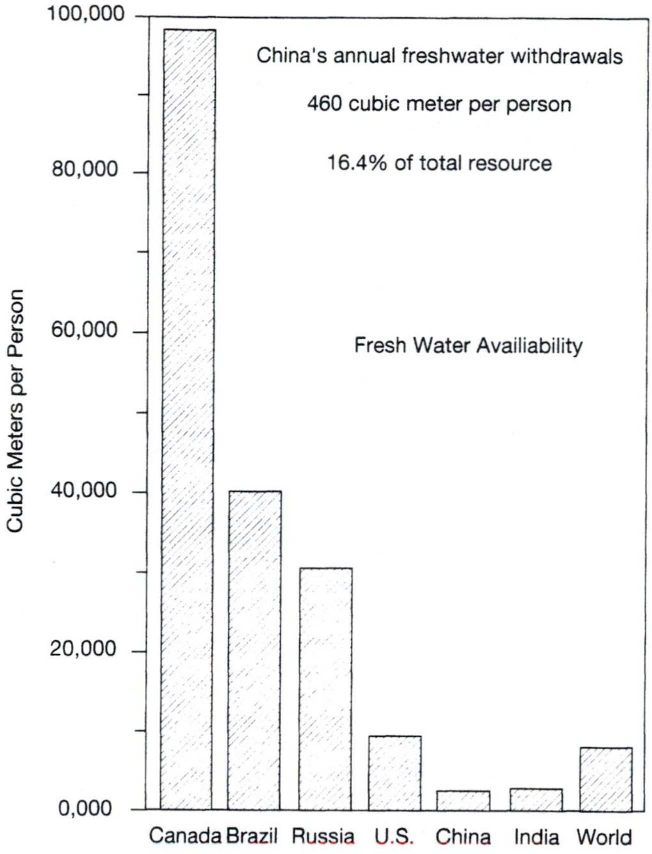

Figure 8–1 China's Water Problems

Data selected and adapted from World Resources, 1996–1997, World Resources Institute.

leading to an increase in the number of shallow wells from a few hundred thousand to 6 million. These have to be sunk deeper every few years to keep up with the declining water levels. Aquifers in some states have been drawn down 20 or 30 meters over a decade. The dry State of Gujarat offers the extreme example, where wells are lowered by 3 meters every two years. Agronomists project a severe water famine in the next decade.

This story of "mining" ground water is repeated in many world regions. The Middle East, with its complex of political boundaries and growing populations, are facing acute water shortages today. Israel diverts agricultural water to supply its urban areas, thereby decreasing food production. The United States also supplies its expanding cities in Arizona and southern California at the expense of its agricultural lands. In fact, water has become such a valuable commodity that an agricultural company purchased land in the California Mojave Desert not to farm but to gain rights to the underlying aquifer. The long range plan is to sell water to the city of San Diego and thus earn more from the sale of water than by planting crops (Sterngold, 1996). Four hundred miles to the east in the middle of the Sonaran Desert, with an annual rainfall of 7 to 12 inches per year, the city of Tucson, Arizona, and surrounding areas supplies its 700,000 residents and 30 golf courses with water pumped from an ancient aquifer that took thousands of years to form. The only way that the home building expansion has been maintained is by taking agricultural land out of production so the city and county water companies could acquire water rights.

This depletion of ancient aquifers is also occurring throughout the Great Plains area, as cotton and grain farms pump deeper and deeper to supply the crops. The United States, as well as countries in Asia and the Middle East, continue this nonsustainable practice with few questions asked, except the fuel costs of extraction. The key question that seems to have been avoided is how deep is the water supply. According to the editor of World Watch, experts know that the level of aquifers are dropping fast but none had the answer to how far down was the bottom or how long the pumping can continue (Ayres, 1998).

Dams, Developments, and Displacements

The global water supply is finite and determines where and how well people may live. There is an unvarying amount on the planet, but some sources are more accessible and useful to humans than others. Surface runoff to the sea is of little use unless it can be controlled or removed somewhere along its course. It is this control of surface water that has been a major enterprise for centuries. In the last 150 years, with the aid of heavy earth-moving machinery, thousands of dams were constructed on every continent. These dams have generated electric power, controlled flooding, and have impounded water for irrigation.

Economic development follows in the wake of dam construction, especially the larger ones. With these vast man-made lakes backed up behind the dam there is a seemingly inexhaustible supply of water and electric power for cities, industries, and farms. Water may be released when needed or held back to prevent floods. Along with the benefits there are negative feedbacks, some just being acknowledged. The reservoirs cover millions of acres of land, often the most productive land in the area and the surrounding environment is radically changed. The Kainji dam on the Niger River, for example, actually contributed to a reduced rice output and the fish production declined by 60 percent. The lake environment may stabilize in the future and fish populations may recover, but the short-term prospects have not been hopeful (Anonymous, 1997).

Another aspect of water control is that silt is no longer deposited downstream to rebuild soil fertility. The silt collects behind the dams, filling the reservoir and thereby reducing its useful time span. Traditional farming practices have to be altered radically, as has been the case along the Nile River since the completion of the Aswan Dam. Not only are farmers more dependent on chemical fertilizers, but land erosion and salinization have become special problems in the delta area of the lower Nile. In addition to environmental impacts, one of the more negative effects of dam building is the displacement of people.

The building of the "Three Gorges Dam" in China, a massive undertaking to control the flow of the Yangtze River, is one of the world's largest hydroelectric projects. When it is completed it will have flooded 24,000 acres of farm land and inundated cities, towns, and villages. A million and a half people will be displaced. The people that have been resettled have many complaints about their low compensation and inadequate homes. These complaints echo those of people still suffering from the results of earlier hydroelectric projects, over the past forty years during which some 84,000 dams were built. Such projects are seen as necessities to meet a country's rising water demands to supply industrial and agricultural growth, but often projects are poorly planned and long-range effects are either unknown or ignored.

The Aral Sea

The diversion of two major rivers in Central Asia to supply cotton growth stands out as a leading example of an unplanned environmental catastrophe. Several rivers flow into the Aral Sea, a salty body of water about the size of Lake Huron in the United states (Figure 8–2). In the 1950s, dams were built on the Syr Daryo and Amu Darya rivers and diverted most of the water to irrigate massive agricultural projects, principally cotton. Soon after the water diversion began, the sea level started its long decline as only one-eighth as much water flowed into the sea in 1989 as had in 1960. The total surface area was reduced by 40 percent and the depth dropped 47 feet. With this decline in water volume, the salinity increased from 10,000 parts per million to 30,000, nearly as salty as ocean water. The Aral Sea had provided a rich stock of fish for many generations but after the river flows declined from 1960 on, the fisheries were gradually destroyed. The shoreline receded and docks and large ships were left stranded on dry land. Cities, once on the shoreline, were now miles from what remained of the Aral (Glantz et al., 1993).

In addition to losing a thriving fishing industry, air pollution became a major problem for the area. The drying sea bed became sterile salt flats, polluted with agricultural chemicals after decades of runoff from the cotton farms hundreds of miles to the south. The high winds of the hot dry summers of this Central Asian plateau picked up and scattered these pollutants

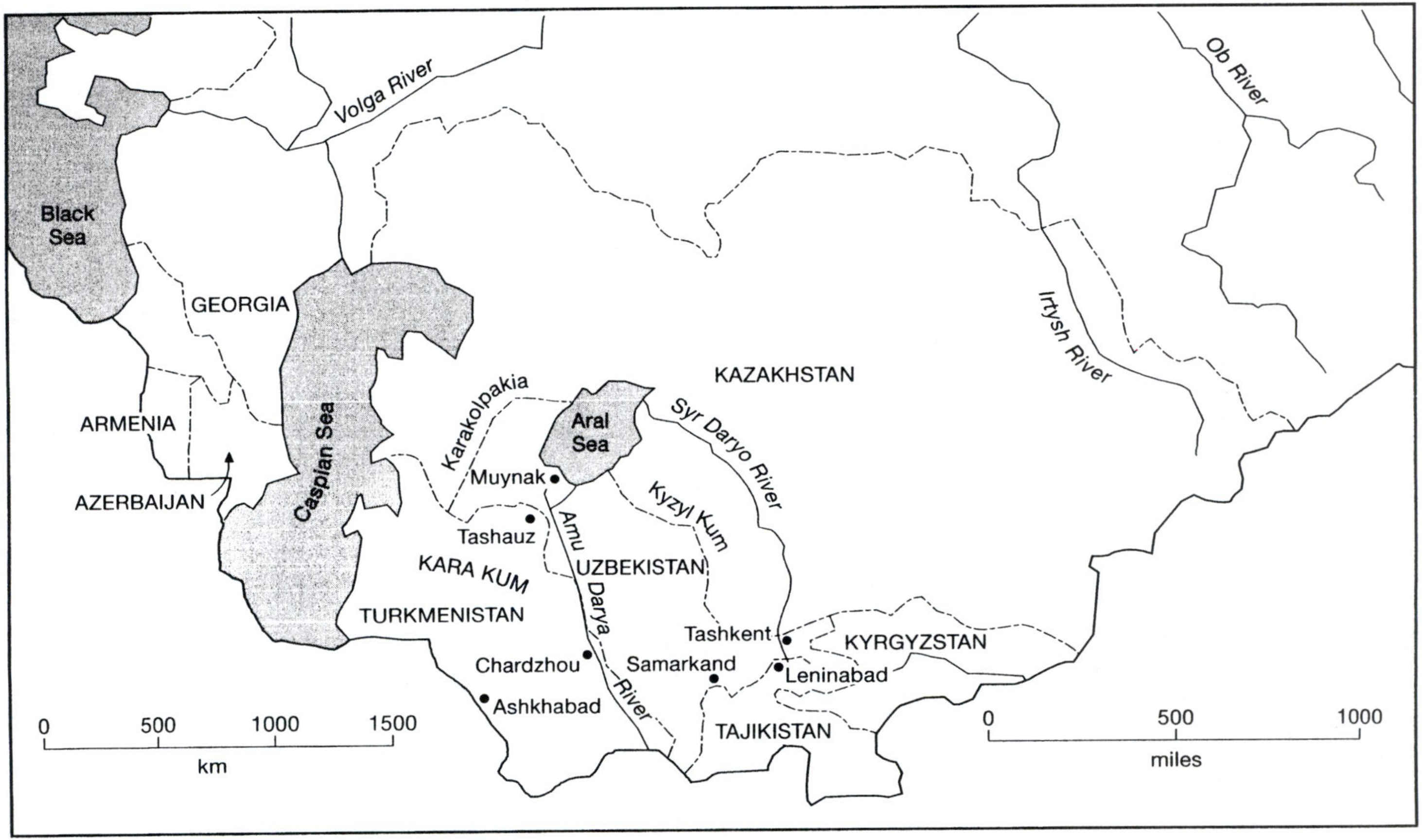

Figure 8–2 Region of the Caspian and Aral Seas

From Feshbach and Friendly, 1992. Eocide in the USSR: Health and Nature Under Seige. Reprinted by permission of Basic Books, Inc.

over thousands of square miles. For the populations living around the Aral, not only was their livelihood destroyed, but their health was threatened as well.

HEALTH AND SOME DEVELOPMENT LINKAGES

The Aral Sea destruction stands out as a leading symbol of environmental abuse and national central planning at its worse; the development projects meant to improve this Central Asian region were an economic disaster. The contaminated windblown dust from the exposed sea bed of Aral polluted thousands of square miles. It was deposited on every surface and found its way into the food chain and water supply. The toxic salt dust fell on irrigated lands and damaged the food crops but, at that time, little thought was given to the affects on the humans who breathed in this dust. The hardest hit were the people living in nearby cities and on the surrounding farms. Their drinking water was polluted and every test result showed that water was contaminated far above any acceptable standard. Hepatitis and typhoid were common infections and probably the contributing cause of an infant mortality rate two times as high as the average for the entire Soviet Union for 1989. Maternal mortality tripled from 1984 to 1989 and eight out of ten pregnant women were anemic.

In certain districts, the health problems were even more acute. The lack of sanitation, clean water, plus the food and airborne pollutants, placed those closest to the Aral Sea at a higher risk for disease and early death than anywhere in the developing countries of the world. Their health was deplorable and inexcusable in a nation that had the technology to develop a nuclear industry and put a man on the moon. The Aral Sea regional populations exceeded USSR averages for the incidences of all infectious diseases. These regions lacked most basic medical facilities; what is ironic in a land with such large irrigation systems was the lack of food.

Milk, meat, and produce were in short supply. Uzbeks were only getting a third or less, considered as a standard for good health. The young bore the brunt of this economic–environmental disaster. Starvation was reported among children in Turkmenistan, though political authorities denied there was any problem and tried to stop stories from circulating in Moscow newspapers. But the 1989 medical records reported that starvation not only existed but began in the uterus of malnourished women. Several separate inquiries showed a high rate of malnourished children, up to 84 percent, in one study. "While the people of the region lacked food, the Aral Sea starved for water" (Feshbach and Friendly, 1992). The result has been both a major change in climate (removal of the moderating influence of the large body of water) and hundreds of thousands of people who have suffered under the impact of ill-planned development.

Dams and Diseases

Waters in the tropics and subtropics carry a number of parasitic diseases, and one of the more widespread is schistosomiasis. This infection is due to a flat worm that is carried for most of its lifecycle by a small freshwater snail. The snail lives in warm muddy water that one finds frequently in small sluggish streams, irrigation canals, and ponds. Larvi of the schistosomes swim freely from its snail host, and humans bathing, wading, or washing clothes in the water can become infected with these free swimming larvi. Some schistosome species infest the veins of the human pelvic area. As the larvi mature into the adult worm stage their eggs are shed in the urine of the infected human. Another type infests the lower intestinal tract and the worms' eggs are dispeled in the feces. Should the human urinate or defecate in or near a water course, then the eggs are picked up by the local snail population. This begins the cycle of transmission all over again. Thus, the persistence and/or spread of the disease depends upon water conditions, snail hosts, and humans using the pond or canal. Because of human mobility, the infection is spread far and wide from infected to uninfected areas.

This disease has been known since antiquity in the Nile; infections have been found in ancient Egyptian mummies. Peasant farmers standing in water up to their knees as they work to clear irrigation ditches soon pick up the flat worm larvi and are reinfected throughout their lives. The carrying of this parasite causes a variety of health problems, but anemia, with the accompanying loss of energy, is the principle one.

When and how the schistosomes spread throughout Central Africa is not known, but the Volta area of upper Ghana was relatively free until the construction of a dam and the impoundment of Lake Volta. The infection rate went from very low to 20–30 percent of the human population of the area. Likewise, the Kariba Dam on the Zambesi River, originally built to generate power for the region, served to spread the disease along with irrigation water. A decade after completion, 69 percent of the children were infected and a total of 16 percent for all ages of the region. The other impounded lakes, Nasser on the Nile and Kainji on the Niger, also serve as sources of schistosomiasis.

This problem is not limited to Africa but occurs throughout Southeast Asia, South America, and the Caribbean, as well. Where its geographical dispersion has been extensive, dams and irrigation works are a prime cause as well as infected migrant workers acting as carriers. Medical geographers make a point that schistosomiasis is a useful marker or indicator for a group of parasitic diseases that are spread by water projects, which include diseases like malaria, filariasis, and leishmaniasis, for example (Learmonth, 1988).

Schistosomiasis infects upward to 200 million people reported in seventy-four countries. Depending on the schistosome species, cystic lesions are formed in the intestines, blood vessels, or liver. In some persons, severe lesions develop in the urogenital region. Often the victim believes these lesions to be due to a venereal disease infection. Women are reluctant to speak of this problem and delay seeking medical treatment because of the stigma of being a carrier of a sexually transmitted disease. In fact they are often misdiagnosed as such and are incorrectly treated. Where schistosomiasis is especially high in parts of Central Africa, these parasitic caused vaginal lesions increase the chance of heterosexual transmission of the AIDS virus, further compounding the problem of its spread (Mtukulo, 1995)

Rivers, Wells, and Disease

Health workers are well aware of the risks of using surface waters for domestic purposes. These rivers, lakes, streams, or ponds carry organisms of cholera, typhoid, dysenteries, and parasitic diseases that are all too prevalent in the developing world. The problem is what to do. Provision of safe water can be costly, especially in densely populated tropical areas. The building of dams and irrigation works has met the needs of agriculture, but these same waters are often dangerous for human use. The solution in many places has been to drill deep wells, tapping underground sources of clean water. This type of water development project to improve the lot of the rural poor has had some unwanted and dangerous consequences.

In Western Bengal of India, some 5 million people live on the Ganges River flood plain along the border with Bangladesh. They plant their crops in the rich alluvial soils and depend on a timely arrival of the monsoon rains to water them. There have been successes and bountiful crops enjoyed, but in some years there were severe losses when the rains failed or arrived late. In the meantime, the villagers took what water they could from the polluted Ganges River and its tributaries for their domestic needs and small gardens. Infectious and parasitic diseases have always been high throughout the region.

The Indian national government, as part of the agricultural development program, began to drill a series of tube wells throughout the area. From 1962, continuing through the next decades, over 100,000 wells were sunk to depths of 500 feet or more. This solved two problems for the millions of poor farmers. The wells gave them an ample, dependable water supply for their farms, and crops could be planted year round, boosting production and, hence, contributing to India's green revolution. Clean water was also supplied for domestic use as a second benefit. For several years the original goals seemed to have been fulfilled but then puzzling skin and lung diseases began to appear.

The wells had drilled through arsenic-bearing rock layers, and as water levels declined with withdrawals, the pyrite bedrock layer was exposed to air. This arsenic-bearing rock began to oxidize, and the arsenic compounds increased in concentration. In effect, the consumers were being slowly poisoned by their own wells. Eventually in 1983, a Calcutta dermatologist traced the cause of the epidemic of skin lesions to waterborne arsenic and described his finding, but official response was slow. The first government action was to drill more and deeper wells. These new wells seemed to help for a time but arsenic concentration returned to former levels and 95 percent of the wells tested positive. Currently there are 1,200 villages at risk of chronic poisoning. Plans are being made to build filtration plants and draw water from the an already overused Ganges (Marshal, 1998).

To the west, across the border in Bangladesh, the people are suffering even more. Some 70 million people, about one-half of the nation, are drinking arsenic-contaminated water. Bangladesh drilled thousands of wells, as did India, to obtain a clean water supply, which was badly needed by this nation of 124 million people living on the Ganges flood plains. How many of these people now suffer the symptoms of arsenic poisoning or will do so in the near future can be only a guess at this time. The nation faces a serious problem and international organizations are helping to trace the arsenic contamination to specific ground water sources. A research center has been founded to study the matter and to devise appropriate filtration methods (Anonymous, 1998). The alternative, a return to full reliance on surface waters, is not attractive because of severe pollution and the frequent flooding of the nation during the cyclone season.

The various affects of arsenic have been known for centuries, and in small doses it had been used in tonics to treat various ailments. Larger doses block blood cell formation, effect respiration, cause skin lesions, and do severe liver damage. The affects of chronic ingestion is not as well understood, but the victims suffer from skin problems, a general thickening of certain areas or lumps that are precancerous. Also, at advanced stages, lung tissues are damaged, causing bleeding and the victim coughs up blood, often leading to a misdiagnosis of tuberculosis, particularly in those populations where the TB infection rate is high. In addition to being a poison of choice of murderers, arsenic has also been used as a main ingredient in insecticides, especially before the days of DDT. So, there have been quantities of arsenic spread about the environment over the past century. The use of naturally contaminated water only makes matters worse.

An unappreciated fact is that arsenic is widely distributed in nature in several types of minerals, and so it occurs naturally in numerous geologic formations from which we draw our water. A permissible limit has been set at fifty parts per billion, but many communities distribute water with higher concentrations. Ground waters (subsurface deposits or aquifers) that contain varying amounts of arsenic exceeding this permissible level have been reported from the Pacific Northwest of the United States to Hungary, from Chile to Argentina. Chronic poisoning by low levels of arsenic in these areas have been traced to many of these sources (National Academy of Science,

1977). Alternate water sources had to be obtained as increasing evidence linked skin, liver, and lung damage to chronic arsenic ingestion.

Hungary, for example, sunk deep artesian wells in the southeastern part of the country to replace the polluted shallow wells that were the sources for so many towns and villages. These new wells and distribution networks brought a supply of pure water from deep underground deposits to every home. Within a short time it was discovered that a geologic layer, rich in arsenic compounds, had been tapped. The people were getting a high dose of arsenic along with their clean water. These wells had to be abandoned and a system of reservoirs and filtration plants were used instead. The best-intended development projects can and sometimes do bring about undesirable results.

HEALTH OR DISEASE: FOOD SOURCES AND GOITER

Normal growth and metabolism depends on a certain level of thyroid gland function, and, as discussed in Chapter 6, this gland requires a small amount of iodine. If this daily requirement is not met, then a series of physiological problems occur. The low levels of iodine trigger the secretion of a thyroid stimulating hormone by the pituitary gland, which then causes the growth and swelling of the thyroid gland tissue. This increases the gland's ability to "capture" iodine from the blood circulation. Persistence of low levels of circulating iodine continues as a stimulant that leads to larger thyroid growth until a person has a large disfigured swelling, or goiter, around the larynx. The longer the deficiency persists, the larger the gland becomes.

In children deprived of adequate iodine, growth is retarded and, if severe enough, they will only achieve dwarf size when adults. Even in milder cases, mental ability can be affected and the IQ lowered by ten or fifteen points. If women when pregnant are iodine deficient, then embryo and fetal growth is affected. Depending on the severity, the fetus can be born a cretinous dwarf with an impaired neurological system. Such conditions of goiter and dwarfism were once widespread occurrences throughout the world. Now this nutritional deficiency is much rarer than it was a century ago. Still, there are about a third of all humans at risk of suffering from iodine deficiency disease and will have impaired growth and develop goiter if they are not treated. The Progress of Nations (United Nations, 1996) described that a lack of iodine affected the physical and mental health of about 50 million children in 1994, and there were 100,000 cretin births. A vigorous world campaign to add iodine to food, mainly as iodized salt and sometimes sugar, halved this number by 1996. More and more nations of the developing world are cooperating with their food industries to ensure that their people receive iodine supplements in some form.

There are four possible causes of goiter, or hypothyroidism.[2] First, there is a theory, yet to be examined thoroughly, that some type of infection impairs the gland's ability to function. Second, certain goitrogenic compounds are ingested from foods, like cassava, and cruciferous plants—cabbages, turnips, etc. Third, excessive minerals in the water prevent iodine absorption. Finally, there is an environmental deficiency of iodine, the most frequent cause of goiter (Pyle, 1979). A fifth possible cause of hypothyroidism and its sequel of growth and mental retardation is heredity, which was the most often used explanation until seventy-five years ago. Cretinism and goiter were very frequent among the closed communities in valleys of the European Alps, and medical authorities once claimed that the disease was due to highly inbred populations, the frequent mating between close relatives.

The world distribution of goiter in the early twentieth century, when accurate recording began, showed a distribution that related to geographical region. People living in mountainous areas, whether Asia, North or South America, or the Alps, had the highest number of affected individuals. The next distribution noted was the people living on plains consisting of "young soils," that is, soils that had recently formed out of ground rock materials from the pressures and movements of glacial ice. Many of these areas had been covered by glacial ice as recently as 10,000 years ago, so they were the youngest of soils. These land areas of recent glacial action had not been exposed long enough to accumulate a concentration of iodine from the rains carrying microamounts of the element that had evaporated from the world's oceans.

Another distribution of goiter cases was found among tropical peoples who live on soils washed by frequent, heavy rains or covered with periodic floods along some of the major river valleys where humans had settled for thousands of years. Contrary to these distributions were those goiter-free populations who lived on or near the sea coasts and who consumed a quantity of seafood. Other peoples, also goiter free, were those living on soils that had never been glaciated and were not inundated by tropical flooding. These geographical distributions showed that goiter was correlated with certain types of soil substrates and were not a matter of climate. The question of inbreeding as a cause of cretinism had not yet been settled.

About the beginning of the twentieth century the physiologic importance of iodine to thyroid function was demonstrated, and some trial tests were made of goiter patients (Matovinovic, 1983). This information about a simple and plentiful trace element led researchers to test for iodine in the water and soils from regions where goiter was endemic. These samples were

---

[2]Goiter may be caused by several other physiological problems, such as a pituitary tumor that effects thyroid stimulating hormone (TSH), but our discussion will concentrate on the major cause, iodine deficiency. For complete discussion of thyroid pathologies, see Ganong, 1993.

all very low or totally lacking in iodine content. Most of these low iodine samples came from Central Europe and the areas around the Great Lakes in the United States, which was known as the "goiter belt." People were drinking water and eating food grown in these areas that were too deficient in iodine to supply the thyroid gland's requirement. Medical researchers now had a clear demonstration of a trace element function, and its geographic distribution correlated with a severe, debilitating disease. This information showed how goiter could be prevented or, in its early stages, even cured. A mass program of food supplementation with iodine was carried out in the United States and Switzerland with great success. But it was years before other countries accepted these results and put into practice the method of goiter prevention.

This reluctance to adopt such a simple prophylaxis has many facets. One consideration is that not all medical people were convinced of so easy a solution; nutritional research was in its early stages and the effects of trace elements were virtually unknown. Then, too, goiter incidence had been declining over several decades. This decline may be explained by the use of more imported and less locally grown food. Food canning and refrigeration were on the increase in the last quarter of the nineteenth century, and expanding rapidly. People of the "goiter belt" were more likely to eat foods grown on soils with a higher iodine content.

The persistent endemic areas were those more remote, poor farming communities, who were, to put it kindly, out of the national mainstream and out of sight. It was still acceptable in the 1920s to blame a good many of the ailments of such communities on defective heredity, or "bad blood." Further, mass dosing with iodine required some form of food supplementation, which the public was reluctant to accept—witness the problems over the past fifty years regarding water fluoridation.[3] Even today the addition of iodine to the food chain is not consistent. Some nations add iodine to bread, salt, or sugar and even then the supplemented items are not always available for purchase. Thailand adds iodine to fish paste, a popular food, and several other countries add iodine to the water supply.

Today, after nearly a century, iodine deficiency still remains a problem. Despite a cheap and easy solution, nearly 2 billion people still remain at risk. Most of these live in developing countries where much of their food is locally grown. People who can afford to buy food produced in several different areas probably ingest enough iodine. Even such populations have exhibited some problems lately. Goiter is reappearing in the Netherlands among people who, concerned about their health, have reduced bread and salt intakes, both sources of iodine. Government restrictions were relaxed in

[3]As of 1994, only 17 percent of California's population received a fluoridated water supply, and there was vigorous opposition when the governor signed a bill that year to extend fluoridation to another 10,000 households.

Croatia, and farmers were allowed to purchase a cheaper noniodized salt for their cattle. Hence, an important source was eliminated from the food chain.

The form of salt seems to be an important consideration. Portugal waited until 1982 to pass a law requiring iodization but it left enforcement to local authorities. Only the fine grain salt was iodized, and the preferred coarse salt was left unsupplemented (Escobar and Escobar, 1993). In New Guinea, twenty years ago, a much favored coarse salt (lacking in iodine) was brought into certain highland districts as a trade item and soon replaced a local variety distilled from salt pools containing iodine. The result was a rapid development of endemic goiter and cretinism where no problem existed before (Heywood, 1992). So, from industrial Europe throughout developing nations, and to the New Guinea highlands, salt quality has affected and continues to affect health in critical ways. Science is only one part of the story, custom another, and then there is the politics of development.

Development and Disease: A Simple Matter of Salt

The story of the treatment of endemic goiter in Spain, ably told by Renate Fernandez (1990) best illustrates the separation and sometimes isolation among clinical medicine, research, and epidemiologial professionals. This isolation has led to misunderstanding and inertia, especially where prejudices mask or distort the view of a population's needs. Just as in the example when malnourished people, suffering from pellegra, were passed over as hereditary defectives, so too were many of the villagers in the mountainous region of Northern Spain. The leading medical authority of the day, Marañon, an endocrinology specialist, refused to accept iodine deficiency as a cause of the endemic goiter and cretinism, diseases that existed in twenty-two of Spain's fifty provinces in 1927. He was fully aware of the existence of these diseases, and had, in fact, led a commission to visit many of the villages to study the health problems of the area.

Marañon delivered a report to the First International Endemic Goiter Conference in Switzerland in which he described endemic goiter conditions found in Spain. But he refused to endorse dietary iodine supplements as a cure. He still failed to grasp the significance of supplementation even after listening to the several conference papers describing in scientific detail the treatment's successes. Even his guided tour of Swiss alpine villages, where cretins were no longer being born since the iodine treatment, failed to sway his opinion.

The basis for objection may have been his wide experience in the treatment of many cases of thyrotoxicosis.[4] But the simplicity of the treatment may have also influenced him as well. He sought solutions to the health problems of the mountain villagers within a more complex frame of reference. Marañon held to his proposal that economic development was the most effective response to eliminating cretinism and goiter in Spain. The emphasis on economic development as the answer is interesting and one of some complexity that Fernandez (1990) discusses at length. The basis of Marañon's argument seems to be that as a specialist treating thyroid disorders, a small dose of iodine was just too simple a remedy to treat the multitude of ailments that he had seen on his visits to the poor farm villages in the Asturian province. Also, he was of the school and class that viewed these people as a race apart. This seemed to be revealed when Fernandez described how Marañon urged that the Hurdenos (villagers of Las Hurdes) should be protected from non-Hudeno intrusions in order to preserve their human genetic resources. This seems contradictory given Marañon's urging of development for these mountainous areas.

Marañon advocated a more gradual approach of economic development and the elimination of the Asturian communities' isolation to improve diet, health, and, most importantly, put an end to their unhealthy breeding habits. He even went so far as to persuade the king to accompany him on a visit to see at first hand the poverty and suffering of the villagers. It appears that on one hand his humanist instincts were to offer some help but on the other, as a medical scientist, he was not convinced of what course to take despite the results seen in the Swiss data on the effectiveness of iodine supplementation. Whatever his motives had been, his professional status was such that a simple goiter treatment was ignored during his lifetime and for twenty-five years after his death. Of course, this short summary does not do justice to the complex economic and political system of Spain and the power that entrenched senior scientists held over research and treament, but it should alert the reader to the gaps between plans, professions, and science.

HEALTH IMPROVEMENTS: MEDICAL OR ECONOMIC CAUSES

The changes in the health and longevity experienced during industrialization occurred over a long period and depended largely on economic changes followed by improvements in living conditions (see Chapter 4). The sanitar-

[4] There were frequent cases in those days when people would ingest iodine in excess in an attempt to lose weight. Obviously this would not have applied to the poor farmers in isolated villages surviving by subsistence farming.

ians moved rapidly ahead, leading medical developments in the improvement of the lot of Europeans and North Americans. As described by McKeown (1979), several of the major diseases were already declining before the infectious organisms or their vectors were discovered. Mortality declines of some of the so-called childhood diseases (pertussis and measles) occurred about a hundred years before immunization began. We should not, however, overemphasize the dichotomy between environmental and medical treatment—they more often advanced together. Diphtheria, like smallpox a century before, continued to reoccur at high rates until an effective treatment and then a vaccine was developed. For all age groups, declines in tuberculosis and acute respiratory infections were first initiated by environmental improvements and then assisted by medical treatment and vaccines.

The health improvements and mortality declines in the developing world have followed a somewhat different sequence of events. Vaccines, antibiotics, and insecticides have been and are continued to be provided for most of the nonindustrialized countries. Medical training and public health assistance has also been made available to aid national health programs around the world. Millions of children have been inoculated, and medicines have been widely dispensed, especially since the end of World War II. There have been some remarkable successes, along with some failures, but on balance, death rates have been brought down to less than half within the last fifty years.

The earliest success recorded was the initial control of malaria as described in Chapter 7, a success that had a major effect on death rate reduction before the disease's resurgence. Smallpox has been eradicated from the world since 1979 when the last case was reported. It took nearly two centuries and the development of a new form of vaccine to inoculate the children of the world, but victory has been declared. Since 1980, there have been major programs to immunize all children for other major diseases. These efforts are continuing, and the World Health Organization, together with several nongovernmental groups, have been cooperating with local governments to reach even the most remote villages of the less-developed world. The goal to vaccinate all of the 120 million babies born each year is now in sight. All infants need to be given the vaccinations of the DPT serum four or five times during their first year of life to protect them from diphtheria, pertussis, and tetanus. Polio, typhoid, and measles vaccines have also been administered widely, especially to pregnant women. As of 1995, 80 percent of the developing countries' children have been immunized with some or all of the vaccines.

In addition to the childhood vaccines, inoculations for tuberculosis and hepatitis have been added. Table 8–3 summarizes this list of vaccines administered and the prevention successes. Polio dropped by 80 percent between 1988 and 1994, measles deaths have been cut by a third, and mortalities from

TABLE 8–3 Child Immunization Progress

	Annual deaths if no immunization	Prevented	Occurring
Smallpox	5.0 million	5.0 million	—
Diphtheria	260,000	223,000	37,000
Whooping cough	990,000	630,000	360,000
Measles	2.7 million	1.6 million	1.1 million
Neonatal tetanus	1.2 million	0.7 million	0.5 million
Hepatitis B	1.2 million	0.4 million	0.8 million
Tuberculosis	3.2 million	0.2 million	3.0 million
Polio (cases of lifelong paralysis)	640,000	550,000	90,000
Malaria/Other parasitic infections	2.2 million	—	2.2 million
HIV/Sexually transmitted disease	1.3 million	—	1.3 million
Diarrhoea/Enteric fevers	3.0 million	—	3.0 million
Acute respiratory infections	3.7 million	—	3.7 million

Source: Data adapted from Progress of Nations, UN, 1996.

the other major seven on the list have also been reduced significantly. Accordingly, an estimated 5 million fewer children are dying each year. The oral rehydration therapy prevents even more deaths in young children from the wide variety of diarrheal diseases they suffer (United Nations, 1996).

Public expenditures on health as a percentage of gross domestic product (GDP) have doubled or even tripled between 1960 and 1990. The production of more effective vaccines have been an aid as well to the health program's success. What is equally significant is that the same transportation system that moves sick people around spreading infectious organisms also enables health workers with their equipment to reach every community. If an air strip or road will not carry them to the isolated villages, then helicopters can and do transport medical aid to the most remote locales.

A majority of people in the developing world still lack access to safe water, though improvements have been made since 1960. With rapid urban growth, the problem has actually worsened in many countries, however. The transmission of diseases through poor sanitation, air pollution, and crowded living conditions increases annually. Credit for health improvements and decline of the major killer diseases can be taken by the energetic prevention offered by the immunization program and not by the sanitarians, as had been the case during the nineteenth century in Europe.

The results are clear and reported with pride. Without the longtime lag it took for improvements of the nineteenth century, and without the industrial development, villagers in New Guinea, in the Amazon forests, or along the Zambizi River in Central Africa have gained at least some of the benefits of twentieth-century progress. More infants are surviving their first year, and more children are living beyond their fifth birthday. The crude death rates have been halved and halved again since the 1950s. This, of course, has contributed to a new demographic regime in the world.

DEMOGRAPHY, TRANSITIONS, AND DEVELOPMENTS

There are two critical facts that must be restated whenever population and development are discussed in reference to the "European Development" model. First, change originated internally, progressing from a series of innovations, as outlined in Chapter 4. Second, and of equal importance, is that these innovations and the fundamental changes of lifestyle that followed occurred over a long time span of nearly two centuries. The demographic transitions and economic developments in the lesser-developed (or developing nations) are transpiring over a very short time period by comparison, and they have been imposed by external forces. This time element and the sources of stimulus have caused nations of the developing world to confront a population growth rate that had never occurred before in human history.

The high rate of annual increases has reduced population doubling time and has divided humanity as never before into groups of slow growth or rapid growth populations. Figure 8–3 diagrams the world's total population and the relative proportions contributed by each of these two "worlds." Eighty percent of the people in 1998 lived in what are labeled as developing regions, and the gap will widen in the future. This contrast is clearly shown in the graph, and something else is apparent also. The graph, drawn from projections made ten years ago, has proven to be quite accurate for the year 2000; note the world total 6 billion projected for that date.

With the continued fall of death rates, the population gaps have continued to widen. The biggest improvements have been in reduction of infant mortality with most of the large developing countries like India, China, Bangladesh, and Indonesia reducing infant losses by nearly a half between 1975 and 1998. These gains were made by improving childhood health, largely through the inoculation programs and added to a drop in the crude death rates of about 60 percent (from a CDR of sixteen down to nine per thousand population). Over the same period, crude birth rates have remained high, declining only slightly, and many of the developing countries have continued to grow at a high rate. Fertility rates decreased significantly from a high of 6 percent down to 3, but population momentum continued to add new citizens because of the large numbers of women in their reproductive years (see Chapter 5). Between the 1960s to present, some improvements have been made in the demographic profile and,

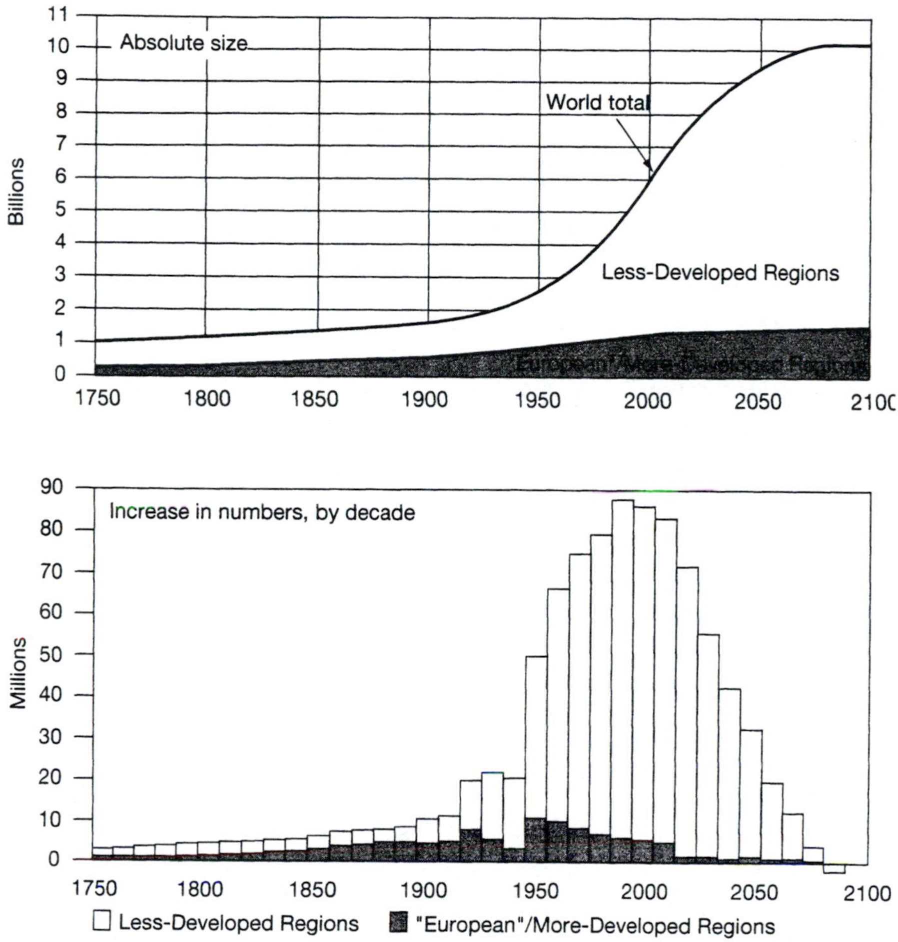

Figure 8–3 World Population Growth and Future Projections

From Merrick, 1986. Reprinted by permission of Population Reference Bureau, Inc.

though growth has slowed, population increases continue at an RNI of nearly 2 percent.

National leaders recognize the consequences of this rapid growth. It depletes natural resources, requires heavier debt burdens for more development projects, and agriculture expands to include those lands that are less fertile and are more expensive to bring into production. Crop yields can only be increased by so much despite greater inputs of chemicals, but even these increases fail to keep pace with food needs as population growth shrinks cropland per capita. Many of the developing nations have been held in phase two of the demographic transition too long and some have entered into a demographic repression. Food must be imported in increasing quantities, and this translates into a decline of income that, in turn, decreases the ability to repay the money that was borrowed in the first place to fund development projects (compare Brown and Kane, 1994; Brown, 1998).

These nations are then caught up in a vicious cycle of debt, production decline, and population increases, requiring more debt followed by further decline. The countries with abundant energy resources and valuable mineral deposits have a chance of breaking out, provided that development is accompanied by an effective family planning program. Besides resources and population growth, the goals as defined by society and implemented by their government have equally profound effects reaching far into the future.

Mexico: Development and Demography

This rapidly growing nation of 98 million people offers an example of the linkages between population and resource development. It has a good resource base of several important minerals plus an oil reserve twice the size of the United States. Though only about 12 percent of its land is arable, it produces substantial quantities of maize, beans, rice, and wheat. In fact, it is the country where the high yielding wheat variety that launched the green revolution was developed. The agricultural lands in the northern part of the country employ the latest scientific technology and irrigation methods. Further, Mexico has a good transportation system and communications. There are modern medical services within reach of all its citizens, and education is free and compulsory through twelve years of age; literacy is 90 percent.

With these resources, the country should be moving out of the "developing" category. Instead, thousands of families migrate into urban areas seeking employment, and thousands more are illegal immigrant laborers in the United States. A major block to progress has been a matter of demographics. Mexico's medical services, food supplies, and access to safe water(in most of the country) have lowered crude death rates and infant mortality. At the same time, fertility has remained high. Over the past two decades, the population growth rate has decreased but still remains above 2 percent. This means that Mexico remains a young, fast-growing population with 36 percent of its citizens under age fifteen despite its many developments over the past fifty years. Mexico's recent history offers some examples for those who wish to consider population as the driving force of development that, in turn, will automatically regulate population growth. In short, the experience of this large country (three times the size of France) offers a way of appraising the demographic transition theory that postulates a fertility decline stimulated by rising of income.

Mexico has suffered a turbulent history ever since its first European contact, which drastically reduced the Native American population from an estimated 25 million down to 7 million, Native and European combined. The country grew slowly over the next centuries to 15 million by 1900, and population appeared to hover at this level through times of revolution, political turmoil, and hunger. In 1910 the crude birth and death rates were about equal and remained so for the next decades. Some gains would be made to be lost a few years later as during the influenza epidemic of 1918, when the crude death rate was forty-eight and the birth rate only forty.

During this time the government took an active pronatalist stance, especially following the revolution and epidemic. There was agreement that, to be a successful modern nation, Mexico's population had to grow. The Secretary of the Interior was empowered to resolve demographic problems. School textbooks and health services promoted large families, there were certain rights and allowances awarded for children, rural clinics were established throughout the country, and prizes were awarded to the most prolific woman of the year. Abortions were outlawed, and advertisements of contraceptives were banned.

Though population growth remained slow for several decades, it was apparent by 1955 that the pronatalist plans had been successful. The change compared to 1940 was plain for all to see. Now the challenge was a call for the creativity to industrialize and build an economy to absorb the rural migrants who were moving out of their native communities in search of work. While industrial plans were going ahead, the achievement of a 3 percent annual population growth rate caught demographers by surprise. They worked out their calculations and projected a population of between 38 million and 45 million by 1970 (it actually reached 50 million). Some officials still encouraged more growth and stated that for the rest of the century Mexico can concentrate on economic development without worrying about births. During the 1960s, in fact, the GNP was 7.3 percent compared to 4.3 percent for their North American neighbor.

There were, however, some officials who were a bit more skeptical. Notes of caution began to be heard that perhaps human welfare could benefit from a 30 percent decrease in birth rate. So began a new era in the Mexican social system when the pronatalist position was starting to be countered by a slower, more cautious approach. By 1972, President Echeverria instituted a family planning policy with the warning that population growth could overwhelm economic development. The policy of family planning has worked. Growth was reduced from 3.2 percent to 2.3 percent within a decade, and the goal was to seek a further reduction to 1 percent by the year

2000 (Bobadilla, et al, 1993). As of 1998, Mexico's RNI remains at 2.2 percent, however.

Mexico presents a puzzling picture for those who look to the demographic transition model, according to Ansley Coale (1973). The recent demographic history of Mexico refutes those optimists who hold the view that development is the best contraceptive (for discussion see Keyfitz, 1994). When rapidly growing nations follow several paths of development, then increases of income or advances in social and economics may not automatically reduce high birth rates, as is illustrated by Mexico. This nation, with more natural resources than most industrialized countries expanded its agricultural output and improved its social services and infrastructure; yet fertility remained high. To add to a complex equation of demography and development, Mexico has one of the second richest oil reserves in the Western Hemisphere.

Compared to this example of Mexico, several much less well-endowed nations have made some major advances in the last few years in their efforts to reduce population growth and improve the health and well being of their citizens. Bangladesh, one of the poorest and most densely populated countries, has reduced its crude death rate by a third in twelve years, reduced its birth rate, and lowered the rate of natural increase to less than Mexico's. All of this was accomplished with some outside aid, of course, but it was done by a nation of mostly subsistence farmers with few resources. Others, like Sri Lanka and the several Central Asian Republics of the former Soviet Union, have achieved population control, bringing the RNI down with further reductions probable in the future. Do these examples or any number of others provide a model for bringing populations in balance with their resources? Is there a single formula or perhaps a universal law of demography and development? We think not, given these and several other examples, plus the experiences of the European nations a century ago.

A matter of social custom, or culture if you will, often enters into the reproductive equation and, hence, exerts its influence on national statistics. The examples are too numerous to list here but the one we discussed earlier is worthy of recalling. During the post–World War II era, the baby boom upset many demographic projections and predictions. Its effects on demographic laws or theories have been best described by Sir Charles Galton Darwin as part of his commentary on social science when he was a participant at a population conference in 1955.

> There seems to be a grave danger that often he(the social scientist) will be confusing what in fact are only fashions with eternal laws. Thus one of the most hopeful prospects that would prevent excessive increases in population seemed until recently to be the observation that the most prosperous countries showed the smallest increases. If then prosperity could be produced in other

countries, that should ultimately stabilize their population. This hope has been entirely defeated by the United States, which has recently shown one of the most rapid increases of all, and in spite of its present wonderful prosperity (in Grebenik, 1955).

SURVIVING ENVIRONMENTAL CHANGE

There will be, there must be, continued development to provide for the present needs of 6 billion people. This development must expand further to provide for the additional 2 billion people projected over the next twenty-five years. This is, of course, a monumental challenge and is made more difficult by the fact that most of the increase will occur in the less-developed world where population growth is already pressing the region's limits. The industrialized world can continue to furnish food and financial aid, but this too has its limits. The regions of rapid population growth will have to expand food production and industrialization to meet its needs. The challenge will be to expand without changing the environment to the point where it will impede the support of future generations. In other words, development will have to be sustainable.

Sustainable development is certainly an ideal goal but perhaps too idealistic. It cannot be achieved universally for all resources. Water use can be conserved by recycling, or impounded by dams and channeled through irrigation works. It may be easily placed in the sustainable category, except that conservation practices are seldom strictly followed. Through indifference and ignorance, a valuable resource is wasted and, as population grows, there will be increased competition for the rights to aquifers and the major river systems, particularly throughout the arid lands.

Land may be farmed for maximum yield with attention to conservation, a maintenance of fertility with minimal erosion. In the case of the use of forests, it will be more difficult to balance the rate of cutting with the rate of reforestation. At this time wood is the major fuel used for cooking in most of Africa and Southeast Asia and over half of the trees cut down are used for firewood. Whole areas have been denuded by a need for fuel. When there are no trees left to strip, then the poor must either buy expensive charcoal (made from wood gathered from some distant place) or use dry cattle dung mixed with grass as a fuel to cook their meals. There are few alternatives in countries like Niger, Mali, or Ethiopia. Such use not only exceeds the sustainability of marginal woodlands but it deprives the farmer of fertilizer for his land (Repetto, 1987). Commercial logging of tropical hardwoods or the intentional clearing of land for roads or for pasture accounts for the balance of deforestation. Mining is another development that disrupts the land form to an extreme degree. Roads must be built, most often through ecologically fragile areas, and minerals extracted, leaving polluted landscapes and waterways extending many miles from the site of mining operations.

The mounting fuel problem may be solved by use of coal or petroleum products, as in the case of a wide use of kerosene (paraffin) widely used in India. Natural gas and propane replaced charcoal as a cooking fuel in the 1950s in Mexico City, just in time, as the charcoal burners were rapidly chewing away the forests in the vicinity. But all of these alternatives require energy to dig for, drill for, or distill, and transport these fuels to the consumer. This means that more oil will have to be pumped from existing fields and new deposits found, and this supply is limited.

The price of all petroleum products doubled and doubled again in the 1970s when, through a combination of politics, war, and a strong cartel, oil production was tightly controlled to limit supply and keep prices high. There seemed to be a permanent oil crisis and a world, dependent on petroleum for most of its energy, appeared to face a bleak future. But as economic theory would predict, the higher prices drove down demand and, at the same time, new drilling technology increased output. The OPEC cartel's control was broken and crude oil came down from its $53 a barrel high to below twenty. Now there seems to be a plentiful supply and conservation of energy is no longer a high priority. The new drilling methods are extracting and adding to the oil storage faster than it can be used in the 1990s. Today, optimism reins with a plentiful supply and low prices, but petroleum is a finite resource and the world supply is projected to peak in fifty or ten or twenty years, depending on which prediction one takes (Science, 1998). After passing the production peak, it will decline and areas around the Caspian Sea will become more important sources, but these oil fields are located in a politically unstable region. What's more, the transport of oil by pipeline must cross the territory of countries that have interfered with the supply before. In sum, petroleum supply has limitations that are sensitive to political manipulations (as always).

The question of sustainability leads to one about the carrying capacity of the earth. Just how many people, and at what level of comfort and health, can the earth support. Various projections have been made and range all the way from 10 to 50 billion. The estimates of carrying capacity are based on expected food yields for a given area and on the energy inputs required. Increasingly, more is written about water as a limiting resource; also, numerous assumptions regarding technological innovations and new energy sources are entered into the equation. The background and history of population projections are given in some detail by Cohen (1995).

Some of the more rapid growth to date has occurred in areas where continued increases in food production are in doubt. Such countries will have to import, and the food exporting countries will expect some payment in return. But those in greatest need will be least able to pay. Besides, the quantity of transport to move the volume of food around the world taxes today's cargo carriers and to expand further would multiply the cost in materials, fuel, and personnel. Considering these factors together with lack of arable land, water shortages, and dependence on human effort and cooperation, the question of earth's carrying capacity is too narrow and theoretical. Carrying capacity must be viewed more in terms of human goals and perceptions of needs and environment. The economists see no problems that invention and innovation cannot solve. Government officials view the question from a political perspective. Biologists stress the limits of the natural environments. Somewhere in between these polar opposites lie projections that may fit the human into an ecological model.

Its been said many times, and in various ways, that there are unintended consequences to human use or manipulation of the environment. Humans have reached a level of environmental sophistication where we realize the web of linkages between human action and the biotic and abiotic resources of the natural world. We also acknowledge that it is management of human effort that drives these linkages today, as depicted in Figure 8–4. It is also management that can equip us to deal with the external factors or the unexpected, as in the case of natural disasters. Also, we can deal with the unexpected and unintended consequences resulting from even the most careful of plans. True, we never do just one thing in the natural world, nor should we.

In a well-managed world, the sequence of inventions and their application would provide for any population likely to come, according to a statement made in a World Bank Report of 1984. Seven years later, Keyfitz (1991) recalled this statement, and noted that there is no overall management in sight. He continued that each stream of invention has had some grave drawbacks (unintended consequences). Some eight years after this observation, many of the same problems confront us, but they are more acute in the developing world. These countries are confronted with the reality of populations pressing against existing limits not any theory of carrying capacity of an ideal world. A key question is will these limits spread to include more world regions? The answer is in how we manage global resources.

There are hopeful signs in the expanding studies and number of concerned citizens. Now we talk of population and development, environment and development, and reproductive health in frequent world conferences whose themes overlap. The direction is now more focused on what Ward and Dubos called "Only One Earth." It is what we have and we now are appreciating that there are limits, though we cannot always identify them. There is considerable talk of a global economy, and we have seen

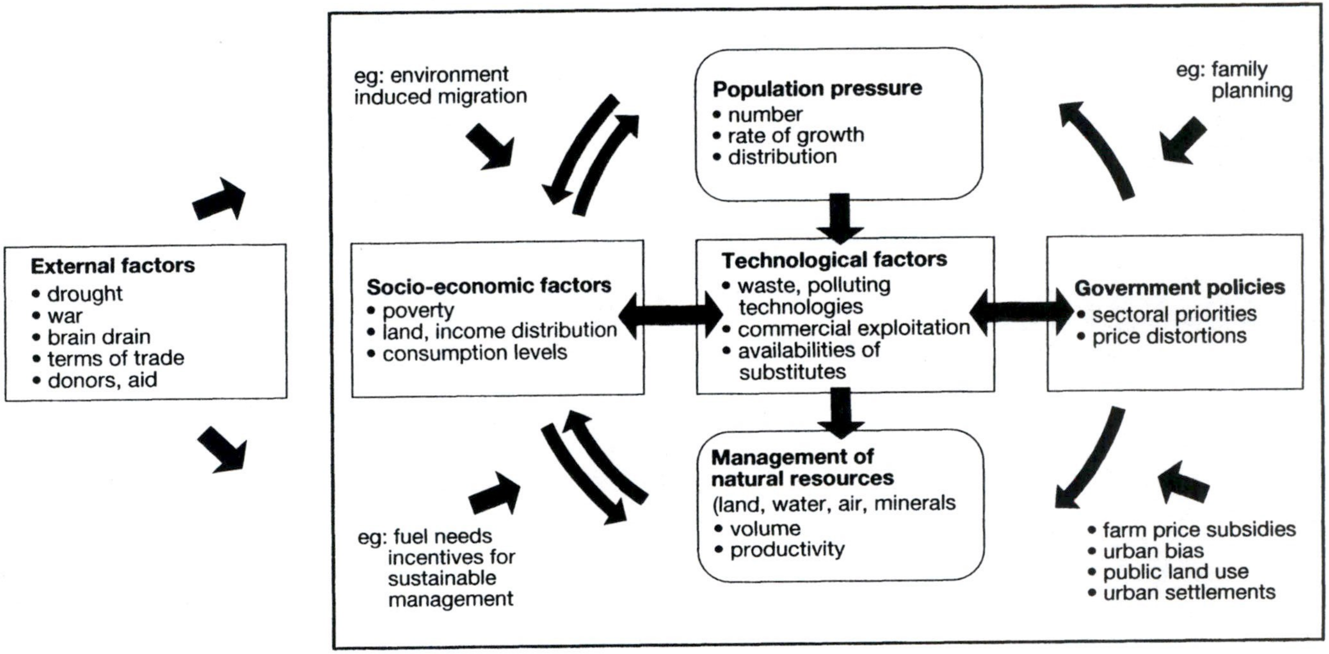

Figure 8–4 The Links between Demographic and Resource Issues

From United Nations Population Fund, 1991. Reprinted by permission of United Nations.

both the positive and negative sides in the past few years. But so far the global part has emphasized resource extraction and pollution rather than a creative innovative approach. Also, consumption is more local than global. Globalization is more than just trade, it means a united effort to wisely use our resources. Humanity entered the twentieth century with billions fewer people on the planet, but they suffered with a higher mortality and much poorer living conditions. We end a century of many improvements. We should expand on these and pass them on to the future generations.

Literature Cited

Ahlburg, D. A. and C. J. DeVita. 1992. *New Realities of the American Family.* Population Bulletin 47(2). Washington, D.C: Population Reference Bureau.

Ames, B. N. and L. S. Gold. 1995. "The causes and prevention of cancer. The role of environment." In *The True State of the Planet*. R. Bailey (ed.) New York: The Free Press, pp. 142–175.

Ames, B. N., L. S. Gold, and W.C. Willett. 1995. "The causes and prevention of cancer." *Proceedings of the National Academy of Science* 153: 760–763.

Angel, J. L. 1966. "Porotic hyperostosis anemias, malarias and marshes in prehistoric eastern Mediterranean." *Science,* 153: 760–763.

Anonymous. 1998. "The next oil crisis looms large and perhaps close." *Science* 281: 1128–1130.

Anonymous. 1998. "Getting a grip on arsenic." *Science* 281: 1261.

Anonymous. 1997. "Dambuilders and dambusters." *The Economist.* April 19, 1997. pp. 79–80.

Appleyard, R. T. 1980. "Economic demography of the twentieth century." In *Changing Disease Patterns and Human Behaviour.* N. F. Stanley and R.A. Joske (eds.) New York: Academic Press, pp. 389–401.

Ashford, L. S. 1995. *New Perspectives on Population: Lessons from Cairo.* Population Bulletin, Vol. 50, No. 1. Washington, D.C.: Population Reference Bureau.

Ashton, T. S. 1986. *The Industrial Revolution 1760–1830.* Westport, Conn.: Greenwood Press (first published in 1948).

Auger, F., P. L. Jamison, J. Balslev-Jorgensen, T. Lewin, J. F. De Pena, and

J. Skrobak-Kaczynski. 1980. "Anthropometry of circumpolar populations." In *The Human Biology of Circumpolar Populations.* F. A Milan (ed.) Cambridge: Cambridge University Press, pp. 213–255.

Ayres, E. 1998. "Digging the ever deeper well." *World Watch.* 11(4): 3.

Bailey, R. (ed.) 1995. *The True State of the Planet.* New York: The Free Press.

Baker, P. T. 1984. "The adaptive limits of human populations." *Man* 19(1): 1–14.

Baker, P. T. and M. A. Little (eds.) 1976. *Man in the Andes. A Multidisciplinary Study of High-Altitude Quechua.* Stroudsburg, PA: Dowden, Hutchinson & Ross.

Balling, R. C., Jr. 1995. "Global warming: Messy models, decent data, and pointless policy." In *The True State of the Planet.* R. Bailey (ed.) New York: The Free Press, pp. 83–107.

Barrett, M. J. and T. Brown 1971. "Increase in average height of Australian Aborigines." *Medical J. of Australia,* 2(23): 1169–1172.

Bayliss-Smith, T. 1985. "Subsistence agriculture and nutrition in the Bimin Valley, Oksapmin sub-district, Papua New Guinea." *Singapore Journal of Tropical Geography* 6(2): 101–115.

Bayliss-Smith. T. 1981. "Seasonal energy relationships and food." In *Seasonal Dimensions to Rural Poverty.* R. Chambers, R. Longhurst, & A. Pacey (eds.) New Jersey: Allanheld, Osmun & Co. Publishers, Inc., pp. 30–33.

Becker, S. and M. A. Sardar. 1981. "Seasonal patterns of vital events in Matlab Thana, Bangladesh." In *Seasonal Dimensions to Rural Poverty.* R. Chambers, R. Longhurst, and A. Pacey (eds.) London: Allanheld & Osmund. pp. 149–153.

Bender, W. and M. Smith. 1997. *Population, Food and Nutrition.* Population Bulletin, Vol. 51, No 4. Washington, D.C.: Population Reference Bureau.

Bennett, J. W. 1976. *The Ecological Transition. Cultural Anthropology and Human Adaptation.* New York: Pergamon Press.

Bentley, G.R., G. Jasienska, and T. Goldberg. 1993. "Is the fertility of agriculturalists higher than that of nonagriculturalists?" *Current Anthropology* 34(5): 778–785.

Berndt, R. M. and C. M. Berndt. 1988. *The World of The First Australians. Aboriginal Traditional Life: Past and Present.* Canberra: Aboriginal Studies Press.

Berry, B. J. L. 1990. "Urbanization." In *The Earth as Transformed by Human Action.* B. L. Turner II, W. C. Clark, R. W. Kates, J. F. Richards, J. T. Mathews, and W. B. Meyer (eds.) New York: Cambridge University Press, pp. 103–119.

Bianchi, S. M. and D. Spain. 1996. *Women, Work, and Family in America.* Population Bulletin. Vol. 51. Washington, D.C.: Population Reference Bureau.

Blurton-Jones, N. G. and R. M. Sibley. 1978. "Testing adaptiveness of culturally determined behavior: Do Bushmen women maximize their reproductive success by spacing births widely and foraging seldom?" In *Human Behaviour and Adaptation*. N. G. Blurton-Jones and V. Reynolds (eds.) Society for the Study of Human Biology Symposium No. 18. London: Taylor and Francis, pp. 135–157.

Bobadilla, J. L., J. Frenk, R. Lozano, T. Frejka, and C. Stern. 1993. "The epidemiologic transition and health priorities." In *Disease Control Priorities in Developing Countries*. D. T. Jamison, W. H. Mosley, A. R. Measham, and J. L. Bobadilla (eds.) Oxford: Oxford University Press, pp. 51–63.

Bogan, K. and R. Crittenden. 1987. "Environment, economic development and the nutritional status of children in the southern highlands of Papua New Guinea in 1983." *Ecology of Food and Nutrition* 20: 29–49.

Borlaug, N. E. 1981. "Using plants to meet world food needs. In *Future Dimensions of World Food and Population*. R. G. Woods (ed.) Boulder, Co.: Westview Press, pp. 101–119.

Boserup, E. 1965. *The Conditions of Agricultural Growth: The Economics of Agrarian Change Under Population Pressure*. Chicago: Aldine.

Bouvier, L. F. & C. J. De Vita. 1991. *The Baby Boom-Entering Midlife*. Washington, D.C.: Population Bulletin 46(3). Washington, D.C.: Population Reference Bureau.

Boyden, S. 1987. *Western Civilization in Biological Perspective. Patterns in History*. Oxford: Clarendon Press.

Brace, C. L. 1995. *The Stages of Human Evolution*. 5th ed. Upper Saddle River, N.J.: Prentice Hall.

Brainard, J. 1990. "Nutritional status and morbidity on an irrigation project in Turkana district, Kenya." *Am. J. Human Biology*. 2: 153–163.

Brainard, J. 1986. "Differential mortality in Turkana agriculturists and pastoralists." *Amer. J. Phys Anthro*. 70: 525–536.

Braudel, F. 1979. *The Structure of Everyday Life. Civilization and Capitalism 15th–18th Century. Volume 1*. New York: Harper & Row Publishers.

Browman, D. L. 1974. "Pastoral nomadism in the Andes." *Current Anthropology* 15(2): 188–196.

Brown, L. R. 1998. "The future of growth. In *State of the World 1998*. New York: and London: W. W. Norton, pp. 3–20.

Brown, L. R. 1997. *The Agricultural Link: How Environmental Deterioration Could Disrupt Economic Progress*. Worldwatch Paper 136.

Brown, L. R., C. Flavin, H. F. French & L. Starke (eds.) 1999. *State of the World 1999*. New York: W. W. Norton & Co.

Brown, L. R. and B. Halwell. 1998. "China's water shortage could shake world food security." *World Watch* 11(4): 10–21.

Brown, L. R. & G. W. Finsterbrisch. 1972. *Man and His Environment*. New York: Harper & Row.

Brown, L. and H. Kane. 1994. *Full House. Reassessing the Earth's Population Carrying Capacity.* New York: W. W. Norton.

Brown, R. 1991. *Society and Economy in Modern Britain 1700–1850.* New York & London: Routledge.

Brown, T. and G. C. Townsend. 1982. "Adolescent growth in height of Australian Aboriginals analysed by the Preece-Baines function: A longitudinal study." *Annals of Human Biology* 9(6): 495–505.

Burkitt, D. F. 1971. "Epidemiology of cancer of the colon and rectum." *Cancer* 28: 3–13.

Burnett, J. 1991. "Housing and the decline of mortality." In *The Decline of Mortality in Europe.* R. Schofield, A. Reher, and A. Bideau (eds.) Oxford: Clarendon Press, pp. 158–176.

Butzer, K.W. 1990. "The realm of cultural-human ecology: Adaptation and change in historical perspective." In *The Earth as Transformed by Human Action.* B. L. Turner II, W. C. Clark, R. W. Kates, J. F. Richards, J.T. Mathews, and W. B. Meyer (eds.) New York: Cambridge University Press, pp. 685–701.

Cairns, J. 1975. "The cancer problem." *Scientific American* 233(5): 64–78.

Cannadine D. and D. Reeder (eds.) 1982. *Exploring the Urban Past. Essays in Urban History by H. J.Dyos.* Cambridge: Cambridge University Press.

Carlton, J. T. and J. B. Geller. 1993. "Ecological roulette: The global transport of non-indigenous marine organisms." *Science* 261: 78–82.

Carpenter, K. J. 1986. *The History of Scurvy and Vitamin C.* Cambridge: Cambridge University Press.

Carson, R. 1964. *Silent Spring.* New York: Crest Books, Fawcett World Library.

Cavalli-Sforza, L. T., A. Rosman, A.S. de Boer, and I. Darton-Hill. 1996. "Nutritional aspects of changes in disease patterns in the Western Pacific Region." *Bulletin of the World Health Organization* 74(3): 307–318.

Chagnon, N.A. 1983. *Yanomamo. The Fierce People.* 3rd ed. Chicago: Holt, Rinehart & Winston, Inc.

Chandavarkar, R. 1992. "Plague panic and epidemic politics in India, 1896–1914." In *Epidemics and Ideas. Essays on the Historical Perception of Pestilence.* T. Ranger and P. Slack (eds.) Cambridge: Cambridge University Press, pp. 203–240.

Chandler, T. 1987. *Four Thousand Years of Urban Growth. An Historical Census.* Lewiston/Queenston: St. David's University Press.

Chao, K. 1986. *Man and Land in Chinese History An Economic Analysis.* Stanford: Stanford University Press.

Chase, A. 1976. *The Legacy of Malthus. The Social Costs of the New Scientific Racism.* New York: Alfred A. Knopf.

Chesnais, Jean-Claude. 1992. *The Demographic Transition: Stages, Patterns, and Economic Implications.* Translated by E.& P. Kreager. New York: Oxford University Press.

Cipolla, C. M. (ed.) 1972. *The Fontana Economic History of Europe. The Emergence of Industrial Societies.Part 2.* London and Glasgow: Collins/Fontana Books.

Clark, C. 1977. *Population Growth and Land Use.* London: The Macmillan Press Ltd.

Clarke, W. C. 1977. "The structure of permanence: The relevance of self-subsistence communities for world ecosystem management." In *Subsistence and Survival. Rural Ecology in the Pacific.* T. P. Bayliss-Smith and R. G. Feachem (eds.) New York: Academic Press, pp. 363–384.

Coale, A. J. 1973. "The demographic transition." In *International Population Conference.* Liege. 1: 53–72.

Coale, A. J., B. Anderson, and E. Harm. 1979. *Human Fertility in Russia Since the Nineteenth Century.* Princeton, N.J.: Princeton University Press.

Coale, A. J. and S. C. Watkins. 1979. *The Decline of Fertility In Europe.* Princeton, N.J.: Princeton University Press.

Cohen, Barney. 1993. "Fertility levels, differentials, and trends." In *Demographic Change in Sub-Saharan Africa.* K. A. Foote, K. H. Hill, and L. G. Martin (eds.) Washington, D.C.: National Academy Press, pp. 8–67.

Cohen, J. E. 1995. "Population growth and earth's human carrying capacity." *Science* 269: 341–346.

Cohen, L. A. 1987. "Diet and cancer." *Scientific American* 257: 42–48.

Colwell, R. R. 1996. "Global climate and infectious disease: the cholera paradigm." *Science* 274: 2025–2031.

Combs, G. F. Jr. and M. L. Scott. 1977. Nutritional interrelationships of vitamin E and selenium. *Bio. Science* 27(7): 467–473.

Condon, R.G. 1991. "Birth seasonality, photoperiod, and social change in the Central Canadian Arctic." *Human Ecology* 19: 287–321.

Connell, K. H. 1975. *The Population of Ireland 1750–1845.* Westport, Conn.: Greenwood Press.

Copeman, R., D. Pashen, and G. Burger. 1975. "The health of the Aboriginal children of Cunnamulla, Western Queensland." *Medical J. of Australia Special Supplement* pp. 8–13.

Cowan, C. W. and P. J. Watson (eds.) 1992. *The Origins of Agriculture. An International Perspective.* Washington, D.C. & London: Smithsonian Institution Press.

Cowgill, U. 1966. "Season of birth in man." *Man* 1: 232–240.

Cowlishaw, G. 1982. Family planning: A post-contact problem. In *Body, Land and Spirit.* J. Reid (ed.) St. Lucia: University of Queensland Press, pp. 31–48.

Cowlishaw, G. 1981. "The detrimants of fertility among Australian Aborigines." *Mankind* 13(1): 37–55.

Crosby, A. W. 1976. "Virgin soil epidemics as a factor in the Aboriginal depopulation in America." *William and Mary Quarterly,* 3rd series 33: 293–294.

Crosby, A. W. 1972. *The Columbian Exchange. Biological and Cultural Consequences of 1492.* Westport, Conn.: Greenwood Press.

Dando, W. A. 1980. *The Geography of Famine.* New York: John Wiley & Sons.

Darlington, C. D. 1969. *The Evolution of Man and Society.* New York: Simon & Schuster.

Davis, C. and M. Feshbach. 1980. "Rising infant mortality in the USSR in the 1970's." *U.S. Bureau of the Census, series, p. 95, no. 74.* Sept. 1980.

Deevey, E. S. September, 1960. "The human population." *Scientific American* San Francisco: W. H. Freeman & Co.

de Herrera, C. D. 1999. "Diabetes rate double for Hispanics." *Population Today* 27(3): 8.

Douglas, G.H. 1996. *All Aboard: The Railroads in American Life.* New York: Smithmark.

Draper, H. H. 1977. "The aboriginal Eskimo diet in modern perspective." *American Anthrop.* 79: 309–316.

Draper, H. H. and C. Wo. 1978. "Metabolic parameters: Plasma vitamin E and cholesterol levels in Alaskan Eskimos." In *Eskimos of Northwestern Alaska. A Biological Perspective.* P. L. Jamison et al. (eds.) Stroudsburg, Pa.: Dowden, Hutchinson & Ross, Inc., pp. 189–197.

Dubos, R. 1965. *Man Adapting.* New Haven, Conn.: Yale University Press.

Dunn, S. 1998. "After Kyoto: A climate treaty with no teeth?" *World Watch* 11(2): 33–35.

Durand, J. 1977. "Historical estimates of world population an evaluation." *Population and Development Review.* 3(3): 253.

Durnin, J. V. and R. Passmore 1967. *Energy, Work, and Leisure.* London: Heinemann.

Early, J. D. and J. F. Peters. 1990. *The Population Dynamics of the Mucajai Yanomama.* San Diego: Academic Press.

Eckholm, E. P. 1977. *The Picture of Health.* New York: W. W. Norton.

Ehrenkranz, J. R. L. 1983. "A gland for all seasons." *Natural History* 6: 18–23.

Ehrlich, P., A. Ehrlich, and J. Holdren. 1977. *Population, Resources, Environment.* New York: W. H. Freeman & Co.

Emerson, K., B. N. Saxena, and E. L. Poindexter. 1972. "Caloric cost of normal pregnancy." *Obstetrics and Gynecology* 40: 786–794.

Emmel, T.C. 1973. *An Introduction to Ecology and Population Biology.* New York: Norton.

Eng, R. Y. and T. C. Smith. 1976. "Peasant families and population control in Eighteenth-Century Japan." *J. of Interdisciplinary History* 6(3): 417–445.

Epstein, D. 1996. "Cholera Epidemic". *ProMed-Digest,* Vol. 96, No. 90.

Escobar, del Rey, F. and G. Morreale de Escobar. 1993. "Iodine deficiency in Spain." In *Iodine Deficiency in Europe.* F. Delange, J. T. Dunn, and D. Glinoer (eds.) New York: Plenum Press, pp. 395–401.

Eveleth, P. B. and J. M. Tanner. 1990. *Worldwide Variation in Human Growth. 2nd ed.* Cambridge: Cambridge University Press.

Ewers, J. C. 1967. "The horse complex in Plains Indian history." In *The North American Indians. A Sourcebook.* R. C. Owen et al. (eds.) New York: Macmillan Co., pp. 494–503.

Fagan, B M. 1992. *People of the Earth. An Introduction to World Prehistory. 7th ed.* New York: Harper Collins Publisher.

Fernandez, R. 1990. *A Simple Matter of Salt. An Ethnography of Nutritional Deficiency in Spain.* Berkeley: University of California Press.

Feshbach, M. and A. Friendly, Jr. 1992. *Ecocide in the USSR. Health and Nature Under Siege.* New York: Basic Books.

Flannery, K. V. 1973. "The origins of agriculture." *Annual Review of Anthropology* 2: 271–310.

Flinn, M. W. (edited with an introduction) 1965. *Report On the Sanitary Condition of the Labouring Population of Great Britain. by Edwin Chadwick, 1842.* Edinburgh: Edinburgh University Press.

Flood, J. 1980. *The Moth Hunters. Aboriginal Prehistory of the Australian Alps.* Canberra: Australian Institute of Aboriginal Studies.

Floud, R.,K. Wachter, and A. Gregory. 1990. *Height, Health and History. Nutritional Status in the United Kingdom, 1750–1980.* Cambridge: Cambridge University Press.

Fogel, R. W. 1982. "Exploring the uses of data on height." *Social Science and History.* 6(4): 401.

Fowden, L., G. A. Gaton, and C. F. Mills (eds.) 1981. *Trace Element Deficiency: Metabolic and Physiological Consequences.* U.K.: London Royal Society.

Frisancho, A. R. and P. T. Baker. 1970. "Altitude and Growth: A study of the patterns of physical growth of a high altitude Peruvian Quechua population." *Am.J. Physical Anthropol.* 32: 279–292.

Frisch, R. E. 1988. "Fatness and fertility." *Scientific American* 258(3): 88–95.

Galvin, K. A 1992. "Nutritional ecology of pastoralists in dry tropical Africa." *Am. J. of Human Biology* 4: 209–221.

Ganong, W. F. 1993. *Review of Medical Physiology.* 16th ed. Norwalk, Conn.: Appleton & Lange.

Garenne, M. 1994. "Mortality in Sub-Saharan Africa: Trends and prospects." In *The Future Population of the World. What Can We Assume Today?* W. Lutz (ed.) London: Earthscan Publ. Ltd., pp. 167–186.

Garret, L. 1994. *The Coming Plague.* New York: Penguin Books.

Glantz, M. H., A. Z. Rubinstein, and I. Zonn. 1993. "Tragedy in the Aral Sea basin. *Global Environmental Change* 3(2): 174–198.

Glass, R., A. Libel, and A. Brandling-Bennett. 1992. "Epidemic cholera in the Americas." *Science* 256(5063): 1524–1525.

Goliber, T. J. 1997. *Population and Reproductive Health in Sub-Saharan Africa.*

Population Bulletin 52(4). Washington, D.C.: Population Reference Bureau.

Golson, J. 1982. "The Ipomoean revolution revisited: Society and the sweet potato in the upper Waahqi valley." In *Inequality in New Guinea Highlands Societies.* A. Strathern (ed.) Cambridge: Cambridge University Press, pp. 109–136.

Gottfried, R. S. 1983. *The Black Death: Natural and Human Disaster in Medieval Europe.* New York: The Free Press.

Goudie, A. 1994. *The Human Impact on the Natural Environment.* 4th ed. Cambridge: The MIT Press.

Gould, J. B. and S. LeRoy. 1988. "Socioeconomic status and low birth weight: A racial comparison." *Pediatrics* 82: 896–904.

Grady, D. 1993. "Death at the Corners." *Discover* 14(12): 82–91.

Grebenik, E. 1955. "The growth of human populations." In *The Numbers of Man and Animals.* J. B. Cragg and N. W. Pirie (eds.) London: Oliver and Boyd, pp. 13–22.

Grigg, D. B. 1980. "Migration and overpopulation." In *The Geographical Impact of Migration.* P. White and R. Woods (eds.) London & New York: Longman, pp. 60–83.

Guppta, R & A. Basu 1991. "Altitude and growth among the Sherpas of the eastern Himalays." *Am. J. of Human Biology* 3: 1–9.

Hansen, J. D. L., D. S. Dunn, R. B. Lee, P J. Becker, and T. Jenkins. 1993. "Hunter-gatherer to pastoral way of life: Effects of the transition on health, growth and nutritional status." *Suid-Afrikaanse Tydskrif vir Wetenskap* 89: 559–564.

Hansen, J. C., N. Kromann, H.C. Wulf, and K. Alboge. 1983. "Human exposure to heavy metals in East Greenland II Lead." *The Science of the Total Environment* 26: 245–254.

Haput, A & T. Kane. 1991. *Population Handbook. 3rd ed.* Washington, D.C.: Population Reference Bureau.

Hardin, G. 1968. "The tragedy of the commons." *Science* 162: 1243–1248.

Hardy, A. 1993. *The Epidemic Streets. Infectious Disease and the Rise of Preventive Medicine, 1856–1900.* Oxford: Clarendon Press.

Harris, M. I. 1990. "Noninsulin-dependent diabetes mellitus in black and white Americans." *Diabetes/Metabolism Reviews* 6(2): 71–90.

Harrison, G. 1978. *Mosquitoes, Malaria and Man: A History of the Hostilities Since. 1880.* New York: E. P. Dutton.

Harrison, G. A., J M. Tanner, D. R. Pilbeam,and P. T. Baker. 1988. *Human Biology. An Introduction to Human Evolution, Variation, Growth, and Adaptability.* Oxford: Oxford University Press.

Haub, C. 1994. *Population Change in the Former Soviet Republic.* Population Bulletin 49(4). Washington, D.C.: Population Reference Bureau.

Haury, E. 1976. *Hohokam, Desert Farmers and Craftsmen: Excavations at Snaketown.* Tucson: University of Arizona Press.

Hausman, A. J. and E. N. Wilmsen. 1985. "Economic change and secular trends in the growth of San children." *Human Biology* 57(4): 563–571.

Heiser, C. B. Jr. 1981. *Seed to Civilization. 2nd ed.* San Francisco: W. H. Freeman & Co.

Heywood, P. F. 1992. "Iodine-deficiency disorders in Papua New Guinea." In *Human Biology in Papua New Guinea. The Small Cosmos.* R. D. Attenborough and M. P. Alpers (eds.) Oxford, New York: Clarendon Press, pp. 355–362.

Heywood, P. F. 1983. "Growth and nutrition in Papua New Guinea." *J. of Human Evolution* 12: 133–143.

Hiernaux, J. 1964. "Weight/height relationships during growth in Africans and Europeans." *Human Biology* 36: 273–293.

Ho, Ping-Ti. 1955. "The introduction of American food plants into China." *Am. Anthropol*, 57: 191–201.

Hostetler, J. A. 1985. "History and relevance of the Hutterite population for genetic studies." *Am. J. of Medical Genetics* 22: 453–462.

Houghton, P. 1996. *People of the Great Ocean.* Cambridge: Cambridge University Press.

Howell, N. 1979. *Demography of the Dobe !Kung*. New York: Academic Press.

Huffman, S. L. 1987. "Women's activities and impacts on child nutrition " In *Food Policy Integrating Supply, Distribution and Consumption.* J. P. Gittinger, J. Leslie, and C. Hoisington (eds.) Published for the World Bank. Baltimore: The Johns Hopkins University Press, pp. 373–384.

Hutt, M. S. R. and D. P. Burkitt. 1986. *The Geography of Non-Infectious Disease.* Oxford: Oxford University Press.

Inaoka, T. 1995. "Health and survival in modernizing Papua New Guinea Societies." *Anthropol. Sci.* 103(4): 339–347.

Jackson, L. C. 1988. "Behavioral effects of chronic sublethal dietary cyanide in an animal model: Implications for humans consuming cassava (Manihot esculenta)." *Human Biology* 60: 597–614.

James, W. P. T. and E.C. Schofield 1990. *Human Energy Requirements.* New York: Oxford University Press.

Jamison, E. and F. Hobbs. 1994. *World Population Profile: 1994.* U.S. Bureau of the Census. Report WP/94, U.S. Govt. Printing Office, Washington, D. C.

Jenkins, C. 1993. "Fertility and infertility in Papua New Guinea." *Am. J. of Human Biology* 5(1): 75–83.

John, B. S. 1977. *The Ice Age.* London: Collins.

Kahn, E. J., Jr. 1984. *The Staff of Life.* Boston: Little, Brown & Co.

Kamien. M. 1980. "The Aboriginal Australian experience." In *Changing Disease Patterns and Human Behaviour.* N. F. Stanley & R. A. Joske (eds.) New York: Academic Press, pp. 254–270.

Kaplan, R.D. 1993. *Balkan Ghosts. A Journey Through History.* New York: Vintage Books.

Kenen, R. H. 1987. "Health status: Australian Aborigines and Native Americans-a comparison." *Australian Aboriginal Studies* no. 1. pp. 34–45.

Kennedy, R. E. Jr. 1973. *The Irish: Emigration, Marriage, and Fertility.* Berkeley: Univ of California Press.

Kevles, D. J. 1995. *In the Name of Eugenics.* Cambridge: Harvard University Press.

Keyfitz, N. 1994. "Demographic discord." *The Sciences.* Sept./Oct, pp. 21–27.

Keyfitz, N. 1991. "Toward a theory of population-development interaction." In *Resources, Environemnt, and Population: Present Knowledge, Future Options.* K. Davis & M. S.Bernstam (eds.) New York: Oxford University Press, pp. 295–314.

King, H. 1992. "The epidemiology of diabetes mellitus in Papua New Guinea and the Pacific: Adverse consequences of natural selection in the face of sociocultural change." In *Human Biology in Papua New Guinea.* R.D. Attenborough and M. P. Alpers (eds.) Oxford: Oxford University Press, pp. 363–372.

Kirk, R. L. 1981. *Aboriginal Man Adapting. The Human Biology of Australian Aborigines.* Oxford: Clarendon Press.

Kirk, R.L., S. W. Serjeantson, H. King, and P. Zimmet. 1985. "The genetic epidemiology of diabetes mellitus." In *Disease of Complex Etiology in Small Populations: Ethnic Differences and Research Approaches* R. Chakraborty and E. J. E. Szathmary (eds.) New York: Alan R. Liss, pp. 119–146.

Klag, M.J., P. K. Whelton, J. Coresh, C. E. Grim, and L. H. Kuller. 1991. "The association of skin color with blood pressure in U.S. blacks with low socioeconomic status." *J. Am. Med. Assoc.* 265(5): 599–602.

Knowler, W. C., D. J. Pettitt, M. F. Saad, and P. H. Bennett. 1990. "Diabetes mellitus in the Pima Indians: Incidence, risk factors and pathogenesis." *Diabetes/Metabolism Reviews* 6(1): 1–27.

Kochanek, K. D. and B. L. Hudson. 1995. *Advance report of final mortality statistics,1992. Monthly vital statistics report;* Vol. 43, No. 6, suppl. Hyattsville, Md.: National Center for Health Statistics.

Komlos, J. 1989. *Nutrition and Economic Development in the Eighteenth-Century Hapsburg Monarchy.* Princeton, N.J.: Princeton University Press.

Kovacs, T. 1977. *The Bronze Age in Hungary.* Budapest: Corvina Press.

Ladurie, E. L. 1975. "Famine Amenorrhoea (Seventeenth-Twentieth Centuries)." In *Biology of Man in History.* R. Forster et al. (eds.) Baltimore & London: The Johns Hopkins University Press, pp. 163–178.

Ladurie, E. L. 1971. *Times of Feast, Times of Famine: A History of Climate Since the Year 1000.* New York: Doubleday & Co.

Lampl, M., F. E. Johnston, and L. A. Malcolm. 1978. "The effects of protein supplementation on the growth and skeletal maturation of New Guinea school children " *Annals of Human Biology* 5(3): 219–227.

Langer, W. L. 1975. "American foods and Europe's population growth 1750–1850." *J. of Social History,* Winter 1975, pp. 51–66.

Langer, W.L. 1963. "Europe's initial population explosion." *Am. Hist. Review* 69: 10–20

Latham., M. C. 1978. "Nutrition and culture." In *Nutrition and National Policy.* B. Winikoff (ed.) Cambridge: MIT Press, pp. 425–430.

Learmonth, A. 1988. *Disease Ecology.* Oxford: Basil Blackwell, Ltd.

Leatherman, T. L., J. W. Carey, and R. B. Thomas. 1995. "Socioeconomic change and patterns of growth in the Andes." *Am. J. Physical Anthropol* 97: 307–321.

Lee, R. B. 1979. *The !Kung San. Men, Women, and Work in a Foraging Society.* Cambridge: Cambridge University Press.

Lee, R. B. 1969. "!Kung Bushman subsistence: An input-output analysis." In *Environment and Cultural Behavior.* A. P. Vayda (ed.) New York: The Natural History Press, pp. 47–79.

Leighly, J. (ed.) 1963. *Land and Life. A Selection from the Writings of Carl Ortwin Sauer.* Berkeley: University of California Press.

Lemarchand, R. 1994. "The apocalypse in Rwanda." *Cultural Survival Quarterly* 18: 29–33.

Leonard, W. R. 1989. "Nutritional determinants of high-altitude growth in Nunoa, Peru." *Am.J. Physical Anthropol.* 80: 341–352.

Leonard, W. R., P. T. Katzmarzyk, A. G. Comuzzi, M. H. Crawford, and R. I. Sukernik 1994. "Growth and nutritional status of the Evenki Reindeer Herders of Siberia." *Am.J. of Human Biology* 6: 339–350.

Leonard, W. R., T. L. Leatherman, J. W. Carey, and R. B. Thomas. 1990. "Contributions of nutrition versus hypoxia to growth in rural Andean populations." *Am. J. of Human Biology* 2: 613–626.

Leslie, P. W. and P. H. Fry. 1989. "Extreme seasonality of births among nomadic Turkana pastoralists " *Am. J. of Physical Anthropol.* 79(1): 103–115.

Leslie, P W., J. R. Bindon, and P. T. Baker. 1984. "Caloric requirements of human populations. A model." *Human Ecology* 12(2): 137–162.

Levander, O. A. 1987. "A global view of human selenium nutrition." *Annual Review of Nutrition* 7: 227–250.

Lieber, E. 1970. "Galen on contaminated cereals as a cause of epidemics." *Bulletin of the History of Medicine* 44(2): 332–345.

Little, M. A. and J. D. Haas (eds.) 1989. *Human Population Biology. A Transdisciplinary Science.* New York: Oxford University Press.

Little, M. A., K. Galvin and M. Mugambi. 1983. "Cross-sectional growth of nomadic Turkana pastoralists." *Human Biology* 55(4): 811–830.

Livi Bacci, M. 1968. "Fertility and nuptially changes in Spain from the late 18th to the early 20th century. Part 2." *Population Studies* 22: 211–234.

Lizot, J. 1977. "Population, resources and warfare among the Yanomami." *Man* 12: 497–517.

Lopez, A. D. 1993. "Causes of death in industrial and developing countries: Estimates for 1985–1990." In *Disease Control Priorities in Developing Countries.* D.T. Jamison, W H. Mosley, A. R. Measham, and J. L. Bobadilla (eds.) New York: Oxford University Press, pp. 35–50.

Lopez, A D. 1990a. "Causes of death: An assessment of global patterns of mortality around 1985." *World Health Statistics Quarterly* 43(2): 91–104.

Lopez, A. D. 1990b. "Who dies of what? A comparative analysis of mortality conditions in developed countries around 1987." *World Health Statistics Quarterly* 43(2): 105–114.

Lotka, A. J. 1956. *Elements of Mathematical Biology.* New York: Dover.

Lourie, J. A. and T. Taufa. 1986. "The Ok Tedi health and nutrition project, Papua New Guinea: Physique, growth and nutritional status of the Wopkaimin of the Star Mountains." *Annals of Human Biology* 13(6): 517–536.

Luke, B., C. Williams, J. Minogue, and L. Keith. 1993. "The changing pattern of infant mortality in the U.S.: The role of prenatal factors and their obstetrical implications." *J. of Gynaecology and Obstetrics* 40(3): 199–212.

Lum, M. K. W., L. R. Knutson, D. B. Hall, H. S. Margolis, and T. R. Bender. 1986. "Decline in infant mortality of Alaskan Yupik from 1960 to 1980." *Public Health Reports* 101(3): 309–314.

McClung, J. 1969. *Effects of High Altitude on Human Birth.* Cambridge: Harvard University Press..

McEvedy, C. 1988. "The bubonic plague." *Scientific American,* 258: 118–123.

McEvedy, C. & R. Jones. 1978. *Atlas of World Population History.* New York: Penguin Books.

McFalls, J. A. Jr. 1991. *Population: A lively Introduction. Population Bulletin* 46(2). Washington, D.C.: Population Reference Bureau.

McFalls, J. A. Jr. 1979. *Frustrated Fertility: A Population Paradox. Population Bulletin* 34(2). Washington, D.C.: Population Reference Bureau.

McGinn, A. P. 1997. "Preventing chronic disease in developing countries." In *State of The World.* L. Starke (ed.) New York: W. W. Norton & Co., pp. 60–77.

McGovern, T. H. 1981. "The economics of extinction in Norse Greenland." In *Climate and History.* T. Wrigley, M. Ingram, and G. Farmer (eds.) New York: Cambridge University Press, pp. 404–433.

McIntosh, S. K. & R. J. McIntosh. 1981. "West African Prehistory." *American Scientist,* 69: 602–613.

McKeown, T. 1979. *The Role of Medicine. Dream, Mirage, or Nemesis?* Oxford: Basil Blackwell.

McKeown,T., R. G. Brown, and R. G. Record. 1972. "An interpretation of the modern rise of population in Europe." *Population Studies* 26(3): 345–381.

McKeown, T. & R. G. Record. 1962. "Reasons for the decline of mortality in England and Wales during the Nineteenth Century." *Population Studies* 16(2): 94–122.

McNeill, W. H. 1992. *The Global Condition. Conquerors, Catastrophes, and Community.* Princeton: Princeton University Press.

McNeill, W. H. 1977. *Plagues and Peoples.* Garden City, New York: Anchor Press.

Malina R. M. and J. H. Himes 1978. "Patterns of childhood mortality and growth status in a rural Zapotec community." *Annals of Human Biology* 5(6): 517–531.

Manti, S.B. 1988. *The India Population Data Sheet*. Slippery Rock, Pa.: Slippery Rock University.

Marme, M. 1993. "Heaven on earth: The rise of Suzhou, 1127–1550." In *Cities of Jiangnan in Late Imperical China.* L. C. Johnson (ed.) New York: SUNY Press, pp. 17–45.

Marsh, G. P. 1965. *Man and Nature; Or, The Earth As Modified by Human Action* (orig. 1864). Cambridge, Mass.: Belknap Press of Harvard University Press.

Marshall, A. 1998. "Poisoned wells, slow death." *World Press Review.* Dec. 1998, pp. 35–36.

Matovinovic, J. 1983. "Endemic goiter and cretenism at the dawn of the Third Millennium." *Annual Review of Nutrition* (3): 341–412.

Matthews, R., D. Anderson, R. Schen, and T. Webb. 1990. "Global climate and the origins of agriculture." In *Hunger In History.* L. F. Newman (ed.) Cambridge: Basil and Blackwell, Inc., pp. 27–55.

Maung, T. 1979. "Cholera in the Gilberts." *World Health,* Jan. pp. 6–9.

Maurice, J. 1991. "Cancer will 'overwhelm' the Third World." *New Scientist* 130: 17.

Maxwell, W. Q. 1956. *Lincoln's Fifth Wheel.* New York: Longmans, Green and Co.

Mayer, J. D. 1983. "The role of spatial analysis and geographic data in the detection of disease causation." *Social Science Medicine* 17: 1213.

Mayr, E. 1982. *The Growth of Biological Thought. Diversity, Evolution, and Inheritance.* Cambridge: The Belknap Press of Harvard University Press.

Menken, J., J. Trussell, and S. Watkins. 1981. "The nutrition fertility link: An evaluation of the evidence." *J. of Interdisciplinary History* XI(3): 425–441.

Mercer, A. 1990. *Mortality and Population in Transition* New York: Leicester University Press.

Merrick, T. W. 1986. *World Population in Transition. Population Bulletin,* Vol. 41. Washington, D.C.: Population Reference Bureau.

Middleton, M. R. and S. H. Francis. 1976. *Yuendumu and Its Children: Life and Health on an Aboriginal Settlement.* Canberra, Australia: Government Public Service.

Miller, C. A. 1985. "Infant mortality in the U.S." *Scientific American* 253(1): 31–37.

Mineau, G. P., L. L. Bean, & M. Skolnick. 1979. "Mormon demographic history II. The family life cycle and natural fertility." *Population Studies* 33: 429–446.

Molnar, S. 1998. *Human Variation. Races, Types and Ethnic Groups. 4th ed.* New Jersey: Prentice Hall.

Montague, K. & P. Montague. 1976. *No World Without End. The New Threats to Our Biosphere.* New York: G. P. Putnam.

Morris, R. J. 1976. *Cholera 1832.* New York: Holmes and Meier Publishers.

Mtukulo, A. 1995. "Finding a hidden disease." *Populi* 22: 5–6.

National Academy of Sciences. 1989. *Recommended Dietary Allowances. 11th ed.* Washington, D.C.

National Academy of Sciences. 1980. *Recommended Dietary Allowances,* 9th ed. Food and Nutrition Board, National Research Council.

National Center for Health Statistics. 1996. *Vital Statistics of the United States, 1992.* Vol. 11, Sec. 6. Washington D.C.: Public Health Service.

National Safety Council. 1977. *Accident Facts.* National Safety Council Publishers.

Neel, J. V. 1994. *Physician to the Gene Pool.* New York: John Wiley & Sons.

Neel, J. V. 1983. "Some base lines for human evolution and the genetic implications of recent cultural development." In *How Humans Adapt.* D. J. Ortner (ed.) Washington, D.C.: Smithsonian Institute Press, pp. 67–102.

Neel, J. V. 1982. "The thrifty genotype revisited." In *The Genetics of Diabetes Mellitus.* J. Kobberling and R. Tattersall (eds.) London: Academic Press, pp. 283–293.

Neel, J. V. 1962 "Diabetes mellitus: A 'thrifty' genotype rendered determinental by progress?" *Am. J. Hum. Genetics,* 14: 353–362.

Neel, J. V., M. Layrisse and F. M. Salzano. 1977. "Man in the tropics: the Yanomama Indians." In *Population Structure and Human Variation.* G. A Harrison (ed.) Cambridge: Cambridge University Press, pp. 109–142.

Neel, J V. and K. M. Weiss. 1975. "The genetic structure of a tribal population, the Yanomama Indians. XII. Biodemographic studies." *Am. J. Physical Anthropol.* 42: 25–52.

Nef, J. U. 1932. *The Rise of the British Coal Industry.* London: Cass.

Newman, L. F. 1990. "Agricultural intensification, urbanization and hierarchy." In *Hunger in History.* L. F. Newman (ed.) Oxford: Basil Blackwell, pp. 103–125.

Nightingale, F. 1987. *I Have Done My Duty: Florence Nightingale in the Crimean War. 1854–56.* Manchester: Manchester University Press.

Nikiforuk, A. 1991. *The Fourth Horseman.* New York: M. Evans & Co., Inc.

Norris, M. J. 1990. "The demography of aboriginal people in Canada." In *Ethnic Demography.* S. S. Halli, F. Trovato, and L. Driedger (eds.) Ottawa, Ontario: Carleton University Press.

North, D. C..1981. *Structure anc Change in Economic History.* New York: W. W. Norton & Co.

Notestein, F. W. 1946. "Population—the long view." In *Food For the World.* T.W. Schultz (ed.) Chicago: University of Chicago Press, pp. 36–57.

Nurse, G. T., J. S. Weiner and T. Jenkins. 1985. *The Peoples of Southern Africa and Their Affinities.* Oxford: Clarendon Press.

O'Brien, G. 1921. *Economic History of Ireland From the Union to the Famine.* London: Longmans.

Odum, E. P. 1989. *Ecology and Our Endangered Life-Support Systems.* Sunderland, Mass.: Sinauer Assoc.

Ogawa, N. and R. D. Retherford. 1993. "The resumption of fertility decline in Japan: 1973–92." *Population And Development Review* 19(4): 703–741.

Ohlsson, R. and T. Bengtsson. 1984. "Population and economic fluctuations in Sweden 1749–1914." In *Preindustrial Population Change. The Mortality Decline and Short-Term Population Movements.* T. Bengtsson, G. Fridlizuis, and R. Holsson (eds.) Stockholm, Sweden: Almquist & Wiksell Int., pp. 277–297.

Ohtsuka, R. 1995. "Carrying capacity and sustainable food production: The facts and prospects from Papua Guinea." *Anthropol. Science* 103(4): 311–320.

Ohtsuka, R. 1983. *Oriomo Papuans. Ecology of Sago-Eaters in Lowland Papua* Tokyo: University of Tokyo Press.

Olshansky, S. J., B. Carnes, R. G. Rogers, and L. Smith. 1997. *Infectious Diseases-New and Ancient Threats to World Health.* Population Bulletin 52(2). Washington, D.C: Population Reference Bureau.

O'Meara, M. 1997. "The risks of disrupting climate." *World Watch* 10(6): 10–14.

Omran, A. 1982. "Epidemiologic Transition." In *International Encyclopedia of Population.* J. Ross (ed.) New York: The Free Press, pp. 172–183.

Oomen, H.A. P C. 1970. "Interrelationship of the human intestinal flora and protein utilization" *Proceedings of the Nutrition Society* 29: 197–206.

Parry, M. L. 1978. *Climate Change, Agriculture and Settlement.* Camden, Conn.: Archon Books.

Pasquet, P. and G. Koppert. 1993. "Activity patterns and energy expenditure in Cameroonian tropical forest populations." In *Tropical Forests, People and Food. Biocultural Interactions.* C. M. Hladik, et al. (eds.) Paris: The Parthenon Publishing Group, pp. 311–320.

Petersen, W. 1982. "The social roots of hunger and over population." *The Public Interest* No. 67, pp. 37–52.

Petersen, W. 1979. *Malthus.* Cambridge: Harvard University Press.

Petersen, W. 1975. *Population.* 3rd ed. New York: Macmillan.

Pianka, E.R. 1974. *Evolutionary Ecology.* New York: Harper & Row Publishers.

Pleket, H. W. 1993. "Rome: A pre-industrial megalopolis." In *The Giant City in History.* T. Barker and A. Sutcliffe (eds.) New York: St. Martin's Press, pp. 14–35.

Polednak, A. P. 1989. *Racial and Ethnic Differences in Disease* New York: Oxford University Press.

Pollock, N. J. 1992. *These Roots Remain. Food Habits in The Island of the Central and Eastern Pacific Since Western Contact.* Laie, Ha.: The Institute for Polynesian Studies.

Population Reference Bureau. 1998. *World Population Data Sheet 1998.* Washington D.C.: Population Reference Bureau.

Post, J. D. 1985. *Food Shortage, Climatic Variability, and Epidemic Disease in Preindustrial Europe. The Mortality Peak in the Early 1740's.* Ithaca, N.Y.: Cornell University Press.

Pounds, N.J.G. 1985. *An Historical Geography of Europe 1800–1914.* Cambridge: Cambridge University Press.

Preslar, D. 1997. "Rabbit hemmorhagic disease." *ProMed Digest* 97(25).

Preston, R. 1994. *The Hot Zone.* New York: Random House.

Prior, I. A. M. 1987. "Cardiovascular epidemiological studies in New Zealand and the Pacific and the Tokelau Island migrant study." *Research Review.* Medical Research Council of New Zealand.

Prior, I. A. M. 1971. "The price of civilization." *Nutrition Today* 6(4): 2–11.

Pyle, G. F. 1979. *Applied Medical Geography.* Washington, D.C.: V. H. Winston & Sons.

Rajan, S. 1991. "Can we explain demography through culture?" *Man in India* 71(2–3): 383–399.

Razzell, P. E. 1974. "An interpretation of the modern rise of population in Europe—a critique." *Population Studies,* 28(1): 5–17.

Reff, D. T. 1992. "Contact shock in the northwestern New Spain, 1518–1764." In *Disease and Demography in the Americas.* J. W. Verano and D. H. Ubelaker (eds.) Washington and London: Smithsonian Institute Press, pp. 265–276.

Rennie, J. and R. Rusting 1996. "Making headway against cancer." *Scientific American* 6: 57–59.

Repetto, R. 1987. *Population, Resources, Environment: An Uncertain Future. Population Bulletin* 42(2): Washington, D.C.: Population Reference Bureau.

Riskin, C. 1990. "Food, poverty and development strategy in the People's Republic of China." In *Hunger in History.* L. F. Newman(ed.) Oxford: Basil Blackwell Ltd. Copyright World Hunger Program, Brown University, pp. 331–352.

Rode, A. and R. J. Shephard. 1994. "Prediction of body fat content in an Inuit community." *J. of Human Biology* 6: 249–254.

Rode, A. and R. J. Shephard. 1984. "Growth, development and acculturation—a ten year comparison of Canadian Inuit Children." *Human Biology* 56(2): 217–230.

Roe, D. A. 1973. *A Plague of Corn.* Ithaca, N.Y.: Cornell University Press.

Roe, F. G. 1955. *The Indian and the Horse.* Norman: University of Oklahoma Press.

Rosenberg, C. E. 1962. *The Cholera Years.* Chicago: University of Chicago Press.

Ross, J.A. (ed). 1982. *International Encyclopedia of Population.* New York: The Free Press.

Saggers, S. and D. Gray. 1991. *Aboriginal Health and Society. The Traditional and Contemporary Aboriginal Struggle for Better Health.* N. Sydney, Australia: Allen and Unwin Pty. Ltd.

Schaefer, O. 1981. "Eskimos (Inuit)." In *Western Diseases: Their Emergence and Prevention.* H. C. Trowell & D. P. Burkitt (eds.) Cambridge: Harvard University Press, pp. 113–128.

Schaefer, O. 1970. "Pre- and post-natal growth acceleration and increased sugar consumption in Canadian Eskimos." *Canadian Medical Assoc. Journal* 103: 1059–1068.

Schaefer,O., J. Timmermans, R. Eaton, & A. Matthews. 1980. "General and nutritional health in two Eskimo populations of different stages of acculturation." *Canadian J. of Public Health* 71: 397–405.

Schofield, R. 1986. "Did the Mothers really die? Three centuries of maternal mortality in the world we have gained." In *The World We have Gained. Histories of Population and Social Structure.* L. Bonfield, R. M. Smith, and K. Wrightson (eds.) Oxford: Basil Blackwell Ltd., pp. 231–260.

Schofield, R. S. 1985. "Through a glass darkly: The population history of England as an experiment in history. *Journal of Interdisciplinary History* xv: 4 (Spring 1985), pp. 571–593.

Schooneveldt, M., T. Songer, P. Zimmet, and K. Thoma. 1988. "Changing mortality patterns in Nauruans: an example of epidemiological transition." *J. of Epidemiology and Community Health* 42: 89–95.

Scragg, R. F. R. 1972. "Medical demography." In *Encyclopaedia of Papua New Guinea.* P. Rijan (ed.) Melbourne University Press, pp. 740–746.

Scrimshaw, N. S. 1987. "The phenomenon of famine." *Ann. Rev. Nutr.*, 7: 1–21.

Scrimshaw, N. S. 1983. "Functional consequences of malnutrition for human populations: A comment." *J. of Interdisciplinary History* XIV: 2: 409–411.

Scudder, T. 1973. "The human ecology of big projects: River basin development and resettlement." *Annual Review of Anthropology* 2: 45–61.

Seiver, D. A. 1985. "Trend and variation in the seasonality of US fertility 1947–1976." *Demography* 22: 89–100.

Sells, M. A. 1996. *The Bridge Betrayed. Religion and Genocide in Bosnia.* Berkeley: University of California Press.

Sharma, V. P. and K. N. Mehrotra. 1986. "Malaria resurgence in India: A critical study." *Soc.Science. Med.* 22(8): 834–845.

Shell, E.R. August, 1997. "Resurgence of a deadly disease." *The Atlantic Monthly,* pp. 45–60.

Shephard, R. and A. Rode. 1996. *The Health Consequences of "Modernisation." Evidence From Circumpolar Peoples.* Cambridge: Cambridge University Press.

Sills, D. L. (ed.) 1968. *International Encyclopedia of the Social Sciences.* Vol. 8. New York: The Macmillan Co. & the Free Press.

Silverberg, Robert. 1969. *The Challenge of Climate: Man and His Environment.* New York: Meredith Press.

Simon, J. 1997. *Endangered Mexico. An Environment on the Edge.* San Francisco: Sierra Club.

Sindiga, I. 1985. "The persistence of high fertility in Kenya." *Social Science Medicine* 20(1): 71–84.

Sinnett, P. and M. Whyte 1981. "Papua New Guinea." In *Western Diseases: Their Emergence and Prevention.* H. C. Trowell and D. P. Burkitt (eds.) Cambridge: Harvard University Press, pp. 171–187.

Sinnett, P. F. 1977. "Nutritional adaptation among the Enga." In *Subsistence and Survival. Rural Ecology in the Pacific.* T. P. Bayliss-Smith and R. G. Feachem (eds.) New York: Academic Press, pp. 63–90.

Sinnett, P. F. 1973. "Epidemiological studies in a highland population of New Guinea: Environment, culture and health status." *Human Ecology* 1: 245.

Slaughter, M H., T. G. Lohman, R. A. Boileau, C. A. Horswill, J. Stillman, M. D. Van Loan, and D. A. Bemben. 1988."Skinfold equations for estimation of body fatness in children and youth" *Human Biology* 60: 709–723.

Smith, F. B. 1979. *The People's Health 1830–1910.* New York: Holmes & Meier Publishers, Inc.

Smole, W J. 1976. *The Yanomama Indians. A Cultural Geography.* Austin: University of Texas Press.

So, Joseph K. 1980. "Human biological adaptation to arctic and subarctic zones." *Ann. Rev. Anthropol.* 9: 63–82.

Sobowale, D. 1997. "Who will feed Nigeria?" *World Watch* 10(2): 4.

Söderberg, J. 1981. "Interrelationships between short-term economic and demographic fluctuations in a period of crisis: South-eastern Sweden, 1866–1872." In *Pre-Industrial Population Change. The Mortality Decline and Short-Term Population Movements.* T. Bengtsson, G. Fridlizius, and R. Ohlsson (eds.) Stockholm, Sweden: Alquist & Wiksell, Intl., pp. 255–276.

Solway, J.S. and R. B. Lee. 1990. "Foragers, genuine or spurious?" *Current Anthrop.* 31(2): 109–146.

Speth, J. D. and K. A. Spielmann 1983. "Energy source, protein metabolism, and hunter-gatherer subsistence strategies." *J. of Anthropological Archaeology* 2: 1–31.

Stebbins, K.R. 1992. "Garbage imperialism: health implications of dumping hazardous wastes in the Third World Countries." *Medical Anthro.* 15: 81–102.

Sterngold, J. "Gauging a grand plan to sell water from the Mojave." *New York Times,* Aug. 11, 1996.

Stocking, G. W. Jr. 1987. *Victorian Anthropology.* New York: The Free Press.

Stringer, C. B. and R. McKie. 1996. *African Exodus: The Origins of Modern Humanity.* London: Jonathan Cape.

Tanaka, J. 1980. *The San Hunter-Gatherers of the Kalahari.* Tokyo: University of Tokyo Press.

Tanner, J. M. 1986. "Growth as a mirror of the condition of society: secular trends and class distinctions." In *A Multidisciplinary Review.* A. Demirjian and A. Brault (eds.) London & Philadelphia: Taylor & Francis, pp. 3–34.

Tanner, J. M. 1981. *A History of the Study of Human Growth.* Cambridge: Cambridge University Press.

Tanner, J. M. 1973. *Growing Up.* New York: Scientific American, Inc., p. 39.

Thomas, B. 1985. "Escaping from constraints: The Industrial Revolution in a Malthusian context." *J. of Interdisciplinary History* 15(4): 729–753.

Thomas, W. L., Jr. 1956. *Man's Role in Changing the Face of the Earth.* Chicago: University of Chicago Press.

Thompson, R. and M. C. Robbins. 1973. "Seasonal variation in conception in rural Uganda and Mexico." *American Anthropol.* 75: 676–686.

Thomson, A. M. 1977. "The development of young children in a West African village: A study in human ecology." In *Human Ecology in the Tropics.* J. P. Garlick and R. W. J. Keay (eds.) London: Taylor & Francis Ltd., pp. 113–126.

Thomson, N. 1984. "Aboriginal health-current status." *Australian and New Zealand of Medicine.* 14: 705–718.

Thorne, A. & R. Raymond. 1989. *Man on the Rim. The Peopling of the Pacific.* North Ryde, NSW: Angus & Robertson Publishers.

Thouez, J. P., A. Rannou, and P. Foggin. 1989. "The other face of development: Native population, health status and indicators of malnutrition—the case of the Cree and Inuit of Northern Quebec." *Social Science Medicine* 29(8): 965–974.

Tobias, P. V. (ed.) 1978. *The Bushmen. San Hunters and Herders of Southern Africa.* Cape Town & Pretoria: Human & Rosseau.

Tolba, M. K. 1995. "Towards a sustainable development." *Ambio* 24(1): 66–67.

Trichopoulos, D., F. P. Li, and D. J. Hunter 1996. "What causes cancer?" *Scientific American* 275(3): 80–87.

Trowell, H.C., and D. P. Burkitt 1981. *Western Diseases: Their Emergence and Prevention*. Cambridge: Harvard University Press.

Truswell, A. S. and J. D. L. Hansen. 1976. Medical research amongst the !Kung. In *Kalahari Hunters-Gatherers: Studies of the !Kung and Their Neighbors*. R. B. Lee and I. Devore (eds.) Cambridge: Harvard University Press, pp. 166–194.

Turner, R. C., A. T. Hattersley, J. T. Shaw, and J. C. Levy. 1995. "Type II diabetes: clinical aspects of molecular biological studies." *Diabetes* 44(1): 1–10.

Ulijaszek, S.J. 1995. *Human Energetics in Biological Anthropology*. Cambridge: Cambridge University Press.

Ulijaszek, S., D. Hyndman, J. Lourie, and A. Pumuye. 1987. "Mining, modernisation and dietary change among the Wopkaimin of Papua New Guinea." *Ecology of Food and Nutrition* 20: 143–156.

United Nations. 1997. *Human Development Report 1997*. New York: Oxford University Press.

United Nations. 1996. *The Progress of Nations*. New York: United Nations.

United Nations. 1993. *World Population Prospects*. The 1992 Revision. New York: United Nations.

U.S. Bureau of the Census. 1997. *Statistical Abstract of the United States 1997.(117th edition)*. Washington, D.C.

U.S. Bureau of the Census. 1995. *Statistical Abstract of the United States. 1995. (115th edition)* Washington,D.C.

United States Government Printing Office. 1997. *Statistical Abstract of the United States 1997. 117th ed.* Washinton, D.C.: U.S. Dept. of Commerce.

Utterstrom, G. 1965. "Two essays on population in Eighteenth-Century Scandinavia." In *Population in History*. D. V. Glass and D. E. Eversley (eds.) London: Edward Arnold Publishers Ltd., pp. 523–548.

Van Noten, F. and J. Raymaekers. 1988. "Early iron smelting in central Africa." *Scientific American* June, pp. 104–111.

van den Eerembeemt, M. L. 1985. "A demographic profile of the Fulani of central Mali with special emphasis on infant and child mortality." In *Population, Health and Nutrition in the Sahel: Issues in the Welfare of Selected West African Communities*. A. G. Hill (ed.) London: Kegan Paul International, pp. 79–103.

Verano, J. W. and D.H. Ubelaker (eds). 1992. *Disease and Demography in the Americas*. Washington and London: Smithsonian Institute Press.

Visaria, L. & P. Visaria. 1995. *India's Population in Transition. Population Bulletin*, Vol. 50. Washington, D.C.: Population Reference Bureau.

Wadsworth, G. 1984. *The Diet and Health of Isolated Populations*. CRC Press.

Wagner, R. H. 1978. *Environment and Man*. 3rd ed. New York: W. W. Norton & Co.

Ward, B. and R. Dubos. 1972. *Only One Earth. The Care and Maintenance of a Small Planet.* New York: W. W. Norton & Co.

Wargo, J. 1996. *Our Children's Toxic Legacy: How Science and Law Fail to Protect Us From Pesticides.* New Haven, Conn.: Yale University Press.

Weekly Epidemiological Record. 1994. No. 3, pp. 13–17.

Weekly Epidemiological Record. 1994. No. 9, pp. 65–66.

Weiss, K. M., R. E. Ferrell, and C.L. Hanis. 1984. "A new world syndrome of metabolic diseases with a genetic and evolutionary basis."*Yearbook of Physical Anthropology* 27: 153–178.

Weller, R H. & L. F. Bouvier. 1981. *Population Demography and Policy.* New York: St. Martin's.

Wenke, R. J. 1990. *Patterns in Prehistory. 3rd ed.* New York: Oxford University Press.

White, I. M. 1977. Pitfalls to avoid: The Australian experience. *Ciba Foundation Symposium 49(new series).* pp. 269–292.

Wilkinson, R. G. 1988. "The English Industrial Revolution." In *The Ends of the Earth. Perspectives on Modern Environmental History.* D. Worster (ed.) Cambridge: Cambridge University Press, pp. 80–99.

Wilmsen, E. N. 1989. *Land Filled With Flies. A Political Economy of the Kalahari.* Chicago: University of Chicago Press.

Wilson, C. (ed.) 1985. *The Dictionary of Demography.* Oxford: Blackwell Ltd.

Wilson, T. W. 1986. "History of salt supplies in West Africa and blood pressures today." *Lancet* 1: 784–786.

Winterhalder, B. 1981. *Hunter-Gatherer Foraging Strategy.* Chicago: University of Chicago Press.

Wohl, A. S. 1983. *Endangered Lives. Public Health in Victorian Britain (sanitary act).* London: J. M. Dent & Sons.

Wolpoff, M. H. 1999. *Paleoanthropology.* 2nd ed. Boston: McGraw-Hill.

Wood, J. W. 1992. "Fertility and reproductive biology in Papua New Guinea." In *Human Biology in Papua New Guinea. The Small Cosmos.* R. Attenborough et al. (eds.) New York: Clarendon Press, pp. 93–118.

World Health Organization (WHO). 1998. *The World Health Report 1996. Fighting Disease, Fostering Development.* Geneva: World Health Organization.

World Health Organization (WHO). 1987. *World Health Statistics Annual.* Geneva, WHO.

Wrigley, E. A. 1990. "Brake or accelerator? Urban growth and population growth before the Industrial Revolution." In *Urbanization in History: A process of Dynamic Interactions.* A.D. van der Woude, Jan de Vries, and A. Hayami (eds.) Oxford: Clarendon Press, pp. 101–112.

Wrigley, E. A. 1986. "Urban growth and agricultural change: England and the continent in early modern period." In *Population and History From the Traditional to the Modern World.* R.I. Rotberg and T. K. Rabb (eds.) Cambridge: Cambridge University Press, pp. 123–168.

Wrigley, E. A. 1983. "The growth of population in Eighteenth-century England: A condundrum resolved." *Past and Present* 98: 121-150.

Wrigley, E. A. 1981. "Population history in the 1980s." *J. of Interdisciplinary History* 12(2): 207–226.

Wrigley, E. A. 1969. *Population and History.* World University Library. New York: McGraw-Hill Book Co.

Wrigley, E. A. & R. S. Schofield. 1981. *The Population History of England 1541–1871.* Cambridge: Edward Arnold.

Yates, T. 1997. "Comment: Chilean hantavirus." *ProMed, Oct. 4.*

Yuan Tien, H., Z. Tianlu, P. Yu, L. Jingneng and L. Zhongtang. 1992. *China's Demographic Dilemmas. Population Bulletin,* Vol. 47, No. 1. Washington, D.C: Population Reference Bureau.

Zemel, B. & C. Jenkins 1989. "Dietary change and adolescent growth among the Bundi (Gende-speaking) people of Papua New Guinea." *Am. J. of Human Biology* 1: 709–718.

Zimmet, P. 1982. "Review articles: Type 2 (non-insulin-dependent) diabetes. An epidemiological overview." *Diabetologia* 22: 399–411.

Index

B

C

D

M

N

O